The Threshold of Manifest Destiny

EARLY AMERICAN STUDIES

Series Editors
Daniel K. Richter, Kathleen M. Brown,
Max Cavitch, and David Waldstreicher

Exploring neglected aspects of our colonial, revolutionary, and early national history and culture, Early American Studies reinterprets familiar themes and events in fresh ways. Interdisciplinary in character, and with a special emphasis on the period from about 1600 to 1850, the series is published in partnership with the McNeil Center for Early American Studies.

A complete list of books in the series
is available from the publisher.

THE THRESHOLD OF MANIFEST DESTINY

Gender and National Expansion in Florida

Laurel Clark Shire

PENN

UNIVERSITY OF PENNSYLVANIA PRESS

PHILADELPHIA

Copyright © 2016 University of Pennsylvania Press

All rights reserved.
Except for brief quotations used for purposes of review or scholarly citation,
none of this book may be reproduced in any form by any means
without written permission from the publisher.

Published by
University of Pennsylvania Press
Philadelphia, Pennsylvania 19104-4112
www.upenn.edu/pennpress

Printed in the United States of America
on acid-free paper
1 3 5 7 9 10 8 6 4 2

A catalogue record for this book is available from the Library of Congress
ISBN 978-0-8122-4836-4

For Linda Barnes Clark and Judith Coren Williams

CONTENTS

Note on Terminology ix

Introduction. Expansionist Domesticity
and Settler Colonialism in Florida 1

Part I. Slavery, Indian Removal, and Expansionist Domesticity

Chapter 1. Property, Settlement, and Slavery 31
Chapter 2. Innocent Victims of a "Savage" War 55
Chapter 3. Seminole Resistance 102

Part II. Gender and Pro-Settler Policy

Chapter 4. Turning Sufferers into Settlers 137
Chapter 5. Gender and Settler Colonialism 162

Conclusion. The Garden and the Spear 194

Appendix 203
Notes 207
Bibliography 249
Index 267
Acknowledgments 271

NOTE ON TERMINOLOGY

I have elected to refer to people of African descent in this book as "black" rather than "African American" because they were not all born in the Americas. I refer to those who were enslaved as "enslaved" persons rather than "slaves" because slavery was a social and legal condition put upon them by whites, not an essential aspect of their being or identity. I refer to people indigenous to North America as "Native Americans" or "indigenous" people or (when accurate) by tribal affiliation (such as Seminole) but rarely as "Indians." I use "Indian" only when referring to U.S. policies and practices that used that label in the nineteenth century, such as "Indian removal" policy or "U.S. Indian agent."

INTRODUCTION

Expansionist Domesticity and Settler Colonialism in Florida

In 1841 a young widow named Elizabeth Berry joined a group of white settlers that the U.S. Army deployed to recolonize north Florida. On August 17, Berry and her children, along with three other families and five single men, moved into blockhouses at Fort White. The U.S. military had constructed the fort in 1836 to protect a nearby settlement from Seminole attacks. By August 1841 the army had abandoned it, but military leaders hoped that installing white families there—the same kind of people the fort had been constructed to protect—would similarly discourage Seminole resistance. It was one of a dozen sites targeted by the army for reoccupation in the winter of 1841. By early 1842, however, the settlers had also deserted Fort White (one army officer blamed the whiskey trade), so Elizabeth Berry and her children moved again. For the second time, she found an opportunity for her family that also served national interests, and they settled near a former Seminole town at Chucochatti, where white settlers had made a successful colony with U.S. military support in February 1842.[1] Elizabeth Berry's story illustrates that making homes in Florida was a political act carried out by white families supported by federal policies, and that white women were key actors in settler colonialism.

Prior to U.S. colonization, Florida was not an uninhabited frontier; it was a prosperous agricultural region where five thousand Native Americans and hundreds of Africans and their descendants lived. In 1823, an American trader visited Chucochatti and several other towns in the region northeast of Tampa Bay, where autonomous Seminoles and Black Seminoles (a group whose status varied from freedom to a form of slavery) had flourished since the mid-eighteenth century. They raised livestock, planted crops in the region's fertile savannahs, and sold their excess produce on the Spanish colonial market. Two turbulent decades later, white families had taken over Chucochatti and much of the rest of Florida. Early in the Second U.S.-Seminole War, American forces burned it along with many other Seminole towns. Several years later soldiers escorted white settlers there, including a handful of widowed or single women like Elizabeth Berry. Many of these early settlers (male and female) filed for free land just after the war under a new homestead law called the Armed Occupation Act (AOA). By 1850 there were 604 whites and 324 enslaved blacks living at Chucochatti, and the region had been renamed Benton County in honor of pro-expansion Missouri senator Thomas Hart Benton, who had championed the new land law. Several waves of U.S. military, Indian, and welfare policies had wrested this productive corner of the continent from Native peoples and installed white families and enslaved blacks on it.[2]

At each stage of Florida's transition from Seminole villages to American farmland, Americans mobilized white women like Berry to support their efforts. Such women provided material labor and cultural support for the growing American settlements in Florida. They represented national growth as the spread of domesticity and civilization and rationalized the violence of territorial expansion as the protection of white American women and their homes. American journalists, settlers, and politicians also told and retold stories that placed white women into threatened homesteads in Florida. "Indian depredation" narratives enabled white Americans to paint the territory as their home, where autonomous Native American and black people threatened their property. Within that rhetorical context, those who predated U.S. settlers in Florida became invaders, while white Americans, who took possession of already settled land, became the victims. Americans naturalized this startling reversal by using racialized notions of civilization and savagery in proximity to white women and children, who were always presumed to be vulnerable innocents. Thus stories about Seminole men's attacks on white women relied on a highly gendered ideology of female vulnerability and domesticity to frame white frontier settlers as innocent homemakers, repurposing domesticity for Manifest Destiny. In this way, white women's domestic work in Florida provided needed physical, material, and reproductive labor and served the fundamentally ideological process of claiming Florida as home to white Americans (many of them slave owners) and not home to Seminole and free black families and communities.

This book examines the central role that gender (masculinity and femininity as understood through domesticity) and race (particularly through white women) together played in the effort to turn Florida into an American place. In the period from 1821, when the United States acquired Florida from Spain, through the Second U.S.-Seminole War (1835–1842) and the decades beyond, American leaders and settlers used white men's and women's physical labor to create homes, farms, families, and communities. The colonization of Florida illustrates how gender ideology—domesticity as well as masculinity—abetted settler colonialism in the early nineteenth-century United States.

Settler Colonialism

As the first territory added after the Louisiana Purchase in 1803 and a frontier that attracted many white migrants in the 1820s, Florida was on the threshold of Manifest Destiny. One of several early experiments in expansion, the aggressive white colonization of Florida provided Americans with a place to test various cultural and political methods of supporting national growth. White settler colonization turned out to be the most effective method, supported by federal policies that granted land to white families.

Settler colonialism in North America began with European colonial ventures. It continued after 1783 in the early U.S. republic in the southern and midwestern borderlands that would become states such as Kentucky, Florida, Illinois, Indiana, and Missouri. While white settlement proceeded differently in each context, American settler colonialism shares much with European colonization elsewhere. In settler colonies such as the United States, Canada, Australia, New Zealand, and Brazil, Europeans expanded their empires through the settlement of families—men and women—who created permanent, mixed societies in which whites dominated native peoples.[3]

In settler colonies, outsiders (white Europeans in many cases) invaded a place and used political, cultural, and economic structures to transform it into their space, turning themselves into its "natives." Intending to stay permanently, settlers used legal and military methods to take and control the land. They also participated in a legal fiction that turned land into property that could be exclusively claimed by (white) individuals under colonial legal structures. Rather than claiming colonial space in the name of a monarch, however, settler colonists often declared their own sovereignty over the land. Many eventually asserted formal or informal independence from their empires of origin (as the United States did in 1776). The permanence of invading white settler families resulted in a perpetual conquest. While whites enjoyed land and citizenship in new territories, for the Native Americans coerced out of these lands, and the Mexicans and blacks denied basic rights and freedoms within them, U.S. expansion hardly felt like liberation. The settler/invaders never left, and indigenous survivors still live under colonial rule in settler societies, as Seminole and Mikasuki peoples do in Florida today.[4]

Unlike other kinds of imperial regimes, large numbers of women from the invading culture helped to colonize settler colonies, providing vital domestic and reproductive labor to create homes and reproduce white families and society. Settler women's work was essential to colonial efforts to dispossess indigenous peoples because they created settlements that were both permanent and dominated by white cultural norms (albeit hybrid colonial ones, distinct from both European and indigenous North American cultures). Other than the presence of a large number of white women, settler colonies were similar to other colonies, and to varying degrees most combined the appropriation of Native land with resource extraction and forced labor.[5]

White settler colonialism in North America placed Native Americans and people of African descent in different positions. Settler societies shared what theorists call a "logic of elimination" regarding indigenous peoples. White settlers rendered land available to themselves by eliminating indigenous peoples; they engaged in violent campaigns to exterminate, assimilate, or segregate indigenous peoples who held prior claims to the space. By contrast, displaced populations of subordinated or enslaved people supplied the labor force needed to build a new society on that land and extract profit from it to benefit the white ruling class. The importation of an alienated and subaltern labor force was fully compatible with settler colonialism, as racial slavery was in the United States. Racial hierarchy arose from white settler colonies' needs for land and labor, which relied on eliminating indigenous peoples and enslaving Africans.[6]

In the United States, settlers often began to unofficially colonize territory through passive, instead of active, expansionist policy. Rather than sending out settlers formally charged with civilizing conquered territory (although it eventually resorted to that in Florida), typically the U.S.

government just failed to prevent settlers from squatting on lands in contact zones, and it later granted them preemption (the right to purchase land before auction) or even free public land. When, inevitably, violence erupted between white squatters and Native Americans, national leaders did not directly bear the burden of responsibility. Thus the government could rhetorically pursue peace with indigenous groups (or assimilation) even as its unofficial colonial army (white settler families) encroached on their lands. The young and cash-poor federal government slowly won more territory without having to officially declare simultaneous wars against all the indigenous peoples in its borderlands, and white settlers acquired more and more land through preemption and other generous federal land policies—policies framed as Jacksonian Free-Soilism, not imperialism. Of course, on many occasions violence between whites and Native Americans in frontier zones erupted to such a degree that the government had to intervene, usually when white encroachment had provoked Native resistance that resulted in the widely reported killing of white settler families. At such points, the U.S. military or state militias, sent to put down indigenous resistance, could be framed as protecting national borders and defending white women and children from the Native Americans, which conveniently made aggressive expansion look like defensive peacekeeping. Land recently wrested from Native Americans and (in the South) open to slavery was the tacit reward for aggressive, individualistic, entrepreneurial behavior. "Settler colonist" may sound more innocent than "imperialist invader," but white settlers were far from harmless.[7]

Florida's history produced a unique version of settler colonialism. Many groups had laid claim to Florida before 1821, so the territory that Americans acquired in 1821 was already home to European colonists, autonomous Native Americans, and free blacks. This mixed population made Americans extremely anxious about their southern border; these groups might ally with foreign empires, or each other, and invade the United States or launch an insurrection against American slavery. A brief summary of Florida's past reveals who lived there on the eve of transfer to the United States in 1821, how these different constituencies provoked white American anxiety, and how each would either be coopted or driven out to make way for American settlers and their enslaved labor force in the decades that followed. White settler colonization, enabled by white women's labor in multiple ways, represented a solution to the threat Americans believed Florida's indigenous and colonial population posed.

Indigenous people had lived in Florida long before Europeans arrived there, but disease, warfare, and the slave trade devastated Florida's first peoples between the 1500s and the 1700s. Beginning in the early eighteenth century, several groups came south to populate this recently emptied region and founded villages in the panhandle and in the interior of north central Florida. Whites began calling all the Native Americans in Florida the Florida Indians and the Seminoles in the late eighteenth century, but indigenous Floridians did not think of themselves as part of one group at that point. Some historians believe that the name Seminole originated from the Spanish word *cimarron*, meaning "runaway." Others believe it derives from a Muscogee Creek word for wild plants and animals. By 1821 their settlements included at least five thousand Native American people as well as several hundred people of African descent. By the outbreak of the Second U.S.-Seminole War in 1835, the "Florida Indians" lived in four regional political communities—Apalachicola, Apalachee, Alachua, and Mikasuki—which were largely autonomous from each other. These groups were also distinct from the Muscogee Creeks (their nearest ancestral relatives) and Europeans. They were farmers and traders who understood kinship through matrilineal clans. Some of them claimed the tribute of enslaved black laborers, which granted them increased status, much as the labor of captives had enriched indigenous peoples in the Southeast for centuries.[8]

In addition to the indigenous people who lived there, there were also a few thousand people of European ancestry. Multiple European rulers had claimed Florida, an attractive territory due to its long coastlines and its strategic location between British and Spanish colonies, close to the Caribbean. The Spanish made the first permanent European settlement at St. Augustine in 1565. Its European population remained tiny (fewer than five thousand people), and by the mid-1700s Spain still exerted little authority outside of St. Augustine. At the end of the French and Indian War in 1763 Great Britain claimed Florida, and most members of the small Spanish colonial population (approximately three thousand people) departed. The British combined part of Louisiana with Florida to create two provinces, East and West Florida, and designated capitals at St. Augustine and Pensacola. The British hoped to encourage the development of profitable plantations in the Floridas and pursued peaceful relations with Native American groups to stabilize them. British colonist Andrew Turnbull, for example, recruited 1,403 Mediterranean laborers (mainly from Minorca) in 1767–1768 to work on his sugar plantation at New Smyrna. Turnbull's experiment with European contract workers failed when disease, grueling labor, violent overseers, and indigenous attacks killed nearly half of them, and the survivors abandoned the plantation in 1777. In St. Augustine the colonial government gave them land. By 1786, their families made up half of the population of St. Augustine and over 70 percent of its white population, because these contract laborers became "white" there, as in other colonies where there were few Europeans and many people of indigenous and African ancestry. Few other British planters were permanently successful, and although Loyalists fleeing the American Revolution added to British Florida's colonial population, most of Florida remained beyond European authority during the British period. Twenty years later, at the end of the American Revolution, East and West Florida returned to Spanish rule, and many of the British colonists evacuated. As the nineteenth century began, Napoleon occupied Spain, weakening it and opening its empire up to nationalist revolutions, which soon spread across South and Central America. Spain therefore had few resources to invest in controlling Florida. As a result, throughout the Second Spanish period (1783–1819), populations of autonomous Native and black people controlled parts of East and West Florida.[9]

There was a significant population of free blacks in Florida because its tenuous position as a barely fortified outpost of the Spanish empire had encouraged liberal immigration policies toward nonwhites since the First Spanish Period. Spain had welcomed runaway slaves and granted them freedom if they converted to Catholicism, swore loyalty to Spain, and helped protect Florida. The Spanish Crown also encouraged slave owners to manumit their slaves and incorporate them into a three-caste society of whites, free blacks, and enslaved blacks. This system allowed individuals to become free so as to discourage a collective uprising of enslaved people. Black and mixed-race residents of Spanish Florida participated in its social and economic life, and the Spanish governor of Florida sent hundreds of them to build and to occupy a fort two miles north of St. Augustine in 1738. Gracia Real de Santa Teresa de Mose, or Fort Mose, became the first free black town in North America sanctioned by a European power.[10]

In addition to the free blacks who lived among European colonists, in the early nineteenth century there were five hundred or more blacks (called *estelusti* by the indigenous people) living among the Native peoples of Florida. Some were runaways or their descendants who had escaped slavery sometime in the past two centuries, while others came into Seminole towns through the trade in enslaved people. They occupied and could move between several different social roles, including spouse, adopted kin, ally, and tributary slave. The Seminoles did not categorically treat enslaved blacks as chattel property. Some of the Black Seminoles, whom elite Seminoles inherited, purchased, or gave as gifts, were treated as property. However, unlike enslaved blacks among American whites, the *estelusti* lived with their own families in Seminole villages or in four separate, but allied, towns where they elected their own leaders, owned property, carried weapons, and chose their own spouses. If they desired to acculturate fully into Seminole society, blacks might do so through intermarriage or even adoption into a clan. The black towns, like all other Seminole and Creek towns, gave tribute and military alliance to the leaders of their mother towns, in exchange for which they received protection and trade privileges. Since Creek and Seminole towns were highly autonomous, having separate towns actually made the *estelusti* more like Seminoles and Creeks. In other ways the Black Seminoles maintained their own culture, practicing Christianity and speaking their own language (as well as English and indigenous languages), but they shared with Seminoles similar agricultural and building methods, clothing styles, some religious practices, and very clear political and military interests. The Second U.S.-Seminole War solidified their alliance due to their common interest in defeating the Americans so that the Seminoles might retain their lands and the Black Seminoles their freedom. Though contemporary whites were concerned about the status of the "Indian negroes" in Florida, the Seminoles were not preoccupied about it. Kinship ties as part of clans or extended families, not status as black, white, or Indian, were the most important categorization for them, at least in the early nineteenth century. Native Floridians thus challenged slavery organized by race even as they practiced a form of it.[11]

Much to the displeasure of American slaveholders, no single regime dominated outside of St. Augustine and Pensacola in the early nineteenth century, and Spain's weak presence left autonomous Native Americans and blacks in the Floridas free to ally with the British, whom the United States was already fighting on its northern frontier in the 1810s. Florida's mixed population also made American slaveholders very nervous. These anxieties drove repeated U.S. invasions of Florida in the 1810s. The Americans lacked a viable legal reason to intervene in Spanish territory, however, and had to withdraw after each invasion prior to 1818, leaving Florida outside of American control. That changed in early 1818 when Andrew Jackson, using reports of "Indian depredations" on white settlers along the Florida-Georgia border as an excuse, led a large American military force (composed of regulars, volunteers, and Lower Creek warriors) into Florida, destroying indigenous villages throughout Middle Florida and capturing thousands of cattle and hundreds of bushels of corn. The Americans began the First U.S.-Seminole War in cultural terms that would become even more familiar in the next twenty years. Cloaking expansionist aggression as self-defense, Jackson justified his actions as vengeance for the deaths of white women and children even as he targeted Seminole homes and families. He defended the invasion as vital to American national interests, since Spain had failed to rid the southeastern borderlands of threats to U.S. sovereignty by autonomous Native Americans, black runaways from slavery, and British agents who aided these groups. Although Jackson's campaign was militarily successful, the Seminoles were too smart to engage his larger force, and most survived to fight another day. Nevertheless, Jackson had exposed Spain's weakness. Treaty negotiations with Spain began in 1819 and Florida officially transferred to the United States in 1821. U.S. forces had finally claimed Florida, but it would take several more decades of war on its indigenous people, and white settler colonialism, before the Americans would fully control the territory.[12]

Due to its unique colonial and indigenous past and its location in the southern borderlands, Florida's version of white settler colonialism differs from that in other contemporary U.S. territories. Much as U.S. economic forces influenced local economies in other Native North American communities, Americans quickly sought profits in Florida. Due to Florida's location in the Southeast, however, the economic interests of slaveholders and land speculators prevailed over those of traders, and early U.S. policy toward Florida focused on removing the threats posed by autonomous Seminoles and free blacks rather than sustaining trade relationships. Thus American rule quickly marginalized the Seminole trade economy. Furthermore, while the expansion of market capitalism touched all American territories in the nineteenth century, the expansion of white settlement usually accompanied the spread of market capitalism in the borderlands. Yet large numbers of American squatters had not settled in Florida prior to 1821, making its colonization different from the process in many other early American frontier territories. While in Illinois and Georgia, for example, white squatters demanded violent federal efforts to remove indigenous residents in the 1830s in order to secure "their" property (in the Black Hawk

War and the Cherokee Removal from Georgia), in Florida the impetus for the First U.S.-Seminole War, which finally forced Spain to cede Florida to the United States, came from slaveholders rather than squatters. Andrew Jackson obliged them and invaded Florida because doing so extended his anti-Indian campaign into Florida and removed the British-Seminole alliance that had threatened the United States during the War of 1812. After 1821 white settlers flooded into upper Florida, and land speculation was popular there; however, the Second U.S. Seminole War—brought on by Jackson's removal agenda in the 1830s—soon discouraged many potential immigrants. In response to the scarcity of immigrants, American leaders enacted several policies during and right after the Second U.S.-Seminole War to attract white settler families to the unsettled parts of Florida in order to pressure the Seminoles to leave. They made policies that enlisted white women in colonization in order to replicate the settlement process unfolding in other territories, realizing that war and removal alone could not accomplish the same colonial goal: permanent settlement.[13]

In other respects, Florida is similar to other American settler colonies built in former Spanish colonial borderlands. In Missouri, as in Florida, the United States removed Native Americans in the early nineteenth century as thousands of white settlers arrived there (with the enslaved laborers they claimed as property) hoping to gain some of the cheap or free public land on offer from the U.S. government. In Texas and New Mexico, lawmakers passed similar public land bills, hoping to attract white settler families as they had done in Florida. Compared to Texas and New Mexico, Florida's southeastern coastal location and its population distinguish it, for it had far fewer white settlers than Texas did by the time of the 1836 rebellion, and a much smaller indigenous population than the New Mexico territory included when the Americans captured it (and the rest of Northern Mexico) in the U.S.-Mexico War of 1846–1848. Pro-settler land policies shaped the white colonization of all these places, and white settler women played an important role in the settler colonialism of all these states, even though their locations and demographics varied.[14]

Most settler colonies, including Florida and other U.S. states, justified imperial violence in the past and disavow it in the present through origin stories that frame settlement as natural, inevitable, or benevolent (for example, Manifest Destiny and the Thanksgiving story). Settler colonial accounts often cast particular imperial actors, such as the monarch, the metropolitan colonizer, and the ethnic cleanser, as the truly guilty parties, while they present settlers as persecuted migrants, refugees seeking asylum, or hardworking pioneers. In doing so, such accounts emphasize settlers' hardships to justify their rewards, while downplaying their role in dispossessing Native peoples. In the United States, settler colonialism had to further distinguish itself from imperialism because the American Revolution left a legacy of anticolonial feelings. However, Americans did not reject colonizing new territory; they just called it something else—such as the spread of democracy. Their stories about territorial expansion sideline settler aggression toward indigenous peoples by focusing on the religious persecution or pioneering valor of the white settlers, who are the heroes and heroines of an inspiring story about overcoming adversity to bring civilization to the wilderness. The brave settlers' sacrifices on the colonial frontier validate their entitlement to the land, which conveniently leaves indigenous peoples with prior claims outside of the main story. Settler stories intentionally marginalize the sustained legal and military battles that whites waged to claim Native land. When settler stories mention conflict with indigenous people, as in stories about Native attacks on white settlers, white narratives blame Native Americans for "bringing it on themselves" (by violently resisting white encroachment), and thus frame indigenous exile or death as the inevitable fate of "savages" who could not coexist with whites (eliding that it is wholly impossible to coexist with neighbors who want to remove or kill you).[15]

Although scholars rarely acknowledge it, the rhetorical frameworks that obscure imperial aggression in settler colonial origin stories often rely on gender. In Florida, female war refugees and hardy male farmers took center stage in the dramatic conflict between whites and Seminoles, and both of those images of Florida settlers helped to paint the naked aggression of Indian removal as a defensive policy to protect "peaceful" settler families. White women especially allowed American expansion into Florida to disappear as chivalrous defense, and at the same time settler narratives naturalized homemaking as woman's duty rather than framing it as imperialist action.

Few scholarly overviews of settler colonial theory analyze gender or examine white women as colonizers. Some lack any gender analysis, while others examine white masculinity or the way colonial regimes targeted indigenous men and women differently. Those insights are important and valuable, but such accounts are incomplete because they do not include settler women and the ways that domestic work drove the political and geographic success of white settlements. As Margaret Jacobs notes, "We must move beyond merely adding (white) women to a simple narrative of heroic triumph over adversity." Rather, settler women must be understood as colonizers who were simultaneously complicit with and subordinated by colonial regimes.[16]

There is a growing literature that fully incorporates women and gender, alongside race, class, and nation, in analyses of the colonial past. Many of these studies build on the insights of postcolonial theorist Ann Laura Stoler, who argues in *Carnal Knowledge and Imperial Power* that colonial regimes invaded intimate spaces and harnessed gender, race, and sexuality to their imperial mission. Margaret Jacobs's *White Mother to a Dark Race*, Adele Perry's *On the Edge of Empire*, and Lora Wildenthal's *German Women for Empire* take up these "intimacies of empire" in settler colonies. These studies put gender and settler women at the center of the colonial encounter. They broaden theories of settler colonialism and challenge previous scholarship in women's history that tended to romanticize settler women as pioneers rather than critically analyze white women as a colonizing force. In order to fully appreciate the role that white women played in imperial expansion, one must frame white female settlers' labor in its colonial context and excavate the roots of the "white woman pioneer" in the narratives that settler societies tell in order to disavow their own imperial pasts. This book joins with these studies to hold white women accountable for their role in settler colonialism and the violence that inhered in it. It contributes to the literature on gender and settler colonialism by critically focusing on white women as actors in a settler colony. It further enriches and complicates settler colonial theory by illustrating how the racial "logic of elimination" intersected with gender: settler colonialism placed women of different races in different positions based on its need for particular kinds of labor as well as land. It depended on the domestic and reproductive power that American culture granted white women to make permanent settlements and to camouflage colonial violence. It also relied on the elimination of indigenous women and the matrilineal societies they reproduced through their children. Finally, white settlers depended on the reproductive and physical labor of enslaved black women, which made slavery profitable and sustainable. It targeted white, indigenous, and enslaved black women and their reproductive power in different ways in order to support settler colonialism.[17]

Due to the narratives that frame settler colonialism as innocent, it can be hard to recognize its imperialist essence. American exceptionalism—the notion that America was different and better than European empires—tends to further obscure this in the U.S. case. Previous generations of U.S. historians argued that the United States was never imperialist so long as its territorial acquisitions were contiguous annexations within the continent; but that argument no longer holds. Scholars of U.S. settler colonialism describe it as a violent imperial mode under which Indian removal and genocide laid the groundwork for subsequent U.S. foreign policy and imperialism. Diplomatic historians now recognize that various iterations of imperial ideology operated well before and after the era of the U.S.-Mexico War, from the expansionist logic among the founding generation of American leaders, Thomas Jefferson and John Adams in particular, to the Latin American filibusters of the 1850s and to the U.S. occupation of Haiti, Cuba, and the Philippines in the 1890s.[18]

While histories of American settler colonialism usually include Florida, its significance in the development of U.S. expansionism has never been fully explored, in part due to the old myth that contiguous expansion was not imperialist. Historians also have overlooked it because the United States acquired it long before Manifest Destiny (the ideology that God intended for the growing population of white Americans to spread over all of North America, bringing Christianity, democracy, and capitalism to improve it) entered popular speech in the 1840s. The U.S. colonization of Florida began in the 1820s, as whites moved west into Missouri and other parts of the Louisiana Purchase, and at nearly the same moment that Moses Austin brought the first Anglo settlers into Mexican Tejas; thus Florida deserves as much recognition in the development of Manifest Destiny. If anything, the colonization of Florida and Missouri led the way, as both were already American territories by the time Cora Montgomery coined the term "Manifest Destiny" in the *United States Magazine and Democratic Review* in 1839. Placing Florida into the history of national expansion before 1840 links settler colonialism to other forms of U.S. imperialism and stretches histories of Manifest Destiny back to its beginnings, well before the conflict over Texas and Northern Mexico crystallized Americans' support for (or opposition to) national expansion.[19]

Florida is also left out of histories of U.S. expansion because of its location in the coastal Southeast far from the western frontier. Historians of the Spanish borderlands include Florida as a northern outpost of Spain's empire, while many U.S. histories include Florida as part of the Old South, even though it was a relatively recent acquisition by the time it joined the

Confederacy. Many historical accounts of expansion begin with the annexation of Texas in the mid-1840s and then follow expansion into the West, but Americans had set their sights on Spain's holdings in North America long before that. In fact, Americans had wanted Florida since the revolution, when John Adams wrote a prototype treaty that demanded Europeans acknowledge the United States as the rightful successor to all of Britain's North American colonies, including Canada, Bermuda, and Florida. Four decades later, when Adams's son, Secretary of State John Quincy Adams, negotiated the Transcontinental Treaty with Spanish diplomat Luis de Onís (ratified by Congress in 1821), he finally fulfilled his father's wishes. In exchange for Florida the United States agreed to pay $5 million in claims that Americans held against Spain, and to concede Texas, which it had claimed (over Spanish and Mexican objections) as part of the Louisiana Purchase.[20]

Expansionist Domesticity

As the border space between public and private, the threshold offers a useful metaphor for theorizing the gender history of American settler colonialism and the relationship between nineteenth-century nationalism and domesticity. As white women remade their homes in disputed borderlands, their domestic work crossed the threshold from private concern to public service—the settling up of the "public land." As Catharine Beecher opined in her 1842 *Treatise on Domestic Economy*, one of American women's most significant roles was to bring Christian domesticity to the wilderness, to install "an ark of civilization amid an ocean of foliage." As Beecher and other adherents of such domestic ideology noted, as the nation expanded, virtuous and well-ordered households (created and sustained by white women) would ensure that new territories and states would become civilized places that supported republican democracy. This belief countered the anxiety that pioneers would "go native" when they encountered "uncivilized" places and societies, or that the peoples that an expanding America swallowed up would challenge American political and social order rather than assimilating into it. Although historians rarely link male political and military leaders to domestic ideology, some of the American national and military leaders in this study also believed that the presence of white women in new settlements would ensure that American virtues would spread outward. Women's domestic roles as workers, mothers, wives, and mistresses required them to submit to patriarchal authority and to instill morality and patriotism in children; they therefore both upheld the patriarchal household model and supported the republic. Many Americans believed that white women were central to the spread of properly ordered households and civilization, just as other colonial regimes had cast European women as civilizing agents.[21]

As they made homes in Florida, white women established that it was part of the United States and home to Americans. The homemaking that they performed operated at both national and household levels, a dynamic I label "expansionist domesticity." Americans rarely explicitly theorized or described this expansionist domesticity because most believed that domestic labor was the work that women naturally provided. Antebellum Americans viewed white women's work in creating permanent settler colonies as their innate, God-given role and rarely commented on it. In historical accounts, white frontier women appear to do the same quotidian labor in a different place, with perhaps more difficulties, fewer comforts, and added loneliness. They seem to have little choice about whether to risk the rewards of frontier living. Yet, as this study shows, male and female migrants into Florida all relied on extended family and kinship networks in order to survive and thrive, in spite of the image of the single, independent male trailblazer favored in popular representations of the frontier. As subordinate partners to male settlers, women (and their labor) could be taken for granted; thus expansionist domesticity underwrote settlement policies and processes in unacknowledged ways. Hence women, even white women, are frequently marginalized or absent from histories of expansion and settler colonialism. Similarly, histories of women and domestic work often remain limited to the world within households, even though territorial expansion regularly counted on women's willingness to cross the threshold and make new homes in contested places.

The continuing assumption that territorial expansion was men's work arises both from the public/private dichotomy that shaped domestic ideology and from ideas about dependence and independence embedded in the antebellum social order. Most Americans, across regional variations, presumed that white men were independent, chivalrous, and responsible for their dependents—women, children, servants, and slaves. The white patriarch derived his power from his position as the independent household head to whom all his dependents owed their labor and loyalty. This patriarchal household social order was central to the framework that policy makers used in Florida. Their policies aimed to restore women and men to their natural roles, a restoration that they equated with the settlement of the frontier. In return, white women benefited from national expansion and were at least complicit with its violence, whether or not they consciously invested themselves in the ideological project of expansionist domesticity. Their dependence limited women's choices and makes it very difficult to locate their agency in history, but because of their role and privilege in national expansion, white women must be considered central actors in accounts of U.S. expansion. While several historians have found that white women often resisted frontier migration, studies such as this one reveal that the work women did once they arrived was no less significant to the expansion of slavery and national territory. In fact, that men compelled white women to go should highlight just how important their presence and labor were to those who brought them (sometimes against their wishes) to Florida and other settler colonies.[22]

Rather than accepting the framing of settler women's domestic work as innocent or even patriotic, we must recognize that white women, like men, were invaders who the nation rewarded for their work along U.S. frontiers, where they effectively expanded the territory upon which their whiteness would grant them a range of privileges based on their alleged superiority to Native Americans and people of African descent. That white women's work was gendered and cast as subordinate to white men's makes it no less significant in the cooperative racial project that was American expansion in the early nineteenth century. In fact, that subordination was part of its significance.

In spite of the ways that nineteenth-century domesticity obscured their significance, white women's lives are reflected in historical records from the Florida frontier; such records even include white women of modest means who did not leave behind journals or extensive correspondence. Land and court records, public and private accounts of territorial Florida, and military and federal policy papers all illuminate the ways their physical labor and symbolic value underwrote American settler colonialism in Florida.

This book approaches the history of white women in Florida differently than many other books on antebellum women. The "cult of domesticity" and its prescriptive notion that women and men occupied separate spheres of influence in the nineteenth-century United States has been a long-standing feature of U.S. women's history. Rather than measuring their political significance by the reform movements they championed or the political parties they supported, this book recognizes, first, that making homes in territorial Florida was a political act even if women were not conscious of it. Women's domestic work had national meanings in the context of territorial and slavery expansion. Second, it suggests that southern white women were not only plantation mistresses or farm wives, but they were also settlers who brought slavery as well as white homes into Indian country. Third, it includes men and masculinity as part of the domestic realm, since almost all households contained both men and women, and because gender ideology relied on the pairing of masculinity and femininity—in oppositional, complementary, and heteronormative ways.[23]

Another implication of this study is that domesticity was not only an ideological construct that shaped national expansion, it was also a material part of the process of Americanizing new spaces. In frontier Florida, white women used their labor (and that of any enslaved people they exploited), household furniture, and kitchen utensils to make new homes and benefited in material ways because they did so. Here this study takes some cues from socialist feminists, who have long recognized the material importance of domestic ideology. Historically this ideology purported that women did not work but "helped"; that women were especially suited for housework or trades that replicated household skills (work always deemed unskilled regardless of its degree of difficulty, and, therefore, always paid less than "skilled" male labor); and that "love" rather than money, independence, or status was the best and most appropriate reward for female work. In this regard, Americans treated women's work for settlement as they did the rest of their labor. It was vital to the reproduction and survival of society but completely discounted as work. Unlike women's domestic work elsewhere, however, their labor on frontiers supported not only their households and the growth of the middle class and modern capitalism but also the expansion of national territory—support that looked apolitical given women's natural role as "helpers." This book categorizes and analyzes women's labor in frontier homesteads as work—domestic and nationalist work—and establishes that white women were important and complicit members of white settler colonies that spread slavery, ended the liberty of free blacks in Florida, dispossessed Native Americans, and attempted to destroy indigenous societies via assimilation, extermination, and removal.[24]

Since this book's central claims about the significance of women's labor depend upon a multifaceted definition of domesticity, the book owes a great debt to scholarship on the antebellum "culture of sentiment." In particular, critic Amy Kaplan has argued that territorial expansion and domestic ideology were partners in a nationalist project that she named "Manifest Domesticity." In Kaplan's view, proponents of domesticity used expansion to give women's domestic literature national and imperial importance. This study expands upon her work to illustrate how proponents of expansion mobilized domesticity in the service of settler colonialism and Manifest Destiny. In Florida, national and military forces mobilized matters typically confined to women's history—domesticity, married women's property law, gender roles—to justify Indian removal, to spread slavery, and to propel territorial expansion via white settlement. Using the tools of social and political history, this book confirms what Kaplan observed in women's domestic literature—that at times the domestic ideal, rather than dividing women and men into separate spheres, united white American men and women around national expansion.[25]

This study also draws upon the vibrant scholarship that analyzes U.S. expansion in cultural history. These scholars have bridged histories of U.S. imperialism with studies of American visual and literary culture, showing that culture not only reflected foreign policy concerns but also helped to shape policy. This study asks not only how U.S. policies in territorial Florida shaped and reflected domestic ideology and cultural beliefs about women but also how those policies affected female historical actors who, in turn, sometimes renegotiated such ideologies and beliefs. It moves beyond texts to consider how expansionist domesticity also operated on a political and geographical stage.[26]

As with settler colonial studies, when histories of national expansion have explored its gendered ideological and material consequences, they have emphasized the ways that white masculinity influenced American foreign policy and imperialism. And for good reason: the idea of martial manhood popular among many nineteenth-century Americans celebrated male exploits in wars fought for territory and framed them as noble violence aimed at the spread of democracy or the defense of women and children. Nevertheless, this important focus on masculinity has overshadowed an equally compelling history of women and femininity. Indeed, only a few studies have looked for women's roles in national expansion. Unlike previous studies, this book does not suggest that women's role was solely oppositional or subordinate to expansionist men. Rather, as whites, white women had much to gain from expansionist policies and actively sought those gains for themselves and their households. In doing so, white women undertook particularly female tasks on behalf of territorial expansion and shared the benefits with white men. Moreover, white women who profitably settled the frontier succeeded for the same reasons men did. The male and female settlers most likely to plant permanent roots and prosper in Florida had usually settled near relatives. In extended families, as in domestic relations, men and women were interdependent.[27]

White women were central to U.S. national expansion and its ideological justifications and effects: they symbolized civilized domesticity, expended the labor that turned frontier dwellings into permanent homes, and gave birth to the next generation of whites in Florida, people who would claim to be its "natives." In this study, then, white women take center stage to highlight their role in American settler colonialism and to emphasize the ways in which white domesticity privileged them and provided essential service to national expansion. The homes that white women built in territorial Florida were the building blocks of a colonial regime that dispossessed Native Americans, as well as places in which people lived under the deeply unequal relations of racial slavery.

Race and the Domestication of U.S. Florida

The gender dynamics of American expansion cannot be separated from the racial projects under way in territorial Florida. The colonization of Florida unfolded as Americans in general began to change their perceptions of Native Americans. Whites viewed people of African descent as irredeemably different from whites, but they had long seen indigenous difference as rooted in environment rather than race. For most Americans before about 1830, Native American "savagery" was a problem that could be solved by "civilization" or assimilation programs, and U.S. Indian policy, at least rhetorically, had reflected this attitude. After 1830 that view began to change, and many white Americans (except for a few Christian missionaries) began to think of "Indians" as a distinct race that would never achieve the same level of civilization as whites or live comfortably among them, in spite of the many examples of indigenous people who did just that. Not only did whites increasingly view Indians as racially distinct and incapable of assimilating but the alliance and occasional kinship between blacks and Seminoles in Florida further inflamed anti-Indian sentiment there.[28]

As white Americans increasingly invested race with immutable meaning, U.S. rule brought a changing racial regime to Florida. American racial systems built on earlier Spanish and British colonial models, and racial categories outside American settlements were somewhat in flux in the early nineteenth century. Florida's middle ground, however, was eroding quickly (along with many others in North America at the end of the Wars of the 1810s), as it became a U.S. territory in which the Native peoples lacked European allies. In the 1820s and 1830s, white settlers began to reproduce the inequalities of patriarchal white supremacy as they settled in Florida, and Seminole and Black Seminole people fought to maintain their land and autonomy. The values attached to differences in skin tone and culture increasingly conformed to the American model, in which the most significant distinctions were between whites (whether of Spanish, English, or other European descent); Native Americans, increasingly cast as undifferentiated "Seminoles" (who Americans believed must be removed); and blacks (who Americans believed must be enslaved). Americans imposed these racial categories in Florida through racial slavery, via the privileging of whites, and in its diplomacy with Native Americans. People of mixed European, African, and/or Native American ancestry would find it much more difficult to maintain their rights and property in U.S. Florida than they had under Spain.[29]

The labor of enslaved people—forced by threat of violence and a dehumanizing racial regime—was central to the creation of white American homes, wealth, and identity in Florida. While the *estelusti* fought alongside their Seminole allies to remain free, enslaved blacks found themselves separated from families and communities and sold or sent to Florida to toil in cotton, sugar, or indigo fields. The number of enslaved people in Florida had already swelled to 15,501 by 1830 and then nearly quadrupled to 61,745 by 1860. Free blacks living in former Spanish colonial towns faced increasing harassment and discrimination after 1821.[30] Meanwhile, white settlers were granted citizenship and property rights, rations, protection, transportation, housing, and cheap or even free land if they helped colonize Florida.

Americans also created a single category of indigenous identity so that all those deemed Indians in Florida could be removed. American negotiators in the 1820s and 1830s regarded Florida's separate bands of Native American peoples as one group, because doing so allowed them to make treaties that (from a U.S. perspective) conveniently bound all of them to one agreement. From a Native American perspective, however, there was no such group or council that could make decisions for all Native people in Florida. In fact, a unified political and cultural "Seminole" identity only solidified in indigenous resistance to American demands, especially in the three wars they fought against U.S. forces. The "Black Seminoles" experienced their own parallel but distinct ethnogenesis in the same conflicts, as they fought to maintain their freedom. U.S.-Seminole diplomacy and conflict thus created new Black Seminole and Indian identities even as they sought to eliminate them.[31]

The absence of a captive trade in Florida also influenced the shift toward American racial hierarchy. By the 1820s the Seminoles were not taking many white captives, for there was no market for them. This made nineteenth-century Florida a far different place—with fundamentally dissimilar relationships between whites, Native Americans, and blacks—than other Spanish borderlands in the early nineteenth century. The captive trade in Pueblo, Plains, Cherokee, and other borderland societies, which continued in the West into the nineteenth century, challenged traditional Native kinship and integrated Native communities into larger capitalist economies there. Intermarriage via captive taking also forged kin connections between imperial settlers and Native Americans in such borderlands, but not in Florida. In the main, the Seminoles viewed whites as enemies and not potential kin, especially since there were plenty of runaway slaves available for adoption as kin or tributary slaves. Instead of taking and trading in white captives, the Seminoles attacked homesteads in order to discourage white migration into Florida. As a result of settler colonialism and the conflicts it produced, whites and Native peoples in Florida increasingly saw each other as fundamentally different.[32]

White Settlers and Ethnic Cleansing

Between the First and Second U.S.-Seminole Wars, the United States signed three treaties with "the Florida Indians." U.S. agents negotiated these agreements in the 1820s and 1830s as white families moved into Florida. American Indian agents conducted these treaties, like almost all U.S.-Indian diplomacy, with a bare modicum of honesty, mostly to create plausible but thin arguments that they were valid. Indigenous people in Florida resisted making and complying with each of these treaties. The first one established reservations for Native Americans in the Florida territory, but subsequent

Table 1. Florida Population by Race and Enslavement, 1830–1860

	1830		1840		1850		1860	
	Territory of Florida	% of whole	Territory of Florida	% of whole	State of Florida	% of whole	State of Florida	% of whole
Total population	34,730		54,477		87,445		140,424[a]	
Whites	18,385	52.94%	27,943	51.29%	47,203	53.98%	77,746	55%
Enslaved blacks	15,501	44.63%	25,717	47.21%	39,310	44.95%	61,745	43.97%
Free blacks	844	2.43%	817	1.5%	932	1.07%	932	0.664%

Source: U.S. Census Bureau, Population Schedules, Florida, 1830, 1840, 1850, and 1860, in Social Explorer Dataset, Census 1830, 1840, 1850, and 1860 [database online].
[a] Includes one "Indian."

documents created a series of impossible and escalating demands on the Seminoles, in particular for land, for the return of the Black Seminoles whom Americans termed runaway slaves, and for Seminole reunification with the Creeks (by now their enemies) on a shared reserve west of the Mississippi River. White Americans were determined to end the freedom that the Seminoles offered runaways and to reclaim their "property" among the Black Seminoles.[33] Chapter 1 analyzes how international treaty law endowed white settler women with separate marital property rights in this period, even as American law also limited the rights of free blacks and shored up racial slavery.

As in many settler colonies, white colonization happened in tandem with Indian removal and the expansion of slavery into Florida. The American population increased quickly after 1821, from a total of 34,730 in 1830 (the date of the first U.S. census of Florida) to 87,445 in 1850. By 1850, migrants from other states comprised over half (56.1 percent) of the free, native-born population in Florida. In that same period, the indigenous population of Florida dropped dramatically, from about five thousand to fewer than four hundred. Many of the whites who settled Florida were slaveholders, and Florida's growing population included nearly equal numbers of whites and enslaved blacks (Table 1). Migrants also built other institutions that nineteenth-century whites associated with civilization: Protestant churches, schools for free white children, and newspapers.[34]

Intending to stay permanently and hoping to become wealthy planters using enslaved labor, the white settler population concentrated in the middle of upper Florida and increasingly limited the rights of free blacks

Map 1. Florida, 1821–1845.

(Table 2). By 1840 over half of Florida's population resided in the region between the Suwanee and Apalachicola Rivers. Attracted by rich agricultural land, whites eagerly flocked to the area, laying out the new state capital Tallahassee in 1824. Middle Florida whites held disproportionately high numbers of slaves, nearly half of all the slaves in Florida in 1830 and more than half of the total in 1840. As slavery increased, the number of free blacks fell (and many fled the territory), especially in Middle Florida.[35]

U.S.-Seminole diplomacy in the 1820s and 1830s culminated in a highly disputed 1833 agreement that the Seminoles would return runaway slaves and move to the Creek reservation in the western Indian Territory by 1835. Those who lived in upper Florida—closest to the whites moving into

Table 2. Florida Population by Most Populated Regions, Race, and Enslavement, 1830–1860

		Population	Whites	Enslaved blacks	Free blacks
1830	**Territory of Florida**	34,730	18,385	15,501	844
	Middle Florida	15,779	4,837	7,587	19
	% of total	45.43%	26.31%	48.95%	2.25%
	East Florida	8,223	4,466	3,438	319
	% of total	23.68%	24.29%	22.18%	37.8%
1840	**Territory of Florida**	54,477	27,943	25,717	817
	Middle Florida	27,556	11,518	15,973	65
	% of total	50.58%	41.22%	62.11%	7.96%
	East Florida	13,126	8,257	4,609	260
	% of total	24.09%	29.55%	17.92%	31.82%
1850	**State of Florida**	87,445	47,203	39,310	932
	Middle Florida	39,461	16,822	22,561	78
	% of total	45.13%	35.64%	57.39%	8.37%
	East Florida	22,442	13,677	8,514	251
	% of total	25.66%	28.97%	21.66%	26.93%
1860	**State of Florida**	140,424[a]	77,746	61,745	932
	Middle Florida	53,200	23,662	29,428	110
	% of total	37.89%	30.44%	47.66%	11.80%
	East Florida	50,667	29,078	21,240	349
	% of total	36.08%	37.40%	34.40%	37.45%

Notes: In 1830 Middle Florida included Gadsden, Hamilton, Jefferson, Leon, and Madison counties; for 1840 data Franklin County was added, it was carved out of Gadsden County in 1832. This table does not include the sparsely populated South Florida region (Indian lands, Mosquito and Monroe Counties) as part of East Florida although they had been included in the British Province of East Florida. U.S. Census, Florida, 1830, 1840, 1850, and 1860 in Social Explorer Dataset, Census 1830, 1840, 1850 and 1860 [database online].
[a] Includes one "Indian."

Middle Florida and already facing violence—capitulated and left in 1834. Elsewhere, especially in East Florida, cycles of borderland violence renewed between indigenous residents and white settlers. These rising tensions erupted into war in late 1835. In November, resistant Seminoles killed Charley Emathla, a Seminole who was cooperating with removal. In late December a band of Seminoles ambushed American soldiers as they traveled between Fort Brooke and Fort King (Tampa and Ocala). On the same day, Seminole warriors killed the Indian agent at Fort King. In retaliation, President Jackson ordered U.S. forces to invade a Seminole stronghold on the

Withlacoochee River. These events formally started the Second U.S-Seminole War.[36]

In the ethnic cleansing campaign that whites called the Second Seminole War, many Seminoles died from starvation, violence, or disease, but their resolve to remain in Florida fiercely challenged their Americans foes. Determined to remain independent and in Florida, but fewer in number and resources than the Americans, the Seminoles fought an effective guerilla war for nearly seven years from December 1835 until August 1842. The United States spent more than $30 million (far more than planned for the removal of all indigenous peoples east of the Mississippi) and sent nearly 1,500 white men to their deaths in Florida during this conflict. The Florida War, as the American press called this conflict at the time, lasted much longer than anticipated, cost more money than any other U.S. war with Native Americans before or since, and resulted in the loss of more American soldiers than any other U.S. war against an indigenous nation. The U.S. military removed about 4,400 indigenous people (including nearly five hundred Black Seminoles) during the Second U.S.-Seminole War.[37]

Most of the military action occurred between the Withlacoochee River and Lake Okeechobee, a region stretching 150 miles across central Florida. That region contained white homesteads as well as Seminole villages, and therefore women and children from both indigenous and white communities were on the front lines. Throughout the war, the U.S. Army attacked Seminole villages, where they killed and captured people and burned homes, goods, and fields. The Seminoles retaliated in kind, attacked troops or white settlers, and then disappeared into Florida's vast coastal plains and swamps where American forces struggled to even locate them. By its second year, the war appeared to be a hopeless effort that Americans, in the context of the economic panic that began in 1837, could not afford to keep funding. Critics did not, however, voice any opposition to the war's aims—just to President Jackson's failure to achieve them.[38]

Critics of the Florida War expressed little sympathy for the Seminoles because, in the 1830s, Indian depredation narratives emerged in the American press, framing the conflict as a war to protect white women and children from "savages" and "barbarians," in spite of the fact that American forces resorted to the same strategy of attacking Seminole homes and families. Chapter 2 examines those stories, the version of this history that has dominated prior written accounts, and their effects on American policy.

Chapter 3 features Seminole accounts of the war and their removal from Florida, a perspective that confirms some aspects of white American accounts but challenges their framing of the conflict. Many whites, fearful of Indian depredations, fled to other states or to military garrisons in 1835 and 1836. Desperate to keep them from abandoning Florida, Congress responded in 1836 by ordering the army to supply rations to any white families, widows, and orphans who stayed in the territory. Chapter 4 analyzes this wartime welfare program.[39]

Although they were essential to white settlements, white women were scarce in territorial Florida, a problem that American leaders would seek to remedy. In 1830 and 1840 Florida had more white adult men and fewer adult white women than national averages. While Florida's enslaved population had a balanced gender ratio and an average age near the national norm, its white population skewed male and its white female population skewed young. If U.S. leaders wanted to populate Florida with white families, they would have to find ways to change this, given the importance of available reproductive-age wives to family formation and white settler colonialism. The influx of white soldiers and the flight of some white women out of the territory during the Second U.S.-Seminole War increased the white gender and age imbalances. In 1840, there were almost twice as many white men in the territory as white women. Furthermore, the enslaved population continued to grow with nearly equal numbers of males and females, so that by 1840 enslaved black women outnumbered white women. As Chapters 4 and 5 reveal, American leaders enacted supportive family settlement policies in the early 1840s as they ended the Second U.S.-Seminole War. As a result, gender ratios among white adults began to equalize. In 1850 the white gender ratio was 1.3 men for every white adult woman (as compared to 1.74 in 1840). By 1860, it approached parity (1.18). As soldiers departed, new white families arrived or formed and white women produced more children. In fact, in addition to migration (voluntary and coerced) and in spite of the relative scarcity of white adult women, reproduction boosted Florida's population in these years. Children under the age of fifteen made up 41–45 percent of the total population in the decades after 1821, and by 1850 Florida had proportionally more white children than the national average and roughly the same percentage of enslaved children (see Appendix).[40]

American leaders created these policies aimed at retaining and increasing adult white female settlers in Florida even as they sought to remove

Seminole families. U.S. forces finally broke the fierce Seminole resistance about five years into the war brought on by the U.S. Indian removal policy. Determined to fracture their alliance, U.S. Brigadier General Thomas Jesup offered the Black Seminoles a deal in 1837. Against white southerners' wishes, Jesup promised them freedom if they agreed to surrender and leave Florida. This gave them an alternative path to liberty and manipulated them into aiding the Americans. As one of their descendants recalled, "They all went together to leave Florida to Oklahoma. . . . You know that they had to do something to be free."[41] In addition to the loss of their Black Seminole allies, the Seminoles lost the war because they ran out of resources and safe places to live. They were rarely routed on the battlefield, but deprivation led many to surrender between 1837 and 1841, while American forces captured others. After their capture or surrender, American military escorts imprisoned the Seminoles at a fort where they waited, sometimes for months, for the steamboats that would take them west. By 1841, most of the Seminoles had been sent west to the Creek Indian Territory. Some Black Seminoles went with them, while others aided U.S. forces in exchange for their freedom. After removal, Black Seminoles found little safety from slavery in Indian Territory, and some traveled further south into Texas and Mexico in search of secure freedom.[42]

In 1841 American military leaders also began to recruit white settler families to reoccupy the frontier. Military leaders believed that white recolonization would induce the remaining Seminoles to surrender. As an incentive to reestablish settlements at abandoned forts, plantations, and farms, the army provided white settler families with rations, transportation, and temporary homes. The white women who participated in this colonization scheme are featured in Chapter 4. Congress passed a bill that awarded free public land to armed white settlers in Florida just as the war ended in late summer 1842. This new law rewarded whites who inhabited and cultivated Florida farms (south of the existing line of settlement) for five years. Chapter 5 highlights the gendered ways in which white settler families operated as armed occupiers under this law.[43]

Ultimately, the U.S. Army never managed to rid Florida of Seminoles completely or to capture all the Black Seminoles and return them to slavery. Several hundred Seminoles remained on an informal reservation in southwest Florida after 1842, distant from white settlements. Nationalists and other proponents of aggressive expansionism found little to celebrate in the Second U.S.-Seminole War and far more to commemorate in the

U.S.-Mexico War, which began four years later. This is another reason why histories of Manifest Destiny sideline Florida. The U.S.-Seminole wars, especially the long and bloody Second U.S.-Seminole War, brought more shame than praise to the American military and government. The war with Mexico, by contrast, was relatively quick and gloriously successful, making it a more favorable context for celebrating national expansion.[44]

As the history of early U.S. Florida reveals, women's history is not separate from histories of war, expansion, slavery, colonialism, and politics. Domestic ideology influenced not only women's lives but also the development of American nationalism and territorial expansion. In the chapters that follow, it will become clear that in political speech, popular representations, and federal and military policy, white women and their domestic labor played an important role in how Americans made Florida part of the United States. Some white women found opportunities on the Florida frontier that were not available to women elsewhere in the United States in the first half of the nineteenth century. Their gains, however, came at a high cost for indigenous and black peoples in Florida.

PART I

Slavery, Indian Removal,
and Expansionist Domesticity

CHAPTER 1

Property, Settlement, and Slavery

> I enclose you the promised deed for the land and negroes, which will have to be executed by your two uncles, the trustees, and then recorded in the court of Leon County, and the sooner you have it attended to, the better.
> —William Wirt to Laura Wirt Randall, December 8, 1827

> By the laws of the Spanish Monarchy . . . your oratrix was entitled to her separate property independent of the control or disposition of the said Defendant, which right has in no wise been changed by the transfer of the Province to the United States, but said property was secured to her by the treaty of Cession and by an Act of the legislative council . . . according to the right and title by which she held it while the Province was under the dominion of his Catholic Majesty.
> —*LeSassier v. Alba*, Escambia County, Florida, May 1831

In 1831 Victoria LeSassier, a wealthy Pensacola widow in her seventies, divorced her second husband, Pedro de Alba. Deeply in debt, Alba had recently threatened to take control of his wife's separate estate, which was worth about $36,000. His financial problems had plagued their marriage since 1819, when LeSassier, suspecting that he had attempted to poison her in order to inherit her property, left Alba's household and went to live with her son. She wrote Alba that she was quitting their marriage because he had treated her so badly that even a slave would have complained, and warned him: "But, Alba, that time of slavery is over. Consider myself your equal in every respect."[1] A slave owner herself, Victoria LeSassier was well aware of the privileges that her whiteness and wealth produced. It was not until Florida became an American territory, however, that she could sue Alba for a divorce (since divorce had been impossible under Catholic Spain). Unlike most other wives in the United States in the 1830s, she was able to keep and control the property that she had brought into their marriage, which made divorce much more attractive. When LeSassier divorced Alba she regained control over several town lots in Pensacola, thousands of acres of land in West Florida, and twenty enslaved people.[2] Her story illustrates how Florida's transition from Spanish colony to U.S. territory resulted in a hybrid legal system that supported white settler colonialism. Legally, Americans did not seamlessly replace civil law with common law; rather they chose to honor some parts of civil and treaty law—even when they challenged common law rules—if doing so favored white settlement in Florida. Under the new regime, white women of property such as Victoria LeSassier (especially those who owned slaves) would benefit in unexpected ways, while Seminoles and blacks would face increasing discrimination.[3]

LeSassier jettisoned her husband but kept her property in Florida because it was a colonial borderland. Before 1821, Spain ruled Florida, and Spanish civil law granted wives separate property rights and half of marital property, not because it supported female independence but rather due to the continuation of their lineage in marriage. While Anglo wives left behind their families of birth when they married, Spanish wives brought familial ties with them, retaining their maiden names in addition to their married ones. Uniquely, colonial-era Florida wives ended up keeping their separate property rights in Florida after 1821 via treaty law. Article 8 of the Adams-Onís Treaty (in which Spain ceded Florida to the United States) upheld the property rights of all Spanish colonists. Since many women had received or inherited property in Spanish Florida, Article 8 confirmed their right to own separate property even though some of them were married and, therefore, would not have had the right to separate property under the common law. The loophole was accidental, as neither John Quincy Adams nor Luis de Onís said anything about women in their correspondence concerning Article 8. In 1822, Florida's legislature adopted the common law and explicitly repealed Spanish civil codes, contradicting Article 8 of the treaty for married women. Historians have often accepted this as proof that civil law no longer applied after U.S. annexation, but in fact it necessitated another law. In 1824, "to obviate any doubts," the Florida Legislative Council specifically confirmed the rights of "husbands and wives" married under civil law to treat their property "in the same manner as they could or might have done under the laws of Spain." Colonial-era wives kept their separate property, and several cases arose in early territorial Florida to test this law. In most cases colonial-era wives prevailed, especially if they were white.[4]

This chapter examines the intersection of race and gender in the application of property law in Florida in the first decades after it transferred into the United States. Using court records to unearth the material contributions that white women made to settler colonialism and the expansion of racial slavery into Florida, I argue that their property was essential to expansionist domesticity, for through their holdings in household property and enslaved people, white women supported Florida's colonization. Due to the advantages that civil law granted them in Florida, many wives were able to amass wealth in their own names, making Florida court records an especially rich source of information on women's property holdings and practices, as women went to court to protect property from competing heirs, creditors, or predatory relatives. Although wives owned all kinds of real and personal property, enslaved human property was more common than any other single type in the court cases involving women surveyed for this study.

Florida's legislature granted a powerful combination of rights to white wives in the 1820s, but it upheld married women's property rights, rather than reversing the loophole to follow common law, in order to honor international law and preserve the treaty with Spain, not in order to protect or empower women. At the same time, Florida law began to limit the civil and property rights of nonwhites in Florida, including free people of color, regardless of whether they were married or women, which suggests that there was more at stake than obedience to international law. Although potentially empowering for white women, the legal hybridity that resulted from Florida's transfer to the United States offered little relief to enslaved people, free blacks, and Native Americans. Many enslaved people—the "property" of whites—were uprooted from their own communities, separated from their families, and sent to labor in Florida's growing cotton and sugar plantations in the early nineteenth century. Indigenous people in Florida, whose removal became an American goal and the object of the three U.S.-Seminole Wars in that same period, had very recently farmed the ground that they worked. For free people of color, including many people in mixed-race Spanish colonial families, the legal and cultural changes that U.S. rule wrought were also devastating. Although there were rare exceptions, typically U.S. courts ruled in ways that benefited whites (whether male or female), while Native Americans and blacks lost property and autonomy. The rights and property of women of color suffered a much different fate than those of white wives because their presence and independence from whites challenged white supremacy. Rather than understanding these only as contrasting experiences, it is helpful to view them as interlocking parts of U.S. settler colonialism, which used property and property law to expand white settlement and slavery into Florida.

Married women's property rights in early Florida seem contrary to antebellum gender norms and the common law, which seemingly subordinated married women totally to their husbands. These rights were consistent with expansionist domesticity, however, which enlisted white women to support colonization. Backing white settler colonialism, American lawmakers and judges supported white property ownership (even for married women), black enslavement, and indigenous dispossession. The property this law protected—land, household goods and furnishings, enslaved people—was useful to the material and cultural process of white settler colonialism. Until 1845, common law rules still limited post-1818 white wives' property rights. Florida passed another law in 1845, the year of Florida statehood, to expand these rights to post-treaty wives. That occurred on the heels of recolonization (1841) and the Armed Occupation Act (1842), policies designed to attract white men and women who were willing to move to a dangerous frontier, recently taken from the Seminoles, and make permanent homes there. In that context, Florida passed the first married women's property acts in any U.S. territory, though again these were not legal reforms intended to empower women.[5] Due to the ways that married women's property (and their legal right to it) supported white settler colonialism in Florida, this chapter places the history of married women's property law within the history of expansionist domesticity on the southern frontier rather than the history of women's rights. Doing so reveals that separate marital property rights were among the benefits of Manifest Destiny for white women, benefits that were explicitly denied Native Americans and blacks.

Married Women's Separate Property Rights

Outside of Florida, most American wives fell under the common law, which designated them *femes covert*, or women without a legal identity. Upon marriage, a husband became the legal owner of a wife's property. The only exception was property set aside in a separate trust in a Chancery or Equity Court, which allowed elite families to circumvent common law coverture. Wealthy parents settled separate equity estates upon their daughters (usually when they married) in order to protect property from unscrupulous husbands and to preserve it for male heirs, rather than to empower the women (much as civil law marital property rules intended). Although elite families benefited from this loophole, American wives as a class did not enjoy the legal right to own property as women under civil law did. Of course, white women throughout the United States brought property into marriages and helped their spouses amass wealth and property during marriage, whether wives owned property separately or not. Separate estates and separate marital property rights, however, render women's capital contributions to their families visible as material contributions.[6]

On a daily basis, the difference between a Spanish wife's separate property and an American wife's separate equity estate was small. Neither typically controlled her own property. For example, Victoria LeSassier's son (and after his death, her niece's husband) managed her estate. However, differences in their access to the courts, consent requirements, and inheritance law meant that when conflicts arose about property, civil law wives had more options than common law wives. They enjoyed direct access to the courts, had to consent to any property arrangements, and could also manage their own property or choose a new trustee. A married American woman with a separate estate usually did not appoint the trustee or consent to the management of her property. If she became concerned about her estate, she could only complain to the trustees, who might or might not agree with her concerns and might or might not choose to pursue legal action.[7]

Floridian Adeline Townsend learned that her position as a married woman with an equity estate was precarious in the early 1830s. Separated from her husband, Townsend had to appoint a new trustee for her estate when the previous one died. Her brother-in-law, Daniel Griswold, "cajoled" her into entrusting her $20,000 estate to him. After becoming her trustee, he "entirely changed his tone" toward her and was "now lording it over her in the most imperious manner." In an exasperated petition to the East Florida Court she complained, "The niggardly sums he has supplied were not even sufficient for her absolute necessities." Noting that she had once had an estate "subject to her own control," she was now "compelled

... to depend upon her own individual labour, and the cold charity of strangers for the common necessities of life."[8] There is no decision in the case file and its outcome is unknown, but this petition illustrates how under common law, even wealthy white women could find themselves at the mercy of a judge and virtually powerless over the trustee of their separate estates.

Inheritance rules also differed. Civil law widows inherited their entire dowry plus half of the property made during the marriage, which they fully controlled. In comparison, the common law entitled American widows only to the use of one-third of the husband's estate during their natural lives. This one-third share, or dower, was a life estate that she could use to maintain herself but which would revert to his heirs after her death. The passing of her spouse meant that a widow faced relinquishing two-thirds of the property to which she was accustomed, since she only got the use of one-third of it. While testators could leave a widow more than her third and give her permanent title rather than a life estate, they could also leave a widow less than a third, a legacy she would have to contest in court. Under these rules, common law widows were subject to the generosity of their spouses rather than entitled to half of the marital property in addition to their own. While civil law required that all husbands treat wives equally, common law made it possible for men to decide how much property and control their widows would inherit.[9]

American rule did expand Florida wives' options in one way. While Spanish law had forced women to remain in unhappy marriages, several (like Victoria LeSassier) sought relief through divorce in the 1820s and 1830s. In the hybrid legal environment of territorial Florida, such women held separate property, received half of the property amassed during their marriages, and were able to divorce—an empowering set of legal rights that were heretofore unavailable in the United States. While women under the common law could petition for a divorce, they were unlikely to do so since they were less secure in their property rights and often had to petition judges to award them property, rather than bringing their marriage contracts and deeds into court (as civil law wives did).[10]

Slavery and Settler Colonialism

White women's property contributed materially to the expansionist project under way in America's newest territory in the 1820s and 1830s. The kinds of property that white women went to court to protect in Florida helps to demonstrate the diverse ways in which they used it to support settlement. The women uncovered in the sample of court records examined for this study lived in Florida during the territorial and early statehood years (1821–1860). They resided in Escambia and St. Johns Counties (which contained the colonial capitals of Pensacola and Saint Augustine); in Jefferson, Leon, and Gadsden Counties (in the Middle Florida plantation belt, around the new capitol at Tallahassee), and in Hillsborough County (where Tampa Bay linked cattle ranchers with ports in the Gulf of Mexico and the Caribbean Sea). Records from these different regions captured cases that concerned the property of colonial-era wives as well as that of white American wives who migrated into Florida after 1821, and involved wives who lived in towns, on farms and ranches, and on plantations. While only those with separate property would end up in court, excluding poorer or propertyless women from this analysis, the court cases included here involved a wide range of female-owned property, from kitchen utensils and cows to acres of land and hundreds of slaves. Women owned the same kinds of property as white men in early nineteenth-century Florida: "real property," such as land, houses, enslaved people, and livestock; and "personal property," the category the law used to describe household goods, apparel, jewelry, and specie (money).

Spanish colonial women often owned land or town lots and houses, particularly in Florida, where the colonial population was likely to vest brides with land in dowries. Victoria LeSassier owned four houses and five lots in Pensacola and over sixteen hundred acres of land nearby. On a smaller scale, when Josephine Gagnet won a divorce from an abusive drunkard in 1829 she was awarded half of his town lot. Comparatively, white wives in the countryside were less likely to own large amounts of land and were a minority among large landholders. In 1827 Laura Wirt Randall received more than one thousand acres in Middle Florida from her father, U.S. Attorney General William Wirt, but hers was an exceptionally large separate estate.

The frequency of different kinds of property in court records suggests, however, that women were more likely to own enslaved people and household goods than to own land or houses. In 1860, by which time plantation agriculture was firmly established in Florida, there were 268 planters in Florida who held thirty or more slaves and sizeable acreage (from 75 to 15,115 acres); only thirteen of them were women.[11] Court records reveal that many women in territorial Florida owned household goods, from humble objects to fancy furnishings. In St. Augustine in 1824, seamstress Eliza Hutchinson found herself in court accused of stealing a shawl, sheets, and eggs from Amelie Nichols. Mary Pemberton took William McVoy to court in 1828, accusing his slaves Lidia and Rachel of stealing clothes from her. Compared to large plantation estates, these matters of personal property appear small, but they were significant to the women attempting to recoup their property. These were also the kinds of property most southern white women of any means held, in part because their families were likely to give them things like clothes or linens, and in part because they probably preferred and felt more entitled to domestic forms of property—the items associated with "women's work" on a daily basis.[12]

Due to their connection with household property, women often asked for it in estate and divorce cases. Carolina Dunham claimed a portion of the furniture and silver from her family's home on the Hillsborough River in 1834. She noted that her mother (Mary) had built a large house in Florida, furnished it, owned several enslaved people, and had died in 1833 without repaying $5,677 that Carolina had loaned her in 1830. Additionally, Mary Dunham had bequeathed Caroline a $350 annuity from her estate. David Dunham, Caroline's brother, the executor of their mother's estate, refused to pay either the debt or the annuity, claiming that the Florida property had been destroyed by "the hostile Indians." Caroline complained to a judge that if the estate had been destroyed, David's neglect rendered him responsible. He had sufficient warning that war was likely, and should have removed and protected the property. Further, Caroline suspected that David had taken the silver, furniture, and enslaved people to St. Augustine and ought to have paid her annuity out of what he had salvaged. She understood the value of silver, furniture, and enslaved human property and believed they could easily be transferred to her or liquidated to cover her inheritance. There is no ruling the record, so it is unclear whether she prevailed.[13]

Similarly, when Nancy and William Johnson filed a joint petition in 1822 to end their marriage, she asked for the return of property she had brought into their household. Both cited mutual "misery and discord," although Nancy's separate petition revealed that William was a drunkard, who "squandered his property at the card table" and openly committed adultery. She claimed that several enslaved people, including "Duranda, Honora, Amanda, Rich, Handy, Eddenborough, and William," some household furniture, and two tracts of land in North Carolina were her own property. William, she complained, had already sold some of it and threatened to sell the rest, turn her out of her rented home in Pensacola, and abandon her. She asked the judge for a divorce, the return of her household furniture, and to set aside seven of the enslaved people in a life estate for her use. No decree appears in this record, but the court did serve William Johnson with a Notice to Appear and sequestered seven enslaved persons and the furniture in preparation for a hearing.[14]

After 1845, more recent migrants also began to enter courtrooms to protect their holdings. Nancy Robards's separate property furnished a well-appointed town house for her family, as befit the wife of a county clerk. The 1848 inventory she filed in Hillsborough County included eight enslaved people, two cows, two horses, a lot in Tampa, a bedstead and furniture, cooking utensils, and forks and knives. In 1849, she added a carriage, more livestock, and fancy furniture.[15]

Nancy Jackson's household boasted fewer luxuries than Robards's, but she too asked a judge to recoup her marital property. When her abusive husband made off with thirty-two cattle in 1846, Jackson went to the courthouse armed with her receipts, evidence that she had purchased and raised the livestock "on account of herself and children." As the wife of a small-time rancher, she was unlikely to have a separate equity estate, but the 1845 extension of separate property rights to all Florida wives allowed her to protect her livestock from her husband, who she claimed failed to provide for his family.[16]

When an impending marriage or an irresponsible spouse threatened the property that white wives listed in courthouse inventories and marriage contracts, they used legal means to protect it. From these legal traces of their domestic lives, one can deduce the many kinds of work white women did on an expanding frontier, from raising cattle to creating hospitable and respectable domestic spaces. Like white women across the South, whether they were married to poor white "crackers," were the wives of "countrymen" (yeoman farmers), or were plantation mistresses, white women in Florida worked hard—probably harder than those who did not live in a frontier territory (while the enslaved people among them often worked harder still). White women did almost every kind of work on small farms except for clearing and plowing new fields (work that enslaved black women were forced to perform). They often raised poultry and dairy cows and had vegetable gardens. Only the most elite did not have to use their own hands to make candles, spin cotton, weave cloth, sew clothes, gather firewood, prepare meals, and plant, tend, and harvest crops. Women, along with their families, cared for children, enslaved people, and livestock. Wealthier mistresses oversaw the labor, clothing, and feeding of their own children and the people their families enslaved, all while enacting the gentility that their class demanded. In Florida, this work was more challenging and was nationally significant because of its frontier context. As the owners of some land, many enslaved people, and a great deal of household furniture and other goods, white women created homes for white families in Florida—the kinds of "civilized" domestic spaces that national policy makers believed anchored white settlers permanently to a territory that would otherwise remain a hostile frontier controlled by indigenous and maroon peoples.[17]

The labor of enslaved people supported new white settlements as well, as Florida's demographic shift toward a population of almost equal numbers of whites and enslaved blacks reveals. Court records make it abundantly clear that, like the Dunham, Johnson, and Robards estates described above, many white Florida wives owned enslaved human property. Enslaved people were also the only class of property to be specifically mentioned in borderlands married women's property laws. Although not specified in the Florida Acts, human property was more common than any other single type in the court cases involving women that were sampled for this study.

Two other early married women's property acts that make clear the importance of slaves on expanding frontiers were laws that legislatures passed in Arkansas Territory in 1835 and in Mississippi in 1839. In the Mississippi law, although the initial part of the bill granted married women the right to own both real and personal property separately, every other section of the law spoke only of enslaved human property. When it expanded its first married women's property act in 1846, Arkansas copied the Mississippi law, adopting a law that protected a wife's enslaved human property from debts her husband contracted after marriage. This emphasis on enslaved property was in line with a long tradition of planters giving enslaved black people to their female heirs. Female slave owners were not unusual in the antebellum South, where women's dowries and inheritances often included human beings.[18]

Throughout the South and in Florida, slavery granted whites, including women, both material and social privileges at the expense of those they enslaved. Slaves were often a white woman's most important and valuable investment: her fortunes in the marriage market, in a marriage to a debtor, or in widowhood often rested upon whether she owned enslaved people and how many she possessed. Whites built respectable households, social status, and "whiteness" out of enslaved persons. Enslaved people's labor saved white women from the most grueling work and also established their white "ladyhood"; these material and social benefits conveyed that white women deserved their status and leisure because they were white. Even for white women in households without enslaved human property, the privileges of whiteness were ensured by the existence of racial slavery. Beyond the social and cultural privileges of whiteness, slavery also produced material advantages for whites. In a new territory like Florida, enslaved people were perhaps a safer investment than land speculation (which men favored), and whites could sell enslaved people quickly if needed. It was not uncommon for white Florida wives to use their human enslaved property as collateral in loans, for example, though that practice also opened the possibility of loss and the displacement of the enslaved people. Women could also easily rent their enslaved property, as labor was in short supply and high demand in territorial Florida. The material value of a slave was not only what he or she would bring at the slave market but also the financial benefits he or she brought an owner when mortgaged or hired out. This practice enabled aspiring planters to clear fields and build homes much faster than they could have using only family labor, or if they had to wait for human property purchased from the Upper South. Rented enslaved people helped build Florida's infrastructure as they labored in sawmills, turpentine camps, and on the railroad. Those hired by the U.S. military during the Second U.S.-Seminole War were even more directly deployed in service to territorial expansion.[19]

Whites benefited from their property rights in enslaved people, but the consequences for enslaved people were dire. Their "natural increase"— children—enhanced the value of a woman's slaveholding over time, but this resulted in the traumatic division of many enslaved families by sale or in wills. While land was static, household and slave property were dynamic and able to literally move with the changing boundaries of U.S. territory. Some wives' enslaved property was the only wealth that enabled their husbands to reach planter status, which was often the goal that prompted migration. Enslaved people suffered, however, when taken away from families and communities to new frontiers. In myriad ways, slaves were vital to expansion and settlement in Florida, but the enslaved people whom whites bought, sold, and hired suffered due to their value and mobility. Florida's enslaved men, women, and children faced harsh working conditions, many were sent or sold away from kin in the Upper South, and all experienced the privations of the frontier and the dangers of U.S.-Indian warfare.[20]

The court records reflect white women's material, and perhaps ideological, investment in slavery. When their enslaved property was threatened or damaged, they actively sought protection or redress in the courts. In a survey of county and circuit civil court records in Escambia County, Florida, between 1821 and 1845, eighty-eight cases involved either a female defendant or plaintiff (or both), and forty-five of these cases also concerned an enslaved person or persons. One-third of seventy-eight cases involving a woman and her property in St. Johns County between 1821 and 1845 included enslaved human property.[21]

For reasons related to their value and mobility, some white women preferred enslaved human property. They often specifically asked for their inheritance portion in enslaved people, or to sell land rather than enslaved persons to satisfy debts against an estate, even though by law enslaved human property was supposed to be sold before land in settling an intestate estate. In Gadsden County in 1833 Sarah Stone petitioned the court to settle her deceased husband's debts through the sale of land rather than enslaved people, as the money she made renting the enslaved people out supported her family. When Margarita Bonifay married John de la Rua, her mother gave her $1,100 in separate property in the form of town lots in Pensacola. In 1832 Bonifay de la Rua became concerned about the depreciation of real estate in Pensacola, so she asked her husband to sell the lots and use the money to purchase an enslaved woman and her four children for her separate estate. He complied.[22]

In the context of national and slavery expansion in the South, white wives' ownership of enslaved people and household property points to their role in the creation of southern households. Such households were rural and patriarchal and were the location of production and reproduction. They required the presence and labor of white women and children and often, enslaved blacks, to produce white mastery and the means of subsistence and profit.[23] Creating such households was directly related to the nationalist project of expansion, as their construction one by one on the Florida frontier eventually created permanent white American settlements.

The separate property of a Middle Florida resident, Laura Wirt Randall, illustrates how white women's property aided white settler colonialism at the expense of enslaved blacks and indigenous people. Randall moved to Florida in 1827, following her new husband, Thomas, the son of an Annapolis, Maryland, merchant who had studied law and served during the War of 1812. The educated daughter of U.S. Attorney General William Wirt, Laura had family wealth and connections that enabled the newlyweds to enter frontier Florida as elite planters. Laura's dowry, set aside in a separate estate entrusted to her maternal uncles, included land, furniture, food, china, crystal, and enslaved people worth $5,000. Furthermore, her father worked his Washington connections to get Randall appointed as a judge to the Florida Supreme Court.[24]

Laura Wirt Randall's parents were careful to legally protect her separate property. In December 1827, her father wrote to her:

> I enclose you the promised deed for the land and negroes, which will have to be executed by your two uncles, the trustees, and then recorded in the court of Leon County, and the sooner you have it attended to, the better. The Judge [her husband, Thomas Randall] will observe that I am guided by a Territorial law of Florida in the form of acknowledgement by your mother and myself, that law adopting the form in use where the parties reside. If there has been any later law which changes the formalities on this subject the Judge will apprise me of it and return the deed for execution anew. If it is desirable for you to have the patents for the land and Tilghman's Bill of Sale for the negroes, these also will be sent. . . . instead of having the *thirteen* negroes mentioned in the original bill of sale you have only eleven: the remaining five hundred dollars which represented the other two negroes, I sent you by the last mail. The negroes I hope will arrive shortly after your receipt of this letter. Your two thousand dollars worth of furniture and provisions will I hope reach you before this letter and put you in better spirits than when you wrote last.[25]

Her father instructed Laura to protect her new property because as a post-treaty (post-1818) wife in Florida, she fell under common law rules, which allowed her parents to settle a separate estate upon her at the time of her marriage by filing an inventory of her property in a Chancery Court (her property was in Jefferson County, which had just been carved out of Leon County in January 1827).

Laura Wirt Randall's separate estate had absolutely disastrous consequences for enslaved people and for Native Americans in the region. Laura and her trustees made decisions about her estate in 1827 that uprooted eleven enslaved people from Maryland and relocated them, against their will, to the Randalls' new plantation, Belmont. When they arrived, the slaves were all sick, a result of their exposure and exhaustion from the long trek to Florida. Many of them were probably also heartbroken. David had been forcibly separated from his wife, Sophy, and their children when Randall purchased him in Maryland. He missed them so intensely that Randall, fearing David "would infest the whole body of the black community with his despondency," asked William Wirt to purchase Sophy and the children and send them to Belmont in 1828. He did so. One of their children, Sally, was so desperately unhappy at Belmont that she attempted to poison the overseer. Laura Wirt Randall's "separate property" included at least a dozen people who suffered physically and emotionally as a result of her power to buy them and move them hundreds of miles to labor for the benefit of her new family.[26]

Belmont's location in Jefferson County also connects Randall's property to indigenous dispossession. Middle Florida was not uninhabited virgin forest when the Randalls relocated there in the 1820s. Lower Creeks from Georgia had migrated into the area around 1715 and founded settlements along the Apalachicola River and around Lake Miccosukee (which was just a few miles north of the Randall plantation in Jefferson County; Thomas Randall purchased corn from "Micausukees" in the late 1820s).[27] The Apalachicolas and Miccosukees were two of three main indigenous political entities in Florida in the eighteenth and early nineteenth centuries. As the conflicts of the 1810s in West and Middle Florida revealed, control over land in Middle Florida had important geopolitical significance. Americans believed these autonomous Native American peoples, once the allies of British and Spanish foes, now posed a threat to the dominance and safety of Middle Florida's planters. The 1823 Treaty of Moultrie Creek, made before the Americans had the power to completely displace them, had established small reserves for the Apalachicola chiefs on the lands they already inhabited along the rivers, as well as a reserve further east for Miccosukees and recent Creek refugees from the Red Stick War. Soon, however, the desires for that land expressed by whites like Thomas and Laura Randall would challenge these arrangements.[28]

Caught up in what Laura called a "mania" for Florida land, her husband, father, and uncles contributed to a booming real estate market in Jefferson County, where land values increased very quickly, from $1.25 per acre in 1828 to $5.00 per acre in 1830.[29] Their investments in land, combined with the large numbers of slaves they brought with them, mirrored the movement of many of their neighbors, who all hoped to become wealthy planters. As Americans streamed into Middle Florida, they overwhelmed the indigenous communities there. By 1840, 50.58 percent of the total American population of Florida lived in Middle Florida's six counties. In Jefferson County, where the Randalls bought land, enslaved people outnumbered free whites (62 percent of total population). The enslaved people on Jefferson County plantations produced 4,639 bales of cotton (15.32 percent of all the cotton grown in Florida in that year). By 1860 enslaved people made up 64.5 percent of the population in Jefferson County, where they toiled in the fields and at the gins that produced 10,847 bales (16.64 percent of Florida's cotton crop in that year). Jefferson County quickly turned from Native ground to a white plantation agricultural colony.[30]

As white demand made the land more valuable, and as the population of whites and enslaved blacks became denser, Americans applied increasing pressure on indigenous peoples to leave. Americans wanted the land for growing cotton and feared that Native Americans would offer freedom to enslaved blacks and attack white settler families in retaliation for white encroachment and theft. As a result, some Apalachicola and Miccosukee people voluntarily relocated. In 1833 Apalachicola bands led by John Blount, Davy Elliott, and Yellow Hair (not the Cheyenne warrior famously battled by Buffalo Bill Cody) departed for Texas. Those who remained suffered continued violence and raids from whites. To secure their own protection, they aided the U.S. government during the Second U.S.-Seminole War and even surrendered their guns, which left them defenseless against white attackers and other Native Americans whom they had angered by aiding the Americans. By 1838 the Apalachicolas were in a desperate situation; starving and facing indigenous enemies, they were also denied aid by their white allies. With no other choice available, the remaining Apalachicolas departed for the West in October.[31]

Laura Randall's separate estate, along with the property that other white wives used to expand slavery and white settlement in Florida, had far-reaching consequences for peoples throughout the American Southeast. The ambitions of whites such as the Randalls resulted in the loss of Native

American land and autonomy, which forced indigenous groups to relinquish key parts of their subsistence and identity. In addition, enslaved black men and women lost their health, their spouses and children, and their ties to former homes in other states. The opportunities that whites found in the southern borderlands relied upon the racial ideologies that undergirded Indian removal and racial slavery.

At the same time, while she was privileged by her wealth, Laura Wirt Randall was not empowered by it. Although her decisions had terrible consequences for nonwhites in Florida, her husband and uncles controlled her estate, and her wealth did not grant her the freedom to do as she liked. She reluctantly married at age twenty-four (practically a spinster in that time), and was never happy about moving to Florida. Raised and educated among the Washington, D.C., elite in the early nineteenth century, she tried to settle into housekeeping and motherhood on an isolated frontier but longed to see her friends and family. Depressed and exhausted after a miscarriage, she became dependent on laudanum (a narcotic frequently prescribed to white women for "female complaints" in the nineteenth century). After four pregnancies between 1828 and 1832, Laura Wirt Randall died in 1833 at age thirty after a lingering postpartum illness. Her unhappiness was in no way commensurate with that of the enslaved families or indigenous people her estate helped to displace, but in contrast to the white men of her class, Laura Wirt Randall was hardly an independent citizen with property. She was the carrier of wealth between men: her father, her husband, and her hypothetical sons. Judge Thomas Randall benefited most from her wealth, for his marriage to Laura Wirt garnered him a state Supreme Court appointment and an entrée into the planter elite. The Randalls illustrate that separate property rights accrued to Florida wives because they were white bearers of domesticity and because white wives' estates generally reinforced the race and gender norms of patriarchy and slavery, not because lawmakers or judges intended to make them the equals of white men.[32]

Though it rarely facilitated their liberation, white wives' property did promote and support white settlement and supremacy in Florida. Enslaved people and domestic property were, like women, mobile. As frontiers expanded seemingly infinitely, women followed, with the things they used to carve "civilization" out of the wilderness. In addition to the material property they brought with them, white women brought domesticity, the cultural ideology that reproduced what Americans believed were white homes superior to the former residences of Native Americans and free blacks. On a frontier, white women's domestic work acquired nationalist consequences. Expansionist domesticity established and policed the boundary between the "civilizing" culture of the colonizers and the "barbaric" culture of those displaced or colonized.[33]

Free People of Color in Court

Enslaved blacks and Native Americans in Florida were not the only people for whom U.S. expansion spelled misfortune. In the territorial period, even as white women's property rights expanded, U.S. law eroded the civil and property rights of free blacks. Many of them were the wives, consorts, or descendants of prominent white patriarchs and had owned property in Florida before 1821. However, in spite of two articles in the Adams-Onís Treaty that might have protected their rights, over the next four decades the very same courts that upheld the rights of married white women under that treaty eroded the rights of free "Spanish inhabitants" of African or mixed racial descent. Article 8 (mentioned above) protected the property rights of Florida's Spanish inhabitants (which turned out to include married women), while Article 6 stipulated that "the Inhabitants" of Florida "shall be incorporated in the Union of the United States . . . and admitted to the enjoyment of all the privileges, rights, and immunities of the Citizens of the United States." While U.S. officials might have interpreted this to include free blacks, who had enjoyed many civil rights in Spanish Florida, they did not. When it came to the rights of free black Spanish colonists in Florida, U.S. courts almost never fulfilled any of these promises of the treaty. This inconsistency reveals that while U.S. courts and legislators cited the requirements of international treaty law when they granted separate property rights to married white women, race deeply influenced their decision to do so.[34]

"White" Spanish wives (those not of African descent) were not denied citizenship rights and retained their rights to separate property. As historians David Weber and Frank Marotti have noted, Americans greeted Spanish inhabitants of European descent who remained after the change of flags as allies rather than rivals because they were few in number, there was a desperate need for "civilized" settlers, and they were united against common enemies: Seminoles and Black Seminoles. This aspect of Florida's transition to U.S. rule illustrates the historical and contingent ways in which race is socially constructed. In the racial landscape of territorial Florida, those who might not have been considered white elsewhere were incorporated into white society because Americans were far more concerned about distinguishing "civilized" whites from blacks and Indians than they were with making distinctions among European Protestants and Catholics. While cultural distinctions remained significant to individual identity, they did not matter structurally.[35]

This was not the case for Floridians of non-European descent, especially those with darker skin. Local and territorial laws quickly limited the right of free blacks in Florida to assemble, bear arms, serve on juries, testify against whites in court, or marry across the color line. By the 1840s, localities unfairly taxed free blacks and required them to have white guardians. Sheriffs coerced them into manual labor projects, whipped them for misdemeanors, and subjected them to curfews. Free blacks did petition or sue for their rights under Article 6, but U.S. courts did not always uphold their rights, unlike white married women's property rights, violating the treaty provisions in law and in practice.[36]

In an increasingly hostile racial environment, many free people of color fought to retain the nearly equal rights and property the Spanish Crown had granted them. Very few of them were successful in court. Women of wealth and status, kin to prominent white men or to powerful Creek or Seminole leaders, met with some success. With the help of several trusted friends and lawyers, Anna Kingsley, the African-born first wife of Scottish land baron Zephaniah Kingsley, managed to protect the enormous legacy that she had helped him build in Florida. In the 1840s, his (white) sister sued for control over the estate, worth upward of $60,000, arguing that because Anna and her children were black they had no rights to property in Florida under U.S. law. A Duval County judge ruled in Anna's favor, and she retained the estate. The judge cited Article 6 of the treaty (the article that promised citizenship rights) as the legal reason for upholding her property rights.[37]

The courts did not consistently uphold the rights of free blacks, however, and American law certainly did not confirm them in a separate statute as it had done for rights of white wives. In 1845, two years before the decision in Kingsley's case, several free blacks in Florida invoked their treaty status to avoid paying a discriminatory state tax. The biracial descendants of another white patriarch, George J. F. Clarke, these litigants were denied citizenship by a disdainful American judge who opined that as "bastard" children born of a black woman, they could not inherit any of the rights their "reputed Father" might have had under Spain. In another case in which the free black plaintiff was the child of two legally married free people of mixed race, the judge ruled that he was still not entitled to the same rights as a "Free White Citizen" because "such a thing" never "would have been admissible . . . and can never be tolerated." Although Treaty Article 6 protected the property of Anna Kingsley and her mixed-race children, other free blacks did not find the same protection under the treaty. Shortly after this ruling, many of the biracial members of the Clarke family began a mass exodus out of Florida.[38]

Furthermore, as did civil law rules for marital property, these legal decisions sometimes directly benefited whites, as unfair taxes often resulted in selling the property of delinquent black taxpayers at auction, where whites could buy it for next to nothing. If they went to court to protest, free blacks (including married women) typically lost their cases and their property. While the treaty had protected colonial wives' property, and the 1845 Florida law protected all wives' property, new racially biased American taxation policies resulted in the loss of property for free blacks.[39]

The story of one of the Clarke descendants, Felicia Garvin (daughter of George J. F. Clarke and his freed slave and wife, Flora Leslie) illustrates how U.S. courts acted in ways that resulted in the loss of black property to whites. In 1842, just before she moved to Philadelphia, Garvin paid Clarissa Anderson $1,000 as down payment on a house in St. Augustine. Garvin instructed her attorneys to pay the remainder of the mortgage with $4,000 from a federal claim, which arrived eight days after she left. However, the attorneys kept the $4,000 intended for the mortgage, and therefore Garvin defaulted. Anderson, a wealthy white widow, kept both the house and the $1,000 down payment when she foreclosed. It is unclear whether Anderson was directly involved in the swindle, but she certainly did not lose anything in the bargain.[40] Although, like Kingsley, Felicia Garvin was related to prominent, wealthy white men, those connections did not help her in court, where U.S. law failed to protect her interests.

The citizenship promised by Treaty Article 6 also potentially included Native American inhabitants, but President Monroe had quickly announced that indigenous Floridians would not become U.S. citizens. Nevertheless a few indigenous women appear in Florida court records. In 1824 "Buckra Woman" (the only name given to her in the case file) sued Philip Yonge for $3,000, money he owed for cattle purchased from her brother, deceased Seminole chief Payne, in 1808. Surprisingly, a jury of white men found in favor of her suit, which was based on a matrilineal pattern of inheritance in which a man's sisters, not his wife and children, inherited his property. However, the American judge dismissed the jury's finding on the basis of "faulty evidence" and on the flimsy technicality that he had no jurisdiction because the case predated the act establishing county courts in the territory (this, of course, had not been a problem for any of the white colonial women whose cases predated 1821).[41] As President Monroe had promised, U.S. courts did not honor the rights of Native Americans who had lived in Florida under Spanish rule as they did the rights of white Spanish inhabitants, even if some of those inhabitants—acting as jurors—thought they should.

Strangely, as they did with civil law precedents in spite of their apparent commitment to American common law, U.S. courts sometimes looked to Native American customary law to decide a case. The disputed ownership of a group of enslaved people that had once belonged to a Creek trader named Philatouche, whom whites called Black Factor, elicited a lengthy court battle in St. Johns County in the late 1820s. Two whites claimed to have purchased the same six enslaved people: twenty-five-year-old Ketty and her two-year-old son, twenty-two-year-old Peggy and her one-year-old baby boy, Fanny (age fifteen), and George (age ten). Margaret Cook and William Everitt each claimed to have purchased them from two different Creeks, Nelly and Nocosilly. Nelly, who sold the slaves to Everitt, was Philatouche's daughter and so traced her inheritance rights through a paternal line. Nocosilly, who sold the slaves to the Cooks, traced his inheritance rights through a maternal line, claiming that as the son of Philatouche's sister he had the right to sell them. This case spanned five years, during which witnesses across Florida, Georgia, and Alabama gave an unusually large number of depositions (over twenty-five). The questions asked in those depositions indicate that the judge's decision, which does not survive in the record, apparently hinged on Creek inheritance law. Creeks were historically matrilineal, but at least one witness claimed that an 1819 Creek law instituted patrilineal inheritance. Since Philatouche died before 1819, according to that same witness, the new patrilineal inheritance law would not have been in effect; therefore Nocosilly was the rightful heir and Margaret Cook the legal owner of the slaves in question. This case only merited all this attention because of the interest that a white woman and man had in it, but it challenges the idea of common law's hegemony. Furthermore, this case also demonstrates that Native American inheritance customs were changing in antebellum Florida as they came in contact with European and U.S. legal practices, a pattern that is consistent with the literature on Native American societies in the early nineteenth-century American South. Rather than unfailingly subjecting Native American property to common law rules, U.S. judges sometimes relied upon Native American inheritance customs to determine the ownership of property. At the same time, patrilineal (common law) patterns were becoming more dominant within Native societies. Finally, when enslaved people were among the "property" in question, the rights of Native Americans (just like those of whites) could have terrible consequences for blacks.[42]

These cases illustrate that U.S. courts were actively, if unpredictably, drawing a color line in the 1830s and 1840s. Although they were not unfailing in their discrimination against free black plaintiffs, American lawmakers and judges consistently upheld and protected whites' claims to property in Florida—especially white claims to enslaved people, land, and the goods that outfitted white households. This pattern exposes that the real goal of territorial government was not to honor treaty rights but to support white settlement. Extending marital separate property to white wives did that, as did denying property and citizenship rights to free blacks and to indigenous people.

Married Women's Property Law and U.S. Expansion

U.S. courts upheld white women's property rights with great consistency in antebellum Florida, even as they increasingly discriminated against free black and Native peoples. What might seem haphazard legal choices appear more logical when one considers the ways that letting white women hold property ultimately promoted the expansion of American settlement and slavery. While the extension of separate property rights to Florida wives was more a passive than an active process, it protected women who lawmakers recognized as vital contributors of reproductive and productive labor to white settlements. White female property holders—many of them also slave owners—not only consistently exercised their rights in court but also used their property to help settle Florida permanently for the U.S. as a slave state. Thus separate property rights for Florida's wives were not just an accident of international diplomacy but part of the structure of white settler colonialism there. That structure, like white women's exercise of separate property rights, had direct and disastrous consequences for enslaved blacks, free people of color, and indigenous peoples in Florida.

In a broad arc across the southern borderlands, from the Gulf Coast to the Pacific Ocean, American territorial growth into former French and Spanish colonies brought married women's property rights into the United States in the early nineteenth century. Although each case differed, Louisiana, Texas, and California, like Florida, retained some civil law traditions and allowed wives to own separate property before 1848. No state other than Florida did so due to a treaty provision, so the influence of the treaty in Florida is unique (and perhaps a learning experience for U.S. diplomats). Southern slave states that neighbored these formerly Spanish or French territories passed some of the earliest married women's property acts in common law states: Arkansas in 1835 and Mississippi in 1839.[43]

Historians of other borderlands where civil law met common law also cite the expansionist benefits of granting white women these rights. It was not the need to support settlement but the demands of those who had already settled that caused the retention of the civil law in Louisiana. Historian Mark Carroll argues that legislators in Texas employed civil law marital property rules in order to support Anglo-Texan women and their families and to dispossess Native Americans and Mexicans of their lands in Texas. In California, preexisting civil law, the recent married women's property law reform in New York, and an imbalanced sex ratio together formed the impetus for granting women separate property rights when married. Delegates believed that the measure would encourage "women of fortune" to come to California. Delegates from majority Californio districts were strong supporters of a married women's property provision and argued for it as necessary to preserve rights already enjoyed by their constituents.[44]

Expansion brought states like Florida, Texas, Louisiana, and California into the United States, where their colonial history of civil law marital property rules challenged the hegemony of common law coverture. While English common law was the most prevalent legal structure in the antebellum United States, its privileged position was not one of total domination. This analysis indicates that the civil law of borderland territories changed the legal rights and perspectives of Americans in some southern states in the first half of the nineteenth century, in spite of their official adoption of common law. This history highlights how expansion changed the nation "at home" even as it remade conquered territories into new American states. The postcolonial insight that colonial encounters usually transform the colonizers as well as the colonized also applies to the legal history of North American expansion.

Expansion provides an alternative historical context for married women's property rights in the United States. Wives in the early nineteenth-century borderlands became legally entitled to hold separate property differently than women in the Northeast, where historian Norma Basch has shown that woman's rights agitation and a desire to protect family households from unstable market capitalism encouraged legal reform. The revision of common law statutes happened first in the South and West, where it was shaped by the distinct contours of frontier life, especially slavery and conflict with Native American peoples. Previous studies have focused on the legal reforms achieved by the woman's rights movement and have dismissed married women's property rights in the borderlands because their outcomes are disappointingly limited in terms of women's empowerment. Taking an intersectional approach reveals, however, that married women's right to separate property in the borderlands did have important outcomes for white expansion and settlement and the growth of racial slavery. This analysis, therefore, places the history of married women's property law in Florida into the framework of settler colonialism and its concomitant results: the expansion of racial slavery and Indian removal. By doing so, it writes white women into the history of Manifest Destiny, where their labor, property, and responsibility have long been acknowledged but rarely analyzed.[45]

Although lawmakers did not target white wives to benefit from civil law marital property rules, political leaders did believe that white women were very important in frontier Florida. As will become clear in Chapters 3 and 4, lawmakers believed that the presence of white women and families distinguished a permanent settlement from a temporary military occupation and was therefore vital to controlling Florida. Similarly, when individual white women used these laws to protect their holdings, they did not understand them as policies or actions that supported colonization. Nevertheless, women used the property protected by these laws in ways that did just that. While domestic ideology coded white women as passive and dependent, it also (somewhat ironically) granted them an active identity as mobile, homemaking agents, and the household and enslaved human property that they owned in Florida facilitated that role. Women's property (along with their labor) was a key component of expansionist domesticity.

While white wives, judges, and lawmakers may not have thought about married women's property as political, it had important political implications. Those stakes are not often obvious in the records themselves, which contain the traces of family and community dramas that sometimes spanned generations. Legal petitions cannot reveal exactly what kinds of ideological investments women, their male kin, or presiding judges may have invested in women's property, nor can they reliably tell us what motivated these actors. While the law epistemologically defines action and actors, it cannot determine behavior.[46] What is clear is that white women did not hesitate to exercise their property rights in the courts of territorial Florida, where American legislators and judges did not hesitate to extend the advantages of this legal protection to whites who used their property to expand national borders and slavery in Florida. Since these rights supported white settler colonialism in Florida, they were inherently bound to have negative consequences on enslaved people, free blacks, and Native Americans.

CHAPTER 2

Innocent Victims of a "Savage" War

> The citizens of Florida . . . have been nightly shot down or tomahawked by the light of their own blazing homes.
> —Delegate Charles Downing,
> Florida Territory, July 10, 1840

> The barbarities have been perpetrated chiefly upon females.
> —*Niles' Weekly Register*, October 1, 1836

At ten o'clock on the morning of September 15, 1836, a band of Seminoles and one black warrior attacked the homestead of Clement and Jane Johns, white settlers in East Florida. According to a sensational pamphlet published in the wake of this assault, the attackers shot and killed Clement, leaving Jane to defend herself, their unborn child, and all their property. The attackers shot and scalped Jane Johns and set her house on fire. Miraculously still alive, she lay still until her assailants left, even as the fire spread to her clothes. Once they had whooped and departed, according to one account, she "scraped the blood from her denuded head in her hands and . . . applied it to the fire," extinguishing the flames consuming her skirts. In spite of her injuries, Johns managed to get out of the burning house, crawling to a shallow pond nearby. Although she had been shot, scalped, and set on fire, Jane Johns remained alive when her father-in-law found her a few hours later. A remarkable survivor, she became perhaps the most famous victim to survive what Americans called an "Indian depredation" in Florida. The *Jacksonville Courier* reported the attack on Johns on September 17, 1836, and several regional and national papers printed the details shortly thereafter. The following year printers in Charleston and Baltimore published it in pamphlet form. Her story garnered national coverage because of its sensational and gory details, which pulled at both domestic and nationalist sentiments with the image of a white woman attacked by Indians and an escaped slave.[1]

Although perhaps the most sensational, Jane Johns's story was not unique. It exemplifies Florida Indian depredation narratives in which white women and their children suffered injury or death and lost property when attacked by Seminoles. These tales glossed over Indian removal and the expansion of slavery and framed the conflict in Florida as a noble war being waged for the protection of innocent white women and children. In countless bloodcurdling stories Americans recast whites as victims, never perpetrators, of violence, and they continually portrayed Native Americans and blacks as the aggressors rather than the victims. The cultural prevalence and emotional power of these stories shaped policy as well as attitudes in and about Florida in the 1830s and 1840s. American leaders used them to justify the Second U.S.-Seminole War and its expense, to raise militia volunteers, and to pass pro-settler welfare and land policies. The focus on property losses in depredation accounts distinguishes them from Indian captivity narratives and highlights the importance of household property in white settler colonies (as does the history of property law). By spotlighting sensational destruction, Florida Indian depredation narratives reveal the central role of white women and expansionist domesticity to the U.S. colonization of Florida.

Reports about Seminole attacks on whites in Florida circulated widely, especially after the United States formally declared a second war on the Seminoles in December 1835. Indian depredation stories, as I refer to these accounts, appeared in private sources such as letters, diaries, and memoirs and in public ones, including newspapers, pamphlets, and broadsides. Typical Indian depredation stories from Florida begin with an attack by a small band of Native American men (usually identified as Seminoles, but sometimes called Creeks, Mikasukis, or Apalachicolas) on white settlers. Occasionally, Black Seminoles or enslaved people appear as assailants or victims in these stories. The scene is typically a white homestead or plantation, but sometimes Seminoles assailed travelers on Florida's rudimentary roadways. Narrators repeated several elements in endless combinations in depredation reports about "the Florida War": innocent white mothers and children attacked at home by Native American and (sometimes) black men, killed or horribly mutilated with "savage" weapons, and their domestic realms plundered and burned. The consistency, ubiquity, and sensationalism of these stories made them culturally powerful and also responded to and re-created certain expectations in their American audience, predicated on assumptions of white female innocence and nonwhite "savage barbarity."

The fact that white women were injured or killed in the Second U.S.-Seminole War proved very important to the ways that American citizens, journalists, and politicians framed the war. As with stories from many other settler colonial regimes, these narratives relied upon gender to justify colonial violence. Depredation stories cast white women and children as the "innocents" whom only barbaric savages would attack; but the presence of white families was a real threat to the Seminoles in Florida. As in most settler colonies, conquest and settlement occurred simultaneously in Florida as settlers arrived before and during Indian removal, and armed conflicts over land coincided with settlement. Most white male settlers brought families and, if wealthy enough, enslaved people with them, while others found wives and formed new families once they arrived. Growing white families competed with indigenous peoples for land, food, and resources, and signaled that soon there would be increasing numbers of whites claiming this frontier as their own "native" home. Women's reproductive and productive labor was indispensable to the creation of new homes and the next generation of Americans on the frontier. The work of enslaved people supported the productive and reproductive work of white women for the benefit of white households.[2] Far more than just symbols of "barbaric" indigenous violence or white "civilization," white women were absolutely vital to white households and growing communities. Since this book aims to clarify white women's part in Manifest Destiny, it is important to note that Florida Indian depredation accounts were part of the historical process of obscuring the importance of women's labor to national expansion. In counterpoint to the image of women as innocent victims in Seminole depredation narratives, this chapter highlights white women's labor as a colonizing force that assisted in Seminole dispossession and in the white settlement of Florida.

Although they deemphasized women's expansionist work, depredation narratives inadvertently offer evidence of its significance, for they paid special attention to the destruction of the families and the domestic spaces that white women created in Florida. A central component of a cultural campaign that represented Florida as already "home" to American settlers, the narratives represent Indian depredations as attacks on the home in two senses: Native Americans stole or destroyed white settlers' property, and many whites faced poverty or fled the territory as a result. Along with the material consequences, depredations were also attacks on white mothers and children, the families who transformed property into a "true home." That cultural labor was significant beyond its sentimental appeal, because it once again framed whites as settlers who had been attacked by a savage enemy rather than as a colonizing force that the Seminoles targeted as a strategy of resistance to removal. This frame presumed, rather than explicitly argued, that whites had a natural claim to their Florida properties as home, and therefore that the Seminoles did not. Sentimental accounts of scorched and plundered frontier cabins had the power to frame Indian removal as the defense of white women and children.

While they gloss white women's work as colonizers and represent women as innocent victims, Florida Indian depredation narratives do illustrate that white women fought on the front lines of the Second U.S.-Seminole War. Many homesteads became battlegrounds as violence erupted in Florida between 1835 and 1842, and many white women's domestic realms became central sites of depredation accounts. Neither military nor women's historians often place nineteenth-century white women on battlefields. Usually they are stoking home fires and observing from the sidelines. This was not the case in Florida (nor was it on most frontiers), because the Seminoles brought this conflict to whites' doorsteps. They refused removal and, since they had fewer warriors and resources than the U.S. military, waged a guerilla war. Since this was a conflict aimed at ousting them from the territory in order to make Florida safe for white settlement and slavery, and because American troops frequently destroyed Seminole homes and families, they resisted and retaliated by attacking white homesteads and plantations, where white women defended their homes.

Florida Indian depredation stories were propaganda rooted in real events. This chapter examines the ways that they shaped perceptions and policies, but they are also evidence that white Americans and Seminole people terrorized each other between 1835 and 1842. Although widely reported, it is difficult to quantify this violence. The rations program that supported Florida's "suffering inhabitants" between 1836 and 1842 (described in detail in Chapter 4) furnishes some information about how many white settlers in Florida lost homes and family members to Seminole attacks. In June 1842, as the war was closing, there were 1,795 people on the rolls of suffering inhabitants drawing rations from the U.S. military. They came from eighteen households that had been "broken up by Indians" (some more than once), while another twenty-three households had lost civilian husbands, fathers, or sons (and in one case a wife) who had been "killed by the Indians," and another fifteen households had lost the support of men who died in military service (from disease, wounds, or in battle). All the ration rolls before 1842 are missing, so it is difficult to estimate exactly how many homes and civilians the Seminoles destroyed, but given the numbers from 1842 the number of households disrupted was probably in the hundreds. In addition to an unknown number of civilian deaths, 1,466 American soldiers died in the Second U.S.-Seminole War (mostly from disease, not combat). The Seminoles suffered even higher losses from whites. Americans burned many villages during the U.S.-Seminole Wars and killed hundreds of Seminole warriors and civilians, although an exact count is unknown. The U.S. removed 4,420 indigenous people and their allies of African descent from Florida during the Second U.S.-Seminole War, and approximately 1,400 died on the journey west.[3]

As it is hard to determine the frequency of all this violence, it is often impossible to verify whether the precise details of a particular Indian depredation story are historically factual. Did Jane Johns really use her own blood to put out the fire burning her legs? It seems unlikely. More important than the veracity of that sensational detail is that white Americans in 1836 found it credible that Native Americans would shoot, scalp, and set fire to a white woman and leave her for dead in her burning frontier home. They would have taken her innocence (in spite of her presence on a contested frontier) and her attackers' savagery for granted. While American accounts placed Seminole violence against whites (especially women and children) in the foreground, they consistently ignored or justified the violence that whites perpetrated against Native Americans and blacks, including women and children. No accounts of "white depredations" upon the Seminoles made their way into print (although the oral accounts passed down among Seminole descendants provide some alternative views of the war, as the next chapter recounts). Regardless of the frequency or verity of Seminole attacks on white Florida settlers, the widespread circulation of depredation accounts in private, public, and political discourse about the Second U.S.-Seminole War testifies that they performed a weighty set of cultural and political tasks in narrating this conflict.

Florida "Indian Depredations"

Resonant with the long-standing genre of Indian captivity narratives, Indian depredation narratives from Florida framed stories about Native American violence on white settlers in the sensationalist language of early nineteenth-century print culture, using a term drawn from federal frontier policy. Under the Indian Depredation Claims system (1796–1920) the U.S. government promised to indemnify all losses that American suffered from "Indian depredations" if the attacks took place outside of Indian territory during a time of peace and if white settlers had not continued the cycle of violence with a revenge attack. In the absence of kidnapping, depredation stories focused on injured white bodies and homes.[4]

In numerous ways, Florida Indian depredation stories followed the conventions of Indian captivity narratives. Narratives of Indian war and captivity were among the major frontier myths in which American national identity and culture originated, and Americans had been recounting the horrific details of Native American violence against whites for hundreds of years. Authors of such stories sought to explain and justify the violent campaigns they waged to take the lands of Native Americans and to establish their fundamental difference from those they eventually deemed racial inferiors. The depredation stories from Florida, like captivity narratives, featured "savage" violence against white (and sometimes nonwhite) men, women, and children, and highlighted scalping and the use of exotic implements such as "tomahawks" and "scalping knives" (known as axes and knives when wielded by whites). The narrator usually decries the attackers as "indiscriminate" for harming white women and children, a label Americans had long used to establish the uncivilized nature of indigenous warfare (and justify their own violence on Native women and children). "Indiscriminate" Indian depredations were cited as early as 1819 in Florida. The presence of vulnerable white women helped make them more sensational and compelling stories, and so narrators highlighted female victims, as when the editor of *Niles' Weekly Register* noted that "these barbarities have been perpetrated chiefly upon females."[5] Following the conventions of antebellum culture, depredation accounts emphasized female passivity, piety, maternity, and domesticity. They invoke particular sympathy for the plight of white mothers who, unable to protect their children, were forced to watch them harmed or killed. Captivity narratives and depredation accounts focused on female victims because this allowed them to invoke emotional, sympathetic responses using gender conventions, which dictated that such victims were innocent and civilized because they were maternal and domestic. The emphasis on domestic spaces and on maternal and infant victims harkened back to captivity narratives even as they made Florida scenes of armed struggle difficult to cast as conventional war zones.[6]

White gender norms prescribed that dominant white men protect vulnerable and subordinate white women, so when white men appeared in depredation accounts authors tended to glorify the bravery, chivalry, and gallantry of white men, contrasted with descriptions of women's vulnerability. Many white men were killed in the initial stage of an attack attempting to protect their families, while others (as the narratives often explain) were away fighting this war on other fronts or had already been killed doing so. Even when a man died in an Indian depredation, it was sympathy for the woman and children he left behind that authors expressed. In accounts of the attack on Clement and Jane Johns, for example, narrators always described the murder of Clement Johns but followed that with sympathy for his widow, not for Clement. This made it possible to evacuate all traces of white aggression from the story: the white men who had invaded Florida were framed as the heads of families rather than soldiers or squatters, and they were gone. Left behind were their families—the women and children whom nineteenth-century Americans understood not as invaders of indigenous lands but faithful followers of migrating husbands and fathers. They were innocent victims, then, of their loyalty to men unable to protect them and of the "barbaric" Seminoles.

Alongside white mothers, white children also appear as victims in Florida Indian depredation stories. If these stories are reliable, white parents left many children at home alone (or with other relatives or enslaved black guardians) in the 1820s, 1830s, and 1840s, for in many stories white mothers return home to find their houses in flames and their children endangered. In some cases this was an embellishment that heightened the sentimental and sensational appeal of the tale, although in other instances it appears that the war left white mothers with few alternatives. Faced with fulfilling the duties of the absent male household head as well as their own work, perhaps white women sometimes risked leaving children at home, particularly since Florida's roads were no safer than their homesteads.

Florida Indian depredation stories also borrowed from the emerging domestic literature and scandalous dime novels of their milieu. The rise of domestic ideology in the northern United States engendered a whole "culture of sentiment." Authors, artists, journalists, photographers, and educators produced sentimental texts intended to make their consumers feel emotions, especially pity, sympathy, and grief. Sentimental culture also presumed that certain people (whites) were those who felt sympathy, while others (indigenous, enslaved) were the objects and recipients of their pity and sympathy. Tellers of Indian captivity and depredation narratives typically expected their audience to feel horror, fear, sympathy, and solidarity with white victims of violence, and they used sentimental language to achieve this end. Unlike slave narratives, however, they did not as frequently suggest that nonwhites deserved sympathy, and almost none of the Florida narratives do. Early in the war (January 21, 1836), the *Jacksonville Courier* included this assessment of recent depredations: "None whose hearts are not ice can hear recitals of such dreadful deeds of massacre, without sorrow and grief. We deeply sympathise with afflicted friends in St. Augustine."[7] Only Americans with hearts of ice could resist the affective impact of these stories, which expected them to feel sympathy for the poor residents of Florida who daily faced Seminole "massacres."[8]

While the Florida depredation stories invoked sympathy for whites, they were less invested in respectable, virtuous, and socially redemptive lessons than many sentimental novels and captivity narratives were, and typically devoted more of their pages to the shocking and horrific details typical of sensational literature, which emphasized materiality and corporeality. In one frequent element, for example, depredation narrators describe a mother and infant killed by the same bullet or felled by a common stab wound, and then express horror at the barbarity of those who would murder a very young "baby at the breast." Sentimentalism's lowbrow cousin, sensational stories filled the story papers, pamphlet novels, and newspapers of the mid-nineteenth century. As innovative publishers and editors capitalized on new technology and began to produce cheaply made texts aimed at the masses, they relied on street sales rather than subscriptions, and so editors chose outrageous headlines full of scandal, crime, violence, and sexuality. The tragic, violent death of a white woman was a favorite sensational subject in the 1830s and 1840s, when the deaths of New Yorkers Helen Jewett and Mary Rogers occupied a great deal of attention. As some readers consumed those dramatic tales, others were reading about the mangled bodies of white mothers left in the wake of depredating Seminoles in Florida. Shelley Streeby argues that U.S. expansionism in the 1840s influenced sensational literature in ways that shaped how Americans constructed norms of class, race, and gender at home and abroad. In the "double vision" of this literature, images of the working-class city and the frontier West colluded to reinforce the boundaries of race, gender, and class that expansion and capitalism sometimes unsettled (and often reproduced) in the nineteenth century. In the sensational story papers and pamphlets, a variety of undesirables populated both seamy urban underworlds and the borderlands of an expanding America: prostitutes, immigrants, Mexicans, Indians, and Cubans, all of them a threat to white women and to (white) "American values." Against these characters, authors arrayed "real" heroic American men, workers, frontiersmen, even filibusters, consolidating white male citizenship against perceived threats to its continued dominance. Popular cultural representations of urban and frontier spaces and people influenced political culture and vice versa. Nineteenth-century popular fiction reveals how Manifest Destiny offered new backdrops for sensational stories that entertained Americans focused on expanding their nation into former Spanish territories in the Americas.[9]

Although Florida Indian depredation narratives shared the sensationalism, sentimentalism, gender ideals, and racial assumptions of other narratives of war and captivity, they also differed, primarily in that they are not stories of white captivity among Native Americans. The Seminoles lacked the resources to feed captives, there was no longer the incentive of a ransom system, and there was no market for trading captives, since the United States would send captive Seminoles to Oklahoma, not trade them back in exchange for a white captive. With very few exceptions, then, these were tales about depredations upon families and property, not about captivity among the Seminoles.[10]

The blacks who sometimes appear in Florida depredation narratives also distinguish these stories from other accounts, which rarely featured people of African descent. Unlike the slavery debate in other frontier states, the Florida debate did not turn on whether slavery would expand into Florida, because it already existed there, and no one doubted that it would continue. Rather, slavery shaped expansion into Florida because proslavery Americans wanted to conquer and remove Native Americans and free blacks from Florida in order to prevent any more slave runaways and because they feared a joint rebellion of Seminoles and blacks. As new Florida resident Corinna Brown put it in 1837, "should the *slaves* rise about this time, it would make glorious work—the horrors of St. Domingo enacted over again in earnest."[11] While the feared slave insurrection never occurred in Florida, the concerns of many slaveholding whites were very real. Some blacks lived and fought with the Seminoles, and some historians classify the Second U.S.-Seminole War as the longest and most successful slave rebellion in U.S. history as well as a war of Seminole resistance. Although they are somewhat rare in depredation accounts, when blacks were present they brought the specter of a slave rebellion clearly into the frame. This heightened the fear of the reader and further justified the war as a necessary defense—in this case, against the implicit threat of a slave rebellion. Judge Robert Reid warned U.S. Secretary of State John Forsyth just before the Second U.S.-Seminole War began that "while we guard ourselves against a savage foe, we should be prepared for an evil—not entirely out of the list of contingencies—yet nearer home."[12] He meant, of course, the slaves.[13]

Another difference from other narratives is that, in Florida Indian depredation stories, after the attack the narratives return to the scene of destroyed domestic space, rather than following white captives into Indian country. To "depredate" is to plunder or rob, and these accounts focus on human victims and their property losses. The Indian Depredation Claims system, designed to limit cycles of retaliatory violence on American frontiers, invited peacetime victims to make claims against the federal government for property losses they incurred from Native Americans. Under this policy, citizens of the United States reported "Indian depredations" to local authorities, agents of the Indian Office, or even members of Congress in hopes that by following the proper bureaucratic procedures they would receive compensation. They rarely did, but the policy codified the "Indian depredation" as an officially recognized form of American settler victimization. If whites settled on the frontier and Native Americans attacked them, the Native peoples and the national government bore responsibility, and white settlers remained innocent of any wrongdoing, even as their encroaching settlements enriched them and enlarged the national territory. In this way, the nation expanded without formally declaring war on the indigenous peoples its citizens displaced. Illustrating how clearly "invasion [was] a structure rather than an event" in U.S. settler colonization, the U.S. government put this policy in place in 1796 and continued it until 1921. Leaders anticipated continuous borderlands violence even during times of formal peace because they knew that expanding white settlements would continually pressure indigenous ones; in fact they counted on it. Although the wartime depredations in Florida were not eligible for reimbursement,

Floridians knew of the claims system and several filed claims for Creek and Seminole depredations alleged to have occurred in Georgia, Alabama, and Florida in 1836 and 1837. In 1837 a congressional committee investigated and rejected their claims. Although the federal Indian Depredation Claims system did not create Florida Indian depredation narratives, the existence of this policy surely helped to reshape traditional captivity accounts into the genre of "Indian depredations."[14]

Fire is an important feature of the typical Florida narrative's focus on the destruction of property. After the Seminoles plundered, they set their victims' property alight. As with "indiscriminate" violence against "innocents," American narrators attributed the use of fire as a practice of the "barbaric" Seminoles, although American troops plundered and burned any villages they encountered during the First, Second, and Third Seminole Wars, setting fire to Seminole homes, supplies, and fields after taking any provisions they desired. Following the violence and the fire, depredation narratives catalogue the property stolen or destroyed in the attack. The details about property damage linked the violence to colonization: how would whites ever settle in Florida if Seminoles kept burning down their farms? Any subsequent pursuit of the attackers, or rumors of the site of their next attack, generally closed out depredation accounts.[15]

Private Accounts

Depredation narratives had the power to transform whites' perceptions of the Florida conflict. Throughout the early nineteenth century Americans in Florida who survived or witnessed depredations recorded those events in letters, diaries, journals, or memoirs. In their accounts it is possible to observe an individual's emotional and political reactions to Native American violence against white women framed as depredation. While some people might express sympathy for the Seminoles in the abstract, once Americans observed a bloody attack they began to view the Seminoles as aggressors, not victims. Operating at an extremely emotional level, depredation stories reframed Indian removal as white defense, one sensational story at a time.

Well before the start of the Second U.S.-Seminole War, Nancy Cone Hagan was so moved by one Indian depredation that she wrote a poem to commemorate the deaths of several white children, "On the Death of Allen

Carr's Children, Murdered by the Indians in 1826 Near Col. Gadsden's in Leon County."[16] On December 6, 1826, a small band of Miccosukee warriors attacked Carr's homestead and killed four white children, their uncle, and one enslaved black man. Allen Carr was a squatter on land "originally that of the Indian," that John Gamble (maternal uncle of Laura Randall) had speculatively purchased in 1823. According to family notes compiled in 1898 by his son (Major Robert Gamble), the Seminoles "were on the eve of leaving the country, and, in the hope of avoiding the necessity a number of the young warriors attempted to embroil the tribe in war, and to that end they murdered Carr's family."[17] Hagan paid no attention to the motives of the Miccosukees fighting to keep their homes, however. The first stanza of her poem contains elements typical of depredation narratives: an absent head of household and a baby at the breast:

Poor Allen Carr was absent, the cruel Indians knew,
Took the advantage of the helpless, their savage rage to show.
The mother too was gone from home, a lucky circumstance,
Which thereby saved herself and son, the infant at the breast.[18]

Hagan's poem and the newspaper reports never offer any explanation for why Allen Carr and his wife left their oldest children with an uncle and departed their home. In the following stanzas Hagan included other typical elements: the "spotless innocence" of the slain white children, the destruction of the Carr's home, and specific mention of instruments of "Indian" violence, the hatchet and the scalping knife.[19] Yet Hagan's poem also suggested—as later accounts would not—that perhaps some compromise with the Seminoles was possible:

But have we no compassion for the savage forest men?
And try to cultivate them? Let mercy be our theme.
Teach them to be more human and teach them all we can.
And tell them of the Saviour and of the gospel plan.[20]

Encouraging a Christian mission to convert the Seminoles (who apparently need to be taught how to be human), she does not only call for punishment. In this, she displays a lingering commitment to indigenous "civilization" policies that policy makers in the Early Republic had embraced—plans to assimilate Native Americans rather than remove or kill them. With the rise of scientific racism and the ideology of Manifest Destiny in the 1820s and 1830s, civilization schemes would become supplanted by Indian removal policies. While Hagan responded with some pious sympathy for the unsaved "savages" in 1826, those who experienced Seminole attacks and read depredation stories from Florida in subsequent decades were far less hopeful than even her racist mission plan suggests.[21]

Nearly thirteen years after the attack on the Carr homestead, another Southern migrant recorded Seminole "depredations" in his journal. Daniel Wiggins arrived in Middle Florida in October 1838 to live and work on Judge Thomas Randall's plantation (he likely never met Laura Wirt Randall, who died in 1833). Wiggins was a devout Methodist and a millwright from Randall's hometown of Annapolis, Maryland. Encouraged by Randall, who perhaps needed someone with his skills to expand his cotton plantation, Wiggins left a wife and children behind in Annapolis (her parents were ill and she did not want to leave) to ply his trade in Middle Florida, in spite of the ongoing war. Wiggins sent his tools ahead on a schooner, collected twelve enslaved people whom Randall had recently purchased in Maryland, and escorted them to Belmont, Randall's Jefferson County plantation. The monthlong journey began on the *Duchess of Baltimore*, which sailed from Baltimore to Savannah, and then continued overland, where, Wiggins noted, "the Indians have massacred many families."[22] Wiggins complained about the lack of religious society on the journey and in early Florida; often passed judgment on those who drank, played cards, and danced; and attended religious meetings whenever possible. Throughout his first winter in Florida rumors of Native American attacks swept Florida, and he frequently mentioned them in his diary. In January 1839, he wrote, "Many tragical seigns [scenes] have been acted in and about this neighborhood, the relating of which is enough to make the blood run cold—men women & children indiscriminately massacred by the savage foe. I intend as I may have opportunity to collect some of the particulars and write them down."[23] Perhaps he planned someday to publish them (although he never did), as did others who recognized that an audience existed for stories about Seminole attacks on white women. His accounts share many details with published narratives, as his attention to "indiscriminate" violence suggests.[24]

Wiggins's opinion and attitude about the Seminoles and their plight was forever changed by his exposure to a depredation. He had arrived in Florida with some sympathy for the Seminoles, mixed with a liberal dose of fear and racism. On a Sunday in early January 1839, just a few weeks after he had arrived, he wrote in his journal that some whites had attacked a nearby Seminole camp and killed several people, including a young girl. "It makes me feel sorry," he wrote, "to hear of the poor heathens being butchered, especially the females and children, yet I feel glad that they are routed."[25] Wiggins's limited Christian sympathy for the indigenous peoples of Florida was *almost* mobilized here for a Seminole girl—due to her age and gender, a victim most likely to earn an American's sympathies. Yet after another month in the war-ravaged territory, he did not feel the slightest twinge of sadness on behalf of the Seminoles, even women and children. On February 20, 1839, Wiggins personally witnessed the aftermath of an attack on a white woman for the first time:

> I . . . beheld a melancolly and shocking sight—a mother and her sucking child lay a corps on the same board. . . . They were killed yesterday by a herd of bloodthirsty savages—she was shot in two places and stabbed and tomahawked—and then throat slightly cut, besides her arms much bruised and pinched; and the poor harmless child bruised all over the face and tomehawked in three places on the head. . . . I pray the Lord protect me in this land of cruel death. . . . That poor woman and child were apprehensive of danger where they were and had set out for their father's which was about 10 miles north-east. . . . [Rescuers] found the woman dead and stript almost naked and several bags of oats piled upon her—the child was also stript and was not quite dead.[26]

This experience ended any equivocation Wiggins had about whether or not Native American victims deserved his sympathies. The bodies of Mrs. Swan and her "sucking child" are minutely described, illustrative of the brutality of the indigenous attackers. The victims' defenselessness is highlighted by the infant's tender age (so young that he was still nursing) and by their "stript" bodies. The male frustration that they could not be protected—even as they journeyed to safer ground—is palpable. Wiggins clearly feels Swan's death as unjust on gendered grounds—not only was she a woman, and therefore an innocent noncombatant, she was also a mother attempting to protect her child. This potent combination elicited his sympathy and grief both as a chivalrous husband and as a protective father. The attack on Swan occurred near the site of the recent attack on Seminole families, but Wiggins did not mention that the attack on this white woman might have been in revenge. In fact, he began to dehumanize the Seminoles, referring to them as a "*herd* of bloodthirsty savages" in contrast to the brutally killed white (human) family. Through stories like this, Americans rewrote the conflict over Seminole removal into a story of unwarranted Native American brutality against white women and children, without any mention of the violence perpetrated by white Americans.

A month later, in a separate passage, his attitude toward Native Americans had become even more racist, and no longer contained even a hint of sympathetic Christian mercy:

> I pray the Lord to give succor to our army that this otherwise delightful land may no longer be cursed with these hoards of bloodthirsty monsters. The people are now held as prisoners by a mean, cruel, and degraded race—not one hardly worth the name of human—still we are compelled to submit to this degradation. It is thought that government is too lenient towards those savages, they have repeatedly proved themselves to be a treacherous and deceitful race and thereby themselves unworthy of the privileges of honorable warfare and should be hunted and entrapped as wild beast[s] of prey and when taken immediately killed or transported to a distant land.[27]

While when he first arrived he had felt some empathy for the Seminoles, mixed with his fear of them, after seeing the corpses of Swan and her baby and living in daily fear of facing a Seminole attack himself, Wiggins believes the Seminoles to be inhuman and can find no reason to sympathize with them. In fact, he is now a firm believer in Indian removal. As he became a white "Floridian" and lived in terror of an attack, Wiggins likely conversed with other whites on this frontier and began to identify with them and to hate Native Americans. In the passage above Wiggins not only expresses that the Seminoles are "savage beasts" who must either be killed or removed, he also invokes the idea of white captivity by Native Americans—the *whole territory* is being held against its will. This firmly places the Americans in the victim position and constructs the Seminoles as the aggressors, never the prey. Furthermore, in the context of the constant rumors and reports of yet another Indian depredation, the victims that Wiggins observed did not appear to him as a singular event. Rather, he could not help but view their deaths as one example among many of what happened to whites in the "land of cruel death," and as a just reason to use violence against the Seminoles. Wiggins suggests in this passage that the Americans should feel justified in capturing, removing, and even slaughtering Seminole women and children because the "treacherous and deceitful" Native Americans deserve not to be treated as honorable foes.[28]

In spite of his constant fear, Daniel Wiggins survived his sojourn in Florida during the Second U.S.-Seminole War. He died in 1850 during another adventurous attempt to reap the rewards of American expansion. After returning home from Florida to his family in Maryland, he accompanied Thomas Randall on a trip to the California gold fields, but died of an unspecified ailment on board a ship before they arrived.[29]

When Americans privately recorded their encounters with or fears of Seminoles and the Second U.S.-Seminole War, they also recorded their own emotional reactions. They were fearful, angry, and frustrated, and they experienced terror and panic, sorrow and grief.[30] Other letters reveal that many Floridians assumed that their relatives elsewhere had already heard about the Seminole depredations in Florida, since these tales were widespread: Mary Macomb preemptively wrote her mother in Ohio in December 1835, "We are now in great alarm from the Indians. You will see it in the papers or I would not make you uneasy."[31] As Macomb knew, these stories filled many pages of newsprint in the 1830s and 1840s.

Migration and Settlement

Although depredation accounts emphasized white women's victimization *at home* in Florida, most of the population of the territory were recently arrived migrants. While there were a few holdovers from Spanish and British colonization, most of the people of European descent in Florida in the 1820s–1840s had, like Nancy Cone Hagan and Daniel Wiggins, migrated there from elsewhere. Many women came unwillingly with husbands or fathers, while others came as widows with extended kin in search of a better future. Before they faced Seminole attacks or labored to settle the territory, however, they had to get there.

Many women survived difficult trips into Florida. Planter women's trips to the antebellum southern frontier were long and dangerous, many fell ill on the way, and some did not survive. Jane Woodruff left Charleston with her family in January 1823 and arrived in Florida over a year later, by which time she had survived nearly drowning, "dreadful" roads, dysentery, cold and uncomfortable nights sleeping on the ground or the deck of a boat, and a six-mile walk. Laura Wirt Randall wrote her cousin that her journey "exceeded everything I had pre-imaged, tho' I thought I was prepared for the worst."[32] Planter women's complaints have survived in their letters, but others had worse hardships to endure. While white men rode horses and white women and all children rode in carriages or wagons when traveling over land, most adult slaves walked between fifteen and twenty-five miles each day on journeys into Florida. Whites slept in tents, but enslaved blacks slept under open skies and in all kinds of weather. Black women cooked for everyone in the caravan while whites rested. White women who experienced migration while pregnant or nursing were relieved when they and their newborns arrived, but many enslaved women were not so fortunate, and some miscarried on the forced walk to Florida. All enslaved people lost weight on the journey, and some died of accidents or disease.[33]

Separation from family, friends, and the creature comforts of home made white women sorrowful and reluctant trailblazers. As widowed, destitute, yeoman migrant Mary C. Johnston wrote from Florida in 1843, "Mine is the frequent lot of women: poverty, loneliness, and a broken heart."[34] Laura Wirt Randall found the isolation almost unbearable. "I am really very solitary here," she wrote from Tallahassee, "Tho' every lady comes to see us—there are few to come."[35] Forced by their dependence on men to accompany them to the southern frontier, women experienced migration as a brutal reminder of their position as obedient helpmeets with little power to shape their own futures. Their letters and journals contain extensive evidence of how keenly they felt this loss of connection to friends and kin.[36]

Forced migration was even more painful for enslaved people, who called it "being stolen" from their families and communities.[37] Torn away from parents, children, spouses, and siblings (mostly in the Upper South), enslaved people in frontier Florida experienced the social dislocation of migration without the hope of personal gain that drew whites to Florida. Since it was becoming illegal to teach blacks literacy in the antebellum South, slaves enjoyed very few letters from home, unlike the whites who forced them to come. Most knew that they would never again see or even correspond with those they had left behind. As Edward Baptist notes, "In contrast to the migrations of planters and common whites which relied upon and reinforced kinship, forced removal to the plantation frontier attacked and dissolved the family bonds of enslaved African Americans."[38] In reaction there were sometimes suicides and infanticides by enslaved people on the frontier. This was, perhaps, what Thomas Randall feared for David, the enslaved man whom his wife's dowry settlement had separated from his wife, Sophy, and their children.[39]

Having survived the journey, and mourning their losses, white women and the slaves their families "stole" into Florida began the work of creating new homes there. White men proudly seeking independence on the frontier depended upon the labor of white women, children, enslaved people, and male kin. Only the wealthiest white families owned land or could afford to buy it immediately, and women in such families frequently contributed some of the money used to secure land, slaves, and farming equipment. Most yeoman and poor whites either had to raise cash or squat on land they did not own until they had saved enough cash to buy it, risking their futures on the likelihood of preemption or the whims of land speculators. Nancy Cone Hagan sold a slave and her land in South Carolina in order to buy land in Leon County. Other yeoman families sold livestock, crops, or their own labor to raise the cash, ventures to which women had usually contributed labor. For slaves, whites' need for cash in order to buy land and supplies sometimes meant that they had survived an arduous journey to Florida only to be sold again, further severing family and community ties. Some slave owners purposely brought younger slaves to Florida, where they knew that labor would be intense and hot, and left older enslaved people behind. Florida's slave population in 1830 was mostly between age ten and age thirty-six but had an almost equal gender ratio, suggesting that age and not gender mattered most in assigning work.[40]

Upon arrival at their final destination in Florida, white women anxiously awaited the building of their new homes. As those tasked by antebellum prescriptive literature with making homes, they felt a great responsibility to create new domestic spaces that approximated those they had left behind. Many slept in tents or crude, dirt-floored cabins until their households had the time, money, and labor to build a house. The adjustment for planter families was largest, and at least one Florida family found it impossible to become accustomed to "living in a cabin and sleeping on the floor."[41] As their lists of household property indicate, women in early Florida counted a variety of household implements and furnishings among their property, and they certainly put them to use in new frontier dwellings.

Laura Randall found her first accommodations in Florida abysmal, but she was hopeful that the future would bring better living. Her parents sent "the handsomest and best" china, crystal, and furniture to provision her new home.[42] Mary Dearing, a New Hampshire native, funded a frame house with her nephew Charles Brown and other kin near Mandarin, Florida, during a lull in the Seminole War in 1838, christened it "Llangollen," and set about furnishing it.[43] More of the work of setting up a household fell to well-to-do women in Florida than in more settled places, because clearing and planting demanded all slaves' labor, including those who might have otherwise been forced to work for white mistresses in the house.[44]

Poorer white women had little hope of ever living in mansions, but their labor also supported domestic spaces and household production. The "diggins" (early yeoman settlements in Middle Florida) were "a few openings of raw dirt in the woods, three, four or more log cabins close to each other. . . . In the fields, one might see men and women, often both black and white, digging and hoeing together."[45] Yeoman women were often observed spinning thread, shucking corn, grinding cane, or picking the seeds from cotton. Women close to Seminole settlements did their chores with a shotgun nearby. Many planter and yeomen households were also supported by the labor of enslaved people, including women and children. In the midst of war with Native Americans, white women set about the work of making Florida home. Part of an invading (if sometimes reluctant) force, white women performed important work on the journey and in making new settlements.[46]

Seminole Depredations in American Newspapers

Americans could hardly have read a newspaper during the Second U.S.-Seminole War without finding some report of an "Indian depredation" on whites in Florida. Nineteenth-century journalism typically blurred the line between factual news and sensational entertainment, and this was certainly characteristic of the reports on Indian depredations that ran in regional and national newspapers. These stories ranged from brief mentions to detailed accounts of gruesome slaughter and farmsteads ablaze. Few editors or stories objected to the *goals* of the war (causing frustrated abolitionists to dub it "the silent war") and these newspaper stories share a common gendered and pro-removal framework regardless of the political affiliation of the paper or its audience's degree of refinement.⁴⁷ Florida newspapers such as the Whig *St. Augustine News*, the conservative Democratic *Florida Herald* (St. Augustine), and the Democratic *Tallahassee Floridian* ran depredation stories. So did newspapers in neighboring states, which tended to be Jacksonian and Democratic, proslavery, and pro-removal, including the *Charleston Mercury* and the Savannah *Daily Georgian*. Northern and national papers also ran depredation accounts, typically reprinted from the southern papers. These ranged from the genteel *National Intelligencer* to the abolitionist *Liberator* and the widely popular *Niles' Weekly Register* (Baltimore) and *Atkinson's Saturday Evening Post* (Philadelphia). Indian depredation accounts also showed up in the *Army and Navy Chronicle* (a weekly that reported miscellaneous military news from Washington, D.C.), the *New-Yorker Magazine* and the *Jeffersonian* (both published by Horace Greeley), the Democratic *Times and Commercial Intelligencer* (New York), Baltimore's *Sun* (Jacksonian), the *Boston Recorder* (an evangelical Christian paper) and the *Family Magazine*, a monthly aimed at middle-class readers published in Cincinnati, Ohio.⁴⁸

Newspapers reported depredations as "War News," as part of the war, not a consequence of it. Americans from Boston to New Orleans read about them alongside information about recent battles, military decisions, and troop movements. Americans could, then, treat the injuries that depredating Seminoles inflicted on civilians as a violation of the warfare conventions supposedly shared by civilized nations and use it to justify their own scorched-earth methods against the Seminoles. While this again illustrates how blurry the line was between invasion and colonization in American settler colonies like Florida, at the time this practice reinforced white women's central role in the story, presumed their "innocence," overlooked their work as colonizers, and thus helped to frame the war as domestic defense. Since newspapers treated them as war news, depredations appeared to be not an effect of the war but actually the rationale for the war itself. Enforcing Seminole removal became, in this framing, the solution rather the cause of the war. American aggression became American defense.⁴⁹

In 1836, a prospectus for the *Jacksonville Courier* pledged to promptly report on the ongoing horrors in Florida, which included depredations and military reports: "The Interests of this distracted and bleeding portion of our Territory—the varied scenes which are being acted—the tragic parts performed—the untold wants and sufferings of our homeless, houseless citizens . . . intelligence of the movements and operations of our army in

Florida, and of the doings of the Indians, their visitations upon our settlements, now here, now there, will at the earliest dates be found in the columns of our paper."[50] The publishers of the *Courier* were aware of the national audience for news of the war and they hoped to capitalize on the fears of Floridians, who could read reports of Indian depredations and military operations in its pages.

Reports continued to appear in the newspapers throughout the war. In July 1836, *Atkinson's Saturday Evening Post* reprinted a report that Native Americans on their way to Florida were "murdering our defenceless citizens with their helpless wives and children." This account offered details on the bodies of a dead woman and child: "Mrs. Jones was found by the side of a fence, with a small child by her side, the child had its head broken."[51] The Savannah paper carried news of depredations near Tallahasse in March 1837, where a wife and children were "inhumanly mudered by the savages."[52] In July 1838, a Charleston paper reported that the Gwinn family of East Florida "fell victim to savage barbarity; a father, mother and two children were found murdered at the residence . . . a daughter about 13 years of age is missing."[53] In July 1839, the *St. Augustine News* reported an attack on the home of Green Chaires outside Tallahassee, where the Native Americans had killed his wife and "burnt his infant children in the consuming dwelling."[54] In 1840, the same newspaper recounted depredations near Micanopy and New River.[55]

The newspapers were not just profiting from readers' thirst for sensational violence. Depredations were indeed a central part of this conflict. Rather than fight formal battles against an enemy that vastly outnumbered them and had more resources, Seminole warriors frequently attacked settlers and sometimes ambushed U.S. forces. As much a political as a military affair, guerrilla wars are usually fought by a weaker group against superior numbers and resources, as with the American patriots against Great Britain during the American Revolution. As Congressman Joseph R. Underwood of Kentucky noted in 1838, "Do you suppose that the Seminoles are silly enough to come out from their hiding places, and to meet your *thousands* with their *hundreds* in open fight?"[56] As Underwood suggested, attacks on settlers were strategically effective. When Seminoles attacked white settlers (whom they considered invading colonizers), damaged or destroyed their farms and homes, and enticed away their slaves, they were destroying the domesticating property that whites used to colonize Florida. As a result, whites fled in fear from the lands that the Seminoles claimed and hoped to reclaim, and military leaders could not predict or prevent the next attack. As long as enough Seminoles survived to mount another surprise attack, the war continued.⁵⁷

Newspaper and magazine accounts usually included the same elements that recurred in privately recorded depredation stories: Florida was the scene of terrible, indiscriminate murders by "savage" Native American and black men. They featured mothers and/or children whose bodies and homes had been horribly mangled, and they listed wounds and property losses in detail. The papers also covered the deaths of white men, especially if they were maimed in especially horrible ways or could be framed as military heroes attempting to rescue or protect mothers or children.⁵⁸ As the newspapers told and retold depredation accounts, they began to frame them each as "yet another" depredation. In early October 1836, the Savannah *Daily Georgian* reported depredations at the home of the Uptegroves in East Florida, "another instance in our vicinity of Indians committing barbarities upon females."⁵⁹ This reflected both the ubiquity of these stories and the fear that they would never end.

Press accounts sometimes implied that the "Florida War" also served to control the free and enslaved blacks in Florida and throughout the rest of the South, who might launch an attack on slavery as part of their participation in the Seminole resistance. The editors of the St. Augustine paper expressed in 1841:

> The South . . . have rights not to be disregarded. It is a well known fact that a large negro force have lent their cooperation to the Indians during the war—that many of these were slaves of the enemy, claimed to be free, or were runaways from neighboring states, and, when once among the Indians, abandoned themselves to every license in the perseverance of this murderous contest. And what is to prevent, if the Seminoles are to be allowed a residence, Florida from becoming the retreat and abiding place of every runaway slave in the South?⁶⁰

Seminole removal was important to protecting slavery and the South, and therefore so was the success of this war.

Abolitionist editors, among the scarce opponents of the war, also noted the significance of blacks to the conflict in Florida. In 1837 the *Liberator* reminded its readers that it was an "Indian *and Negro* War," in which the "negro Indians" were key allies of the Seminoles and a large part of the reason that they could survive and resist.⁶¹ Abolitionists' solution was to end slavery, of course, which would make the war unnecessary (since they opined it was really about slavery, overlooking Seminole resistance to removal); deprive the Seminoles of important allies; and stop the bloodshed. Abolitionists joined with proslavery voices in condemning Native American violence against whites, as it would have been politically unwise to sympathize with Seminoles and escaped slaves who attacked white women and children. A particular newspaper's stance on slavery influenced its reportage about slave rebellion, but all agreed that the Florida war was as much about protecting the interest of slaveholders as it was about displacing the Seminoles.

Events left out of depredation stories reveal as much about their cultural work as the details they repeated. Although whites across the political spectrum appeared to have no sympathy for Seminole people, throughout this period the Seminoles were fighting for their lives, homes, families, farms, and sacred places. By the end of the Third Seminole War in 1858 the United States had forced between four and six thousand Seminoles from Florida onto the Creek Reservation in Oklahoma. U.S. troops used violence against Seminole men, women, and children, set fire to their homes and crops, and tortured them for information about the location of warriors and other villages. Of course, American newspapers reported none of those details. The widely reported stories of Seminole attacks on whites, however, served to justify and frame the war as one of defense, glossing Indian removal with chivalrous calls to rescue white women and children from Native American attackers.⁶²

These stories from Florida were reported alongside "depredation" accounts from other frontier conflicts that occupied North Americans in the 1830s and 1840s, when the United States fought the Black Hawk War, the Second U.S.-Seminole War, and the U.S.-Mexico War, and removed many Native American people from the Southeast to Oklahoma. Though it was far shorter and less expensive, the Black Hawk War shared much with the Florida conflict, including its causes, conduct, outcomes, and the cultural texts Americans produced and consumed about it. In May 1832, U.S. forces (14,000 strong) moved against 1,100 Sauk and Meskwaki (Fox) resistors under Black Hawk who refused to vacate Illinois, and defeated the resistance in early August. The United States spent between $3 and $8 million to defeat Black Hawk and his people, 77 whites died, and U.S. forces killed 450 to 600 indigenous people. American editors sometimes compared Osceola, the Seminole whom Americans believed led the resistance in Florida, to Black Hawk, and whites framed both men as "noble savage" freedom fighters in later years.[63]

The Black Hawk War was also the source of American reports of Indian depredations (many committed by indigenous people who were not part of Black Hawk's band) and a captivity narrative that rehearsed the same melodramatic elements as previous stories and subsequent Florida tales. Reports of the Indian Creek Massacre, the most famous Native American attack from the 1832 conflict, included information on the "depredations of the Indians" but followed the older model of captivity narratives more closely than the Florida stories, because it culminated in the kidnapping of two "highly respectable" white teenage sisters, Rachel and Sylvia Hall (called "Frances" and "Almira" in a published pamphlet). After a two-week journey to an indigenous village, during which the sisters lived in terror of becoming wives to Native American men, the war ended and the sisters were ransomed and returned. The pamphlet that reported this "inhuman barbarity" shared much with similar stories from Florida: "Savages . . . engaged in the work of human butchery on the frontiers" attacked "defenceless inhabitants;" they "mutilated . . . without distinction of age or sex!" The author emphasized the "mangling" of the bodies of whites killed in the attack, the exposure of other women's bodies after death (one report claimed they were hung upside down from fence posts so that their dresses fell off and exposed their bodies), as well as the use of "tomahawks," "scalping knives," and other "tortures." The captive Hall sisters witnessed the division of plunder among their attackers, but (in contrast to Florida stories) any property considered valuable by whites was overshadowed by the interest of their "savage" captors in the "bleeding scalps which they had, ere life had become extinct, torn from the mangled heads of the expiring victims!" The author of this account was far more interested in such "shocking proofs of savage Cannibalism" (sic) than in enumerating the property losses of white frontier family households. Even in a section titled "Indian depredations" this account focused exclusively on harm to persons: "Their tomahawks have, literally, been made drunk with innocent blood! the virgin's shriek, the mother's wail, and infant's trembling cry, has proved music in their ears!" Reports of these atrocities against white women and children were used to raise militia volunteers from Kentucky and Illinois and to convince any doubters from the East that extermination was the only course of action against the resistant Sauk and Meskwaki. Although some Americans in the Northeast expressed sympathy for Black Hawk's cause (as very few would do a few years later regarding the Seminoles) this and other accounts of Indian depredations on whites in Illinois quickly silenced them. Although it operated in the same register as the Florida narratives that came a few years later, this narrative paid more attention to injured bodies and captive teenage girls than it did to the disruption of white domestic spaces, suggesting that the Florida depredation narratives represented a refining of Indian War stories into a new focus on the destruction of white domestic spaces as well as bodies.[64]

On a larger scale than Illinois or Florida, the American and Mexican press also reported on hundreds of devastating Comanche, Kiowa, and Apache "depredations" on settlers in Northern Mexico in the 1830s and early 1840s. Unlike Northern Mexico, North Florida was not reduced to a man-made desert by Seminole raids on white settlers. Groups of one hundred to four hundred Native American warriors raided in Northern Mexico, and they captured or killed thousands of civilians. These depredations depopulated the region and destabilized Euro-American nation-state power there. Mexican officials failed to address this cross-border warfare until it was too late, which ultimately aided U.S. efforts to take the region from Mexico. Florida was geographically smaller and the Seminoles were fewer in number, and whites outnumbered them very quickly (unlike the dwindling population of Mexican settlers outnumbered by Plains Native Americans in the Southwest), due to federal military and policy support for white settlements.[65]

The larger Southwest borderlands conflict continued into the U.S.-Mexico War (1846–1848), during which the United States spent nearly $75 million to field a large force that eventually totaled more than ninety thousand soldiers in order to invade Mexico (over thirteen thousand died, though fewer than two thousand in battle). In significant contrast to its coverage of the U.S.-Indian Wars, the antiwar American press published accounts of American soldiers' depredations in Mexico, where they murdered, raped, and plundered those they considered their racial inferiors in search of the promised rewards of Manifest Destiny. Although the Seminole stories about the "White Wars" retold in Chapter 3 of this book make it clear that American soldiers committed many atrocities upon the Seminoles in Florida, the press did not publicize these as it did during the war with Mexico. While white atrocities against Seminoles in Florida were either ignored or excused as necessary for the protection of white women and families, the papers framed the Mexican War soldiers who committed atrocities against Mexican mothers and children as greedy reprobates who plundered for their own gain, not to defend innocent white women and children. Therefore, their murder, rapine, and plunder was harder to ignore or justify and even called the superiority of white manhood into question.[66]

Seminole removal from Florida was only one of five tragic sagas of indigenous dispossession in the U.S. Southeast in the 1830s. Under duress, Choctaws and Chickasaws left Mississippi, Creeks left Alabama and Georgia, Cherokees left Georgia and North Carolina, and Seminoles left Florida. The United States used devious diplomacy, coercive treaties, cash payments, and violence to ethnically cleanse about seventy thousand people out of the Southeast and move them onto reservations west of the Mississippi River in the 1830s and 1840s. On what a Choctaw leader named the "trail of tears and death," as many as seventeen thousand of these people perished. All of these groups had adapted some assimilationist strategies and practiced some form of black enslavement prior to removal, and they expanded racial slavery into Indian Territory. None besides the Seminoles resisted removal with war, but all resisted, and members of all these groups remained in the Southeast in spite of the pressure to leave, where their descendants still reside today. The United States set aside $500,000 to effect their removal in the 1830s but eventually spent far more than that. Although some evangelicals and reformers in the Northeast objected to Indian removal, Americans who lived in the West and the South supported it wholeheartedly. They lived in close proximity to Native American people and so had much to gain directly from their dispossession, and more firsthand experience with the frontier violence featured in bloody narratives of "Indian depredations." Americans who read about Seminole attacks on white mothers, children, and homes in Florida understood that violence as part of a much larger campaign of national expansion and Indian removal, one in which hundreds of white soldiers, thousands of white settlers, and millions of American dollars were already invested.[67]

Women and Work on the Florida Frontier

It is a truism of women's history that during wartime women have been called upon to do unusual kinds of work usually reserved for men. It is also the case that women on frontiers often worked harder than women elsewhere and at some tasks considered men's work in more settled parts of the country. In wartime and on frontier zones, then, American women have found grueling labor as well as opportunity to prove their competence at "male" employments and perhaps parlay that into future rights or freedoms. In frontier Florida, these two historical patterns merge and cannot be disentangled. Women's work on this frontier was part of the conflict itself. The work they expended to reproduce and sustain white households *was* the work of expansion, and through making white homes, women completed the appropriation of indigenous land. As they made homes, planted crops, birthed babies, and nurtured communities, women in Florida were establishing—on the ground and in narrative—that this contested territory belonged to them and to their families. Just as attacks on them were considered war news and reported alongside military engagements, women's work contributed to the invasion, colonization, and settlement of Florida, including what had recently been Seminole land. While depredation stories portray white women as victims and never aggressors, without white women American settlement was impossible.

Although antebellum prescriptive literature trumpeted domesticity as a woman's true calling, almost all women labored both inside and outside of their homes, especially in new frontier settlements. Due to the domestic gender ideal, this is work for which they rarely get credit, and even the domestic work they performed is discounted as somehow less important or difficult than "real" work. Openly admitting that they were tan and strong from outdoor work exposed both male dependence on women's labor and opened women up to losing respectability for doing men's work. Nevertheless, all women worked in frontier Florida. As historian Tracy Revels argues, "To be female in the antebellum south was to be a laborer."[68] Only a tiny elite group escaped physical labor entirely, and even planters' wives worked to care for all the children and slaves in their households. Such women had much better lives than poorer and enslaved women, but few were truly ladies of leisure.

In the small urban centers of early Florida, white and free black women earned wages and participated in trade. White women worked as housekeepers, seamstresses, tailoresses, pattern makers, mantua makers, milliners, music teachers, nurses, and tutors. Free black women also plied the needle or performed laundry, housekeeping, cooking, or childcare work. White and black women sold the produce of their gardens and kitchens in markets. In Florida's towns and in some of the industrial outfits in West Florida a small portion of Florida's enslaved people worked as hired laborers, their wages paid to the whites that claimed to own them. The labor shortage in antebellum Florida encouraged this, and some enslaved women worked as domestics or in military facilities, lumber companies, textile mills, and brickyards.[69]

Outside of Florida's towns, white yeoman and tenant-class women worked in the cotton, indigo, sugar, corn, and potato fields. In the vast majority of Florida, where migrants hewed homesteads out of forests and former Seminole settlements, everyone in every household worked toward that goal, including women. As Baptist argues in his study of Middle Florida yeomen, "Women's labor was as essential as that of adult men. Consigned by custom and law to the direction of the male head of household, women performed almost every kind of task on small farms."[70] There are no accounts of white women felling trees and clearing land in antebellum Florida (although enslaved black women did), but they did everything else on farms. Planter's daughter Ellen Call Long noted that "the 'cotton patch' or 'potato hills'" left "no time for ornamental gardening" for the common white women of Florida.[71] Indeed, women worked alongside men, children, and any slaves they owned, tending livestock, crops, and gardens. Free and enslaved women gathered firewood, raised poultry, grew vegetables, and produced goods at home such as candles, cloth, and clothing. Most Florida farms grew some cotton to sell, corn to eat and to sell, and a variety of other crops and subsistence foods. Revels notes that "visitors to Florida commented on the industry of farm women, usually portraying them as far more enterprising than their men." In comparison to their more refined sisters, poor white or "cracker" women knew how to shoot and hunt, drank whiskey and smoked tobacco, were not sheltered domestics, and often worked for wages, took in boarders, or drove a hard bargain in the market, Revels notes. In these ways, they fought for their own and their families' survival. This labor created and sustained white households on former Seminole land where they had not existed just a few years before.[72]

Planter class white women also worked in new white settlements. One plantation mistress noted that her neighbor looked "weather-beaten" even though she ran a household with the help of enslaved people. Unlikely to work in fields, white mistresses typically managed large households, a task that they found especially strenuous in a newly settled wilderness. Many cooked for large numbers of whites and enslaved blacks every day. Jane

Woodruff prepared daily meals for over one hundred slaves in North Florida and shared their food even when it was meat infested with maggots. Laura Wirt Randall, although she had at least three household servants or slaves, sowed vegetable seeds herself for a kitchen garden and frequently attempted fancy desserts when she was entertaining. Most planter women delegated weaving to slaves, but many cut, dyed, and sewed clothing. They nursed sick and injured slaves and supervised both white and black children. On less wealthy plantations, white women performed more of the household production, making candles, sewing, and cooking or baking foods themselves. The women of the Brown family, who relocated from Rhode Island to East Florida in the 1830s, relished the opportunity to establish their own "enterprises" and planted orange and mulberry trees and attempted to cultivate silkworms. Although they came from an urban merchant class background (their deceased father had been a shipbuilder and privateer), and commanded some assistance from slaves and servants, Ellen and Corinna Brown did some domestic work and nursed their kin when they fell ill (which happened frequently). Their brothers planted acres of cotton, corn, and potatoes, and their aunts Mary and Ann Dearing cooked and did some field work. Planter and merchant class women's expanded workload on the frontier prompted one planter to opine that even planter class women became "domestic industrious housewives" since labor alone was the only employment "to cheer up life in this dreary solitude."[73]

All white households relied on women's work, while those who owned enslaved people also exploited the labor of enslaved people for the benefit of white families. Planters depended on enslaved people's abilities in order to achieve plantation self-sufficiency: whites needed slaves not only to grow the cotton, but also to pick it, clean it, spin it, and weave it into cloth. In their quest to make their own "independent" fortunes, white owners made no distinctions to protect enslaved women from the demands of "men's work." Larry Rivers found that on the large plantations and small farms of territorial Florida enslaved men and women performed all the same tasks. They prepared new ground for planting, plowed and hoed fields, and sowed and harrowed over seeds. While some of the fields that early migrants planted had been farmed by Native Americans before them (early maps and land parcel descriptions mention the "old Indian fields" that white settlers claimed), new fields had to be cleared as cash crop cotton agriculture expanded into Florida. In Florida, as elsewhere on the southern frontier, slaves of both genders and white men and boys had to fell trees, roll and burn logs, remove stumps, dig ditches, and plow before they planted.[74]

Enslaved women performed all that backbreaking work of settlement while continuing to provide cooking, nursing, child care, sewing, and other female tasks for their own families and for the whites that claimed to own them. In addition, some served as midwives, "conjure women," and preachers in Florida. Many had to cook morning and evening meals for themselves and their children and kin, and on large plantations it was usually a bondswoman who cooked at midday for all the slaves and the whites as well. Women also shared with enslaved men (if they lived with their spouses) the work of grinding their own cornmeal, tending chickens and vegetable gardens, and mending clothes. All this work inspired one enslaved woman to declare in 1862 that she would "rather be whipped to death than worked to death" on a Putnam County plantation in East Florida.[75] The labor of enslaved men and women was vital to the growth of white settlements in Florida, but only whites benefited, while enslaved people suffered terribly from the trauma and exhausting labor that white settlers exacted from them.

Devastated Domesticity

Given the effort that making and sustaining white homes required, it is no wonder that Americans spilled so much ink decrying their destruction in Florida Indian depredation stories. The focus on the devastated homestead and dead mother was a crucial part of the way these tales used gender and domesticity to reframe a war for Indian removal as a matter of domestic defense. American publishers printed several narratives of female suffering and salvation in Florida during the first two years of the Second U.S.-Seminole War. In narratives published outside newspapers and sold for profit, a tragically disrupted domestic scene is a major trope. This was not typical of captivity stories, in which the scene of the story followed white captives to their indigenous captors' village. White women in depredation narratives, however, flee their homes, running away from their attackers and toward a hiding place. Rather than staying with the victims, the narratives typically return to the scene of the attack, and describe the destruction of the home in symbolic terms. Authors often used destroyed homesteads and wounded maternal bodies as interchangeable signs mobilized to mourn the loss of domestic harmony as well as valuable property. The preoccupation with lost property emphasized that white Americans were at home in Florida and had already established homes and farms there.

Florida Indian depredation tales sold as pamphlets and broadsides contained the same elements as depredation narratives in newspapers, journals, and letters, but they were longer than other accounts, more embellished with sentimental observations and sensational details, and three included engraved illustrations of depredation scenes. As did newspaper reports, narrators treated these attacks as part of the war; in fact, usually the woman's narrative of suffering made up only a small portion of the whole pamphlet, with most of the pages dedicated to summarizing the causes and events of the war up to the date of publication. They typically included text taken directly from newspaper articles as well as excerpts from "authentic" letters and journals (probably fictional), and sometimes other depredation narratives as well, so that one pamphlet brought together all the individual emotional reactions, sympathy for white mothers and children, war news and war framing, and devastated domesticity featured in other Florida Indian depredation narratives. Since there were so many Seminole attacks included, the narratives published for profit repeated the violence and its tragic outcomes until it seemed as though their pages dripped blood.[76]

As the most sensational accounts, these narratives illustrate how publishers and authors used race and gender norms to manipulate readers. They offered readers scenes of devastated domestic tranquility as sensational proof that the Seminoles had violated all of the family and domestic relationships that Americans held to be sacred and natural, just as stories of captivity had violated those same norms and elicited the accusation that indigenous warriors were "indiscriminate" in their choice of victims. It is clear that publishers expected American audiences to feel sympathy for white women who watched children die and homes burn to the ground, and to feel rage and horror at the "savages" who were responsible. They also reveal the that Americans would pay, or at least publishers hoped they would pay, to read these horrifying tales of Native American attacks on white women and children in the 1830s.

The "Captivity and Sufferings of Mrs. Mason, with an Account of the Massacre of her Youngest Child" appeared in a broadsheet illustrated with two images and embellished with a poem sometime in 1836 (the sheet is undated but references events in the spring of 1836). The author or publisher probably composed Mason and her story out of several different accounts since she does not appear in the newspapers or the Florida census. A sensational vehicle for pro–Indian removal and pro-war propaganda, the tale invoked sympathy and horror in the reader. Mason returned home one day to find her home on fire and her child asleep inside. She picked up "dear Ellen" and ran for their lives, but a Seminole "lay in ambush," and with this "uplifted tomahawk" he killed Ellen. Mason fainted next to her daughter's "mangled corpse" and awoke to find her attacker mysteriously "lying cold" and "shot by some unseen hand." Shortly thereafter, as she fled toward a nearby plantation, a group of "squaws" beat Mason and took her clothing. She escaped from them two days later and wandered alone and barely clothed for five days before she reached a settler's home and was saved. Her salvation does not end the tragic story, however, because Seminoles soon burned out the settlers with whom she had taken refuge, "a wife and five children savagely butchered," just three days after she left them. In the space of a few brief paragraphs, the typical elements of a Florida depredation narrative appeared: Native Americans attack a woman and her child, the mother watches her child killed by an indigenous warrior with a tomahawk, she flees, faces exposure and hardships, and, in this case, is even briefly captured. Further violence to other whites and their property rounds out the terrifying story.[77]

Two engravings illustrated the Mason broadsheet. At the top of the page, a woman defends her daughter from an attacker with an axe as a house surrounded by warriors burns in the background. The second scene, below the text, is of a battle between the Seminoles and American militia. The necessity of this war in order to protect white women and children is visually argued as readers look down the page. The text leads them to the same conclusion.

The Mason account is unambiguously racist. Mason recounts many instances of Seminole "barbarity" and "savagery," from the initial attack to her encounter with the violent indigenous women, to the destruction of the home where she had sought safety. Her encounter with the "squaws" would undoubtedly have "terminated in [her] death" by exposure and abuse if not outright murder, and no sympathy for them is even implied although they were likely starving and in need of clothes as a result of the American war to force them west.

Mason's letter is followed by a poem that uses sentiment to reinforce racial and cultural differences between Native American and white people,

Figure 1. Captivity and Sufferings of Mrs. Mason, with an account of the murder of her youngest child. This image headed the 1836 broadside. Courtesy of the Newberry Library.

particularly in terms of family and domesticity. It includes this tribute to motherhood and loss:

> The prayer of women availeth not,
> They plead to hearts of stone,
> The babe is wrenched from its mothers breast,
> She hears its dying groan—
> > These savage hearts are all unmoved,
> > By mother's wail, or beauty's tone.

Feelings separate the Indians from the whites in this poem: the helpless mother's plight moves the presumably white readers to feel sympathy,

Figure 2. A Battle with the Indians. This image appeared at the bottom of the 1836 broadside. Courtesy of the Newberry Library.

which distinguishes them from unsentimental "savages" whose hearts are "all unmoved." Separated families and feeling mothers are counterpoised to unfeeling "stone-hearted" Native Americans, whose women were opportunistic harpies in this story, not loving mothers. American readers feel their racial and cultural difference from the Seminoles, for reading Mason's story has surely elicited sympathy, horror, and fear from them.

The destruction of "home" is also featured in the poem, just as this theme appeared in the images and in the narrative. The "ruined home" is mourned in the stanza that follows the one above, which also ends the poem:

> The eastern sky was light and red—
> The sun rides proud on high,
> Its beams fall on a ruined home,
> Where dead and mangled lie—
> And smoking embers tell the tale,
> Of ruthless savage butchery.

Readers are invited to return to the scene of the burned home on the morning after, where they observe not only dead bodies but destroyed domesticity.[78]

The destruction of white domesticity is also prominent in "A True and Authentic Account of the Indian War in Florida, Giving the Particulars Respecting the Murder of the Widow Robbins, and the Providential Escape of her Daughter Aurelia, and her Lover, Mr. Charles Somers, After Suffering Almost Innumerable Hardships," printed in New York in 1836. This pamphlet recounts a Seminole attack on a widow, her teenage daughter, and the daughter's bethrothed. Although the fiancé and hero, Charles Somers, tries to protect them, the Seminoles barge into the home, kill the widow, pursue the young lovers into the swamp, and then return to set the house on fire. The Robbins account includes twenty-six pages of text, of which only four pages covered the title story, while the rest repeated stories of military encounters and other Seminole attacks, maximizing the number of Seminole "murders" of white women and children within its pages. As with other pamphlet narratives, this one rehearses the elements of the typical depredation narrative, reminds the reader that Seminoles practiced "indiscriminate slaughter," and establishes the spotless innocence of the white families living in Florida.[79]

The narrative focuses in on the tragic end of the Widow Robbins and her home. From their hiding place, Aurelia Robbins hears the attackers whoop as the house goes up in flames, and in that moment the narrator claims that she *forgets that the Seminoles killed her mother*, and exclaims, "Oh my God! shall my poor mother perish in the flames?" As her memory returns, she sobs "What did I say?—I have no mother."[80] The loss of her mother and the house are collapsed into one great loss, and Aurelia sinks dramatically into Charles's arms. Her fiancé is all that is left, now that her family and home are destroyed. Following this tragedy, Charles Somers and Aurelia Robbins survive a night in the swampy forest and are saved the next day by the arrival of a detachment of Florida volunteers, affording the author an opportunity to laud the bravery and honor of white men.

This pamphlet included a striking image, "The Indians and Negroes Massacreing the Whites in Florida, in January 1836," in which flames pour out of a burning home, as Native American and black men attack white settlers (even though no Black Seminoles are mentioned in the narrative).[81] A composite representation of the war rather than a picture of what happened to Aurelia Robbins, this image may have illustrated other narratives as well. The usual elements are prominently featured in the picture.

Figure 3. "The Indians and Negroes Massacreing the Whites in Florida, January 1836." This image followed the title page in the Robbins depredation pamphlet. Courtesy of the Strozier Library at Florida State University, Special Collections and Archives.

Seminoles wield axes and knives ("tomahawks" and "scalping knives") against several white women and men, as others lay bleeding on the ground. The central action is the struggle between a Seminole man and a white man engaged in hand-to-hand combat, flanked by violence on all sides. On the far edges of the image, Native Americans attack white women, so that as one views the image from left to right, the visual story begins and ends with indigenous violence against white women and children. On the left, a supplicating white mother with several children begs a Seminole woman to relinquish an infant. Next to her, a black man stabs a white man. To the right, smoke and flames billow out of the windows of a burning house, as indigenous people grasping axes and knives massacre white women and men. Behind a woman who has been forced to the ground, another Native American threatens to scalp a white man who is on his knees. Embellishing the image with some color, the illustrator used red ink to make the blood of the white victims stand out. All of the blacks and indigenous people in the frame are attackers, not victims, while most of the whites, and all of the white women, are prostrate before them. A burning home serves as the backdrop for the violence in the image. Thus Florida was visually portrayed as a place where combined forces of blacks and Native Americans destroy white homes and attack white families.

The remainder of the Robbins booklet includes more tragically ruined white homes. The author makes broad sentimental appeals for sympathy on behalf of the poor, suffering whites who had expended years of toil to create the homes in Florida now demolished by Native Americans. In a description of the depredation at New River and Cape Florida, for instance, the author lists "houses, barns and cribs of grain," livestock and chickens, "furniture, clothing, bedding, agricultural implements, and even breadstuffs sufficient to sustain" whites lost to Seminole depredation. Yet, the author notes, all those property losses pale in comparison to the loss of one's home. Terrified families flee without "a single article of domestic comfort. . . . On this account the sufferings of many families were augmented to a degree almost beyond the endurance of nature. All but life—all that could render life desirable, was unavoidably left to the merciless savages. The results of years of hardy untiring industry became the prey to Indian fires."[82] As in all these accounts, this focus on property loss presented Florida as a home belonging to white Americans, not the Seminoles and blacks who attacked them.

In addition to her survival of stabbing, scalping, and fire, Jane Johns's story also featured her wrecked homestead. In the spring of 1837, Dr. Andrew Welch, who cared for Jane Johns after the 1836 attack, published a pamphlet "for her benefit" and took her on a speaking tour in Charleston and Savannah. This lengthy account was published in Charleston in early 1837 and reprinted in Baltimore later that year. The "Narrative of the Life and Sufferings of Mrs. Jane Johns, Who was Barbarously Wounded and Scalped by Seminole Indians, in East Florida" includes extracts supposedly taken from Doctor Welch's journal and an account credited to the victim herself. Welch sandwiched these two versions of the attack between several chapters that included details about her parents and her life before this attack, as well as accounts of other "depredations" and general news of the war in Florida. His attention to her family history and her destroyed homestead were especially effective domestic propaganda.[83]

Andrew Welch was a medical doctor from England who arrived in Florida in the early 1830s. Whether he genuinely wished to aid Jane Johns or only wished to profit from her narrative is difficult to determine, but he later published narratives about an adopted Seminole son and another about an escaped slave, which indicates his interest in sentimental and sensational subjects, or at least in their potential to generate a profit. His attitude about Native Americans and enslaved blacks shifted between these publications (rendering his sincerity somewhat doubtful), but he consistently wrote in ways intended to mobilize readers' sympathies. Welch was also involved in land speculation in the territory, so he had a vested interest in clearing the land of Seminoles, as well as perhaps pecuniary motives for publishing sensational tales.[84]

Perhaps with potential profits in mind, Welch added several sensational details that had not been included in the newspapers. Welch claimed that Jane Johns was pregnant when attacked and subsequently miscarried. This addition magnified the tragedy and responded to audience expectations that women in depredation narratives would be mothers who lost children. Welch also added some family history, which entwined Johns's story with American expansion into Florida: Jane's parents, a Mr. and Mrs. Hall, barely survived an 1813 Native American depredation, at a time when Florida was preoccupied by the "Patriot War." Filibusters from Georgia invaded Spanish Florida in March 1812, and the conflict lasted until 1814. Mrs. Hall gave birth to Jane immediately after their escape, hence both mother and daughter survived Seminole attacks while pregnant, and Jane's miraculous escape was foreshadowed by the circumstances of her birth. In April 1821 Jane's brother was killed, an uncle wounded, and female neighbors were "butchered" by Seminoles. Welch's narrative thus begins with a series of attacks that disturbed the domestic peace of Jane Johns's childhood, events that foreshadow her story and imply that the Seminoles had been disrupting Johns's family since before her birth.[85]

As in many other depredation accounts, Welch employed the "indiscriminate" use of violence against white women and children to differentiate between whites and Native Americans. The circumstance under which her father-in-law discovered Jane Johns (another detail added by Welch) highlighted purported white civility in contrast to supposed Seminole barbarity. According to Welch, when her father-in-law first spied her, lying unconscious with a coffee bag on her head, he almost shot her, thinking her a "squaw with a red handkerchief upon her head." At the last second, a male companion stopped him from firing, and "entreated him to forbear, and not to take away the life of a defenceless woman."[86] The tale of her discovery illustrated the difference between gallant, civilized white men who supposedly never harmed women, and the "barbaric savages" who scalped, shot, and set them on fire. Civilized men purportedly took pity on helpless women, even Seminole ones, and would never shoot one.

Welch's twenty-seven-page pamphlet also afforded him space to reflect upon the Johns's destroyed homestead, which he used to hyperbolic effect. As in the Mason and Robbins accounts, the devastated scene of the whites' ruined home is the subject of sentimental grief:

> The house in which he and his affectionate young wife had so lately dwelt in all the bliss of early wedded love, was now nought but a few smouldering ruins, in the centre of which a few bricks pointed out the spot where lied buried . . . the remains of one who but a few days since, lived in health and high hope of reaping the fruits of his honest labor—the surrounding cultivation shewed evidence of his industry and enterprise. Never did I behold a more melancholy or wilder scene that that on which I now gazed in sadness—in one spot I saw some calcined human bones left unsepulchred, being too fragile to remove—they pulverized at the touch. In another place, I noticed fragments of glasses, plates, and other articles for domestic use, from which, but a few hours previous, this fond young couple had received in thankfulness, their daily sustenance—upon the stump of a pine tree I found some remains of hair—here the murderous villains had severed from the scalp of the yet-living young widow, her long, and lately so much admired tresses.[87]

Alongside the industrious settler's ashes and his widow's scalp are fragments of brick, glass, and porcelain, which attest to the civilized home they had built in Florida. These were signs, Welch notes, of their marital bliss. Long hair was the crowning glory of young white womanhood, symbolizing youth, sexual attractiveness, and, in this context, also operating as a key indicator of Jane Johns's whiteness. The attack destroyed the home that Clement Johns's "honest labor" and "industry and enterprise" had created for them (though surely she labored as well). This cluster of white, heteronormative symbols of domesticity established that, despite the nearby Seminoles, the industrious Johns had built a home in Florida and were the innocent victims of a depredation that had robbed them of it.

After her wounds healed, Jane Johns traveled to Charleston and Savannah with Welch, where he lectured on the benefits of a vegetarian diet (a timely health reform topic), and they sold copies of her narrative, reputedly for her financial support. As an exhibit of Seminole cruelty, Johns and her scalped head no doubt drew large crowds at Welch's lectures, in spite of the incongruous topic and expensive tickets, which cost $1.00 each. On March 29, 1837, the *Charleston Mercury* ran an advertisement for the upcoming appearance, and specifically noted "Mrs. Johns will attend in person."[88] On April 1, 1837, the Charleston paper added, "Ladies are particularly requested to attend."[89] One imagines that white women in the South's jewel cities made up the majority of the audience. Surely they ogled her scalped head while contributing donations to her support, displaying their benevolent Christianity and sympathy while consuming the spectacle. The lecture tour that Welch and Johns made in 1837 likely boosted political support for Seminole removal and what was becoming a very unpopular war, by reminding Americans that it was necessary to protect innocent women and children in Florida from "Indian depredations." Perhaps their response extended into pressure on their husbands and sons to help tame Florida and bring it into the southern fold. It is sobering to imagine that the ladies of Charleston and Savannah would engage in this kind of informal political activity as their more radical contemporaries in the North began to enter politics via opposition to Indian removal and slavery. Women's desires to embody virtue, through sympathy or through diet, crossed party and sectional lines but did not always extend across the color line and could be mobilized in many ways. Perhaps Welch believed that diet reform provided a common ground for women of all political persuasions.[90]

Authors represented white women in Indian depredation narratives as innocents whose homes and families were long-standing residents of Florida, where Seminoles had tragically destroyed their domestic lives. Indigenous and black attackers violated or exposed a woman's home and body in some fashion in these for-profit stories, so that wounded female bodies and ruined domestic property become overdetermined symbols for devastated domesticity. This attention to the scene of the attack highlighted, again, that indigenous people hurt women and children, that whites were already "home" in Florida and were defending themselves, and that the Seminoles, uncivilized as they were, hardly deserved to make their own homes in Florida permanently. Removing them thus became the answer rather than the cause of the violence.

Women's Reproductive and Community Labor

Children were as important to the sentimental work of depredation narratives as white women. Surely no other victims of Native American violence were as innocent, sympathetic, and tragic. Where all those white children came from, and the labor it required to gestate, feed, clothe, nurse and sustain them, comprises another portion of women's work in early Florida—work that was elided as *sentiment* in depredation stories and in American life.

In addition to their work in homes, fields, churches, and communities, all women performed important work as mothers. While for planters children represented the fulfillment of a patriarch's expected role, for yeomen families children were a future labor force. For slave-owning whites, the birth of enslaved children promised future wealth and labor, while for enslaved parents, children who were already someone else's property were at best a bittersweet joy and at worst a reminder of sexual violence. To Native Americans, of course, growing numbers of white and enslaved black children signaled that whites would continue to expand their claims to land in Florida. Like white women, white children were important symbols of their intentions to create permanent homes and farms in Florida. Not only innocents without any fault or claim in Florida, settler children were also the white future of Florida.[91]

Children were not easily created and sustained. Women knew that pregnancy and childbirth were dangerous and taxing, especially on a remote frontier, where proper nutrition and medical care were difficult to procure. While the perception of the risk of death in childbirth was greater than the actual risk in the eighteenth and nineteenth centuries, women at the time were products of a culture that often spoke of pregnancy in the same breath with death, either of the mother or the baby. However rare it was, some women sacrificed their own lives in creating new life. Others spent most of their adulthood pregnant and nursing on a frontier where poor diet and lack of good medical care ground them down. Young children also faced high disease rates in Florida, and many died in their first few years. Laura Randall miscarried her first pregnancy in 1827 and then had three daughters in rapid succession between 1828 and 1831. By the third pregnancy, she was taking laudanum to avoid a second miscarriage (a tragic irony), and to escape the demands of two infants. She wrote to her cousin that "the cares of maternity, and of housekeeping fall very heavily. . . . Three babies in less than three years are enough to make one tired of babies, I think: at least, so I generally say when my feeble health makes me feel the toil of nursing and the loss of rest with particular heaviness."[92] Laura Randall died in 1833 following the birth of her fourth child, who also died. Even wealthy white women in antebellum Florida faced childbirth with few medical aids and little hope of survival if something went wrong.[93]

Women's reproductive labor was of paramount importance to their families, households, and masters. Men were well aware of the benefits of women's presence and labor, since in addition to their work on farms and in homes, women birthed the children who grew into laborers and into the adults who would support parents in old age. Many of the women who came to Florida in the 1820s, 1830s, and 1840s had children soon after arriving, eventually producing large families. Nancy Cone Hagan's daughter Elizabeth gave birth to two daughters in her first two years of marriage and probably also worked in the fields alongside her husband, younger brothers, and the family's female slave. Although women's reproductive labor is often taken for granted as "natural" and inevitable, it involved work and sacrifices that many women feared. Although most women expected to conceive, carry, birth, and raise children in their lives, that made it no less terrifying or natural. While fertility rates fell in the United States overall in the nineteenth century, large families remained common in the South, where maternal mortality rates remained higher than in New England and the Mid-Atlantic.[94]

Women's reproductive work created an impressive number of white and black children in Florida. By 1850 there were 21,148 whites under age fifteen (41 percent of the total white population) and 17,384 enslaved black children under age fifteen (45.4 percent of enslaved blacks). Whether these children were born in Florida or came with migrant households, they indicate how powerfully women's reproduction and work to raise children contributed to the expansion of American communities in Florida. Without the women who risked their lives to bear these children, nearly half the population of Florida would not have existed in 1850. While mothers and children starred as the most sympathetic victims of Native American violence in depredation narratives, they were also responsible for the fastest growing segment of Florida's population in the territorial period. They were, therefore, an essential part of the American threat to the Seminoles' future there.[95]

For enslaved mothers, childbearing was an even heavier burden, as it enriched white masters by creating children whom parents could not protect from the terrible emotional and physical burdens of slavery. As Jennifer Morgan has demonstrated, from the earliest days of New World slavery, whites invested in female slaves because of their ability to reproduce the enslaved labor force, augment white wealth in human property, and also perform hard work in fields. In this way, women were the most productive and lucrative slaves. Unlike in some parts of the South, the gender ratio among Florida's enslaved population was relatively even throughout this period (large plantations had slight male majorities, smaller farms had slight female majorities). Both whites and blacks encouraged and supported family formation among enslaved blacks. White slave owners sometimes selected the "strongest and best" to breed together. One former slave remembered that his mother, Fannie Parish, was regarded by her owner as a "breeder," whose tasks were specifically limited to bearing and caring for children on the plantation. Enslaved women in Florida began bearing children early, sometimes as young as thirteen, and most bore their first child between age fifteen and age sixteen. Childbearing did not spare most women from field work, and many of them returned to the fields only one or two days after giving birth. As elsewhere, some enslaved women in Florida were raped or engaged in consensual, though highly unequal, relationships with white men, and children born of such unions became slaves as well. The children produced by slave families added to the wealth of whites, but they were also testimony to enslaved people's determination to maintain their own humanity in the face of their legal status as property. While family ties were an important way to combat the dehumanizing reality of slavery, children might also be used to manipulate or punish recalcitrant adults or sold away someday to another distant frontier, and a slave's children had little hope of someday becoming free. Perhaps because of this, in 1829 a slave named Jane killed her infant and was hanged at Tallahassee. When death or migration loomed, and as white children came of age, white owners rarely hesitated to sell slaves and that often disrupted family units. Rivers estimates that between 50 and 60 percent of runaway slaves in Florida left in order to reunite with family members.[96]

The reproduction of both white and black families in Florida was vital to the growth of American settlements there. Every white or black baby born in Florida marked the expansion of Americans in a territory in which they competed with Seminoles for land, homes, and rights. Whites born in Florida grew up to be "natives" who would call Florida home and claim rights equal or superior to those of the Seminole Natives, whose claims to

Florida as home were violently contested in the 1830s and 1840s. The enslaved children born in that generation would, against their will, serve those whites and support their dominance over Seminoles. Yet when Seminoles attacked white homes in depredation narratives, narrators frame white women and children in purely sentimental terms, neglecting their importance to the social and political development of the territory, a pattern continued by romanticized histories of the American frontier. It is important to interrogate that framing in order to hold white women accountable, and to connect the voluntary and involuntary labor of women to the processes of settlement, expansion, and removal. The women who created the first generation of Americans in Florida, some willingly and others under coercion, reproduced American families and American slavery on new soil in the midst of a violent contest over the territory itself.[97]

Women created communities as well as families. Through their social activities in homes and churches, women established new networks of reciprocity, kinship, friendship, and political alliance. In doing so, they reestablished the social order that migration had forced them to leave behind by choosing those with whom they would trade, associate, entertain, snub, or show deference. As women wove new communities out of separate strands of migrants and neighbors, they created the networks that responded to the challenges of life in Florida—loneliness, disease outbreaks, and, of course, attacks from "depredating" Native Americans. Women's work building these community ties is implicit in depredation narratives, when they flee their burning homes to take shelter among their neighbors. Creating those connections, however, required much work.[98]

Although community building was certainly not exclusively women's work, white men depended upon white women's work as hostesses, neighbors, and agents of domestic economy. Rich or poor, they engaged in community-building activities, some of which looked more like leisure than work but required the labor of many people (including that of enslaved people) to support travel, entertaining, and caring for new friends and adopted kin. This essential service was probably less wearying, if no less valuable, than their physical labor. Women's work, whether coerced or freely given, knit together new communities out of migrants settling the territory. Through their work, they aided in the taking of that land from indigenous women and groups.

Planter women worked to establish their family's status via social connections. As the Randalls built a home at "Belmont" in the late 1820s, for example, Laura Randall knew that it was her duty, as the wife of a judge and planter, to entertain. The Randalls regularly hosted "land hunters" who had come to Florida to look at parcels of land for potential investment. By hosting prospective neighbors (or speculators), they cultivated subsequent migration, contributing to the expansion of American settlement beyond the borders of their own plantation. As more whites settled nearby, they hosted dinners, dances, and family parties, social opportunities that created work for Randall (and more work for her enslaved servants) and also marked her as a woman of elite status. Entertaining provided the opportunity to display wealth, which set elites apart from poor whites and from the blacks who served them. Reinforcing these social hierarchies was especially significant on the frontier, where exigent circumstances sometimes blurred the lines. When elite white women upheld social distinctions in their new communities, they were "civilizing" a new country while at the same time establishing social (and often political) ties between the most powerful and wealthy white families.[99]

Labor in support of their farms and families brought poorer white women together. Yeomen women shared quilting, shelling peas, making cloth, caring for the sick, and helping other women through childbirth. Working together lightened each woman's load and made a social occasion out of daily labor. They were going about what one historian calls "the business of subterranean community-building." Older and widowed women who had fewer demands on their time did important work through and in their churches. Through visiting, older women provided connections among new congregants even outside of church, creating communities out of disparate households. Women made up the majority of church members in antebellum Middle Florida, and probably in the rest of the state as well, given their preponderance in southern churches. Nancy Cone Hagan visited neighbors and kin to spread the gospel and also in her capacity as a midwife. Fond of visiting friends, she wrote:

> O how delightful is the day
> When friends together meet
> They sit and chat the day away
> Not fearing what they speak.

Women's joy at spending time with friends served their communities as well. When Florida yeomen protested planter power in 1839, their churches were the primary place where they met to register their dissatisfaction with the Union Bank, which refused to extend credit to them and overvalued the currency they had to use to buy land. Women's work building community ties made it possible for yeomen to coalesce politically. Through networks of visiting and working together, yeoman women knit their new communities together, found pleasure in doing so, and supported political and social alliances among their families.[100]

Within the society of enslaved people, women supported communities so that all enslaved people might resist and survive the terrible burdens of slavery. Although every new baby born into slavery and every enslaved person, nursed through illness, fed, and clothed, was another hand to clear fields and pick cotton, enslaved families and communities also reaffirmed the human dignity of their members. Kinship also supported many forms of resistance to enslavement. Women and men held in bondage cooperated in carrying out work slowdowns or vouching for those claiming to be sick. The record is silent about the women or men who may have supported Celia Bryan, who killed her Florida owner with a hoe when he tried to punish her, but other slaves defended those who resisted violent physical punishments. Some enslaved cooks, who were usually women, attempted to poison owners and overseers who mistreated enslaved community members, an act that would require help to obtain, administer, and then cover up the toxin. Furthermore, kinship and community influenced some enslaved people to run away. Given the proximity of Seminoles, Black Seminoles, and unsettled lands, many believed Florida had the highest runaway rate in the South. Most of the time runaways headed for their old homes in Georgia, the Carolinas, and Virginia, where they hoped to reunite with family members. In such cases, community networks of enslaved persons worked against owners' interests. On the other hand, the creation of new communities in Florida might have also kept enslaved people from leaving. While enslaved communities enriched whites to the extent that they made slaves healthier and happier, they also empowered enslaved individuals to resist and survive brutal work regimes, violent punishments, and the dehumanizing effects of being treated as the property of another.[101]

Among free whites and among enslaved blacks, women's work created new lives and new communities in Florida, and this work (whether freely given or compelled) guaranteed that new American settlements would continue. It is no wonder, then, that white politicians praised these efforts and sought to support white, often slaveholding, families with new policies in

Florida in the 1830s and 1840s. It is also therefore obvious why Seminoles targeted white homes, including women and children, in their "depredations." Not only were they returning the violence that Americans committed against their own homes and families, they were striking at the heart of the future of white communities in Florida, those who daily carried out the labor of dispossessing them of their own homes.

While Jane Johns and other female victims appeared in print as victims and stalwart survivors of terrible violence, they were very busy going about the work of making Florida home in the 1830s. White men brought their families and, if they had the means, enslaved people to Florida, and their success and "independence" completely depended on their ability to compel wives, children, and enslaved blacks to perform vital productive and reproductive work. Where they succeeded, whites created communities, families, and households that were stable enough to support economic and political development in the 1840s and 1850s. Although white women were often not enthusiastic about moving to Florida, and enslaved men and women were forced to go, their work there made Florida home to white Americans. White families benefited from their labor, while enslaved ones suffered. Their own motivations and the cultural investment in protected domesticity aside, white women were just as much "colonizers" as their male kin and masters, and women and their work was no less significant in winning Florida for Americans and taking it from Seminoles. As migrants, workers, mothers, slave-owning mistresses, and neighbors, they made a future in Florida for white Americans and for slavery. Their significance reached well beyond their role as the victims of "Indian depredations."

CHAPTER 3

Seminole Resistance

> Referred to the Secretary of War that forthwith Genl Clinch be ordered with his whole concentrated force move into the Indian Towns seize the women & children and inflict meritted chastisement for these atrocious murders so unprovoked.
> —Andrew Jackson, December 16, 1835

> Many meetings were called by the white man trying to persuade the chiefs to leave this ancient land of ours. . . . Because of the resistance that our people put up, they had to be on guard for the white devils night and day.
> —Mrs. H. M. Weiss (Bird Clan), Florida Seminole

While the terrifying tales white Americans told of Indian depredations emphasized the violence white women and families faced in Florida, they neglected to mention the hundreds of Seminole women and families who suffered during the ethnic cleansing of Florida in the late 1830s. This chapter fills that breach with Seminole accounts of war and removal, from their oral tradition, which refute some of the racist invective of white Indian depredation narratives and offer indigenous perspectives on the conflict. In the 1970s a Seminole elder shared the stories her grandfather told about the "White Wars" in Florida (as indigenous people call the U.S.-Seminole wars), stories in which whites were clearly the aggressors: "As time went by the wild killer instinct . . . came to dominate the white man's thinking. . . . We learned to be suspicious and careful of the white man. When evil possessed him, he began to attack the Indians' villages by night or by day. My grandfather said the cruelties they practiced on the Indians were beyond description."[1] Her grandfather's stories are part of the collective Seminole memory of the violence engendered by white settler colonialism in Florida. In their stories, Seminoles memorialize the violence and trauma of removal, justify their ancestors' resistance, and assert their continuing existence in spite of the historical attempt to eliminate them. They confirm that there was an exchange of violence between white Americans and Florida's Seminoles, one that often included women and children, but challenge the American framing of the conflict as a war to protect white women and children from "savage Indians."

By putting the violent conflict over Florida into an indigenous perspective, Seminole stories make clear that expansionist domesticity was not a peaceful, romantic endeavor, although white rhetoric about gender, family, and civilization often framed it that way. Americans pursued aggressive expansionism, not home defense, in 1830s Florida, and their legal, military, welfare, and land policies resulted in grievous consequences for indigenous people: the United States removed nearly 6,000 indigenous people and their allies of African descent from Florida between 1820 and 1858; approximately 1,400 Seminoles died on the journey from disease or in a steamboat explosion, and many more were seriously ill at some point in their journey. Those who survived the journey west faced disease, hunger, white swindlers, and conflict with their Creek and Cherokee neighbors in the first years they resided in Indian Territory. This chapter also includes evidence from letters and journals written by contemporary whites to support Seminole accounts. I read white accounts against the grain alongside Seminole oral accounts to recover a Seminole history of the U.S.-Seminole Wars, one that includes the experiences of indigenous women. All this evidence serves as a reminder that although white Indian depredation narratives focused on white settlers' property losses, the conflict in Florida was actually an American campaign to dispossess the Seminoles of their land so that white families could settle on it. In terms of property, deaths, and cultural and political sovereignty, the U.S.-Seminole wars resulted in far heavier losses for Seminoles than for whites.[2]

In order to make their own overwhelming losses apparent, Seminole storytellers provocatively reverse white narratives. In a rhetorically resistant reversal of white Indian depredation stories, Seminole accounts frame white settlers and soldiers as the savages—brutal, greedy, and unjust invaders who looted Seminole homes and committed terrible violence upon helpless

Seminole elders, women, and children. Seminole stories echo the intersection of race and gender in white Indian depredation narratives by prominently featuring the mistreatment of women and children by white soldiers and settlers. Seminole women and children struggle against hunger, insufficient clothing, captivity, and violence in these accounts. Seminole storytellers justify their ancestors' violent resistance in the same way white Americans justified their war on the Seminoles: as defense of their homes and in retaliation for the violence already perpetrated against women and children. They also share some of the gory sensationalism of Indian depredations retold in white American sources, and Seminole accounts similarly emphasize white violence while downplaying or justifying the violence that Native Americans in Florida employed against whites.

Other aspects of Seminole accounts are not reversals of white narratives but wholly unique. Seminoles often become captives in these accounts, unlike Florida whites. Frequent sexual violence also distinguishes these accounts from white Indian depredation narratives. In Seminole stories whites often rape Seminole women and girls, something that published American sources never mention and that whites never accused Seminole men of doing to white women. Many colonizing regimes employed sexual violence against indigenous women, as did the American racial slavery system against enslaved black women. This chapter includes analysis of rape in this unique and historically contingent context, in which it operated in symbolic and material ways as part of the ethnic cleansing of Florida. The frequent and widespread mention of rape in Seminole oral tradition further illustrates how white Indian depredation stories operated in context. By emphasizing the danger that the "Florida Indians" posed to white women and families, white stories displaced the terrible violence white soldiers were perpetrating on Seminoles women and girls.

As the frequency of sexual violence in them suggests, Seminole women are some of the most important symbolic bodies in Seminole narratives about the violence of the White Wars. Seminole identity and cultural survival relied on women. As clan mothers, reproductive beings, and farmers who provided sustenance, women created and sustained Seminole society. Parallel to white American claims to Florida made via domesticity, but distinct from white American gender norms, Seminoles understand kinship and land rights through their own matrilineal clan lens in their stories, and frame white families as individualistic, greedy, and barbaric (not civilized).

As Seminoles tell about the lived experiences of their ancestors who resisted American expansion, they are repeating cultural narratives in which their own ideas about gender and race (through kinship) resist the narratives whites told to justify Indian removal.

Seminole stories of the White Wars also demonstrate that frontier zones are places where people from different cultures form their own identities in reciprocal relation with the other. Whites and indigenous people clashed not only over land but also the very categories their societies use to determine who can claim that land. Just as whites constructed notions of their own superiority and "civilization" via the racial narratives that undergirded slavery and Indian removal, Seminole racial and national identity emerged from this violent frontier zone, where Native peoples sought a future for themselves separate from Creek interference and white settlers, alongside the runaway slaves who were their allies and sometimes their kin. Although U.S. Indian removal policy aimed to eradicate them, the U.S. campaign against them unintentionally helped to produce a collective Seminole racial and national identity in Florida. Although indigenous peoples had lived in Florida for many years before 1821, they resided in autonomous towns and had not understood themselves as part of one common culture or nation. U.S. Indian removal policies changed that by treating all of them as "the Florida Indians" and giving them a shared enemy. In a process that anthropologists call *ethnogenesis*, the Seminoles emerged through the alliance of many different indigenous groups who had sought refuge in Florida since the early eighteenth century, recently joined by about two thousand Creek refugees from the Redstick War. Some argue that their identity consolidated during the Second U.S.-Seminole War, but other scholars believe that even by the time of their removal that process was still incomplete and would continue along parallel but separate routes in the new Seminole Nation in Oklahoma and among the remnant population in South Florida. Some historians and anthropologists include the people of African descent among them, while others argue that parallel Seminole and Black Seminole ethnogeneses occurred, producing distinct identities for the Native Americans and blacks who fought American forces in Florida.[3] For clarity I refer to indigenous people in Florida as "Seminoles" in this chapter, although that identity may not have been fully consolidated at the time. Importantly, Seminole stories about the White Wars are also Seminole origin stories, tales that take Seminole identity for granted during a conflict in which it was actually being forged.

While there are few white women in Seminole stories about the White Wars, white men often committed the violence against Seminoles remembered in them in the name of avenging or protecting white women and children. Whether they intended to harm Seminoles or not, white women were part of the settler society that did so, and their presence was repeatedly used to justify violence and removal. The violence in these stories is thus an inherent consequence of the expansionist domesticity that white women carried with them into Florida.

In spite of the violent ethnic cleansing that white Americans pursued, Seminole women endured and their families and clans continued long after removal. Importantly, Seminoles' stories about the White Wars always conclude with a reminder that their ancestors *survived*. Today there are just over four thousand Seminoles and six hundred Miccosukees in Florida. In 1957 one group of descendants organized and achieved federal recognition as the Seminole Tribe of Florida. Although the Seminole Nation of Oklahoma excluded Black Seminoles from claiming Seminole identity in a 2000 election, denying them tribal monetary benefits, there are people today who identify as Black Seminoles. A smaller group of indigenous descendants who had settled along the Tamiami Trail in South Florida achieved federal recognition as the Miccosukee Tribe of Indians of Florida in 1962. Still other Indians in Florida belong officially to neither tribal entity. More than memories of victimization, when Seminoles remember their ancestors' stories about war and removal, they proudly assert that their resistance was successful, and therefore Seminole culture and society continue in the present.[4]

Truth, Memory, and the Oral Tradition

For the last 180 years the history of the U.S.-Seminole Wars that whites recorded has been the dominant version, especially in print. This chapter includes Seminole oral accounts that complicate and contradict the dominant narrative. Oral historical sources are indispensable in crafting Native history, since using the white written record to narrate Native American experience is often, in the words of ethnohistorian Patricia Galloway, like "trying to wring blood from the stones of European incomprehension and representation of Native behavior and testimony." Accounts from the Seminole oral tradition are not necessarily any more or less biased than documentary accounts, but they are historical sources that were never written down and therefore may have changed with each retelling. Importantly, they are the only records of the Seminoles' forced deportation that are not filtered through the pens of nineteenth-century white Americans.[5]

Like written documents, oral historical accounts are a record not only of the past but of how people have interpreted that past.[6] Many of the events described in Seminole narratives of the White Wars occurred, as did some of the Indian depredations described by whites. Their interpretive framing and embellishment depend greatly on the narrator's point of view, of course. White historians and anthropologists, along with a few Native Americans, recorded many of the oral histories included here in the 1970s, when activists from the American Indian Movement were vociferously protesting the past and present mistreatment of Native American people in North America. That context likely shaped these retellings. As with white Indian depredation narratives, it is nearly impossible to say exactly where these oral accounts stray from true events to portray the sensational "truths" of cultural memory. Although soldiers and settlers may not have literally turned into "white devils," Seminoles came to believe that whites were greedy, violent fiends who would lie, cheat, and kill to take their land. Although white Americans believed their actions were justified, they did use terrifying violence to take Florida from the Seminoles. In 1835, Andrew Jackson ordered Colonel Duncan Clinch to seize indigenous women and children, establishing even before the war formally started that Seminole families were targets.[7] There is plenty of other evidence in military histories of the Second U.S.-Seminole War that the U.S. Army targeted Seminole families, plundered corn and cattle from Seminole stores, and burned down Seminole homes, farms, and villages. A white soldier's journal confirms that there was a culture of rape in the U.S. Army as well, during what he termed the "squaw-kissing war."[8]

Indigenous rhetorical strategies also shape these accounts and their retelling. Scholars of Native American rhetoric note that Native people discover and apply the "available means of persuasion" most likely to influence whites, an audience that presumes its own superiority. Native Americans therefore often adapt white rhetorical strategies in order to combat anti-Indian attitudes and policies. In doing so, Native Americans establish their equal humanity with whites, encourage whites to identify with Native people, and challenge "savage" stereotypes. Native Americans also have "an acute awareness of audience," that is, they are far more aware of white cultural norms than whites are acquainted with indigenous cultural norms (as with many colonized peoples). It is not surprising, therefore, that Seminoles used some of the same sentimental elements from Indian depredation narratives in crafting their stories of white attacks on Native Americans.[9]

Seminole Stories: Treaties and Lies

While white narratives of Indian depredations always faulted the Seminoles for creating war by violating treaties and refusing to leave Florida, Seminoles believed that their ancestors' resistance stemmed from American greed, dishonesty, and violence. An elderly Seminole man explained in the 1970s:

> The transgressors said, "You must move west. You can no longer be living here." And they would promise the war leaders, saying that things would be better further west. But you see, they have lied so many times. They had captured Wildcat, Osceola, and others in the name of the white flag of truce. They had burned villages, plundered, raped and killed our people. How can we trust and believe in them? . . . They said our chiefs had said it was all right to move to the West. . . . Back in Grandfather's days it was the total intention of the United States Army to exterminate our people. That's why there aren't very many Seminoles today. . . . In spite of all the treachery and deception . . . the Seminole is not destroyed—his spirit is alive today.[10]

Although historical sources written by white Americans do not frame U.S.-Seminole diplomacy as lies intended to exterminate the indigenous population in Florida, most recognize that the treaties leading up to the Second U.S.-Seminole War were dubiously negotiated and created a series of unreasonable and rising demands on the Seminoles, in particular for removal and for the return of the Black Seminoles, whom Americans considered runaway slaves. For example, in 1823 the Treaty of Moultrie Creek stipulated that all Native people in Florida relocate to a reservation south of Tampa Bay, return the runaway slaves among them, and no longer harbor new runaways. The proposed reservation was almost all uncultivable swampland, and the Seminoles protested that they could not subsist upon it. To overcome their opposition, Americans bribed six of the most influential indigenous leaders with $5,000 each, livestock, and his own reservation along the Apalachicola River in his current homeland in North Florida. Enough indigenous Floridians signed the treaty to satisfy the Americans that it was legal, but since the new reservation proved as barren as feared, most of the Native people stayed in their North Florida homes along with those who had been granted reservations there. They continued to farm and hunt there and to welcome and protect black allies. Inevitably, conflicts over land, livestock, and Black Seminoles erupted with the white Americans who began moving into Florida after 1821.[11]

Andrew Jackson won the presidential election of 1828 and mandated Indian removal east of the Mississippi River in 1830. Under his leadership, the United States hoped to capture the Black Seminoles and turn them over to slave owners who claimed them as property and to settle the Seminoles on lands located in the Creek reservation in Oklahoma. To coerce them, the Americans planned to give the Seminoles' annuity payments (compensation for their land in Florida) to the Creeks to distribute, a move that would force them to recognize Creek authority. Although many indigenous Floridians had Creek ancestry, the Creeks had recently become their enemies by allying with U.S. forces against them. The Redstick emigrants who made up about a quarter of the Seminoles in 1835 were refugees whom joint U.S. and Lower Creek adversaries had defeated during the Creek War of 1813–1814. Creek warriors, moreover, had just fought against the Seminoles in the First U.S.-Seminole War in 1817–1819. Seminoles and their black allies also feared that the Creeks would reenslave the blacks, some of who had escaped Creek masters whose slavery practices were more similar to American slavery than the independence they enjoyed among the Seminoles. Thus the Seminoles had no intention of subsuming themselves under Creek authority.

A terrible drought in 1831 brought starvation, however, rendering many of them open to negotiation. They did not give in completely but agreed to consider removing to the west in exchange for food, clothing, and blankets. Under the terms of the 1832 Treaty of Payne's Landing, Seminoles sent a delegation of Seminole men and two Black Seminole interpreters to Indian Territory to examine the lands that the United States intended them to inhabit on the Creek reservation. Indigenous Floridians understood that this group had no power to make further agreements but would report back to a Seminole council in Florida, which would decide. The Florida delegation sent to Indian Territory in 1832 did not find the arrangements acceptable, but the United States overcame their opposition with outright fraud and forced them to sign the Treaty of Fort Gibson in 1833. Americans changed the language of the preamble to the treaty to suggest that the delegates *did* have the power to finalize the Treaty of Payne's Landing for all the indigenous peoples in Florida, and coerced them into stating that they found the proposed settlement in Creek country satisfactory. Under this treaty, the Americans announced that all the Indians in Florida had agreed and had three years to remove to the West.[12]

The Americans' insistence on enforcing this underhanded treaty brought about the Second U.S.-Seminole War, which broke out in December 1835. From a Seminole perspective, the threat of Creek domination and the loss of identity and property it portended, combined with the history of unreasonable and deceptive treaties with the Americans, added up to one solution: violent resistance. About five hundred black allies who had fled slavery joined in their struggle in hope of retaining their own freedom. Even after many of these people were removed, large factions of Seminoles and Black Seminoles refused to move onto Creek land or submit to Creek authority in the West.[13]

As the treaty disagreements illustrate, American whites and the Seminoles talked past each other about the racial and ethnic makeup and meaning of Native American identity in Florida. While kinship and alliance (which they did not share with Creeks) were the most significant factors for the people in the process of becoming the Seminoles, ideas about blood and ancestry influenced white notions of who these Native Americans were, so the Americans kept trying to turn them into Creeks in treaty documents. The presence and status of people of African descent among the Seminoles further complicated this cross-cultural misunderstanding. While white Americans labeled the Black Seminoles "black," not "Indian," and therefore appropriately enslaved rather than removed, Native Americans in Florida approached people of African descent quite differently. Seminoles pursued relations with blacks that varied in context and were not solely dictated by skin color. They sometimes married, adopted, allied with, or purchased *estelusti* as tributary slaves. The *estelusti* might live in Seminole villages or in their own independent, tributary villages. Indigenous Floridians thus challenged and partially rejected American ideas about race. Their distinct racial and slavery practices set them apart from other southeastern tribes and, of course, from whites, who believed the Seminoles' alliance with runaways and maroons posed a major threat to the United States and to slavery, and therefore required their removal.[14]

In late December 1835, as U.S. troops moved against Native American and Black Seminole towns, the Seminoles ambushed Major Francis L. Dade and his men, killed the Indian agent, and executed those among them who cooperated with Americans. In the long, expensive conflict that followed, the U.S. ultimately broke the Seminole resistance through attrition. The American military fought a few major battles, in nearly seven years of warfare, but mainly sought to capture the Seminoles and any "negro Indians" as prisoners of war, or starve and terrorize them into surrendering. To deny them subsistence, Americans burned Seminole homes, destroyed hundreds of fields of corn and pumpkin, and pillaged herds of cattle and horses. After taking any livestock and food that the army could use, American soldiers razed homes and crops. The Americans coerced captives into providing the location of remaining villages and camps; threatened and abused Seminole women, children, and elders; and destroyed sacred objects and sites. From a Seminole perspective, life during the White Wars consisted of trying to elude capture and sustain life under increasingly difficult circumstances, while mourning those who had already been lost.

Clan Mothers, Targets, and Survivors

A Seminole woman named Mary Huff said to Jean Chaudhuri (a Muscogee-Creek woman who collected many of these stories), "It has been told to me that when the white soldiers would come to a village, finding only women and children, they would kill most of the people, all except the young girls, and they would rape them, leaving them to die."[15] Attacks on Seminole women and homes were representative, according to Huff, of the treatment that all Seminoles expected from whites in the nineteenth century: "Those were the days when the white men have not yet learned how to be human. . . . He had only one thing on his mind, and that was to kill the Seminoles—to kill them on sight, kill them, don't let them any of them live."[16] Women are important symbolic bodies in Seminole narratives about violence (as they were in white stories). For the Seminoles, however, violence against women signified an attack on all Seminole people not because they were domestic and maternal homemakers but because, like other southeastern Native peoples in the nineteenth century, the Seminoles defined all social relationships through matrilineal clan membership. Women carried the future of their people in their reproductive bodies and cultural roles. For Seminoles, attacks on women were not just proof of white brutality, they also constituted attacks on all Seminole people—present and future—due to women's central place in the clan system.

Matrilineal clans are composed of an extended family that shares a female ancestor. Mothers transmit their clan to their daughters and sons, and their daughters in turn pass clan membership on to their children. Clans dictate available marriage partners (who must come from a clan other than one's parents' clans) and provide social position for all individuals. Political, spiritual, and social power is distributed through clans. For example, town leaders were traditionally men who came from a particular clan, and the successor was usually the eldest son of the deceased leader's eldest sister. Clans perpetuated knowledge and identity and regenerated them in response to threats. Women headed clans and led each clan's camp within a town.[17]

As clan mothers, Seminole women were responsible for nourishing people. The story of Corn Woman, the spiritual origin of Seminole women's roles, is common to many indigenous peoples in the Americas and demonstrates women's spiritual connection to nourishment. The woman responsible for bountiful gardens, Corn Woman "gave food to her people."[18] Among the Seminoles, ideal women "tilled the garden, and were very hospitable to guests and relatives. They made sure there was ample food on hand for their visitors and relatives."[19] For the good of their people and the honor of their clans and towns, Seminole women endeavored to be good farmers and hostesses.[20]

These cultural beliefs about women and their roles shaped Seminole women's work, the importance Seminoles attached to it, and the significance of its destruction by whites. Early nineteenth-century Seminole women were farmers and traders who raised many crops (corn, beans, squash, melons, honey, rice, sugar cane, orchard fruits) and traded what they produced in excess of their family needs. When weather, animals, or warfare damaged their food supply, women sustained the people with wild cabbage palms, potatoes, and coontie, a starch processed from the roots of *Zamia integrifolia* or arrowroot. Seminole women also tanned hides, made pottery and baskets for storage, wove cloth and made clothes, and raised children. As trade with Euro-Americans brought racial slavery into Florida, some Seminole women (and men) claimed a corn tribute from enslaved people they claimed to own among the Black Seminoles, which further enriched them. By the time the United States claimed Florida in 1821, the economic power that commercial crops created had enhanced some women's roles. However, as trading and intermarriage with whites entered southern indigenous people's lives more deeply over the course of the nineteenth century, the accumulation of personal wealth tended to empower individuals rather than clans, which eroded tribal women's power.[21]

The White Wars further diminished indigenous women's status by making it much harder for them to fulfill their roles. When white soldiers burned the crops that indigenous women had planted in the 1810s and 1830s, they did more than deny the Seminoles food. Burning their fields, destroying their food stores, and overturning their pots also wounded the women because it culturally and socially displaced them. When they had to flee to hide in the swamps, they left the ground that belonged to the matrilineal clan. When white soldiers raped Seminole women they usurped women's power to choose their own sexual partners and to decide whose children would share membership in their clan.[22]

Since men were responsible for making war (in addition to hunting, herding, and leading towns), the increase in warfare that Seminoles faced after 1821 exacerbated the gender imbalance. Men not only made key decisions during war, white officials consulted only with Seminole men. Whites ignored, and thereby rendered much less powerful, Native women's power in decisions about land and resources, and the system of reciprocity in which they operated. For this reason, whites rarely identified Seminole women by name but instead by their relationship to a man: for example, Osceola's wife, Jumper's sister, or Old Charlie's squaw. In white eyes, clan or skills did not determine Seminole women's importance, only which warriors they claimed as kin did.

In spite of the challenges that trade and war with whites created, the clan's power endured. During the war Seminole men often told American leaders that they could not make the decision to relocate without consulting women. Others requested gifts or tribute for female kin. Ultimately, when the warfare ceased, the trauma of war and removal may have even helped to strengthen clans. Proud of their heritage, the Seminoles remained attached to their matrilineal society because it was distinct from Anglo-American culture. Matrilineal kinship continued to structure Seminole life in Florida after the Seminole Wars, when the remaining Seminoles lived in clan-based camps headed by the eldest woman. Today there are eight matrilineal clans among the Florida Seminoles.[23]

Nineteenth-century *estelusti* women were also farmers and traders. They collectively tended fields of corn, melons, beans, peanuts, pumpkin, rice, sugarcane, tobacco, and fruit orchards, and raised hogs and poultry. They foraged for wild foods and herbal remedies, tanned hides, produced clothing, wove baskets, and sometimes made pottery. After feeding their own people and setting aside the tribute they owed to the Seminoles who claimed them, they, too, traded their excess produce. Although they were not matrilineal, they often lived in matrifocal households. The Black Seminoles valued all the labor that sustained their lives outside of enslavement to whites and celebrated the opportunity to have children who would not be the property of whites. As white Americans threatened their families and crushed their towns in the 1830s, they mourned the loss of their produce and feared for their freedom.[24]

Under distinct but related racist colonial pressures, Seminole and *estelusti* women provided vital labor that sustained their people. When the "white devils" attacked their bodies and destroyed the homes they created and maintained in Florida, the Seminoles and Black Seminoles understood American soldiers as threats to the whole community. As progenitors of Seminole clans, or of free people of African descent, women represented the future of Seminole and Black Seminole identity and culture. Their destruction threatened nothing less than the social and cultural annihilation that removal or enslavement portended.

White Devils

In the 1970s, an older Seminole man retold his grandfather's story about the American attempt to expel his ancestors from Florida. His story typifies many of the accounts of the White Wars in the oral tradition. Like photographic negatives of "depredating Indians," the white soldiers and "scavengers" of this story star in a reversal of a white Indian depredation narrative. Other elements are also reversed, as whites savagely attacked Seminole families and homes.

Long ago, "on a bright, beautiful day," white soldiers appeared and launched an unexpected attack on a Seminole village while the warriors were away (mirroring the white families surprised by Seminole attackers in depredation stories). The warning to run and hide came too late for "the women, the children, the sick, and the old ages," who scattered before white soldiers on horseback. "Vicious" brutes, the white soldiers murdered helpless Seminoles and set their homes ablaze. Questioning their honor, just as whites labeled Seminole warriors "savages" for attacking women and children, he continues: "They were the brave, courageous soldiers . . . fighting helpless women and children, and the old people." As in white Indian depredation tales, his story emphasizes the destruction of property that symbolized and sustained Seminole domestic life: "The soldiers would turn over the cooking things where the women had been cooking; they would go into their corn bins and destroy all their corn." This story even matches white Indian depredation narratives in its sensational violence, with flying "chips of bone," "the smell of blood flowing like brook water," throats slashed, bodies riddled with bullets, and bayonets plunged into corpses. As in white narratives of the Seminole wars, civilians were also fully involved in the conflict, though here they are white invaders eager to steal Seminole land and resources: "Sooner or later, as always, the scavengers would come to pick up the leftovers. . . . The white settlers . . . would come in, look over the place, gather the few scattered pigs, horses, hogs—gather anything they could find and claim them for their own. These heartless, cruel people would look over the village and stare at the dead bodies. But this meant nothing to them. . . . After looting the dead, they would go back to their little, respected homes." The narrator frames white settlers' unfeeling theft as evidence of their hypocrisy. Whites decried the depredations on their own homes as outside the bounds of civilized warfare and proof of "Indian savagery," yet they committed the same crimes against Seminoles. Finally, as in white narratives, the storyteller cites all this indiscriminate violence against Seminole homes and families to justify the resistance and retaliation carried out by Seminole warriors, who returned home to find smoking ruins and murdered families: "All the hatred and revenge seethed through their bodies." They, like white men reacting to Indian depredations, felt frustration, anger, grief, and sorrow in the wake of the attack. As in other Seminoles accounts, this narrator did not include descriptions of Seminoles attacking white settlers, just as white accounts avoided mentioning the violence American soldiers used against Seminole families and homes. Seminole stories—like white ones—explain the era of war and removal as a time when their ancestors rightfully fought to protect their homes and their families.[25]

Given the numerous parallels with white Indian depredation narratives and the nearly direct reversals of their elements that Seminole accounts contain, I argue that Seminoles tell these stories to respond to and refute the stories told by whites. The storytelling is itself a form of resistance. Seminole stories broaden the historical record and reframe the conflict as a story of white violence and greed, in which whites are the barbarians. Narrators explain and justify the violent resistance of the Seminoles by citing white aggression.

There are three major ways, however, in which Seminole stories are not perfect reversals of white Indian depredation stories. First, after descriptions of the initial attack, Seminole accounts become stories of captivity among whites, since Americans were capturing Seminoles in Florida. In many stories, after the initial attack, American soldiers force captives to march for many days to Fort Brooke near Tampa Bay (or to another post on the way to Tampa), where they imprison the Seminoles. Then they wait, sometimes for months, for the steamboats to arrive and take them around the Gulf of Mexico to New Orleans, and then upriver to Creek territory. While they wait, Seminole stories (and U.S. military records) note that Indian agents and Seminole leaders negotiated livestock trades, slave catchers searched for Black Seminoles they could claim were runaways, and white soldiers brought in more captives.

Second, Seminole stories nearly always end by acknowledging the continuing existence of their people, a tribute to their resistance and survival, and a reminder that the "Indians" have never disappeared in spite of white efforts (both rhetorically and militarily) to erase them. No one, of course, needs to be reminded that whites survived Indian depredations and continue to live in twenty-first-century Florida. As the elder concluded his grandfather's story: "What a struggle they had to come through so that my generation today could still yet remain in their ancestral land. The grief and sorrow that my ancestors inherited was not in vain. Because of their steadfastness, we, the Seminoles, are living on our mother earth."[26] Seminole narratives of the White Wars reframe the Americans' attempt to ethnically cleanse them from Florida as a narrative of past and continuing resistance. In retelling the stories of their forebears' suffering, they preserve and renew the resistance of their ancestors.[27]

Third, the "white devils" are not symmetrical reversals of the "Indian savage" stereotype, for they include characteristics that whites did not attribute to Native Americans. Race itself is under construction in these stories, as it was in white Indian depredation accounts. As whites and Seminoles established and reinforced their racial and cultural differences, they chose unflattering attributes of the other that starkly contrasted with their own values: whites celebrated the individual and his work ethic within a hierarchical society they called civilized, and therefore painted Native Americans as lazy and indiscriminate. Indigenous Americans valued reciprocity, generosity, and hospitality and therefore found whites to be aggressive monsters driven by greed to commit terrible violence. The "white barbarian" is insatiably acquisitive, a characteristic that indigenous peoples in eastern North America had attributed to whites for centuries but not one that whites usually ascribed to Indians (whose lack of private property marked them as uncivilized to whites).[28] One Seminole woman, Mrs. Weiss, explained white violence as a "killer instinct" that took "everything":

> As time went by the wild killer instinct of the white man came to dominate the white man's thinking and as a result he went berserk and started to spread himself like fire, burning and taking everything that was in his way. We learned to be suspicious and careful of the white man. When evil possessed him, he began to attack the Indians' villages. . . . My grandfather said the cruelties they practiced on the Indians were beyond description. They would take the breasts of women and cut them off and make tobacco pouches out of them. They would mutilate the rest of the bodies; the men would lie about with their heads split open and their bodies broken into many parts. Sometimes the white man would get their pleasure from castrating the men.[29]

As their greed drove whites mad, Seminoles believed they practiced horrible forms of torture and mutilation on indigenous people, including sexual ones such as the removal of breasts and genitals in this story. White greed even stretched into the commodification of brutalized Seminole bodies, as here indigenous women's breasts were fashioned into bags for tobacco, pouches with a particularly grisly cultural appeal to whites who believed that Indians were a source for skins, closer to animals than people. Weiss also cites this violence as one cause of Seminole resistance to removal: how could the Seminoles possibly accept white promises about life in the West given how dishonest and brutally violent they were to Seminole people?[30]

Rape is another element that sets Seminole stories apart. Whites rarely accused indigenous men of raping white women, and in fact many whites believed that Native American men never committed this crime against indigenous or white women. This may be because it did not happen, due to incest taboos, warrior abstinence, their greater esteem for women generally, or views of sex as properly based in reciprocity rather than dominance.[31] There is ample evidence that white soldiers raped Seminole women during the war and removal.

In his diary, U.S. Army private Bartholomew Lynch named the conflict in Florida the "squaw-kissing war" and portrayed U.S. Army officers as tyrants who combined the conquest of land with the conquest of women.[32] Stationed near Tampa Bay, where the army imprisoned most Seminoles before they were shipped west, Lynch witnessed the interactions of soldiers and Seminole captives. His peers and superior officers treated him terribly because he was a recent Irish immigrant, but as an indignant outsider he included very frank observations about *their* drunkenness and abuse of women—topics that most soldiers found either unremarkable or unmentionable in their letters and diaries. On October 6, 1838, Lynch wrote, "If the officers in Tampa would be half as mad to fight Buck Indians as they are to buck Indian Squaws, they would unquestionably be the bravest and gallantest officers in the world. The way they pitch into the squaws is a sin."[33] A month later he recorded that two officers had gone hunting out in the bay, "an Indian squaw each for his own use."[34] In March 1839, Lynch's wrote a tongue-in-cheek ode to Tampa:

Tampa, Tampa, what a beautiful heavenly luscourious [sic] spot thou are, what will those officers do when they leave you? where they have only to say to the soldier-slaves "go and fetch me a turtle," and they go; and they say "go and bring me some large fat oysters" and they go. What a miserable life officers do lead while campaigning in Fla.—
The squaw kissing war
The deer hunting war
The turtle soup and stewed oyster war
The war of snug places without clashing sabers
The joy of speculators—Sweet Florida War.[35]

As Private Lynch brought together in verse, Americans linked sexual violence and Indian removal—the Second U.S.-Seminole War was both a "squaw kissing war" and "the joy of speculators." From his perspective, the Florida War was a federally funded campaign of rape and feasting, at least for the men in charge. One did not find "clashing sabers" in the cozy frontier outpost, where profligate American officers were apparently too busy "pitch[ing] into the squaws" to chase after Seminole warriors. Other soldiers echoed Lynch's observations of drunken officers and mentioned the Seminole women prisoners in their midst, though none with Lynch's candor.[36] The historical literature on the Seminoles and the Second U.S.-Seminole War has never addressed the historical trauma of martial rape. Military historian John Mahon suspected that it was widespread but never made that claim in print, perhaps because most of his sources on the subject were Seminole accounts.[37]

Former chief and tribal storyteller for the Seminole Tribe of Florida Betty Mae Tiger Jumper recounted a removal story for her 2001 biography. It describes the capture, removal, rape, and escape of her female ancestors, through whom she traces her roots in the Snake Clan. The story describes sexual assault three times from the perspectives of different female forebears. Like many others, Jumper's family story operates as a resistant rhetorical reversal of the Indian depredations recounted by whites.[38]

The story begins when American soldiers surround and kidnap a camp of old men, women, and children while the younger men were away hunting, taking the Seminoles by surprise, as the Americans had told them that they were at peace. Following their capture, Jumper's great-grandmother and her three daughters were kept with other captives in a pen at Fort Brooke. Her great-grandmother soon began to worry "because the soldiers had begun using the younger women. . . . Then, she and her oldest daughter were raped, and she became consumed with a plan to help her youngest daughters escape." The worried mother dug a hole under the fence, pushed the girls through it to freedom, and then began to sing loudly to distract the soldiers, while she sat over the hole to hide it. Using their knowledge of natural signs, the girls swam away and walked home, where they reunited with their father and brothers in central Florida.[39]

Just as expansionist power linked rape and conquest, these Seminole women understood their escape as resistance both to removal and rape. This is made clear when the older sister tells her two younger sisters:

> Go like Mother says and don't stop. See me. The soldiers will start on you two next, so leave when Mother says. These men have no pity on anyone, young or old. They are like wild beasts. They treat us like animals. They laugh and kick you around while raping you

and make a big joke out of it in front of others. They drive us like cows on the trail. You have seen when older people get sick or too tired to walk. They fall. They get whipped and are made to get up. If they are too helpless to get up and walk, the soldiers shoot them. If babies cry too much from being hungry, the soldiers throw them in a creek or pond and drown them or hit them against a tree to kill them. . . . Leave! Run for your lives. You'll be free![40]

Similar to white Indian depredation stories, this Seminole story deplores atrocities perpetrated on female bodies (as well as violence against children and elders). It evokes an emotional reaction, positions Seminoles as the injured party, and constructs white soldiers as the "wild beasts" who practice barbaric violence. The accusation that soldiers hit babies against trees to kill them operates as a specific reversal here, for whites frequently accused depredating Native Americans of killing white babies in this way.[41]

The third discussion of rape in Jumper's story comes from the girls who escaped. On their journey home, they feel anxiety and sadness because they had left their mother and sister behind. "They cried as they thought of the suffering of their older sister, who had been raped so much that she could hardly walk. The girls envisioned their mother carrying her. They could only hope that they were dead." Death was perhaps the only escape from the suffering brought by the White Wars (this theme also recurs in Seminole stories, as discussed below). The trauma of rape and other abuse haunts the young girls, even though they escaped. Their emotional reactions contradict white depredation narrative images of stoic "squaws" by revealing the emotional ties between a Native American mother and her daughters. White authors often foreground mother-child relationships in Indian depredation stories to maximize the demonization of "unfeeling Indians" who harmed or killed children in front of their mothers. Resisting that stereotype, the Snake Clan girls express deep and enduring attachments to their mother and older sister. By reversing some aspects of the white depredation genre, Seminole stories like Jumper's contest assumptions not only of white innocence but also of indigenous "savagery." The specific form of that savagery, rape, is not a reversal, however.[42]

Other Seminole oral accounts attest that during removal Seminole women anticipated rape by whites, and all Seminoles lived in terror of "white devils." Mary Huff told Jean Chaudhuri a story about some white men who chanced upon a group of Seminole women who were swimming.

The whites gang-raped them, and (in another gruesome reversal) the storyteller describes the women's injured bodies in detail. She concludes, "This is one incident of many that happened," telling listeners that this was common.[43] Charlie Gopher concurred: "Young Seminole maidens were ill-used. Twenty men forced themselves. This is what I've heard, and this is what has been handed down—that one has to be alert for these white devils."[44] Although there are no statistics about the number of American soldiers who raped Seminole girls and women, it happened often enough for Seminole storytellers and white soldiers to mention it as a form of violence that American soldiers regularly practiced.

In the oral tradition, rape appears to have been a common experience, not an unusual or unexpected occurrence. There are no accounts that link one particular rapist to a specific Seminole victim, nor any formal charges of rape filed in court records.[45] However, the narrators who tell stories about the culture of rape cross social lines—white and Seminole, male and female, nineteenth-century contemporary, and twentieth-century storytellers. Together, these accounts form a persuasive set of evidence that there was a culture of rape among white soldiers during the U.S.-Seminole Wars.

It is not clear whether Black Seminole women were subject to the same kind and degree of sexual violence that Seminole women were. Although it seems likely that military men targeted them during removal, descendants interviewed for Shirley Mock's ethnographic study do not mention sexual violence during removal. Bartholomew Lynch wrote in his Second U.S.-Seminole War journal that officers would censure soldiers who took liberties with any woman claimed by an officer, including a "Negro girl," which suggests that all kinds of women at Fort Brooke were vulnerable to white sexual assault.[46] Captive Black Seminole women, whose parents or grandparents had fled slavery, or who had fled slavery themselves, knew that white men frequently used sexual violence against enslaved women. Whether or not whites raped them in their villages or in the removal camps is not clear in the record.[47]

As feminist theorists and historians have long understood, rape is an expression of power (not desire) used to communicate and maintain dominance. In the context of war, it communicates the authority of one adversary over another in a deeply gendered way, and perpetrators intend it to terrorize and humiliate its victims as well as those who care for them. In Florida, when white soldiers raped Seminole women they communicated to the Seminoles that they were under the complete control of the American military, that their women and girls did not merit the same protections and respect that white women and girls did, that they were all powerless to protect themselves from white violence.[48] Rape was a terrible crime against individual women, but it had much broader consequences and resonances. When white soldiers raped Seminole women they also attacked the clans, because the child of a Seminole woman whose father was white would become a full-fledged Seminole with the potential to use that power in detrimental ways. Rape thus threatened the system through which Seminole people controlled membership in their community and sustained a culture that honored Seminole values. Rape, therefore, was not only an attack against one woman, or even all women, but also an attack on all Seminoles, because it threatened to either disperse or extinguish the clans. It was also a form of martial rape, or rape employed as a tool of war, which seeks to destroy family and community bonds and to drive out or disperse entire peoples, failing their complete extermination.[49]

Martial rape also operates to solidify bonds among warriors. Those in command likely tolerated the widespread rape of Seminole women because of its usefulness to the overall war effort.[50] Bartholomew Lynch believed that American officers' abuse of women was an expression of bonding and white male privilege. In March 1839 Lynch recorded his disgust when a guard robbed someone and officers did nothing. His tirade reveals how central sex was to the culture of privilege among white officers: "Such is the state of morale in the U.S. Army that every crime is overlooked except passing your officer without saluting him and any other contempt is punished with great severity. Or if you take liberties with any squaw, soldier's wife or Negro girl who is under the protection of an officer, you are fiercely fixed for it."[51] Officers demanded respect they did not deserve, Lynch believed, and by asserting their right to "protect" or claim particular women, they communicated their dominance over other men (white, black, and Seminole), as well as over women, children, blacks, and indigenous people. The dominance and bonding aspects of rape characterized its practice under American slavery as well.[52]

Numerous colonial powers deployed sexual violence against indigenous and enslaved black women in service to empire, but the rape of indigenous women has valences particular to their location at the intersection of colonialism, racism, and misogyny. Theorizing rape at the confluence of these forces, American Indian feminist activist and theorist Andrea Smith argues that rape and land conquest have been part of a larger American colonial process in which the demonization and rape of Native American women served to reinforce patriarchal rule both among whites and among the colonized. Whites viewed Native Americans as "impure" and therefore available to sexual violation without consequence; indigenous women are "rapeable," while "pure" white women are not. Native American women suffered this abuse not only because of racism but also because of the threat they posed to patriarchy. As women in a more egalitarian society, Native American women offered white women an alternative to patriarchy, one that white men destroyed in order to maintain their own dominance. Those who wished to exterminate indigenous people targeted Native American women (for death, rape, involuntary sterilization) because women were the people who would give birth to the next generation of indigenous Americans in matrilineal and matrilocal societies. Conversely, American leaders promoted white female settlement for corollary reasons: because white women would give birth to the next generation of white Floridians and instill white cultural values in them, including female subordination to men. Sexual violence as conquest not only reinforced the racial and cultural assumptions of white supremacy but also aimed to brutally ensure white patriarchal domination.[53]

As Smith's trenchant analysis illustrates, the Seminoles were not unique. There is ample evidence that Europeans and Americans employed sexual violence against Native women before Seminole removal and continued to do so after, and scholars have noted evidence for martial rape in other indigenous oral traditions. Historians such as Kathleen Brown and Theda Perdue have explored the ways that European "conquest and colonization had their own sexual dynamic."[54]

Captives and Diplomats

Whites viewed Seminole and Black Seminole women through a very different cultural lens than indigenous communities did. Misogyny, racism, and colonialism combined in the image of the "squaw," the ugly Native American drudge (foil to the beautiful "Indian princess") whose features came from a long history of white stories about indigenous peoples in North America. As this book has argued, whites mobilized an understanding of white women and children as innocent victims, and of indigenous men as savages, as they waged a propaganda war on the Seminoles in the 1830s and

1840s. The focus on white women and Seminole men marginalized Seminole and *estelusti* women, and whites invoked them very rarely, but when they did so whites mobilized familiar stereotypes to justify their own actions—actions that whites would have called atrocities if committed by Seminole men against white women. Whites made few observations about Black Seminole women; while they often described "squaws" or "Indian negroes" they never commented on "Indian negro women," giving the false impression that all the women were Seminoles and all the Black Seminoles were men.[55]

When they commented on Native women, white men pronounced Seminole women a combination of unfeminine traits, including ugly, coarse, insufficiently dressed, and wretched. The "squaw's" differences from white standards of femininity created racial difference out of divergent gender norms and emphasized the superiority of white people, who allowed women (all women in cultural ideology, though only relatively wealthy ones in reality) to pursue their "natural" roles as mothers and homemakers, not farmers and traders. U.S. Brigadier General Thomas Jesup observed that "Alligator's daughter" was "an ugly disgusting looking squaw, excessively dirty, and constantly scratching her head, and spitting on the floor."[56] Another soldier remarked of the female captives who arrived at Fort Mellon on their way to Tampa, "They are the most destitute beings we have yet seen. Most of them are almost naked."[57] Army surgeon Jacob Motte observed a group near Jupiter Inlet, and recorded, "From their appearance, I should judge the burden of the war to have principally fallen upon the female portion of the natives. . . . The squaws . . . presented a most squalid appearance . . . many having nothing around them but the old corn bags we had thrown away." Motte implied that Seminole women shouldered more of the burden of this war than they should, or perhaps presumes that white men would have somehow shielded their own families from wartime poverty more effectively. He also noted that while the Seminole men smoked tobacco "the squaws engaged in the less dignified employment of picking up the corn which our horses dropped from their mouths."[58] Desperate to feed their people, women sifted the kernels from the dirt and pounded them into *sofkee*, a cornmeal mush and Seminole staple. "Squaws" failed to live up to white standards of female propriety and beauty, but their desperation originated in the poverty that the White Wars brought upon them.

In view of their awful condition and obvious desperation, whites expressed surprise when they found Seminole women just as obdurate as the warriors. According to Motte, the Seminole women who gathered around his tent in search of food "declared that if their great father said they must go, go they would but that they only petitioned to have a slip of the vast country that once owned them masters. They would be contented with the swamps, the hammocks, the barren spots, nay 'the everglades,' so that they might live and die in their native wilds."[59] Historian John Mahon noted, "White men watched them weep openly many times, yet oddly enough considered them more intransigent than their men. A squaw widowed by the conflict would sell her husband's ammunition for hunting, but give it away for war use."[60] Newspapers reported similar resistance from women. In the spring of 1839 when 250 Seminoles boarded a ship at Tampa, the *St. Augustine News* reported, "The women were very reluctant to go, and upbraided their men with cowardice, in refusing to die upon their native soil."[61] This was perhaps ritual shaming driven by grief, and the indignity and disrespect that whites visited on them. Ironically, white political and military leaders had endorsed an 1836 welfare policy aimed at keeping white women and their families from leaving war-torn Florida (the subject of the next chapter). When Seminole women expressed determination to stay, they appeared to be stubborn, unladylike "squaws." Race marked the difference between patriotic pioneer women and intransigent indigenous ones.

Other white observers found Seminole women remarkably stoic. Lieutenant William Tecumseh Sherman described a small girl who remained silent in spite of a gunshot wound in her back, and another woman, riddled with buckshot, who kept quiet out of her fear of the whites.[62] Seminole women may have stayed silent to remain unnoticed by whites, because they refused to give their tormentors the pleasure of seeing them suffer, or because they had trained themselves to remain silent at all costs in order to avoid discovery. To whites, however, their silent endurance marked them as unfeminine and therefore racially inferior. White male perceptions of Seminole women as wretched, resistant, and stoic constructed white women, in contrast, as fragile, subordinate, and well protected, and this allowed whites to justify their own aggressive actions as those of a benevolent and civilized society against a violent and barbaric one.

Although whites were clearly not unbiased witnesses, if one reads between the lines of their observations one finds many traces of Seminole women's experiences as captives, diplomats, guides, and survivors of sexual and physical trauma. For whites, captive Seminole women and children symbolized the subjugation and conquest of the Indians, and so Americans celebrated the capture of Seminole women and children in published reports throughout the war. According to military and newspaper sources, captive women were among those who supplied information to the U.S. Army during the war. Lieutenant Colonel William Foster reported in early 1837 that a captive named "Sally," Cloud's (Yaholochee's) niece "according to promise showed us . . . the hiding place for the pack saddles & the landing place for the canoes of the village where she was taken." Foster probably hoped that Sally would lead them to Yaholochee and the rest of his band, and perhaps she did: Yaholochee negotiated their departure with Brigadier General Thomas Jesup shortly thereafter, and his band departed Florida in December 1837.[63]

Women like Sally guided the American army under several possible circumstances. They perhaps understood that power lay in the ability to mediate between enemy groups and used information as currency. Some female prisoners of war feared becoming victims of sexual violence, and perhaps they used information as a way to avoid that. It is also likely that army personnel coerced this information from them, either with violence or with the threat of violence against their children. In December 1840 American army colonel William Harney threatened to hang captive women's children if they refused to lead the way to a village. Yet they declined and he never carried out his threat, which suggests that terrorizing them was not a successful way to negotiate.[64] Finally, as food became scarcer and safety less possible, Seminole women probably cooperated as a last resort and method of survival. It is also possible that indigenous women were supplying the Americans with false or partial information, as sources did not always indicate whether the information they gave proved useful.

Captive women who supplied information to the enemy conjure up the white fantasy of the "Indian princess." The alternative to the dirty, abject squaw in white American representations of Native American women, Indian princess narratives displace the white aggression that actually resulted in the loss of Native American land and blame the fickle Indian maiden for her people's losses. In a typical Indian princess tale, she falls in love with a white man and betrays her own people to save him, and thus plays a role in a white victory over her people. She thus takes the blame for the fate of Native Americans, releasing whites from responsibility so that they can proceed with a romantic fantasy of their own ancestors' role in history.[65] Since the Indian princess so nicely absolves them, whites usually give an Indian princess a name. Milly Francis, for example, became known as the "Florida Pocahontas" for saving a Georgia militiaman's life during the Second U.S.-Seminole War.[66] While the captive women who cooperated with their captors may seem to play this role, they were actually resistant survivors, whose actions enabled their own survival and therefore the survival of their clans and people. Despite the ways whites may frame their stories as popular romance, it is important to recognize that this is another form of resistance, as it defeated the ethnic cleansing policies that threatened to remove or exterminate all the Seminoles.

Madeloyee (also called Polly Parker) is one such survivor. A Seminole woman from Bird Clan, she did not have a white lover, but some interpret her actions as traitorous and some whites called her the "Evangeline" of her people in the late nineteenth century, after the Henry Wadsworth Longfellow poem in which a young woman was separated from her lover when the British expelled the Acadians from Nova Scotia.[67] During the Second U.S.-Seminole War Madeloyee and her Seminole husband Chai worked for the U.S. military as guides to Seminole camps. The U.S. Army allowed them to remain in Florida after 1843 because they feared retribution. They ran a trading post until the Third U.S.-Seminole War in 1855, when Madeloyee again guided American troops. This time the Americans betrayed her and sent her west, too. When the steamer she traveled on stopped, she escaped and returned to South Florida. She died there in 1921 (she must have been a very old woman, if the stories about her participation in the Seminole Wars of the 1830s–1850s are correct). Madeloyee refused to submit to removal, and guided or traded with whites if it meant her own survival, regardless of the consequences for other Native Americans (always "her people" to the whites).[68] Since the United States eventually tried to remove her, her story works less well to absolve whites of responsibility for removal but may still reassure some that indigenous people were just as responsible for Seminole land loss as white Americans.

Whites made fewer observations about Black Seminole women than Seminole ones. It is clear that many Black Seminole women were present, since they appear in court cases over disputed slave claims and on the rolls of indigenous people removed from Florida. The *estelusti* experienced deprivations similar to the Seminoles during the White Wars. They banded together into multigenerational, matrifocal households and camps during the war. Unlike Seminoles, *estelusti* families faced not removal but slavery if the Americans captured them. Many Black Seminole women carried guns

Figure 4. This postcard image of Madeloyee, captioned "Aunt Polly Parker, the Oldest Seminole Indian in the State, Florida," dates from the early twentieth century. Courtesy of the author's collection.

to protect themselves from slave raiders in particular. In 1836 slave traders kidnapped Rose Factor, a runaway among the Seminoles, and her children. (Creeks had originally captured Factor after she had escaped Spanish owners in St. Augustine. Her husband Sam, son of Black Factor, subsequently freed her.) Factor and her son Billy escaped and returned to Florida. She worked as an interpreter and courier for the Americans during the war, in hopes that they would rescue the rest of her children from enslavement in Georgia (they never did). She sought to migrate west with the Seminoles in the late 1830s, but a series of legal battles with her former Spanish owners prevented her from doing so until 1841, when the U.S. Army reimbursed her for her services during the war, which released her to leave.[69] After removal, some Black Seminoles traveled further south into Texas and Mexico in search of land and a more secure freedom. As among the Seminoles, women were vitally important to Black Seminole survival. Cora Montgomery observed that the women who arrived among a group crossing the Mexican Border in 1850 "seemed objects of special care."[70]

The Black Seminole woman best known to nineteenth-century white Americans probably did not exist. American abolitionists loved to tell the story of Osceola's part-black wife, "Morning Dew," who was supposedly kidnapped into slavery. This event purportedly motivated Osceola's participation in the war and resistance to removal (not his desire to remain in Florida or protest dishonest treaties). The legend allowed antislavery reformers to reduce Seminole resistance down to a desire to protect their black kin from enslavement, and to blame the U.S.-Seminole Wars on slavery, which was politically useful. Yet there is little evidence that either of Osceola's wives was a woman of any African descent, let alone one whom Americans kidnapped and sold into southern slavery.[71]

Seminole and Black Seminole women also played diplomatic roles during the war, as had many Native women since the beginning of the European invasion of North America.[72] *Estelusti* women served as translators, as some Black Seminole men did.[73] Seminole female elders sometimes appeared to broker peace. On February 24, 1838, a female elder opened a council meeting with U.S. Brigadier General Thomas Jesup. As surgeon Jacob Motte looked on, she pointed to the warriors and said that "they were all her children . . . she was tired of the war; that her warriors were slain; her villages burnt; her little ones perishing by the road side. . . . She desired that the hatchet should be buried forever, between her children and her white brethren." Representing the mothers of the people, this woman invoked the language of kinship—her children and their white brothers—to encourage the Americans to make peace. Jesup replied by "expiating on the 'maternal' affections of their great father at Washington, there being no great mother for his red children." According to Motte, "The chiefs were then asked if they were willing, as they had promised, to abide the will of their great father the President." Perhaps Jesup did not understand that fathers did not grant the same kind of relationship that a mother did in the Seminole worldview, or perhaps he was insisting on a relationship of dominance rather than reciprocity.[74] Although Jesup may not have recognized it, the female elder's role in the attempt to broker peace reveals that Seminole warriors continued to acknowledge the clan mothers' decision-making power. Traditionally Seminole towns and clans made decisions about relocating and about war collectively, and women's voices would have been heard in town or camp councils.

Two years later, as the war continued in October 1840, another female elder, perhaps sent by her clan to broker a temporary peace, invited General Walker Keith Armistead to speak with several Seminole war leaders. She appeared one day with sixteen sticks to indicate that her band would be ready to negotiate in sixteen days. Perhaps Seminole war leaders, recognizing white gender and age norms, sent an older woman to negotiate because they knew that white soldiers might listen to her rather than shoot her on sight.[75] When the day for the arranged talk arrived, male Seminole leaders claimed that they wanted peace on behalf of their people. Americans had destroyed their corn, and their women were "broke down with labor in preparing *coontiroot*." They were starving and unable to continue the fight, they said, but maintained that the land was theirs and the Americans had no rights to it. The war of attrition was a war on women, and it was working.[76]

When Seminole leaders struck agreements with American officers, they often cited the suffering and exhaustion of their families as a primary motive for their surrender, as the 1838 and 1840 exchanges indicate. A group of Seminoles who surrendered for removal in 1837 told American officers that their families would only come into the fort once they were properly clothed, probably because they knew that women not clothed to white standards would be targets of white sexual assault. They insisted on camping outside of Tampa until they received rations and cloth, which the women quickly turned into meals and raiment. The Seminoles also expressed concern in negotiations for removal about the treatment their women and children would receive on the journey west.[77]

Legacies of Conquest

At the end of the Second U.S.-Seminole War in 1842, Brigadier General William Jenkins Worth signed an agreement that allowed the few Seminoles who remained to occupy five million acres in southern Florida, land originally negotiated by General Alexander Macomb as a temporary reservation during the brief cease-fire he achieved in 1839. Due to the traumatic experiences of the Seminoles during the White Wars, they retreated into the Everglades, and whites did not see them in Florida for at least one generation. Avoiding conflict with whites became a Seminole way of life for those who remained in Florida, and that meant avoiding any unnecessary contact. Only in the 1870s did Seminoles reemerge to trade with whites in South Florida, and whites rarely encountered Seminole women at trading posts or even in Seminole camps. William Stiles, a curator for the Museum of the American Indian who had been in contact with Florida Seminoles since 1929, confirmed in the 1970s that it was improper for whites to enter a Seminole camp when the men were gone, and if they did, they would find it empty, because the women and children would have fled. Contact between women and white men was especially limited, as half-white children with full clan status might result from such unions. Some Seminole traditionalists believed that "half-breeds" were "bad spirits" who threatened their communities, and even young Seminoles who sought a formal "white" education faced censure from older traditionalists.[78]

Historical trauma left other legacies as well. Many attest that the Seminoles preferred to kill their own kin rather than allow whites to rape or torture them. Mary Huff recalled, "My grandfather used to say it was better to kill one of our own when there was no other alternative."[79] Similarly, Mrs. Weiss remarked: "An Indian would rather fight until death than to be taken captive at the hands of white man."[80] One of few Seminole men to comment on rape, Charlie Gopher recounted in May 1971: "Whenever the girls were raped, and left there dying usually, a relative of another Indian would crawl back into the area and kill the girl in order to relieve her pain."[81] Descendants also reveal that their ancestors killed women who consorted with whites and any children that resulted. According to Gopher, "If a girl was lucky enough to survive these brutes, and was pregnant by them, if the child was of white ancestry, the tribe would kill the child."[82] Rape was so common and so traumatic that the Seminoles developed policies of euthanasia and infanticide in the aftermath of white sexual violence to spare the victims and their families from further suffering.

These practices began as responses to violence and terror during removal and became more rigid policies for clan and tribal preservation among the few Seminoles who remained in Florida in the twentieth century, as they sought to prevent further disruptions to their community. Social policies of euthanasia and infanticide are a response to what Claudia Card has called the "genetic imperialism" of martial rape. Victimized communities may identify a child conceived in rape with an enemy group and fear that the child will undermine clan and community solidarity. The rejection of any children that resulted from the rape (or consensual union) of Seminole women by white men was widespread into the twentieth century. White rapists caught by tribal members were executed, and sometimes the children who resulted from rape (or consensual sex with whites) were also killed. Although it happened rarely, the women of her clan also might punish or kill a Seminole woman who willingly engaged in sexual relationships with white men. In the late nineteenth and twentieth centuries, Seminoles rejected the children of white men and Seminole women, whom the elder women of the group often drowned. By contrast, they often accepted (with some conditions) the children of black and Seminole unions, especially when they had Seminole mothers, or if black mothers had been adopted by a clan.[83]

When Seminoles remember that whites abused women and hurt children, they are recording trauma, invoking horror, and using their own rhetoric to resist a long, racist legacy of white narratives. By telling about the violence that Seminoles experienced at the hands of whites, Seminoles contest the white version of this history, the version popularized in Florida Indian depredation narratives in the 1830s and 1840s that justified violent removal as the defense of white women and their homes and families. Seminole stories argue, against that tradition, that Indian removal was the result of white greed and aggression. Even as Seminoles emphasize the victimization of their forebears, they are resisting stereotypes of their people as "savages" and pointing to the barbaric hypocrisy of the whites who, in the name of protecting their "homes and families," destroyed Seminole homes, raped Seminole women and girls, and murdered Seminole families. Seminole stories strip away the sentimentalism of expansionist domesticity and reveal its violent, political nature, albeit with a dose of cultural bias against whites equal to the anti-Indian prejudice of depredation narratives.

While telling and retelling Seminole stories of the "white devils" was and is resistant, observing that effect should not obscure the fact that these were stories of horrific and inexcusable violence. While it is important to recognize Native American agency, white Americans also had agency, and they used military, political, and cultural power to overwhelm Native American resistance in Florida. Recognizing that Seminoles are still in Florida is important, but it is perhaps more important to note (as many of the Seminoles in this chapter have) that there would be many more of them there today if Americans had not upheld and carried out ethnic cleansing in the southeastern United States in the nineteenth century.

Survival and Endurance

Somewhere between New Orleans, Louisiana, and Vicksburg, Mississippi, on board the steamboat *South Alabama*, five captive women gave birth in May 1838. These women were part of a large group of people from Florida, forced travelers on the Seminole Trail of Tears. There were 1,127 people in their party, making it over one-quarter of the roughly 4,420 people whom U.S. forces removed from Florida between 1836 and 1843. Two hundred and forty-nine of them were Black Seminoles. Since leaving Tampa Bay, they all had experienced terrible conditions, and over half of them had become sick in the stockade at Fort Pike (New Orleans) while waiting for the steamboats that would take them north to Oklahoma. Between their departure from New Orleans on May 22, 1838, and their arrival in Vicksburg four days later, forty-seven people died. But these five women lived, and brought new life into the world.[84]

What was it like, giving birth aboard a floating prison on the way to an unknown future? How did they bear childbirth while people became sick and died all around them? Did the white soldiers watch to assess whether or not Seminole women really had pain-free births, unburdened by Christianity? Did the women groan and scream, or were they stoic in the face of their pain? How did they manage, without the ritual separation from society and spiritual cleansing that usually accompanied birth in Seminole villages? Did their babies survive? Did they name them for recently lost kin? Such questions are impossible to answer because these women were nameless statistics to the officer in charge.[85]

Their unknown stories might hold great joy or countless sorrows. These women conceived their babies sometime in late summer or early fall 1837, a tumultuous time for the Seminoles. Brigadier General Jesup began to offer freedom to any "Indian negroes" in 1837 that agreed to removal as part of a divide-and-conquer strategy. On September 8, 1837, American troops captured King Philip's large band south of St. Augustine, including women whom army surgeon Jacob Motte described as "miserable, blackened, haggard, shriveled (smoke-dried and half-clad) devils."[86] Shortly thereafter, Coacoochee, Osceola, and others either surrendered or Americans captured them (under the flag of peace, which brought Jesup infamy).[87] Some of the people on the *South Alabama*, therefore, could have been in American custody since the previous fall when these five women became pregnant. Perhaps each woman had desired a child and sought to carry the legacy of a beloved warrior with her into Oklahoma. In the face of war and death, maybe nurturing a new life was her way of nourishing her people and resisting their destruction. Given the context, however, these five women might have been raped, since they would have been vulnerable to white soldiers at several points between capture or surrender and their arrival at a U.S. fort. The record is silent about who fathered these children, and whether their mothers were glad to meet them.

These five mothers, whether willing parents or not, illustrate Seminole women's importance to cultural survival. Through them, and because of their persistence, Seminole clans and families continued. Because Seminole women endured, new Seminoles came into the world, in spite of all the efforts of the United States to eradicate them. Although they suffered during this period, Seminole women—and therefore Seminole people—survived.

PART II

Gender and Pro-Settler Policy

CHAPTER 4

Turning Sufferers into Settlers

> The question now is, whether the women and children of respectable planters . . . driven from their homes by a merciless and savage enemy, and forced into your military cantonments, to escape the tomahawk and scalping-knife, are to be left to starve?
> —Delegate Joseph White, January 30, 1836

> I cannot hear the hartrending cries of the women and children who are slaughtered on our borders, and I would make any sacrifice of men or money to give them protection.
> —Florida governor Richard Keith Call, May 20, 1839

As violence escalated into war in Florida, whites terrified of "Indian depredations" fled the countryside. Some took refuge in Jacksonville and St. Augustine, while others left the territory. In January 1836 Joseph White, the Florida Territory's delegate to Congress, asked federal leaders to consider the plight of whites in Florida.[1] Fearful that white settlers afraid of or displaced by wartime violence would abandon Florida, Delegate White lifted images of threatened, "respectable" white women and children and settler homes from the pages of Indian depredation narratives and used them to convince Congress to enact a welfare policy that would protect and retain white frontier families. He succeeded, and Congress passed a resolution to "Aid the Suffering and Indigent Inhabitants of Florida" on February 1, 1836.[2]

This program granted food rations to people made homeless, widowed, or orphaned by the Second U.S.-Seminole War. The U.S. Army distributed these rations to hundreds of individuals between 1836 and 1841. Following the early failures of the Florida War and the economic panic in 1837, Americans came to view this policy as too expensive, so military leaders leveraged white settlers' dependence on rations to shift policy in the summer of 1841. The new policy required whites to "recolonize" the Florida frontier as members of "armed families" if they wanted to continue to receive rations or other aid. They had to re-create the homes they had lost in order to continue to receive aid. These policies represented an expansion of the political power of Indian depredations. No longer stories that justified Seminole removal or helped to raise volunteer regiments and federal funds for war, they became the basis for social welfare and, in the next chapter, land policy. This chapter follows the passage and implementation of the suffering inhabitants and recolonization policies in Florida, and follows several of the beneficiaries into the decades following the Second U.S.-Seminole War when many became successful Florida farmers and planters. Such successful settlers indicate the degree to which these policies achieved their expansionist aims.

The history of these policies reveals that between 1836 and 1842 congressional and military leaders harnessed gender to expansionist policies in Florida. This began with a welfare program aimed at war widows and orphans because, although the United States went to war to remove the Seminoles, the conflict threatened to drive white settlers out as well. Over time that aid policy transformed into colonization and land schemes. As federal welfare policy evolved as a tool of expansionism, policy makers employed expansionist domesticity to naturalize and justify its development. Over the course of six years, leaders first used notions of gender to enact policy in the name of chivalrous charity for displaced white widows and orphans, and subsequently to frame it as support for independent men at the head of settler families and households. As recipients of federal aid changed from "suffering inhabitants" to "armed settlers" between 1836 and 1842, each aid program aimed to restore white women and men to their "proper" household and family roles, which policy makers assumed would settle the frontier. In these ways, policy makers used ideas about men's and women's ideal roles to naturalize and justify federal spending in Florida. Gender made it possible for them to debate policies aimed at ending the Second U.S.-Seminole War as if those policies were federal social provision for the benefit of deserving white Americans. Expansionist domesticity allowed American leaders to begin a welfare program for war victims and subsequently change it into a policy of land entitlements for deserving settlers.

There were also gender challenges policy makers had to meet. Many believed that settlers were more effective than soldiers at colonizing and holding land in Florida, yet it was a dangerous frontier where Seminoles harmed and killed white women and children and burned down their homes. American politicians thus cast white women in two expansionist-domestic roles: the innocent victim and the civilizing agent. As Chapter 2 illustrated, as victims of Seminole violence white women were highly visible in the American press, and their vulnerability was widely employed by politicians to justify the Second U.S.-Seminole War. American support of the war in Florida was cast as a defense of white women and their families, regardless of public dispute on expansion of slavery or the removal of Native Americans. In their role as civilizing agents, white women became less visible. Behind protective male household heads, policy makers tacitly recognized women's presence in language about families. In the midst of these rhetorical changes, some women adeptly played both roles; widowed "sufferers" under one policy became "settlers" under another, and some single women filed land claims as heads of families.[3] Beyond the gendered rhetoric, many white women and men benefited from these policies. The choices made by the white men and women who received these benefits shaped these policies, as did the ideas about male and female roles held by men in Congress and the military.

Antebellum gender ideology, rather than masking white women's roles in frontier settlement, freighted their roles with new meanings. Nineteenth-century domestic ideology did not prevent white women on the Florida frontier from getting rations and land directly from the government. Rather, gender operated as a way for politicians and military leaders to recognize women—"the women and children of respectable planters"—as settlers with a direct claim on the nation's resources. It was precisely their domestic contribution that was used to justify food aid and, subsequently, free land. In a war-torn territory where Seminoles killed male providers, the army stepped in to provide for the sustenance of widows and orphans. As that program became too expensive and counter to the goal of populating the frontier with white homes, congressional decision makers shifted to a new free land policy, one that relied on the ideas that settlement was permanent only when male-headed "families" occupied land, built homes, and began to farm. Patriarchal expansionist domesticity, American politicians believed, would guarantee permanent settler colonialism.

This was not the first time that policy makers mobilized gender and social provision to support national expansion, nor would it be the last. Generous land policies for veterans, land donation and preemption rights for squatters, and distribution and graduation schemes all happened before or concurrent with these policies in Florida. Beginning in the Early Republic, entitlements such as land grants and veteran pensions enabled and largely accomplished the geographical expansion of the country through military and civilian conquest. Importantly, these policies (in Florida and before) preceded many of the social provisions that scholars such as Susan Sterett, Theda Skocpol, and Linda Gordon examine in the late nineteenth and twentieth centuries. This suggests that a longer and wider of view of welfare history in the United States is necessary, one that looks at how land, Indian, military, and expansionist policies also provided for needy Americans. Studies of social provision have long recognized how welfare enlarged the state and its bureaucracies, but American social spending also required recipients to serve expansionist roles, roles that required them to participate in the dispossession of Native Americans from their land and the expansion of racial slavery. A longer, broader policy history reveals how social provision in the United States was rarely just about need and was often a tool used to draft citizens into service toward national goals.[4]

Debating Aid for "Sufferers" in Congress

The resolution "for the relief of the indigent and suffering inhabitants of Florida" enacted by Congress in early 1836 ordered that rations "from the public stores" be given "to the unfortunate sufferers who have been driven from their homes by Indian depredations." Like Indian depredation stories, the policy debate focused on the ways the war had displaced white settler families from their Florida "homes." This focus on "homes" reiterated that Florida was already home to white American families, eliding Seminole claims to Florida homelands. The consistent invocation of lost homes also brought domesticity directly to bear on expansionist policy, as the public outcry against Seminole attacks on white settlers and their homes motivated congressional leaders to act. A January 13, 1836, memorial to Congress from the leading citizens of St. Augustine requested rations for citizens who had been dispossessed by Seminoles or who had lost male providers killed in action. White Floridians referenced and retold depredation stories in other petitions and letters as well, demanding more military aid. On the eve of the war, Judge Robert Reid (who would lead Florida's first constitutional convention in 1838 and become governor of the territory in 1839) recounted a depredation story in a letter to U.S. Secretary of State John Forsyth, requesting more arms and soldiers for Florida.[5] In the spring and summer of 1839, Governor Richard K. Call lambasted the military for not doing enough to protect white settlers and noted recent attacks on whites living near the Apalachicola River. Call concluded, "I regret exceedingly the necessity of drawing a militia force from our population at a season of the year when labour is so much required for cultivation. But I cannot hear the hartrending [sic] cries of the women and children who are slaughtered on our borders, and I would make any sacrifice of men or money to give them protection."[6] Sympathy for the victims of Seminole violence was one motivation for congressional action, but Florida leaders also believed that stabilizing and increasing the population of white families moved Florida closer to statehood, something that affluent planters in Middle Florida hoped to achieve in the 1830s. Americans had been encouraging white settlers to come to Florida with generous land policies since the 1820s. Congress passed the Donation Act in 1824, which allowed squatters to claim up to 640 acres in Florida. In 1828, Congress passed a law allowing squatters to preempt public land auctions and purchase land they had settled on for $1.25 per acre. The continuing frontier violence had now displaced some of these early settlers and discouraged new migrants from coming. Congress acted to restore settler families to their "Florida homes" through policies that provided for white settler women and children and, eventually, reinstated them on the Florida frontier.[7]

The federal response focused on aid to women and children. In Congress, support for the resolution was overwhelming but not unanimous: 178 representatives voted for it while 14 opposed it. While some representatives issued partisan attacks, ultimately they did not vote along party or sectional lines. Regardless of party and region, members of Congress relied on gendered ideology to inform their votes. Members invoked a range of arguments: sympathy for victims (widows and their children), a need for civilizing women to create homes on frontiers, honorable men's duty to provide for the needy, the moral blamelessness of the indigent (which depended on gender and age), and the construction of white settlers as innocent bystanders in wars between the United States and Native Americans (which rested on the assumption that Americans were dependent on a paternal nation). Many Congressmen invoked women and home in the debate without explicitly defining either term, safely presuming that their fellow lawmakers shared their own sentimental understandings of gender roles and proper, civilized domesticity, powerful social categories in the early nineteenth century. As the debate and the implementation of the policy will reveal, they meant white women and children and white settler homes.[8]

The gendered nature of this debate about supporting settler colonialism had historical roots in American discourse regarding aid to indigent people. Beginning in the Early Republic, gender ideology—assumptions about independence and dependence rooted in the social norms of patriarchal household order—influenced which public payments counted as charity and which were well-deserved rewards for patriotic service. Policies aimed at male workers and at mothers shared an underlying belief in paternalist family structures, as both supported male-headed households or replaced absent men with public support. The policies that the United States enacted in Florida in the 1830s and 1840s shared this commitment to a patriarchal norm. The suffering inhabitants policy aided women and children only because they were without male providers, justifying the government's role as a stand-in paternal provider and reinforcing notions of feminine helplessness.[9]

During the January 30, 1836, House debate, several representatives presented the government, or perhaps the nation itself, as a paternal figure that should provide for the white victims of the Seminoles and the Florida War. The war had created a situation in Florida in which individual patriarchs could not protect or provide for their families on the Florida frontier. Representative Francis Granger, a New York Whig, decried the government's impotent response: "The war-cry is up in the woods, the tomahawk glitters in the sunbeam, the scalping-knife is urged to its cruel duty, the flower of your chivalry is strewed along the plain, and yet every department of this administration is as dumb as the bleeding victims of this inglorious contest." Representative Granger was issuing a partisan attack, but he did so in highly gendered terms. If militant masculinity had allowed the "flower" of its "chivalry" to be killed, then the nation absolutely had to act to rescue survivors, as well as its own pride and manhood. Having failed to protect them, the nation moved to provide for their widows and children.[10]

Pitiable widows inspired much public sympathy in the nineteenth century and often received public aid. Although they were women independent of male household authority, widows had fulfilled their proper family role by marrying and (usually) bearing children. Americans expected widows to be helpless in the aftermath of their husbands' deaths but also anticipated that they soon would competently shoulder their new household responsibilities. While many of the women who benefited from the government programs in Florida in the 1830s and 1840s were widows who subsequently proved themselves competent as household heads in a frontier territory, the policies themselves did not require them to be widowed. Rather, political leaders used the sympathy-generating category of "widow" as the opening wedge to propel policies forward, without restricting either rations or land programs to widows only. In addition to widows, many married women (as well as men) and some single people took advantage of them.[11]

As justification for this aid, and to heighten their colleagues' sympathies, many congressmen repeated stories of Seminole attacks in Florida during the debate. Several cited female victims and their children who were attacked at home and torn from their secure domestic spaces. They also repeatedly invoked the "tomahawk and scalping-knife" as symbols of the cruel methods of the "savage Seminoles." Representative Amos Lane of Indiana (Democrat) described Florida's frontier as "a scene that can but call for the commiseration of every sympathetic bosom," in response to "the cries of women and children" as "the scalping-knife is urged to its bloody office." Sympathy for women and children, in addition to calling on a national paternalism, also identified the speaker as "civilized" in contrast to the "savages" who attacked these pitiful white settlers with exotic weapons. Rhetorically, gender framed policy makers as feeling and paternal protectors, and aid recipients as damsels in distress.[12]

The suffering inhabitants policy was designed to prevent whites from fleeing Florida in search of food and shelter, and thus used rations to support existing white settlements and their future expansion. By 1836 East Florida's white American residents faced food scarcity. The flight of farmers to the safety of towns and forts and the arrival of American troops in need of supplies quickly led to a shortage of provisions in Florida. Even for those with means, there was not enough food to buy. This necessitated government intervention because, as Representative Granger noted, without aid the few inhabitants left in Florida who had been "driven from their homes" would "inevitably perish." The alternative to starvation and Indian depredations was to leave the territory, an option that would create a flow of migrants in precisely the wrong direction. Giving rations to widows and orphans not only satisfied a paternalistic urge, but it also served national interests by encouraging Americans to remain in Florida.[13]

More than recipients of paternal aid and sympathetic innocent victims of Seminole aggression, women were considered by policy makers to be vital to the process of building successful and permanent settlements. Single male settlers with guns were hardly distinct from soldiers, since without families they were less likely to settle permanently. As Senator Samuel Stokely of Ohio (Whig) later opined during the debate over the Armed Occupation Act in July 1842, "The presence of the families would bind the settlers to the soil," and women had "a most happy effect in stimulating the courage and enterprise of their male relatives." The senator took for granted that white women were necessary for settlement, as did many of his peers, who were rarely so explicit. Since white women were fundamental to American settlement, granting rations and protection to them was a shrewd method of encouraging them to stay in the territory. More than a paternalist response to needy women and children, the rations program was also an investment in the colonization of Florida, where women's presence would make white communities permanent and prevent the Seminoles from gaining ground.[14]

Placing Floridians in the category of "sufferers" implied a connection to others who had received federal disaster aid. As Michele Landis Dauber argues, disaster relief was "the first sustained, organized social welfare program." Beginning in 1789, the United States sent aid in various forms to victims of earthquakes, floods, fires, Indian depredations, and, during the War of 1812, British attacks. Politicians discussed these precedents, including relief of victims on the Niagara Frontier after the War of 1812, and aid the American government had sent to victims of earthquakes, floods, and Indian and British depredations. The debate over suffering inhabitants shares much with the disaster relief precedents of the first three-quarters of the nineteenth century, including concern about setting precedents, invocations of charity above precedent, the moral blamelessness of the victims, the assertion that the government was partially to blame, and (in the case of Indian depredations) a focus on the "savage" nature of the Seminoles. Unlike previous sufferers, those in Florida were the first white Americans to receive food and shelter as a group from the army during an ongoing war, though Congress had granted aid for individual petitions during and after other armed conflicts. For example, Congress partially reimbursed the Niagara victims for property losses suffered due to British attacks during the War of 1812, granting them cash payments after the war.[15]

Congressmen also (ironically) discussed Indian treaty provisions as a pertinent precedent. Many treaties granted displaced Native Americans rations and annuities in exchange for leaving their land. Supporters of the suffering inhabitants policy cited this as one rationale for providing similar aid to its own citizens; if indigenous enemies had received help, surely white families deserved as much. Delegate Joseph White of Florida (as a federal territory Florida sent a nonvoting delegate to Congress) noted that even as Congress debated this resolution, the army was feeding the Seminoles awaiting removal at Fort Brooke (Tampa Bay). The United States had also promised the Seminoles money, equipment, and clothing (though it did not always fulfill its obligations). In the long history of U.S.-Native American diplomacy, the United States granted annuities to many indigenous tribes in exchange for their land, which again indicates that provisions for welfare (of Native Americans as well as white frontier settlers) were policies aimed at supporting national territorial expansion, and that such policies created dependence on the federal government that often proved useful to policy makers when they decided to change course and needed a way to coerce recipients to follow. In Florida, the U.S. government used aid to Americanize Florida in multiple ways: to encourage Seminoles to leave and make their homes in the West (or at least to make treaties appear fair and just), and to encourage white settlers to stay in Florida until the conflict subsided and they could rebuild their homes in new or repopulated white settlements. It proved far more enticing to whites than to Seminoles, but of course white settlers had more to gain and far less to lose.[16]

Given the extensive precedents in disaster relief and Indian policy, congressional leaders tried to foresee how their actions might inspire future policies. Many anticipated that Americans would continue to spread south and west. They worried this resolution would result in a legislative precedent for taking "a hundred millions" from the Treasury to aid settlers who suffered in frontier wars against Native peoples. Their concerns were prescient. Just four months later, following a debate in which lawmakers cited the suffering inhabitants policy, the House of Representatives approved rations for whites displaced by Creek attacks in Alabama and Georgia.[17]

While lawmakers concerned about setting precedents worried that aid to settlers would expand inevitably along with national borders in the age of Manifest Destiny, others took up the question of social provision and moral responsibility. Some congressmen worried that this policy would make Florida's residents lazy and dependent. Representative Richard Hawes of Kentucky (Democrat) proposed amending the resolution by replacing "sufferers" with the phrase "women, children, and men unable to bear arms," in order to avoid creating dependence. "Feed men up, stuff them with rations, and . . . there is no fighting. . . . Let them be hungry at times, and then they will fight fast enough."[18] Gender and age were two criteria for establishing that a victim was not responsible for his or her own suffering. Dependent white women, children, and disabled men could not possibly be responsible for their situation.

The concern about creating dependence came directly from debates about poverty relief in the early nineteenth century. Americans disagreed about the relative superiority of "outdoor" relief (assistance to poor people living in their own homes) or "indoor" relief (aid that required poor people to live and labor in institutions). Those who attacked outdoor relief believed that giving the poor aid without surveillance undermined their work ethic and encouraged idleness. Deliberations in Congress regarding the Florida victims never directly addressed outdoor and indoor relief because there was no option for indoor relief. Florida was an overwhelmingly rural federal territory. It lacked the state agencies and the urban centers in which benevolent agencies typically operated. The suffering inhabitants policy offered white settlers the option to live at a fort if they sought a safe place to dwell, but it did not require them to do so (and the evidence from the previous chapter suggests that army forts were not necessarily safe for women and girls). The policy also excluded "ablebodied men" in order to satisfy skeptics such as Representative Hawes. Rather than debating whether to build poorhouses in Florida, the congressional debate took up questions about moral blameworthiness, disaster relief, and precedents. Each of these concerned the gendered paternalism of the federal government: if victims were dependent women and children, then they were not to blame. Since Seminoles had killed their male providers, the national government should step in to help them. Further, if the paternal nation had offered aid to other sufferers following disasters, then surely the Americans in Florida deserved similar help. Finally, if there were already precedents for national paternalism in Indian treaties and other disaster relief measures, then Congress members did not have to worry about setting a new precedent by aiding Florida's citizens.[19]

The question of moral blame was also distinct from contemporary poverty debates because Florida was a frontier where Indian warfare, rather than the tax burden created by poor people, was the problem. It was easier, therefore, for lawmakers to blame forces other than the victims themselves for their situation. Supporters of the policy put the responsibility on the Seminoles and the American government. Delegate Joseph M. White of Florida opined: "This bloody war, now raging on our frontier, was not produced by any acts of the people who were plundered and murdered, nor by causes which they could, by any foresight or courage, control or prevent. It grew out of the relations between the Government of the United States and these Indians." When the Seminoles violated the terms of their treaty with the United States, they "commenced this scene of destruction upon the peacable [sic], unsuspecting, and unoffending inhabitants of Florida."[20] Although surely the Seminoles recognized the presence of whites as very clear proof of American aggression, this view maintained white American settlers' innocence by relying on sentimental notions of home and gendered relations of power. It presumed that white Americans were people who were simply "at home" in Florida, rather than settlers actively engaged in national efforts to wrest control of the territory from Seminoles and Black Seminoles. It also presumed that Americans were dependent on the paternal nation, unconnected to the government's diplomatic endeavors, and therefore innocent of any aggression. Conveniently, it held that whites were victims of their government's statecraft rather than its perpetrators and beneficiaries. Although no one expressly cited it, the federal Indian Depredation Claims System probably contributed to this framing of the conflict, because it rewarded private citizens who suffered in the process of territorial expansion and made the government responsible for losses they suffered in frontier conflicts with Native Americans.[21]

Although some placed responsibility on the government, others pointed out that white settlers went to the frontier because they stood to benefit. Representative Joel Turrill, a New York Democrat, believed that Floridians were no different from other pioneers "whose spirit of enterprise has stimulated them, with the hope of gain, to press their settlements into the wilderness, where savage tribes still linger . . . with a full knowledge of the hardships and privations, of the difficulties and dangers they have to encounter." As such, they had "no particular claims over other pioneers."[22]

Turrill proposed an image of the hardy, bold, presumably male pioneer as an alternative to the assertion that the Florida victims were dependents without responsibility for their own suffering. In his view, settlers were taking a calculated risk from which they stood to gain, and, therefore, were responsible for themselves and the losses they suffered. Although this opposition failed in debate, it foreshadowed the gendered shift that took place as policies changed in the early 1840s. When Congress passed the suffering inhabitants resolution on February 1, 1836, gendered arguments for sympathy, nationalist paternalism, and white women's vital role in colonization overcame concerns about creating precedents and idle dependents. Gender also shaped how the military executed this policy.

Morality, Dependence, and Social Provision

Anna Maria Dummett, daughter of a sugar planter, narrowly escaped an 1836 Seminole attack on her family's plantation and weathered the remainder of the war in St. Augustine, where she collected rations as a "Suffering Inhabitant." She recalled, "It might be said we lived under 'martial law.' It was not safe to ride half a mile out of town, for the Indians were at times very near. . . . A very strict guard was kept up."[23] Many other white refugees arrived in towns in 1836 and 1837, where they faced food shortages, overcrowding, and disease. Hundreds drew rations at Garey's Ferry, established in early 1836 as the principal depot for the army in Florida. During the war between seven hundred and eight hundred people camped there in open-sided shanties, after surviving a depredation or abandoning their homes in fear of a Seminole attack. One 1836 visitor noted that in all of the three hundred huts he visited he found two or three people sick with measles, cholera, or influenza. Army surgeon Jacob Motte concluded that Garey's Ferry was "remarkable for nothing except flies, fleas, and heat." The settlers camped in this squalor were the sufferers Congress intended to aid.[24]

President Jackson delegated the execution of the rations program to the army, which was the only organization in Florida with the infrastructure and resources to provide aid. This meant that American military leaders decided who was worthy of support as they attempted to support settlement and defeat the Seminoles. Since the army's goal was to end the war with at least a claim of American victory, it designed an aid program that encouraged behaviors that were likely to help win the war and limited those that might hinder their efforts.[25]

Secretary of War Lewis Cass employed Anglo-American social norms to establish who was an eligible sufferer: women, minors, and enslaved people (those considered dependents in southern households), who survived a Seminole attack, fled their home in fear of one, or lost a white male provider in the war. Heads of families drew rations for their families as a unit. They had to demonstrate a stable moral character and attest that they could not find supplies to purchase. Although they did not have to formally prove that they had had a home before the war began, the ration rolls suggest that the neighbors who applied for aid alongside them confirmed their stories of loss. The army also required able-bodied men to serve in the military if they wanted access to rations, since if they were otherwise employed then they ought to be supporting their families. Those who joined the army had to support their own families, except for their children under fourteen and slaves under ten, who were allowed half rations (presumably children and young slaves could not work to support themselves). Rations included flour or bread, meat, salt, vinegar, beans, coffee, sugar, soap, and candles. Free and enslaved "colored" persons "whose owners could not procure provisions for them" received partial rations—of bread, meat, and salt.[26]

As anticipated in the language of the resolution and its implementation, the lists of suffering inhabitants were limited mostly to white women and children, but widowers, displaced families, and elderly and indigent residents who had no other means of support also drew rations for their families. The president had initially authorized the War Department to supply rations to sufferers in Florida (anyone unable to maintain themselves) until October 1, 1837. Although rations continued after that until the end of the war, they were increasingly limited to the "aged, infirm, the widow and the orphan" at the discretion of the Florida command. The army was ordered to find employment for able-bodied adults so as to avoid the "pernicious moral influence" of welfare, and to avoid diverting rations and other supplies away from the war effort. At the end of the war in June 1842, the one surviving list of suffering inhabitants included four hundred individuals drawing rations at five different forts or garrisons located in northern Florida (Map 2). By the time army officers created this list, the program had shifted toward rewarding settlers who returned to the frontier, and the army had already removed many people from the rations rolls. These four hundred people comprised a small fraction of the hundreds who had received rations in the previous six years. Of the four hundred aid recipients remaining on the rolls in 1842, most were white women and their children;

Map 2. Selected forts and towns in Florida, Second U.S.-Seminole War. Sufferers received aid at St. Augustine, Jacksonville, Garey's Ferry, Micanopy, and Fort Robert Gamble.

seventy-five women (mostly war widows) accompanied by two hundred children and about fifty slaves. At least sixty of these women were widows of the war or survivors of a Seminole attack. "John Beasley's widow" and her four children, for example, drew rations at Jacksonville, because her husband had been "killed by Indians." Charlotte Joyner and her two children drew rations in 1842 as well. Her husband was "killed in service" in 1836, and she was "very old and infirm," so the military officer in charge of distribution recommended that she and her children continue to receive rations. In addition, about forty white orphans and another fifty enslaved people rounded out the rolls of suffering inhabitants at the end of the war.[27]

Despite the increasingly limited rules of eligibility articulated by the War Department, the officers in charge of the ration rolls used the discretion the Secretary of War granted them to make exceptions. Some of the widows lost husbands before the war but benefited from the aid program anyway. Other families who had lost property and fled their homes after an attack also received rations, although their male providers were still alive and able-bodied. Elderly men and women drew rations, too. Many of them were not the direct victims of war or Seminole violence but presumably had lost the ability to provide for themselves because of wartime scarcity. Some of these people might have been destitute before the war. For instance, two women abandoned by their husbands, Mary Adams and Martha Tippin, drew aid for themselves and their children. Thus, under the suffering inhabitants program, the federal government even took care of women and children whose male providers had failed them for reasons unrelated to the war. Here, the government's role as paternal provider and protector is especially clear. The military was attempting to stabilize a chaotic frontier community so that white Americans would stay and eventually become self-sufficient again. To do so, it provided for families who had lost their homes and/or their ability to support themselves, as a "civilized" home provided physical shelter and daily subsistence, as well as moral health (as the exclusions discussed below reveal). The aid program yielded the national benefit of securing new territory and served a sympathetic cause that reaffirmed stable gender roles on a frontier of broken families.[28]

The enslaved and free blacks that received aid under the suffering inhabitants program included about fifty "negroes" at the end of the war. As the property and dependents of whites, keeping them alive protected white private property. Further, slave labor would be needed for colonizing Florida when the war finally ended. Almost all of them were enslaved people whose rations were given to the white householder who claimed to own them. Army officers distributed rations for enslaved persons almost exclusively at rural posts, but thirteen free blacks drew rations in St. Augustine or Jacksonville. If whites abandoned free or enslaved blacks to starve, they might run away to fight with the Seminoles.[29]

In September 1837, the army issued new rules to regulate aid, hoping to cut costs in the midst of a major economic downturn and public attacks on the expensive and so far failed war effort in Florida. The new regulations reveal what kinds of sufferers the War Department considered worthy, as well as those it sought to exclude. Anyone caught wasting or selling their rations was permanently stricken from the rolls. The army instituted a procedure to prevent recipients from doubling their rations by drawing at two places, which apparently some had done. It excluded others for moral reasons, including selling whiskey, running gambling houses, or being "notoriously immoral." Frances Snowden lost her rations for "living with a man not her husband." Such women and men, violators of family norms and national interests, were not the kind of civilized colonists that the United States hoped to retain in Florida.[30]

Historical records are incomplete, so it is impossible to offer any statistical assessment of the success of the suffering inhabitants policy, but at least some of those who drew rations during the war remained and settled in Florida. Although it is difficult to trace women in nineteenth-century public records, a few of the widows and orphans can be tracked in land and census records, and their stories illustrate the paths that "sufferers" followed as they became "settlers" in the 1840s. At least nine of the thirty-one female sufferers of St. Augustine, for example, continued to live in Florida until 1850 and remained until 1860 and beyond. Several became fairly prosperous with estates worth $250 to $4,250 according to the 1860 census (roughly equivalent to $6,760 and $115,000 in 2010). The other twenty-two female household heads had disappeared. They may have moved out of state, died, or remarried.[31]

Jane Baya may have been one of the widows who remained in Florida after the war. A woman identified only as "Antonio Baya's widow" and five of her children drew rations in St. Augustine during the war. Yet someone named Antonio Baya continued to appear in the St. Augustine census in 1850 and 1860. It is unclear whether this is a different man with the same name or if reports of his death in 1842 were intentionally fraudulent or sincere but premature. Jane and Antonio Baya were quite successful following her time on the rations rolls, assuming she was the widow and he the same man reported dead in 1842. Not only did Antonio apparently come back from the dead, but he rose from the rank of town butcher worth $500 to a farmer worth $3,000 who owned enough land to necessitate the labor of at least a dozen enslaved people. Since Jane may not have truly been widowed and Antonio may have been able-bodied, they might not have been exactly the victims targeted by the 1836 policy, but they certainly became the kind of respectable citizens that Americans wanted to settle Florida: they owned enslaved people, moved out of the town into the county where they planted, and together raised another generation of white Floridians.[32]

Eleven of the families on the St. Augustine ration rolls at the end of the war had Minorcan or Italian surnames, indicating that their ancestors were among the laborers recruited by Andrew Turnbull to work on his sugar plantation at New Smyrna in the 1760s.[33] The women who drew rations and remained in Florida after the war included six widows of Minorcan descent. Antonia Geneva, Mary and Antonia Medici, Rafaelle Goff, and Antonia Marine owned between $400 and $600 in property in 1850 (comparable to $11,500 to $17,300 in 2010). By 1860 their average wealth had increased, ranging from $250 to $3,850 (comparable to $6,760 to $104,000 in 2010). Their circumstances improved over time, and none of them were completely destitute in the decade after the war. Perhaps since their families had once relied on help from the British colonial government (when they fled Turnbull's plantation), these St. Augustinians were inclined to rely on the American government for help as well.[34]

The other St. Augustinians who remained in Florida included Jane Long, Mary Kelly, Louisa Fatio, and Mary and Anna Maria Dummett. While Kelly and Long came from unknown circumstances (Long had some property in 1850; Kelly worked as a domestic in 1860), Fatio and the Dummetts came from slave-owning, landholding colonial era families. They, more than any others, embodied "the women and children of respectable planters" whom advocates of the resolution in Congress had cited. In 1860, Mary Dummett reported $1,250 in property (approximately $33,800 in 2010) and owned one enslaved person. Her son Douglass claimed an estate worth $15,000 (equivalent of $406,000 in 2010) and owned twelve enslaved persons. Daughter Anna Maria Dummett, who ran a boardinghouse in St. Augustine where she raised ten orphaned nieces and nephews, owned eight enslaved persons in 1860 in addition to her townhouse.[35]

Louisa Fatio also ran a boardinghouse in St. Augustine following the war, as did many other single and widowed women in the nineteenth century. Fatio was the granddaughter of Francis Philip Fatio, who arrived in British East Florida from Switzerland in 1777 and founded a ten-thousand-acre plantation on the St. Johns River. His descendants became prominent members of Florida society. In 1842, the widowed Louisa Fatio drew rations for herself at St. Augustine. She never remarried but remained in St.

Augustine where she, too, prospered, ran a boardinghouse, and raised orphaned nieces and nephews in a house on Aviles Street. She and the Dummetts attest that in 1842 even women from extremely wealthy planter families could not find food, even if they had the resources to buy it. Rather than leaving Florida and their land and connections behind, they weathered the war in St. Augustine, survived on government rations, and emerged in the 1850s with some of their wealth intact.[36] Collectively, all the women who drew rations in St. Augustine in 1842 illustrate that the suffering inhabitants policy, while it may have assisted some who were not totally indigent, did ensure that at least some of the white women and children widowed, orphaned, and displaced by the war stayed in Florida and raised successful children.

The rations recipients of St. Augustine were not the only aid recipients who behaved as policy makers hoped. Some of the women who drew rations at rural posts also stayed and eventually thrived. Rachel Board, Frances Wood, and Ann Monroe were neighbors near Garey's Ferry in 1840. All three women were widows by 1842. Rachel Board was in her twenties, drawing rations for herself at the post. Frances Wood was in her forties and received provisions for herself and three young children. Ann Monroe was the oldest, in her late fifties in 1840, and lived with a grown son but still received food for herself. Twenty years later, in 1860, all three still lived in Middleburg, the town built around Garey's Ferry. They remained neighbors for many years as their families intermarried and the numbers of children and grandchildren grew. All three women flourished on the eve of the Civil War, with property holdings in 1860 worth between $600 and $1,280 (roughly equivalent to between $202,000 and $430,000 in 2010). Board and Monroe, as well as Monroe's son, purchased their own land in the 1850s.[37] Although they were widows in need of aid during the Second Seminole War, each of them ended up as successful Florida farmers. Women willing to remain in Florida, like the widows of St. Augustine and Garey's Ferry, simultaneously mobilized a combination of two seemingly contradictory roles for women—as suffering victims and as successful, prosperous, civilizing colonists. Their children benefited from their risks and efforts, as did the nation.

Turning Sufferers into Settlers

Colonel William Worth, in command in Florida, wrote to Major David Wilcox, the officer in charge of the suffering inhabitants' rations rolls in the summer of 1841: "I desire to encourage those who have been compelled to abandon their farms or plantations to reoccupy the same, believing a few sturdy frontier settlers will operate a powerful influence upon the savage." Remarkably, Worth explicitly named settlers as part of his military campaign against the Seminoles and laid out a plan in which the military would continue to protect and provide for them on the condition that they return to abandoned farms or join new settlements. He suggested that settler-colonists should be protected by the military on their journeys back to the frontier, and that the federal government not only continue their rations but also give them guns and (most surprisingly) soldier's pay. Clearly he and other military leaders viewed male-headed family households as a replacement for troops or a corollary force for U.S. conquest.[38]

When the army began this shift from aiding victims to supporting settlements, it recruited some women from the lists of suffering inhabitants into resettlement parties with the threat that their rations would end if they did not go. They arrived with other families to parts of Florida recently abandoned by whites or forcibly vacated by Seminoles, often places where the military still could not guarantee their safety from Seminole attacks. Floridians had helped to prompt the recolonization program. As early as August 1839 Florida governor Richard K. Call had suggested the "government should invite people to settle in the territory and let them occupy the forsaken plantations free of rent or tax and also pay them monthly wages and furnish them with arms and ammunition to defend themselves and others. In this way there would be a gradual advance upon the Indians which would soon cause them to give up the contest." In the summer of 1841 the army adopted Governor Call's plan and advised Florida aid recipients to start making resettlement plans because their rations would soon end (unless they were especially pitiable). If they did leave for the frontier and planted immediately upon arrival, rations would continue through the next crop season.[39]

In July 1841 the War Department accepted the premise of this plan but rejected Worth's generous proposal of incentives, including the soldier's pay for armed settlers. Instead of paying them, military leaders used the dependence that the rations program had created to compel "sufferers" to become settlers. It continued to support the most indigent people with rations, but military leaders decided to stop rations altogether to push them to go find some other way to sustain themselves. Those who were able and willing to resettle the frontier therefore had to return to the frontier and begin planting, as the army would no longer give them rations simply to sustain them during the war. They had to earn their bread by permanently settling on the frontier.

The War Department's decision was likely motivated by political and gender concerns. While the expediency of the plan to pay settlers appealed to those serving in Florida, paying settlers to occupy Seminole territory would have admitted that white settlers risked their lives not simply for their own gain but in order to dispossess Native peoples and expand the United States, making explicit that they were hardly innocent bystanders in the conflict between the Seminoles and the United States. While expansionists touted freedom, independence, and the spread of democracy as the benefits of expansion, the act of paying colonists would have communicated that they were agents of a national force (not to mention the precedent that such a policy might set for other frontiers). It also would have indicated that the government was willing to put white women and children at risk to further expansionist policy goals. Paying civilians to settle would have challenged gender norms by revealing that policy makers believed families (including white women and children, and enslaved persons) were more effective than troops at wresting the Florida territory from the Seminoles.[40]

The new resettlement policy proved popular among Florida's displaced white residents. Although some of the aid recipients who had been promised soldier's pay balked when the War Department withdrew that incentive in July 1841, most eventually cooperated. Some widows, along with single and widowed men and married couples with children, joined resettlement parties headed by men (often veterans of the Second U.S.-Seminole War). The recolonization parties occupied nineteen sites in Florida, many of them vacant army forts and burned out Seminole towns, a material manifestation of the replacement of soldiers and Seminoles by settled families. In August 1841, for example, William Cason lead a party of white settlers to Fort White (see Figure 1) that included his own wife and children, seven other male-headed families, and widow Elizabeth Berry and her two children. By June 1842 there were over 1,400 people receiving rations from the army under the resettlement program. In addition to the nineteen groups making new settlements, 39 families returned to their abandoned farms. Among those "reoccupying plantations" and "making new settlements" there were 250 white women, 348 white children, 394 black enslaved people, and 446 white men. These individuals and families appeared on lists sent to military commanders in 1841 and 1842 along with the June 1842 accounting of the remaining 400 recipients, indicating which dependents (white widows, white children, and enslaved people) on the resettlement rolls had moved over from the list of those who received rations as "suffering inhabitants." Military leaders hoped that the new settlements including white women and children and enslaved blacks clearly signaled to the Seminoles that the whites had come to stay.[41]

Although they did not get soldier's pay, eventually these settlers received far more aid than the War Department originally intended. Rather than just a month's rations, they received rations to sustain their families and slaves through the next growing season, when they could once again feed themselves. They traveled with military guards and borrowed military horses, wagons, boats, and ferries to get to their new farms, passing through or inhabiting blockhouses and traveling down roads that the army expressly constructed for their safe passage. The American military literally cleared the way and protected them as they made their way to the settlements. After they arrived the military remained concerned about the moral character of those receiving government benefits. In the resettlement reports, officers noted that alcohol had negative effects on settlements, and the most successful ones were isolated from the trade in "ardent spirits."[42]

The strategy that Worth put in place in mid-1841 shifted the government's relationship to the white inhabitants of Florida from one of charity for worthy victims to one of reciprocal benefit, and therefore refocused attention on male settlers, away from female supplicants. Under the new policy, the government armed and supplied settler families because they were colonizers and civilizing agents who furthered national and military goals. Although both men and women populated the new settlement parties, the military emphasized that those who led and benefited from the resettlement policy were citizens—men with a stake in national expansion who could be explicitly drafted into the war effort. Without any fanfare, 250 white women joined them, in spite of the assumptions about female vulnerability. These women, alternatively understood as the indigent sufferers whose terrified cries had motivated and justified the suffering inhabitants policy, left the rolls of sufferers to join military-sponsored resettlement parties, drafted by the threat of starvation. The change restored individual men as "heads of families" to their role as providers and protectors. By transferring responsibility for white women and children back to male settlers, this policy reinstated gender and family norms in Florida, moving it closer to "civilized" status.

At the same time, by including former "suffering inhabitants," the military implicitly drafted women into the war effort. Women—their labor and the symbolism of their presence—were vital to the resettlement policy. Without women, children, and enslaved persons, the resettlement groups would have looked pretty similar to American troops, whose presence thus far had done little to sway the Seminoles. Yet chivalrous men were supposed to protect women, not deploy them in wars, and so policy makers and military leaders had to narrate their presence as "families" accompanying sturdy settlers. Although in 1836 Florida policy sought to aid and protect female victims, by 1841 it relied on the fact that women were brave colonizers (under the leadership of men, of course) who would enable the United States to finally take Florida from the Seminoles. In 1842, resettlement policy shifted again, as the next chapter discusses, with further emphasis on independent pioneers and limiting federal costs.

While it is clear that gender shaped these policies and changes in strategy, it is less clear how individual women reacted to them. Women were, in some ways, the pawns of policy makers and military leaders, who relied on their dependence and vulnerability to justify war and aid programs, and on their labor and symbolic power to make American homes in Florida. Yet policy makers were not all-powerful. Without white women's cooperation and complicity, (whether as direct recipients of aid or as the mothers, wives, sisters, and daughters whose labors sustained their households) the aid, resettlement, and armed occupation policies would have failed. White women took advantage of American policies in Florida, both as sufferers and as settlers. Along with white men, these women survived the war and then built and rebuilt homes and families on the Florida frontier. Their combined efforts displaced over four thousand Seminoles who surrendered to the army between 1836 and 1843.[43]

The shifts in Florida policy in 1841 were not only practical strategies to end the war and establish white settlements, they were also characteristic of American patterns of social provision and expansion. For example, the fear that entitlements encouraged idleness and dependence often resulted in reforms requiring aid recipients to work, and in this case many of those who continued to receive federal benefits had to recolonize a dangerous frontier. Americans historically rewarded citizens who supported national goals with entitlements, and in Florida some citizens who settled in dangerous country received food, transportation, and home-building assistance. Benefits for military service in wartime comprised a massive portion of social provision in the nineteenth century, and American defense spending has always funded "loyalty benefits," or social and medical provision for military service members, veterans, and their families. The rations provided to Second U.S.-Seminole War victims in territorial Florida are one example of welfare spending in the American military budget. Although the War Department did not approve it, Worth's 1841 proposal to compensate Florida settlers with soldier's pay also would have granted benefits usually reserved for soldiers to settlers who served on a violent frontier.[44]

Some historians argue that there is a connection between war spending and social spending. Libertarian Murray Rothbard uses the term "welfare-warfare state" to describe how the American state enlarged itself using social welfare provisions and emergency war measures that it never fully retracted. Furthering national expansion on a violent frontier rendered one a worthy recipient of federal aid in Florida, which illustrates the historical connections between the growth of social provision alongside national boundaries. Many of the military conflicts of the nineteenth century—when this pattern in social welfare policy began—were directly related to expansion and fought to dispossess and remove Native Americans.[45]

In the context of a broader policy history, the Florida aid programs of 1836–1841 illustrate how political and military leaders used deeply gendered federal social provisions as expansionist policy, a pattern of policy making that shaped national growth before, after, and beyond Florida. Federal social spending in frontier Florida illustrates how closely domestic welfare aligned with expansionist policies, not a surprising result once one takes into consideration the significance of white women and domesticity to settler colonialism and Manifest Destiny. Americans who wanted to expand national territory, oust Seminoles, and support permanent white settlement and patriarchal families understood that they needed white women to accomplish those goals. The evolution of policy in Florida suggests three important conclusions related to the linkages between welfare, expansion, and gender.

First, gender has shaped expansion and welfare so profoundly that locating their historical connection requires challenging social assumptions about men and women. Politicians and pundits typically do not classify men as "welfare" recipients. The entitlements granted to American men are presumed to be deserved rather than charitable. Women rarely appear as significant actors in territorial conquest; they are usually the victims or pioneering helpmeets. As this chapter about a short period on a specific frontier has revealed, aid programs aimed at women were part of a larger military strategy of conquest, and military policies aimed at supporting male-led settlement parties were also a form of social provision. As this chapter argues, the United States used "domestic" matters such as the welfare of widows, orphans, and families to support military efforts to enlarge the nation. Highlighting this illuminates how social policy enlarged not only the welfare state but the territorial nation as well.[46]

Illuminating the connections between welfare and expansion highlights how gender shaped policies that supported national growth. While welfare studies have historically attended to the influence of gender, studies of federal expansionist policies have not, in part because policy makers often implicitly included women, while they explicitly recruited men to be pioneers. As political and cultural speech, policy cannot be trusted to be completely truthful about either its intents or outcomes. In Florida highly gendered expansionist policies supported both Indian removal and white settlement because gender naturalized female recipients' dependence and cast federal support for men as empowerment for "independent" household heads. In many other contexts, Americans used land, disaster relief, and veteran's benefits policy (including land bounties) to settle frontier zones, but the degree to which gender underwrote those policies is unexplored in many studies. A second important conclusion, then, is that histories of national expansion will benefit from gendered analyses of expansionist policy making, because policy makers justified and naturalized material support for expansion using gender (protecting women, enabling hardy men). Products of antebellum culture, they had very powerful expectations about how properly gendered, white households could serve national goals of settlement, expansion, and Indian removal.

Finally, looking at the histories of gender, welfare, and expansion together brings women into focus as historical actors complicit with American imperialism. The literature on social provision emphasizes that women were often its beneficiaries; connecting that history to national expansion makes it clear that white women were also important to efforts that ousted Native Americans and enlarged the country. A third conclusion, then, is that white women were important subjects and actors in national expansion, not just helpers or civilian casualties. While this has been clear to historians of women for a long time, histories of expansion that focus on military campaigns, federal policy, and foreign affairs have yet to incorporate women and their labor (what I call expansionist domesticity) fully into narratives of American expansion and Manifest Destiny. Much as they have shaped federal policies, gender norms have shaped historical scholarship about frontier settlement, making it difficult to conceive of the presence of female settlers as politically significant. The growing body of scholarship about gender and expansion has begun to address the role of manhood and womanhood in U.S. expansion. As this and other studies have noted, the version of manhood most useful to national expansionist goals required a complementary womanhood and the presence of white women and children. White women's active complicity with aggressive expansion has been highlighted by historians such as Jean Stuntz, Amy Greenberg, and Robert May, who have linked several white female boosters to the Manifest Destiny of the 1840s and 1850s. As they and other historians of women and gender have already illustrated, women operated as actors and agents, as well as sympathetic victims and symbols of civilization, in American history. This should be no less true in political and military studies of territorial expansion.[47]

The suffering inhabitants and recolonization policies spent federal resources to support expansionist domesticity—the settlement of white American families—in Florida. The rhetoric and programs that linked social spending to national interests in Florida relied on gendered logic and on the presence of white women in frontier Florida, whose number increased as a result. Beyond the individuals and families on the ration and resettlement rolls, Florida's overall white population increased after 1840 (from 27,943 to 47,203 in 1850), and the number of white females increased more than any other group (adding 10,011 white females between 1840 and 1850). This population growth accompanied the policies described in this chapter as well as the increase in settlement following the Armed Occupation Act, discussed in the next chapter. These policies were precedents for later federal entitlements that supported national expansion, and thus helped establish that U.S. policy makers would provide for the welfare of citizens who furthered national goals, not simply those in need. Through expansionist policies, America leaders established the roots of the modern welfare state, supported white settler colonialism, and reinforced white patriarchal gender norms. The history of white settlement in Florida suggests that expansionist domesticity, in addition to concern for social welfare, shaped early patterns of social provision in the United States. As U.S. soldiers terrorized and removed Seminole families in the 1830s and 1840s, they actively replaced them with white ones whom they fed, protected, and championed as the leading edge of American civilization.[48]

CHAPTER 5

Gender and Settler Colonialism

> The country wants settlers, not an army.
> —Senator Thomas Hart Benton, January 7, 1840

> Since the close of the war . . . hundreds daily flock into the country to look up lands to speculate on & take up those tracts offered by the government under the armed occupation law. . . . In a very few years this territory will be more thickly settled than any of the Southern states & far more prosperous.
> —Corinna Brown Aldrich, April 30, 1843

In July 1842, as the Second U.S.-Seminole War was finally winding down, members of the U.S. House of Representatives considered a land bill that would arm white settlers and reward them with free land in exchange for colonizing Florida. Following a long and expensive war, national leaders sought a plan that would settle the territory with the least federal investment, absolve the nation of responsibility for defending it, and exploit its natural resources to the greatest effect. Proponents of the bill believed it would put an end to Indian depredations, "the atrocities which so frequently harrowed up our feelings," and "assist in stimulating a new state into the Union." Also, the law would avoid "the disgrace of being beaten by a few savages" by securing the border "as a rampart against the encroachments of the Indians." Opponents of the law called it a "fraud on the public" that would arm settlers who would "turn sportsmen, and range at pleasure . . . in pursuit of game." Supporters retaliated by deleting the section of the bill that furnished guns and ammunition. They replaced it with a remarkable provision that granted additional land for settler's wives. John Pope (Kentucky Whig) contended: "By encouraging men to take their families with them, a more permanent settlement would be effected. Men who were not able to buy land, would be willing to fight for it; and, by giving their wives a sufficient inducement, they would be willing to go with them." David Levy, a Democrat and the Florida Territory's delegate to Congress, also favored giving the proposed land bounty to the wives, "not only on account of it being due them for the hardships and privations they would have to encounter, but because this inducement to families would give permanency to the settlements."[1]

Thus white American leaders continued to believe that white women were essential to their colonization plans. Although they presumed that settlers were men (as their references to settlers and their wives reveals), they also believed that ideal settlers were married, and that they needed to offer incentives to attract married white women to Florida. In the previous decade, U.S. policies aimed at creating permanent white settlement had made Florida attractive to white women by entrenching a proslavery and pro–white settler legal regime that granted women property rights, and by offering them rations and safety during the war brought about by the Indian removal policy intended to clear the way for their safe and permanent settlement. The new law built on previous "suffering inhabitants" and recolonization policies, while it also recruited new residents with the promise of land. White wives in Florida gained the opportunity to receive free "public" land alongside white men in hopes that this would bring even more of them south into Florida.[2]

The land bill that finally passed into law differed slightly from the version debated in the House in July, as the provision for wives disappeared in conference, but white women remained eligible for free land in Florida. Signed by President John Tyler on August 4, 1842, the Armed Occupation Act (AOA) stipulated that any "head of a family" or single man over eighteen, able to bear arms, could claim 160 acres of public land south of the "line of settlement" in Florida, and that upon building a house and cultivating five acres over the course of five years, the government would grant armed occupiers permanent title to the land. The language of the AOA bill made single or widowed women tacitly eligible for its benefits if they claimed to be heads of families (just as women had been implicitly included in resettlement parties).[3] The passage of the bill and its effects in Florida reveal how a subtle shift in rhetoric rendered white women less openly visible in Florida policy, while their implied role actually enabled some white women to claim their own land. Forty single women sought to claim free public land in Florida in 1842 and 1843. Five of them, ironically, were widows who had qualified as suffering inhabitants in June of 1842.[4] Many more widows, daughters, and sisters eventually inherited land originally applied for by male kin. These women and their families and neighbors furthered U.S. territorial goals in Florida even as they built wealth for themselves on land very recently inhabited by Seminoles.

As members of Congress negotiated the new land policy, they once again drew on assumptions about white women and men and the skills they would bring to colonizing Florida. U.S. leaders believed that unsettled land was not fully secured, and that single white male settlers would be unsuccessful without the family members who would provide the labor necessary to permanently colonize the soil (and it appears they were correct, as most successful settlers were members of extended family groups). Settlers' wives were necessary because they ensured that white men were domesticators as well as conquerors, but white women were not explicitly hailed as colonizers. Single and widowed women's implied eligibility left an opening for them to support settlement in Florida, and get free land for doing so, without violating gender norms with an explicit invitation. Thus Congress quietly enlisted white women to help permanently colonize Florida.

As policy makers moved away from welfare for victims of Seminole violence, and toward land entitlements for settlers, they continued to support patriarchal families and expansionist domesticity. The suffering inhabitants policy had replaced absent men with public support. In keeping with their desire to support family settlement in Florida, members of Congress designed the AOA to directly support white households headed by married couples, believing in the power of expansionist domesticity.

Gender must not be overlooked in the dynamic relationship between welfare, land policy, and national expansion. Policy makers often implicitly included women in pro-expansion policies, while they explicitly recruited men. The desire to support independent men and help dependent women shaped the debates, content, and implementation of policies (while also making it easy to overlook male "suffering inhabitants" and female "armed occupiers" by using gendered assumptions about who suffers and who settles to pass aid policies). While the Armed Occupation Act appeared to recognize only white men as potential beneficiaries, in reality white women benefited from it as they did from other expansionist entitlements. As political and cultural speech, policy (like Indian depredation narratives) cannot be trusted to be completely truthful about either its intents or outcomes. The AOA's vaguely gendered policy language exploited white women's work for settlement without explicitly rewarding women or acknowledging the importance of their domesticating labor, but it did allow individual women to capitalize on expansion. It also finalized the dispossession of the Seminoles and Black Seminoles and ended the freedom Florida had once offered to people fleeing slavery.[5]

Congress Debates Giving Away Land

Originally suggested to military leaders by Florida governor Richard K. Call, the idea of awarding frontier settlers with land had been championed by pro-expansion senator Thomas Hart Benton (Missouri Democrat) since the late 1830s. The idea was very popular among Florida's territorial leaders and residents, but Benton found less support in Washington. He tried but failed to pass free land bills for Florida in 1839 and in 1840.[6]

In the late 1830s, Florida's future was uncertain, but Americans remained invested in its potential. As Senator Benton proposed the 1840 version of the bill, he reminded his opponents in Congress that Florida's natural resources were vast and promising; many thousands of acres of land for farming and logging were at stake, as well as important ports on the Atlantic and the Gulf of Mexico. The federal government also stood to gain from the sale of public land if Florida could be made attractive to white settlers and speculators. White citizens hoped to settle farms and plantations in Florida, where the labor of their families and slaves would make them comfortable and even wealthy. The problem, of course, was that a force of Seminoles and Black Seminoles threatened those white settlers already in Florida, and so far an expensive and protracted war had not succeeded in ousting them. Florida, in 1840, was costing a lot more money than it was generating. Many Americans were confident that the Seminoles and their black allies would soon be defeated and removed and that the territory would soon enter the nation as a slave state, but neither of those things was yet accomplished.[7]

As the measure stalled in Congress, Charles Downing (Florida's territorial delegate to Congress, 1837–1841) brought a resolution to Washington from Florida's territorial government that proposed that the U.S. cede all the public land in Florida to the Territory, which would sell the land to settlers to raise funds for a volunteer army to fight the Seminoles. Frustrated with ineffective federal and military policies in Florida, territorial leaders supported liquidating Florida's land wealth to fund the war, and believed such a strategy could combine Indian removal with white settlement. If this resolution had passed (it was tabled in the House) the Florida Territory, rather than the United States, would have profited from the land sales. Since the Northwest Ordinance of 1787, national leaders had planned to finance the federal government with public land sales, and they did not change course in Florida.[8]

As Floridians pressured federal leaders to act, Benton returned to the Senate with another version of his bill. Advocating for this new law, Benton emphasized the influence that white settlers would exert on Seminole resistance: "The heart of the Indian sickens when he hears the crowing of the cock, the barking of the dog, the sound of the axe and the crack of the rifle. They are the true evidences of the dominion of the white man; these are the proof that the owner has come, and means to stay; and then they feel it is time for them to go."[9] White women were conspicuously absent in the colonization tableau that Benton illustrated for his colleagues in the Senate. He did not explicitly hail women as the cry of a new baby or the sound of a dinner bell might have done. This absence is striking, given that the bloodcurdling screams of women and children under Seminole attack had so lately filled the Florida soundscape. Previously Benton had invoked a patriarchal version of domesticity as key to a healthy republic. "The tenant has, in fact, no country, no hearth, no domestic altar, no household god. The freeholder, on the contrary, is the natural supporter of a free government, and it should be the policy of republics to multiply their freeholders," he had argued in 1826.[10] Benton emphasized the importance of "the hearth" in creating a republic of settled, white patriarchal households. By 1842, that emphasis on domesticity continued but shifted to focus on the male householder: the "people" he invoked to take and keep possession of the land were men with guns, axes, roosters, and dogs—armed men, but domesticated ones. Implicitly, as will become clear, they were men with families, whose hearths featured domestic altars and household gods.

Benton's choice to focus on male settlers represented a gendered rhetorical strategy. While previous policies in support of expansion in Florida had relied on white women's vulnerability to justify federal spending, support for this measure faltered when politicians invoked white women attacked by Seminoles. Given nineteenth-century gender conventions, how could they justify sending white women into an ongoing Indian war in the hopes that their presence would bring that war to an end? As the dependents of white men, women were supposed to be protected, not recruited to be members of an occupying force. Leaders like Benton believed, however, that families were necessary to creating permanent settlements, and they recognized that populating Florida's southern peninsula with white settlers required some incentive to convince families to take the risk. Florida was largely wilderness and swamps and still inhabited by a few Seminoles. The Second U.S.-Seminole War had been brought on by, justified with, and narrated as a series of Seminole attacks on white women and children. If politicians suggested that the Native Americans were gone and the territory safe for women and children, they forfeited the original justification for the policy—that armed settlers would finally defeat the Seminoles. If there were no more Seminoles, then (their opponents asked) why should the government give settlers free land? To persuade opponents of the bill, therefore, Benton and his allies refocused the policy on armed male settlers, deemphasizing Seminole threats to white women and children. The ideal male settler was, however, definitively located within a domestic realm in which he had a family life and pursued political and economic strategies to protect and provide for his family.

To persuade their opponents, pro-AOA congressmen rhetorically erased Seminoles, their free black allies who had escaped slavery, and women, while their opposition highlighted them. This strategy is clear in the changing titles of proposed Florida land policies. The law proposed in 1839 was titled "A Bill to Provide for the Armed Occupation and Settlement of That Part of Florida which is Now Overrun and Infested by Marauding Bands of Hostile Indians," which was followed by the House resolution titled "A Bill More Effectually to Protect the Lives and Property of the People of Florida, and to Bring the Seminole War to an End." While Indian removal, an active war, and the protection of white Floridians were clearly the justifications for these earlier bills, the final statute was entitled "A Bill to Provide for the Armed Occupation and Settlement of the Unsettled Part of the Peninsula of East Florida," a title that emphasized settlement over warfare, and did not reference the Seminoles at all.[11]

These different framings of the debate about Florida policy turned on several questions, each of which had both gendered and racial significance.

One central question in the debate was the government's proper role in territorial expansion: should it protect or reward those who risked their lives extending its frontiers? Opposition to the AOA came from southern conservatives and abolitionists who objected to anything framed as federal aid in Florida, though for different reasons. Elite southerners did not want the federal government to favor small landholders over powerful planters and land speculators, while antislavery leaders argued that the AOA would inappropriately spend federal resources to quickly settle another slave state, strengthening the position of proslavery interests in the country. To counter them, proponents had to reframe the policy as a reward for those who expanded the country, rather than an expensive aid program. This choice was highly gendered; aid would have implied that Americans were dependent on their government, as women were dependent on men, and implicitly suggested that federal policies properly targeted women and children for aid (although recipients might be male or female). Policies framed as reward, however, implied that settlers served the country, indicating that men were the proper targets for policy (through whom women and children would benefit).

I argue that Benton failed to win support for the bill in 1840 because he used the well-worn representation of Florida's white settlers as victims who deserved federal help as they weathered a "humiliating and mortifying" Indian war.[12] The 1840 version had also included a host of added benefits for settlers, such as guns, military protection and transportation, a year of rations and ammunition, grain and vegetable seeds, medicines, and a clothing allowance, in addition to free public land. (These benefits were very similar to some of those offered under the 1841 recolonization program instituted by the military as it phased out the suffering inhabitants program.) All these benefits contributed to the image of this policy as aid rather than reward. Opponents worried that the government might bankrupt itself giving away land and provisions even as it forfeited profits from the sale of public lands, while the settlers gave nothing and received a bounty of land.[13]

A second major question raised in the policy debates concerned the status of the territory: was the war truly almost over? A free land policy for white families was appropriate only if Florida was a safe place for settlers to bring their wives, children, and the enslaved people who supported white settler colonies. In the 1839 version of the bill settlers would receive title to their land whenever the Seminoles were finally removed and the territory peaceful, which implied that it was not yet peaceful. Further, while this seemed logical in early 1839, when the press predicted the end of the war was near, two or three years later Americans no longer assumed that the Seminoles would ever or could ever be completely removed.[14] In early January 1840, Benton reintroduced his bill with a provision that settlers would get the title to their claims after five years of continuous occupancy. Attempting to finesse the question of whether the war was nearing its close, Benton described armed occupation as simultaneously a way to end the war and a way to settle the postwar territory. Anticipating Brigadier General William J. Worth's plan to give settlers military pay in 1841, and hoping to frame free public land as reward rather than aid, Benton contended that the land the settlers would receive would be payment for military service. This implied that the war was not yet over and that settlers would become part of it. At another point in the debate, Benton indicated that armed settlers were needed to settle territory after it has been conquered: "Armed occupation, with land to the occupant, is the true way of settling and holding a *conquered* country.... We want people to take possession and to keep possession." Here Benton placed them on an already conquered frontier.[15] In spite of this, many senators balked at the idea of using settlers—which would include women and children—to conquer as well as to colonize. Some, like Representative Samuel Stokely (Ohio Whig) believed that married men with families settled with the most promise of permanency, as their wives and families bound them to their farms and stimulated them to work diligently.[16] The war, however, was not yet over. Senator William Campbell Preston (South Carolina Whig) wanted further military action in Florida rather than a force of armed settlers. Congress did not have the power to make "armed settlements" as they did to make war, and conquest was a job for men, while subsequent colonization by settlers included women and children. Others agreed, and the bill failed in 1840.[17]

In addition to American troops, the presence of Seminoles and Black Seminoles determined whether or not leaders believed the territory was peaceful enough for white slaveholding families to settle it. Opponents of the AOA made racial threats central to the problem of Florida. One congressman offered a jocularly racist alternative to free land, and suggested replacing soldiers and bloodhounds in Florida with whiskey, which would conquer the Seminoles (portrayed as drunken "savages" unable to control themselves) through liquid means and make a nice profit for American distilleries.[18] To most, however, Seminoles and Black Seminoles were a deadly serious threat in Florida. According to Senator Preston, "The fastnesses of Florida are now filled by a strange intermixture of negroes and savages. It is an asylum for runaway negroes; and do you propose to send a slave population there, who will have every inducement to join the Indians?" Not only was Florida rife with rebellious slaves, Preston also claimed that Florida could not be settled without black labor, because its lands were "low and dangerous to the health of the Anglo-Saxon blood, and inviting only to those who had slaves to perform their labor."[19] Until the Seminoles and their black allies were vanquished, whites could not colonize Florida. Invoking fears of a slave rebellion in Florida, and an increase among the "negro Indians" allied with the Seminoles against the United States, Preston made Seminoles and Black Seminoles visible and direct threats to white people and U.S. interests in Florida. Recognizing the importance of race, Senator Benton explicitly argued for expansion as a racial project. He contended: "We owe assistance and protection to these people from humanity and compassion. *They are white people and Christians*. They are of our own race; they have suffered every extremity and every horror known to Indian warfare. The *mother and the babe, the father and his children, the husband and his wife, the slave and his master*, all, all have been doomed to one undistinguished massacre."[20]

Again relying on the Indian depredation formula, Benton argued that the federal government, and perhaps the whole nation, owed some remuneration to Florida's white settlers who had suffered Seminole attacks. The attacks threatened the social order itself, as household protectors (mothers, husbands, and masters) had been massacred along with the dependents they and the nation had failed to protect (babies, wives, and slaves). Giving them free land would establish civilization in Florida by installing ordered, white, slaveholding households there to replace the violent and disorderly Seminoles and maroons.[21] This argument failed because it represented Native Americans and blacks as present threats in Florida, and because it linked land bounties for whites to their victimization, rather than framing land as reward for their service.

Since whiteness did not recruit more support, Benton tried to deemphasize the presence of nonwhites in Florida. Arguing (again) that the war had accomplished its goals, Benton and his allies dismissed the continuing depredations as the work of a few stragglers, a marauding band of maybe a dozen Seminoles who would eventually die out. "As warriors, these Indians no longer appear; it is only as assassins, as robbers, as incendiaries, that they lurk about. The country wants settlers, not an army." The best way to get rid of them, the senator argued, was to occupy their land, deny them the opportunity to feed themselves, and overwhelm them with white settlements. Benton had begun to understand that he needed to make the Seminoles and rebellious slaves appear to be a contained threat, and to represent settlers as independent men rather than victimized families, before his bill would pass.[22]

He soon shifted to a new argument: that the United States needed some hardy and determined white settler families, who would bring weapons, farm tools, and civilization to Florida. "The blockhouse [a small, isolated fortress] is the first house to be built in an Indian country.... Within that blockhouse ... safe habitations are found for families.... Cultivation and defence then goes hand in hand," Benton opined. While the idea of combining conquest with settlement had not worked in 1840, it did in 1842 because of the shift from deserving war victims to rewarding frontier families. That shift emphasized white male settlers and de-emphasized white female victims and the Seminoles and maroons who threatened them. Benton noted, "While soldiers alone are in the country, they feel their presence to be temporary.... It is the settler alone, the armed settler, whose presence announces the dominion of the white man." Indeed, it was not the settler "alone" but the settler and his wife and family (to the exclusion of the soldier) who would establish white dominion in Florida. Explicitly white, and implicitly partly female, the force of armed settlers that Benton invoked would oust the Seminoles, control slaves, and settle the territory. Offering land in exchange for the danger of settling in territory populated by Native Americans was the most effective and efficient way to settle "new countries," Benton believed. These were proper inducements, and would attract, he hoped, ten thousand armed, white settlers—also hailed as American families—to the Florida frontier.[23]

Although strong, brave, white men were paramount, white women's role in settlement was discussed in debates leading up to the passage of the AOA bill. In the House of Representatives it passed only after lawmakers added the amendment (described at the beginning of this chapter) that recruited female participation in the plan. In support of the 1842 bill, Representative Stokely argued that "the presence of the families would bind the settlers to the soil" and that women had "a most happy effect in stimulating the courage and enterprise of their male relatives."[24] He convinced other leaders that "the hardships and privations to be encountered by the settlers would justly entitle the women to the compensation proposed to be given them."[25] Stokely noted that the extra provisions offered in the 1840 bill (rations, arms, ammunition) had been removed and replaced with a clause explicitly aimed at encouraging women to accompany men. The amendment granted further benefit to the wife or children of the original settler who, with proof of actual settlement, cultivation, and four years continual residence, were entitled to an additional 160 acres of land adjoining that of the initial family settlement.[26] Legislators also decided to reserve the sixteenth section of each township for a school, following a provision for public education included in the Land Ordinance of 1785.[27]

Apparently, what national expansion required, more than hardy male settlers with guns and food, were wives and children to support them and tie them permanently to the soil. White men became effective settlers, U.S. policy makers believed, only when located at the head of white settler families, situated firmly within expansionist domesticity. This domestic location would encourage them to pursue economic and political goals consistent with white settler colonialism, unlike the goals that soldiers, absentee slave holders, or land speculators might pursue as bachelors or patriarchs whose families lived elsewhere. The provision for additional land adjoining the household head's land claim laid out women's proper role in this settlement scheme. Lawmakers presumed that they would assist male settlers; therefore women would be protected from Seminoles and runaway slaves but still deserved the reward of land. Invoking women and families also framed Florida as a home front rather than a war zone. If wives and children were turning Florida into a territory full of homes, then acts of aggression against Seminoles could continue to be recast as acts of self-defense (as they were in Indian depredation stories). Furthermore, regardless of reality, or of federal or military decisions, this indicated that the war was nearly over because in this framing there were no more armies conquering territory or Seminoles attacking farms, just innocent white families building homes. As in typical white settler colonial origin stories, a landscape of supposedly apolitical domestic spaces obscured the presence of a colonial regime backed up by military might.

Sometime before August 4, 1842, when the president signed the new law, the section granting additional land to wives and children was deleted from the bill, perhaps in conference after it passed both houses.[28] This is surprising because the clause "in favor of the women" was stridently defended by several proponents of the bill in a July 18, 1842, debate in the House of Representatives.[29] In contrast, Representative William Cost Johnson (Maryland Whig), by far the most vehement opponent of the bill, had also played to the gender stereotypes of the Jacksonian era when he proposed that the law should not go into effect until the Secretary of War issued a proclamation that "the armed settlers, men, women, and children, provided for in the bill, are more available troops than the gallant army of the United States."[30] It may be that this type of opposition, in defense of the manhood of the military, resulted in the deletion of the amendment, but neither the House nor Senate journal reveals precisely when that happened. Since this provision was eventually removed from the law, no wives filed for adjacent acreage, but women did apply for their own independent permits close to relatives, inherited claims from fathers and husbands, and worked to create permanent homes on claims made by male kin.[31]

The final Senate debate on the AOA was equally gender conscious but focused on the male settlers congressmen hoped the law would attract. Previous opponent Senator Preston finally supported the bill because it would "encourage poor and destitute, but vigorous, energetic, and hardy men, who were filled with enterprise" to go to Florida "and grapple with the Indian, and root him out for the sake of the bounty." Other "industrious and enterprising" southern migrants would be more willing to risk Florida once the AOA had interposed a "hardy population" between them and the Seminoles. Then "they would move there with their families and with their slaves, and settle and cultivate the soil."[32] AOA settlers were the opening wedge for white settlement and the spread of slavery into southeastern Florida, developments that Preston could easily support. Senators were far more focused on recruiting the right kind of man for the job of settling Florida than hailing wives and children as cosettlers. In spite of the House of Representatives' generosity with settler wives, proponents apparently had to shift the focus away from women to secure its passage.

With explicit invocations of strong men, the AOA passed. It promised 160 acres of land to "white settlers, being heads of families, or young men able to bear arms" who settled south of the "line of settlement" (between township lines 9 and 10, roughly south of Gainesville, thus encouraging settlers to move farther south than the more settled region of north Florida). Those eligible included "any person, being the head of a family, single man, or young man over eighteen years of age, able to bear arms . . . who makes an actual settlement." Any gender-unspecified "head of a family" was eligible, a loophole that allowed women to claim land under the AOA, perhaps left open by lawmakers after the amendment regarding women was omitted in the final law. While widows had been ideal images of suffering inhabitants, women were hardly the quintessential image of an armed settler. Lawmakers clearly believed, however, that white women's domesticating and reproductive capacities were needed on the Florida frontier. Thus, they invoked an expansionist domesticity directed by men. Although young, single men were eligible, other stipulations indicated that lawmakers presumed that such settlers would not remain single forever but make permanent homes at the head of growing white families, as discussed below.[33]

The debate about Florida land policy occurred as military policy changed in Florida and as national leaders debated many other land laws. The army began shifting its "suffering inhabitants" aid program into a reward system for those who would return to or make new settlements in 1841, so the military and federal government's desire to colonize more of Florida's territory with whites was already manifest. There were U.S. precedents for generous public land policies for men, including the land bounties granted to veterans. In the 1830s and 1840s, Congress was also hotly debating several other public land policies, including graduation and preemption schemes. Under a graduation policy, any public land that did not sell at the base price would gradually reduce in price. Preemption, which passed in 1830 for previous squatters, allowed those who settled on public land they did not own to buy it before it was offered at public auction at a base government price ($1.25/acre), "preempting" the sale of their farms at auction, which speculators or wealthier pioneers might otherwise buy out from under them. In 1841, Congress passed a law extending preemption to future squatters. The 1841 law remade criminal, trespassing squatters into "the virtuous 'actual settlers' of the Jeffersonian agrarian ideal."[34] Preemption made legal the practices of white settler colonialism that had operated as de facto expansionist policy for nearly a century. Thus, in Washington and in Florida in the early 1840s, leaders were reframing squatters and settlers as the heroic vanguard of national expansion. The Florida Armed Occupation Act of 1842, which extended these measures into free public land for armed settlers, drew on similar ideas: bona fide settlers deserved to get their land for free (or at the lowest government price) because they risked their lives and families to colonize dangerous territories still defended by resistant Native Americans. White settlers' presence created communities of opportunity in the early republic for other whites, and encouraged Native Americans to leave.[35]

As federal leaders developed ever more generous land policies, the passage of the AOA was further aided by the official announcement of the war's end, since this was key to establishing that Florida was now ready to be colonized. On May 10, 1842, President Tyler announced the termination of the Second U.S.-Seminole War and stated that he hoped the Congress would soon authorize a supply of arms, ammunition, and food for settlers willing to migrate south. Benton's AOA bill passed several months later on August 4, 1842. Ten days after that Brigadier General William Jenkins Worth announced an end to the fighting in Florida. Seminole attacks on whites continued, however, and the army captured several Seminoles after the August announcement of the end of the war. The war was not really ended before the AOA passed, although American soldiers had removed most of the Seminoles and Black Seminoles by the end of 1842.[36]

"Armed Occupiers" Colonize Florida

Corinna Brown Aldrich, who had moved to Florida with her sister a few years before the Second U.S.-Seminole War, wrote to her brother about the AOA in September 1842:

> One excellent provision is that no person can hold the bounty of land unless he builds a house upon it, and makes other improvement suitable for a white man to live in. By this means the *mal* [bad] will be kept out, and the country inhabited by respectable people and those who have something to begin with. The land is rich enough for such even to jump at the advantages offered. George [their brother] seems quite delighted at the prospects held out to him. God grant him success—he will deserve it—for he is an upright, honest & industrious young man.[37]

Although she assumed that AOA settlers would be men, Corinna voiced the assumptions about who was civilized and deserved the rewards of settlement in Florida; honest, hard-working and respectable people of some means who would build homes "suitable" for white families (in distinction to the supposedly uncivilized homes of Seminoles or the flimsy cabins absentee slaveholders erected to house enslaved people).

The new law required settlers to get a permit from the land office, reside on his *or her* claim for five consecutive years, erect a house "fit for the habitation of man," and clear, enclose, and cultivate at least five acres of land. The law did not specify a house fit for a *white* family, but Corinna Brown's assumption was surely presumed by lawmakers. Settlers could not claim lands within two miles of U.S. military installations, and policy makers moved the line of settlement even farther south in the final bill. Both of these requirements required settlers to colonize parts of Florida that were not under American control at the close of the war. Settlers also had to provide their own defense, although the United States loaned them guns and ammunition if they could not acquire them. In order to attract new settlers and those who could not otherwise afford to come, the General Land Office specified that eligible settlers could not already own 160 acres in Florida. Enslaved and free blacks and (of course) Native Americans were excluded. Only whites were eligible, and since they had to build a dwelling and live on the claim for five years, absentee slaveholders could not deploy enslaved blacks to fulfill the settlement requirements. As these explicit requirements and exclusions highlight, white women became eligible settlers because they were white people who would help colonize the territory.[38]

Although the language of the AOA left open that female "heads of families" could apply for AOA permits, the land officials tasked with carrying out the AOA found it too vague (just as the language of the Adams-Onís Treaty had stumped the first American lawmakers in Florida regarding the legal rights of married women). In early 1843 the land agent in St. Augustine, William Simmons, wrote to Thomas Blake, commissioner of the General Land Office, that he was not sure whether the law was intended to include women. In response, Blake pointed out that the law stipulated terms for "his or her settlement" at one point, and that settlers were referred to as "he, she, or they" in another part. Based upon the inclusion of these pronouns, Blake admonished the land agent to make sure that the testimony of AOA permit applicants met the law's requirements regardless of gender. For female applicants, those requirements were that they should have sons or enslaved laborers capable of farming and male relatives who could defend them. This would ensure that female settlers had male protectors as well as laborers to provide for them, ensconced in a civilized and ordered household.[39]

While it is somewhat surprising that single women were granted the same land rights as male settlers in Florida in 1842, it would have been more shocking if those rights had been explicitly granted rather than implicitly allowed. Simmons's question about women's eligibility points to the fact that it seemed to contradict the gender norms of the time; why else would he have questioned it in a law that specifically mentioned "his or her" settlements? In response, Blake relied on two instances of female pronouns to decide that women were eligible, which points to implicit mention of women in a discourse that was focused on male settlers. Also, these women did not threaten gender norms because they signified the presence of families, not independent female landholders. Congressmen were wedded to the vision of the hardy yet domestic male settler accompanied by his family, and assumed that any white women who settled under the AOA would be wives, not heads of families. They likely understood the eligibility of "female heads of families" as an extension of aid to war widows, who would claim land that their sons would later inherit. Such pioneer mothers did not threaten the gender order, and they would join the force of armed white families spreading civilization. Finally, attracting white women to the territory helped create an eligible pool of potential wives for unmarried male settlers, and widows with land would make ideal partners for the "arms-bearers" on the frontier. Several female settlers did remarry men who had AOA claims near their own.[40]

In spite of the incentive of free land, continuing violence between whites and Seminoles in Florida initially discouraged many settlers from filing AOA permits. In September 1842, an entire family was wiped out by a Seminole attack in West Florida, and another band of Seminoles killed Charlotte Crum, wife of a Florida militiaman, in Benton County.[41] The remaining threat of indigenous violence in Florida did not discourage settlement boosters, however. They simply used it to justify the AOA as the next step to defeating the Seminoles left in Florida, just as lawmakers had simultaneously argued that the war was over, the territory safe for settlement, and settlement necessary to end the war. While conditions in Florida could have supported a continuing policy emphasis on protecting white women and children, national leaders passed a new law that made male settlers central to national expansion. This was, as Laura Jensen termed it, "a stunning example of the Government's construction of the settler ideal in Jacksonian public policy."[42]

One thousand, three hundred and twelve people filed permits to settle under the AOA in 1842 and 1843, announcing their intention to claim about 210,000 acres of land in the southern peninsula. Only 459 of the AOA settlers got their land title after five years. The relatively low percentage of successful AOA settlers was probably due in part to the difficulty of complying with land office requirements. Settlers had to report to a land office, all of which were in north Florida, three times: initially to apply for their permit; after one year to file proof of settlement; and after five years to attest that they were still living on that farm. Their neighbors had to supply affidavits swearing that the settlers had built a house "fit for the habitation of man" (beyond that there were no explicit specifications) on their selected parcel of land and cultivated crops on it.[43] Heavy rains in the mid-1840s made much of the territory impassable, which meant that surveyors could not get out to survey the land (which was necessary in order to issue permits and patents), and settlers could not travel to land offices in Newnansville and St. Augustine. Impassable or nonexistent roads also meant that there was infrequent mail, which rendered unreliable the only alternative way to file AOA claims at the land offices. Settlers also left families vulnerable to Seminole attacks if they traveled to the land offices, and the power of the continuing threat of Indian depredations was cited by the commissioner of the General Land Office in his 1848 report to Congress. He noted that it was surprising that anyone had managed to comply with the law's requirements given the lack of roads, surveys, and mail, as well as presence of "a bloodthirsty and treacherous foe, who would have taken advantage of the absence of the settlers . . . to destroy their helpless families, and break up their improvements."[44] While congressional leaders represented the Seminole threat as very minor in 1842, officials and settlers in Florida still expressed concern.

Many of the problems and confusion with the AOA stemmed from the fact that, due to the war, most of Florida was unsurveyed as of 1842. This meant that government surveyors did not survey many AOA lands until after settlers had made and improved their claims. As a result, some settlers found that their land actually already belonged to someone else, based on a private claim that had not ever been surveyed before. Also, Seminoles sometimes came behind surveyors and wiped out their markings, an effectively simple way to resist white settlement. Further, while settlers used natural landmarks to delineate their claims and chose the best available land in the area, surveyors disregarded natural landmarks. The official survey laid an invisible grid over the land that centered on Tallahassee, hundreds of miles away. The survey, therefore, often placed individuals' claims into multiple squares of the grid, or into several "quarter sections" of a township. The government's solution to this was to have the settlers shift the lines of their claims to conform to the survey, so that their land fit into one quarter section of a township (one subdivision of a square in the grid). This sometimes meant that a settler would have to choose between claiming the land he farmed and the land he lived on; she might be forced to abandon some of her improvements in order to keep her fields.[45]

Some threatened to sue the government over this problem, and many were outraged by the inflexibility about quarter sections. Rebecca Munden, a war widow who had received rations as a suffering inhabitant at Fort Micanopy during the war, had settled an AOA claim in Marion County (then still part of Alachua County) in 1842. After her land was surveyed, it turned out that her farm stretched across two quarter sections of the surveyed grid. She wrote a hostile missive to the deputy surveyor in March 1844: "I will not abide by section lines or select either quarter section that my Permit interferes with, as you have requested, but am determined to retain the land allotted to me by my Permit. I therefore forbid you from trespassing upon my premises." The surveyor's map of Munden's claim reveals the source of her adamant refusal: she had settled and cultivated land that straddled the border between two quarter sections, and all of the best land in each was along their shared border. If she moved the boundaries of her AOA claim to conform to either of the surveyed quarter sections she would lose half of her best land, gaining only less desirable scrub. She may have once appeared as a needy war victim, but Munden was now a determined settler.[46]

Still other settlers faced a different problem. They had claimed land before they had actually seen it; stopping at the land office on the way south or sending in an AOA permit quickly before the two hundred thousand square mile cap on donated land was met. This sometimes resulted in more than one claim for the same land. Others discovered that the land they had selected was unfit for farming. Other permits were canceled for land that had been reserved for military purposes, including all the islands off the Gulf Coast. Widow Eliza Crews, for example, tried to file a claim for land on Boca Grande Island, where she had previously lived, but was denied. In this instance, the military defense required by national expansion took precedence over white settlement.[47]

The difficulty of complying with all the requirements of the AOA prompted Congress to pass two amendments after the initial settlement period expired in 1843. In 1844, Congress voted to allow settlers to change their claims if the first parcel they chose was defective for some reason, to claim their 160 acres as fractions of several quarter sections (rather than

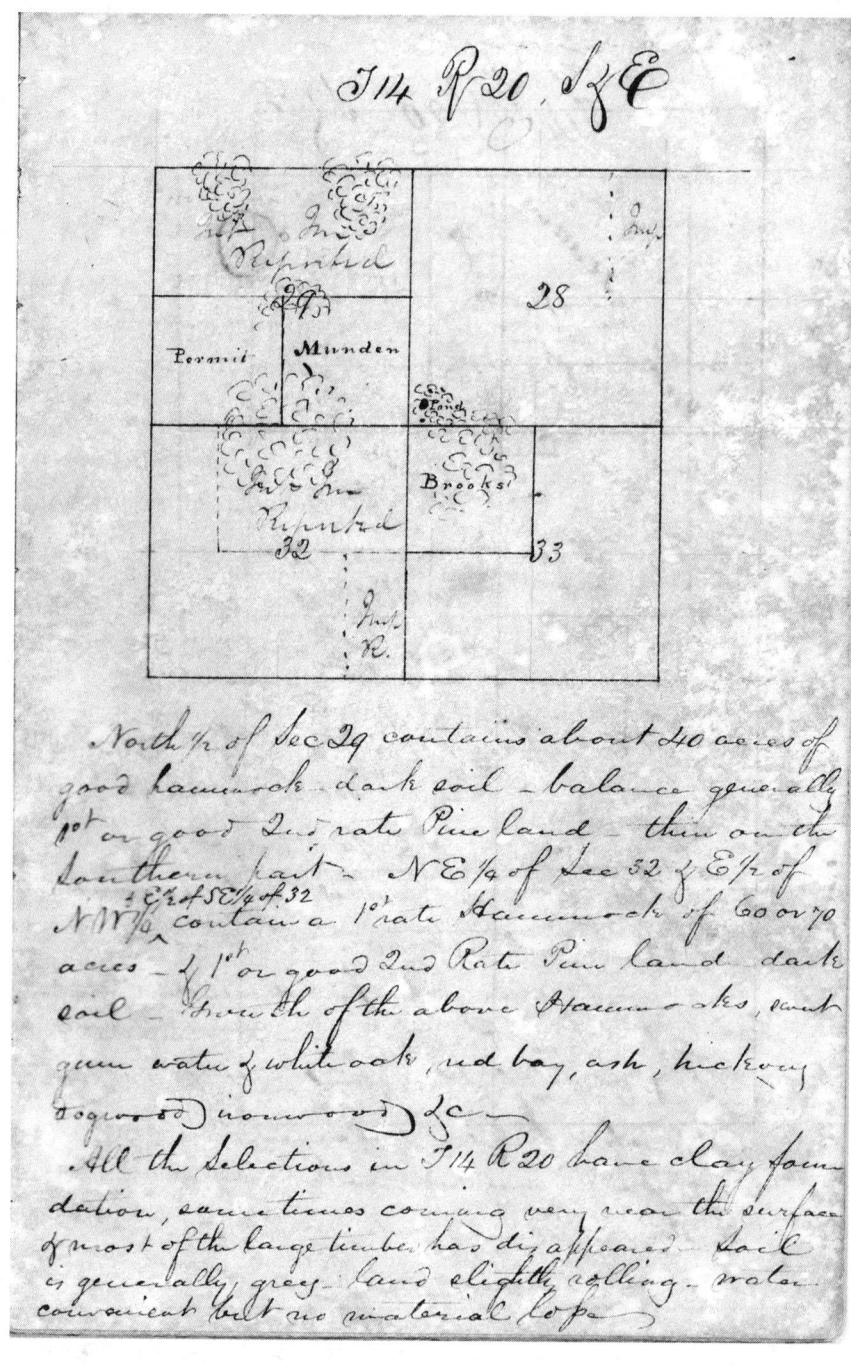

Figure 5. Hand-drawn map of Rebecca Munden's land claim in Marion County, showing that it straddled two quarters of section 29, township square 14 south, range 20 east. Courtesy of the Title and Land Records Section, Bureau of Survey and Mapping, Division of State Lands, Florida Department of Environmental Protection.

abide by post-settlement survey lines), to reside on a plot of Florida land other than that which they had purchased, and to purchase their claim for $1.25 an acre if they wanted the title before they had lived on it for five years (a version of preemption for AOA settlers). In 1848 a second bill was passed allowing those who actually settled and cultivated, but had never properly filed an AOA claim, to do so retroactively. If their land had been sold out from under them because they had established no legal claim, they would be offered a different quarter section of land in the township.[48]

These amendments suggest that policy makers wanted to protect bona fide settlers who had come and established settlements on the frontier, and that they had learned much from the process of crafting this policy and wanted to correct their mistakes in Florida, where they had just completed a grand public land donation experiment. These amendments are significant because they provided an opportunity for lawmakers to change the rules of the AOA, and if it had not been their original intent to allow women to claim land under the AOA, they could have easily amended the law to exclude them. Yet they did not, continuing to allow the inclusion of female pronouns and the vague phrase "head of a family" to set a precedent for later U.S. land laws. As a result, women would prove just as eager, capable, and complicit in U.S. expansion as their fathers, brothers, and sons.

The Impact of the Armed Occupation Act

Although only 35 percent of AOA settlers secured the title to their land after five years, many migrants came to Florida following passage of the bill in 1842. Some purchased public land directly, and others squatted and later preempted government land auctions, purchasing their farms for the base government price of $1.25 per acre. The impact of the AOA on the population of Florida reached well beyond the 1,312 AOA permit applicants. The AOA attracted many new settlers, especially from upper Florida and neighboring states, and created settlements that attracted more whites as they prospered.[49]

The AOA helped to increase Florida's population of white women most significantly. In 1840, there had been more enslaved black women than free white women in Florida. By 1850 the population of white women had almost doubled, and they outnumbered enslaved black women. The total population of Florida, now a state, increased overall between 1840 and 1850, and white men still outnumbered white women (1.2:1), but no other group had increased as much as the population of white women (see Appendix).[50] Although only forty single white women applied for AOA land independently (at least seventeen succeeded and received title after five years), as these changes in population illustrate, many more arrived in Florida in the 1840s.[51] Some were married to male settlers and therefore are difficult to account for, since they were subsumed in male-headed households. Female heirs ultimately received title to the AOA claims of at least twenty male AOA settlers who had died during the first five years of settlement. Seminoles killed Martha Barker's husband in an attack on his Indian River settlement in July 1849, for example, but she received the title to her AOA land in April 1850. Other survivors failed to complete the requirements of the law. Susan Baker's husband had drowned accidentally in 1845, shortly after settling on his claim, and his widow left Florida after his death to eke out her living as a seamstress in Philadelphia.[52]

Other white women arrived in the 1840s and bought land rather than settling on an AOA claim, or accompanied husbands and fathers who purchased land. Land sales, including preemptions, continued in the 1840s alongside AOA settlers, and then began to increase significantly in the 1850s. Not only did relatively cheap land, preemption, and the AOA encourage many whites to settle in south Florida, the Military Bounty Land Act of 1850 brought many veterans into Florida's land offices. In 1854, the Graduation Act added further incentive for settlers, as it reduced prices over time for any public lands that had not yet sold. After the passage of the 1862 Homestead Act, male and female homesteaders also claimed public lands in Florida.[53] All of these generous, pro-settler national land policies followed the AOA, which had opened the floodgates to white settler families in the territory.

With cheap or even free land available, many flocked to Florida, especially Middle Florida's plantation belt. By 1860 Florida's population had risen to 140,424 people; 78,679 of them were free and white, while 61,745 were enslaved blacks. White men and boys continued to outnumber white women and girls, 41,128 to 36,619, or 1.12 male to every female. The gender ratio among enslaved people was fairly even, with 31,348 men and 30,397 women, or 1.03 enslaved men and boys to every enslaved woman or girl.[54] As lawmakers and Florida boosters had hoped, whites brought families and enslaved blacks into Florida in the 1840s and 1850s, hallmarks of what Americans called "civilization."

As lawmakers like Senator Preston from South Carolina had hoped, these white settlers helped to install a new racial order in Florida. In addition to the thousands of enslaved blacks laboring there by 1850, free people of color experienced a drastic reduction in their rights and opportunities compared to those they had enjoyed under Spanish rule. As people who defied the association of dark skin with enslavement and who might aid rebellious slaves and Seminoles, free blacks were explicitly excluded from settling under the AOA. The free black population remained very small in the 1840s and 1850s: it increased from 817 to 932 people between 1840 and 1850, and held steady at 932 in 1860.[55] As unwelcome in Florida as they were in the rest of the antebellum slave South, many free blacks left Florida in this period. Some of those kin to powerful white families from the Spanish colonial period, such as the mixed-race Clarkes of St. Johns County, left for the urbanizing northern United States. Under less voluntary circumstances, almost all of the Black Seminoles left Florida in the late 1830s, traveling to Indian Territory, Texas, and Mexico in hope of securing land and freedom.[56]

As policy makers intended, most of the growth in Florida's population occurred south of St. Augustine, where the presence of white colonists effectively brought much more of Florida's wilderness under American control. The 1840 population of the counties where AOA lands would soon become available (counties south of the 9/10 township line) was only 11,657. By 1850 the population of these counties had grown to 40,872, an increase of over 29,000 people, and 87.8 percent of the overall increase in the Florida population from 1840 to 1850. With free or cheap government land available, white families and their slaves flooded into the unsettled southern peninsula in the 1840s. While one cannot know whether these people would have come to Florida without the AOA incentive, populating Florida's southern peninsula with white settlers did require some enticement. Without some inducement to move that far south, it is likely that in the years following the Second U.S.-Seminole War most whites would have stayed in the northern tier of the state. North Florida boasted rich agricultural land and established white settlements, where new migrants might have taken up homes and farms much closer to the "civilized" United States (and to the kin they might have left behind), rather than risking their lives to carve out homes, farms, and towns farther south.[57]

Widows, Slaveholders, and Settlers

Forty women applied for and received AOA permits in their own names, and seventeen of them (or their heirs) ultimately received title to their claims. Although they were a minority of those who claimed AOA lands, and a small fraction of the women who settled Florida in the 1840s, these independent female claimants are the most visible women among white settlers in historical records. Not implicit members of male-headed households, female "armed occupiers" provide direct evidence that women also found free land in Florida an attractive incentive and aided U.S. efforts to colonize former Seminole territory. Their stories suggest that they succeeded for the same reasons male settlers did: settling near extended family was likely to net both male and female AOA settlers affirmative land claims.

Female heads of families claimed AOA lands all over the region where claims were available in southeast Florida. All of the women who tried to settle claims south of Tampa Bay failed, some because the land was reserved for federal military use, others because southern Florida was just too difficult to survive before the Civil War (few men settled there either). Women who attempted to settle claims farther north were more likely to succeed, but eleven of them also failed. Although women were a very small proportion of AOA claimants (3.2 percent), their success rate was higher than the overall average; 45 percent of female armed occupiers eventually received title to the land they claimed under the AOA, compared to 35 percent of all claimants. Perhaps women proved more permanent settlers because they had fewer alternatives than men, or the few women who filed for AOA permits were already a self-selected group of hardy pioneers equipped to succeed.[58]

Women (and men) who succeeded at getting the title to their land usually settled near extended family members. At least ten of the seventeen women who were successful came out with very enterprising extended families (of origin and marriage) in which multiple members settled AOA claims.[59] Several of them also married at about the same time that they filed their claims, typically to men who filed claims, so that the newly created family doubled its land claim size.[60] Successful female AOA settlers also migrated from within Florida. Twenty-three of the forty women who filed permits stated that they had been in Florida since the 1820s or 1830s, and fifteen of the seventeen women who received title to their claims were among that group.[61] Those who had been living in Florida for at least a few

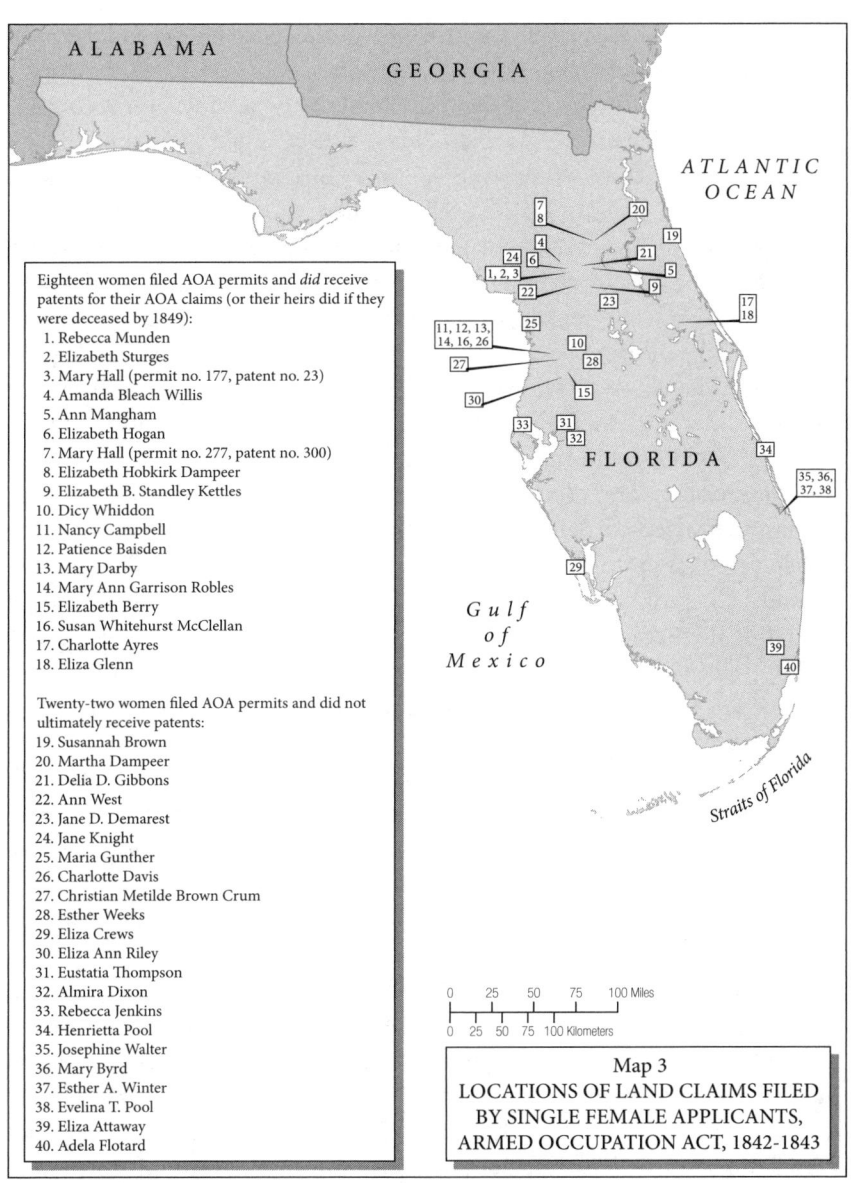

Map 3. Lands claimed by single female applicants under the Armed Occupation Act, 1842–1843.

years had better information about which of the available lands under the AOA were most promising and least dangerous.

The Chucochatti region of Benton County attracted the largest concentration of single female AOA settlers, where twelve single women filed AOA permits.[62] Five of these women filed permits for land in the same township square (22 south, 19 east). Of the twelve women who applied for land claims in this region, six eventually got the patent to their AOA claim (one-third of all the female AOA claimants who were successful).[63] U.S. land policy attracted single white female settlers, even if they were not the "independent" (male) settlers or less-visible dependent wives envisioned by legislators. The single women who joined this settlement were taking the same risks for the same benefits as male-headed families, and they also contributed to the white colonization of Florida.[64]

These women and their fellow settlers occupied a region that had very recently belonged to Seminoles, a stark illustration of the benefits that Indian removal granted to whites—both male and female—following the Second U.S.-Seminole War.[65] Lieutenant Henry Prince recorded burning several of the Seminole towns in this area on a march from Camp Izard to Tampa in the spring of 1836. As American soldiers hunted Seminoles and burned their towns they followed well-worn Native American paths, relying on the existing system of trails to guide them on their way south to Tampa. Seminole traders and hunters had made those trails, although of course the Americans chose to represent them as savages, not business-minded agricultural entrepreneurs.[66] Military officials attempting to move "suffering inhabitants" back out to the frontier had recruited settlers, armed them, and sent them out in the spring of 1842 (before the war officially ended and prior to the AOA). The largest party was led by John Curry and settled at "at the head of the Chocochattee Savanna." It included twenty-four families (some of which were headed by widows) peopled by 73 white men, 41 white women, 44 white children, 32 enslaved men, 17 enslaved women, and 28 enslaved children. These early settlers lived several miles apart in three blockhouses built by the military specifically for their use and protection. They were well aware of the former Seminole inhabitants of their new community. They selected fields formerly "belonging to Tiger Tail's band" for cultivation in their first year. Military reports noted that the land was of "excellent quality," crops were growing, and there was good range for cattle. These slaveholding whites made new settlements over the Seminole towns destroyed by the war, and planted fields first cleared by Seminoles and Black Seminoles, with aid and protection from the U.S. Army.[67]

The community these female settlers helped found in Benton County was as tumultuous and unpredictable as any frontier town. The market and taste for whiskey created a problem. Although this group included "many men of wealth in search of a better country, taking with them their wives, children and cattle," in April 1842 the military liaison to this settlement reported that the settlers there were "in the habit of keeping on hand and disposing of at sale whiskey and spirituous liquors forbidden by the Act of Congress regulating trade etc. in the Indian country." Beyond this legal infraction, the alcohol trade was also likely to "retard and otherwise injuriously affect the settlements now forming," not to mention the disorder it was likely to cause among the troops (the war was not yet concluded). The army threatened to stop rations to anyone caught selling liquor in the settlements, and the military liaison for the recolonization program reported that "many persons have been stricken from the [ration] rolls, for trafficking in this article."[68] If these measures did not take care of the problem, then any individual selling whiskey from the area would be forcibly removed. So chastened, by the summer of 1842 the settlements in Benton County were "generally in a prosperous condition, particularly those far in the interior, where the facility for obtaining ardent spirits are less than in the settlements in the neighborhoods of towns."[69] Thus the women who joined this community in early 1842 ventured forth to a frontier that was threatened not only by Seminoles and runaways from slavery but also raucous whites, if the military concern about liquor was any indication. Leaders, assuming that white women would bring a civilizing moral influence with them, had hoped that family settlements would be less susceptible to such problems, and perhaps white women did help control the whiskey problem. Of course, they might also have enjoyed liquor as much as men did.

After the AOA went into effect many of these initial settlers filed AOA permits for land in the area. Others soon joined them. In the six square miles at the center of the Chucochatti settlement, thirty-three AOA settlers patented land, and another twenty-seven settlers paid cash for land there between 1852 and 1860 (including one woman).[70] Perhaps this was a predictable policy outcome in the county that elected to rename itself for Thomas Hart Benton, champion of Manifest Destiny and the Armed Occupation Act.

The six women who patented their claims in this area were between the ages of nineteen and forty-seven in 1843, and represent both young women who married (or remarried) and formed new households and older widows who cooperated with grown sons to build family farms.[71] Most came with extended families, and several married after they arrived. Mary Ann Garrison and Charlotte Davis were the first of the single female AOA settlers to arrive in Benton County, although only Garrison eventually received title to her claim. Both had come with John Curry's initial group under the military reoccupation program. Elizabeth Berry had gone out with another military resettlement party to Fort White (northwest of Gainesville) before deciding to settle near the Chucochatti group. Mary Darby, Nancy Campbell, Susan Whitehurst McClellan, and Patience Baisden all arrived in late 1842 or early 1843. These women all filed their AOA permits between December 1842 and June 1843. Two of them had lived in Florida since the mid-1820s, and the rest had arrived in the territory by early 1833, so they had all weathered the war, and most had lost a husband in it.[72]

As lawmakers expected, most of the single female settlers were widows. Widows in the nineteenth-century South frequently took over the duties of their deceased husbands, a role that was acceptable for a woman who had fulfilled her wifely duties but lost her spouse. In this instance lawmakers had left open their eligibility with language that indicated that they were probably widows acting in place of men, and most fulfilled AOA requirements as "heads of families" with sons and/or slaves. Widows Mary Darby, Elizabeth Ann Berry, Nancy Campbell, and Susan Whitehurst McClellan (and Patience Baisden, who was probably a widow) settled AOA claims and left land legacies to their children as a result of their success as armed occupiers. Mary Ann Garrison was only eighteen years old, single, and child free when she applied in 1843, so she was hardly the "head of a family" with sons or slaves. She married Joseph Robles and bore a child very soon after she filed for AOA land, however, which suggests that she had filed just before marriage in order to double her family's land holdings. By 1850, Mary Ann and Joseph Robles, a Spaniard with his own AOA claim nearby, had three sons.[73]

Although she was not a widow, Mary Ann Garrison illustrates how important extended family connections were to successful AOA settlers. She came to Benton County with her kinsmen Richard, William, Joseph, Michael, Isaac and Seaborn Garrison and their wives and children, many of whom had arrived with John Curry's party in the summer of 1841. Mary

Ann was likely among them, but it is impossible to tell since only the male household heads were named. Her farm was a few miles south of the former site of the Seminole town at Chucochatti "near an Indian old trail" in "Garrason's Prairie" next to the claim of her father, Isaac. Her uncle Michael Garrison was a land surveyor who had scouted land for the extended family, and her father Isaac Garrison later served as courier for the family and community, taking many AOA applications and other documents to the land office at Newnansville in 1844 and 1849. In August 1849, "Mary A. Garrason," Isaac, Michael, and William Garrison all got their land patents (the title to their AOA claims) on the same day. In the vanguard of American expansion into this region of Florida, Isaac and his second wife, Laura, were also the proud parents of the "first white child" born in the county, a son named for Isaac, to whom Laura gave birth in 1842 (a year before Mary Ann Garrison Robles gave birth to her first son). Given their clear investment in building a future for the Garrison family in the region, male kin must have encouraged Mary Ann to stake her own AOA claim in the area, in spite of the fact that she was young and single at the time.[74]

Most of the other single female claimants also migrated with some kin. Susan Whitehurst McClellan was a twenty-nine-year-old widow when she, her father, and a brother applied for AOA permits near each other in Benton County. Elizabeth Berry settled with the help of her children and got the title to her land in August 1849. Members of her son-in-law's family settled AOA claims nearby, so Berry and her children likely supported and benefited from the support of his kin.[75]

Although in many ways these settlers behaved exactly as lawmakers hoped they would, many of them did not stay in Benton County after their required five years of residency. In order to get free public land, they had furthered national expansion by occupying what had formerly been a Seminole village, but they did not stay permanently. Many of the Benton County AOA settlers, including most of the single women, parlayed their new land claims into comfortable lives elsewhere. Only one of the single female AOA settlers, Mary Darby, remained in Benton County until the end of her life.[76]

Many others moved south to Tampa in the decades after 1850. Nancy Campbell, Susan Whitehurst McClellan and most of her extended family, Elizabeth Berry's son, and Mary Ann Garrison Robles and her family all migrated south to Tampa shortly after they received title to their AOA claims. Perhaps they bequeathed those lands to their children, but it is also possible that these women and their kin were speculating, and sold or rented their lands in Benton County after they received the title.[77] Women were probably pleased to move closer to Tampa, where they could earn a living, if single, and enjoy the safety and social life of a town. A Seminole attack in which a white woman died in September 1842 frightened many, and perhaps fear of indigenous violence remained a concern even in the late 1840s.[78]

Several other young widows did not get the title to AOA land they claimed in Benton County, perhaps because they lacked extended family support or because the frontier remained a challenging place to settle. Christian Brown, in her early thirties and mother of a young son, filed for AOA land in early 1843. Sometime after that she married AOA settler Richard Crum, the widower whose first wife Charlotte Piles Crum had died in the Seminole attack in Benton County in 1842. Since he had served as quartermaster of the Florida Militia during the Second U.S.-Seminole War, it was likely no accident that the Seminoles targeted his wife in this attack, which occurred shortly after the official end of the war. Although Christian Brown Crum helped her second husband establish a farm, she never got the title to her own claim and may have been forced to abandon it when she married. Nevertheless, she augmented the white female population of the region and supported another AOA settler who did patent his claim, along with other members of his family.[79]

Although small in number, these single white female AOA settlers near Chucochatti are historically visible in the land records, and their stories allow some analysis of female AOA settlers. They suggest that female AOA claimants' success (and perhaps decisions to move away) depended on support from extended family members. Although vital to white settler colonialism in Benton County, these women were not gender rebels. Their significance as supporters of U.S. expansion enhanced their domestic role and did not challenge their subordination to white men, just as it upheld their superiority to indigenous and black Floridians. These female settlers built homes and farms close to extended families and used their land to help their children succeed. They brought sons and other kin with them and together built, cleared, and worked the land. It is impossible to discern what kind of authority or submission each displayed in her household, but it is clear that white women (like men) succeeded in cooperation with larger kin groups and together helped to dispossess Seminoles and spread racial slavery. One might interpret the importance of kinship support as evidence that women had to obey the whims of their male providers, but many sons and brothers also benefited from the support of their kin, including female kin, whose contributions were implicit in the discourse of the time and are invisible in historical land records. Yet there were many women and girls in these early settlements in Benton County; 244 white women and girls in Benton County by 1850. Their labor contributed to households that also included 360 white men and boys. Thus it is important to view both the women and men who filed their own AOA permits not as individuals but as members of nuclear and extended settler-colonial families, and partners in the domestication of Florida. Male settlers also migrated in large groups of extended kin, relied on each other for support, and depended upon the labor of everyone in their households to make successful claims.

When they settled among extended family members, whites on the frontier, whether male or female, were more likely to make permanent settlements. When their extended families migrated elsewhere, settlers (whether male or female) were more likely to follow. In conclusion, in spite of gendered ideas about domesticity and female vulnerability, single female settlers were likely not very different from male pioneers; their success depended on the support of their families and communities and their contributions to their households and communities helped their kin and neighbors make permanent homes in frontier Florida.[80]

White settlers also depended upon the labor of enslaved blacks, and by 1850 whites had brought 324 enslaved people into Benton County. While some of their female neighbors owned land, only four women owned human property in their own names, and they claimed only 34 of the 324 enslaved people. Although white men outnumbered blacks in this largely yeoman community, the labor of these coerced migrants was also vital to their establishment and eventual success. Although blacks, unlike white women and children, would never reap the benefits of frontier settlement and receive the title to the land the cleared and planted, their work was just as significant. Their presence was also symbolic, as it signaled that Florida had become a territory where slaves might be safely taken and used to make wealth for white families. Whites and the slave labor they commanded displaced the Seminoles and their black allies, making way for slaveholding white settlers.[81]

Once the United States had violently removed most of the Seminoles and Black Seminoles, the federal government instituted a new land policy designed to attract white families to frontier Florida. The female settlers who filed their own AOA claims, and the enslaved people their families and neighbors owned, are historically visible reminders that white women and black men, women, and children helped colonize Florida, even though they were implicit or excluded in policy discourse, and even though the vast majority of women and blacks were subsumed as dependents within white male-headed households. Beyond their subordination to white men, of course, their similarities ended. White women benefitted directly and mightily from expansion and slavery, but expansionist domesticity only served to cement the enslaved status of the blacks forced to migrate into Florida and clear and cultivate its soil. As the Benton County armed occupiers found, colonizing postwar Florida was a cooperative venture, regardless of the image of the fierce and independent white male settler that mobilized support for the new land policy in Congress. New settlers needed a support network of kin, friends, and neighbors if they were to survive disease, deprivation, weather, wildlife, and the potential threat of violence from the Seminoles they were displacing. The whites that brought slaves or could purchase them would find even further wealth and benefit once they had survived the initial risks of settling early Florida. Together, white men and women were advancing their own families, national interests, and American territory, and (often) racial slavery. As they did so, Native Americans and enslaved blacks lost land and an avenue to freedom.

The expansionist domesticity that underwrote the white colonization of Florida expanded its reach into the rest of the country, where American settlers continued to spread their culture and grow their families on lands wrested from Native Americans in the late nineteenth and twentieth centuries. The pro-expansion policies deployed in territorial Florida—the suffering inhabitants aid program, the 1841 military recolonization scheme, and the 1842 Armed Occupation Act—were political precursors to expansionist land policies in the West, which rewarded frontier settlers with national land resources when they helped to populate and defend a new frontier against Native American rivals. Two decades later the U.S. government instituted a very similar policy to populate the interior of the continental United States. The AOA, justified as part of winning the Second U.S.-Seminole War, served as a blueprint for the 1850 Land Donation Act (Oregon) and the 1862 Homestead Act (any unappropriated public land). These new land laws greatly expanded previous war-related free land policies, the entitlements that originated in the land bounties that the United States first granted to veterans of the American Revolution and War of 1812. As the AOA had done, the 1862 Homestead Act promised 160-acre parcels of "public land" to any citizen or intended citizen who was twenty-one years old, the head of a family or a veteran, and who resided on the land for five years and made improvements. Unlike the AOA, black citizens, many of them recently emancipated from slavery, were also eligible.[82]

CONCLUSION

The Garden and the Spear

In 1833, after the Treaty of Payne's Landing, but before American forces removed most of the indigenous population, an editor in *Atkinson's Saturday Evening Post* noted that Florida had been rejuvenated in its second marriage to the United States: "Florida is no longer to remain under a cloud—her territory has been touched with the spear of American enterprise, and her gardens begin to blossom; she is fast putting off the widow's weeds, and merging to take her place at the head of the table of a new family." This hopeful and highly gendered vision of U.S. expansion into Florida, complete with metaphors about marriage, penetration, and fecundity, promised that American Florida would leave behind its colonial past to embrace American values and prosper under U.S. rule. This vision gendered the whole territory as female to establish "her" subordination to her new husband, America, eliding the significance of individual women in that process. Yet, as these gendered and sexualized metaphors suggest, and as this book has argued, women were at the nexus of American colonization in Florida. This analysis should encourage all historians of the nineteenth-century United States (not just those who study women) to recognize that ideas about women, and women themselves, were instrumental in territorial and slavery expansion, both ideologically and materially. Expansionist domesticity supported national growth in multiple ways.[1]

The Americanization of Florida illustrated to Americans and their government the dangers, challenges, and opportunities involved in removing Native Americans and settling new slave territory. While those who would become "Americans" had been participating in this process since the first Europeans landed in North America, expansion into Florida occurred on the threshold of what would become a massive westward expansion. Years before the Texas rebellion and the war with Mexico, white American settlers (many of them slaveholders) moved south and west into territories such as Florida and Missouri, which were recently acquired from Spain. Although Missouri achieved statehood in the same year that Florida entered the United States as a territory, their development proceeded apace. Thousands of white American migrants arrived in both territories in the 1820s and 1830s. In conjunction with their arrival and the Jacksonian belief in white supremacy and progress, the United States removed most Native Americans from both the confluence region (as Stephen Aron calls the area where the Missouri, Ohio, and Mississippi Rivers meet in the middle of North America) and the Southeast by the end of the 1830s. In both regions, the indigenous peoples who were ethnically cleansed in the 1830s had already been displaced by whites along earlier frontiers and had come south or west at the behest of Spain, fleeing white encroachment. Meanwhile, white settlers brought thousands of enslaved blacks with them. It was a foregone conclusion that racial slavery would continue in Florida, whereas in Missouri the debate over the expansion of slavery nearly split the new nation and necessitated the Missouri Compromise in 1821. Following the Panic of 1819, which had resulted in popular demand for debtor relief, Missouri lawmakers followed on earlier French, Spanish, and British land grant policies, attracting settlers with cheap or even free "public" land (often land still inhabited or recently cleared of Native Americans). Senator Thomas Hart Benton first proposed many of the generous public land policies used in Florida in his home state of Missouri in the 1820s. Benton understood that slavery and Indian removal went hand in hand alongside white settler colonialism, and he argued that in Missouri, "to remove the Indians" would "make room for the spread of slaves."[2]

Texas also invites useful comparisons with Florida, as the influx of American immigrants began there in the 1820s, and it is most often invoked in discussions of Manifest Destiny. In Texas and Florida, slavery and autonomous Native American threats motivated U.S. aggression, but unlike in Florida, large numbers of white settlers led American expansion into Texas. In the 1820s, the Mexican government invited Anglo and Native American immigrants to occupy eastern Texas, which Mexican settlers had abandoned due to Comanche raiding. Much as Spain had welcomed runaway slaves and displaced Native Americans in Florida, Mexico invited Anglo and Native American immigrants in hopes that they would help to pacify the borderland. The new Texans were primarily white, though, and many of them owned slaves. Although Mexico tried to close the border in the early 1830s, Anglos continued to come, and they quickly outnumbered Mexican residents. By the time the Anglo-Texans rebelled in 1835 and declared their independence, there were more than 30,000 whites and an estimated 5,000 enslaved blacks in Texas, as compared to about 7,000 Mexicans and 4,500 Native Americans. In contrast, indigenous and free black people together outnumbered European colonial residents in Florida before 1821. Slavery, which Mexico had outlawed in 1829, was one of the major motivations for the Anglo-Texan independence war in 1835, as Anglo-Texans had already begun to make their new Texas homesteads into profitable cotton plantations that relied on enslaved labor. Although Texas shares slavery and conflict with Native American groups with Florida, Texas is distinguished by the leading role that American emigrants played in its settlement, as it is by the continuing practice of captive trading and raiding.[3]

In New Mexico, which came into the United States later (in 1848, three years after Texas and Florida achieved statehood), geography and demographics created a different process of Americanization. First, white settlers and enslaved blacks were rare in territorial New Mexico, so although the question of whether slavery would be allowed in the lands just ceded from Mexico soon erupted in the Civil War, slavery did not drive American aggression in New Mexico as directly as it did in Florida or Texas. Second, Florida's population was quite small when it entered the United States (approximately 4,500 Europeans, 6,000 Native Americans, and 500 Black Seminoles), but New Mexico had a large nonwhite population of 115,000 Mexican and indigenous people, including Christianized and assimilated Pueblos as well as groups (Utes, Zunis) that retained their own cultural autonomy. They outnumbered white settlers for several more generations, and as a result American colonization created a distinct and ambiguous race called Mexicans, which historian Laura Gómez describes as a "wedge" group between whites and indigenous people. In Florida, this class of Hispanic Americans, between whites and blacks, never emerged. Americans fit the few colonial residents who remained in Florida (from either the Spanish or British periods) into the white and black categories so important to buttressing southern slavery. There were many fewer Hispanics in Florida, many owned slaves and land, and the United States upheld their property rights unless they also descended from Africans. Free blacks soon found Florida inhospitable, but many European colonial families (such as the

"Minorcans" of St. Augustine) became white, rather than ambiguously second-class citizens who were above Native Americans but below whites. Finally, although they definitely resisted U.S. colonial practices, the Native American population of New Mexico did not openly war against the United States as the Seminoles did in Florida, because Americans did not insist on their removal. By that time the U.S.-Mexico and Civil Wars had reshaped the Union, Indian removal had fallen out of favor, besides which the American frontier had now reached Native American populations in New Mexico. Americans believed that they needed to be assimilated, exterminated, or put on reservations to clear the way for white settlers and the progress they heralded, not removed further west.[4]

Compared to Texas and New Mexico, Florida's location, its early entrance into the United States in 1821, its small European colonial population, and its resistant populations of Seminoles and free blacks distinguish it from other former Spanish colonies added to the United States in the nineteenth century. Importantly, warfare, diplomacy, and federal policies in territorial Florida gave the Americans experience with hostile Native American and free black populations as they sought to expand both slavery and the nation's borders, and they would apply those lessons in Texas, New Mexico, and in other Spanish borderlands. White women played roles in each stage of developing national solutions to taking, holding, and settling new territory in Florida. Their domestic labor proved vital to the efforts of the United States government to claim and control it. The imperialism of the late nineteenth century, enshrined in the Dawes Act (which privatized indigenous land) and in American policies in the Philippines, drew upon the policies that Jacksonians instituted in Florida in the 1830s.[5]

This book has argued that white women and expansionist domesticity were crucial factors in the growth of American settler colonialism, as evidenced in the case of Florida. In spite of its distinct colonial past, Florida is frequently remembered as part of the "Old South." It had only been U.S. territory for four decades when it seceded from the Union in 1861, but many Floridians eagerly rewrote its past to match the rest of the Confederacy after the Civil War. Antislavery forces also continued to concentrate on the significance of slavery in Florida's past, especially in the three U.S.-Seminole Wars. In the wake of the slavery crisis, Florida's role in establishing Americans' "Manifest Destiny" faded from view. This examination of Florida's history before the Civil War reveals its importance in the development of the culture and policies that created and sustained American imperialism in the settler colonial model of the nineteenth century (in which slavery played an important but partial role).[6]

It has also illustrated that not all women experienced the "spear of American enterprise" in the same way. As white women arrived, behind or alongside American "spears," to make homes and reframe U.S. violence as peaceful domesticity, they forced enslaved blacks to migrate and labor in service to their own households. On the receiving end of the American spear, Seminole women and their families encountered terrible violence from Americans, who attacked their bodies, homes, and kin. Within two decades Seminoles lost much of their Florida land. There was no place for them (or for free blacks) at the "table of a new family" in U.S. Florida.

As expansion continued beyond Florida, ideas about women and their reproductive labor continued to undergird the white supremacist domesticity that justified, supported, and resulted from Manifest Destiny in the 1840s and 1850s. Expansionists in favor of the assimilation of Texas, for example, theorized its Americanization in two major ways: either Anglo-Saxons would make nonwhites better able to participate in democratic self-rule, or racially superior Anglo-Saxons would outpopulate racial others, an ethnic cleansing that would make newly Americanized spaces civilized. This belief that U.S. economic penetration would hasten the outbreeding of inferior races by American whites revealed the centrality of white women, since white fecundity (rather than aggressive policy and violence) would ultimately triumph over the inferior races supposedly destined for extinction.[7]

In the 1840s and 1850s, supporters of Manifest Destiny continued to mobilize expansionist domesticity, naturalizing expansion with familial metaphors invoking white fecundity. During an 1846 congressional debate about Oregon land donation, Andrew Kennedy, an Indiana Democrat, declared: "Go to the West and see a young man with his mate of eighteen and [after] a lapse of thirty years, visit him again, and instead of two, you will find twenty-two. That is what I call the American multiplication table. . . . How long, under this process of multiplication, will it take to cover the continent with our posterity?" Kennedy was invoking the "American multiplication table" first celebrated by Benjamin Franklin in the eighteenth century but deploying it here for an American (not British) empire. This view of natural reproduction as colonization was a common theme in the 1840s, when boosters of the nation's Manifest Destiny believed that large white families revealed God's design for an Anglo-Saxon North America.[8]

Through metaphors such as the American multiplication table, white women's reproductive contributions to expansion helped cover over its callous political and military structure. Rather than highlighting the federal policy decisions and violent military campaigns that targeted Native Americans, including women, the American multiplication table offered a jocular, heterosexist metaphor about frontier couples "just doing what came naturally" to make expansion look like "nature taking its course." Metaphors about white frontier fecundity outpopulating Native American families suggested that indigenous families would slowly disappear naturally in the face of proliferating whites, obscuring the use of violence against Native Americans. By celebrating the white couples' (re)productivity, such language mobilized whites' sexual choice behind expansion, glossing over the culture of rape that denied Native American women sexual choice, just as slavery stole it from enslaved black women. The allusion to sex and the vision of large white frontier families living in domestic harmony also buried the material and symbolic importance of white women's work in national expansion underneath a rhetoric that made their work seem natural, inevitable, and unremarkable.

This study has sought to reverse these assumptions and to reveal that gender and sex were not simply "what came naturally" in the process of territorial expansion. Just as political and military forces were important to expansion, politicians and military leaders actively drafted white women into staying or coming into Florida, while Seminole and free black women were abused, coerced into leaving, or enslaved. White women played several indispensable parts in the aggressive expansion of U.S. borders and slavery, roles that political and military leaders recognized as necessary and exploited as agitprop. Their significance ought not be taken for granted or simplified as natural.

Throughout the period examined in the previous five chapters, white domesticity rendered American expansion necessary, justifiable, natural, and inevitable. In matters of domestic and human property, in depredation narratives, in Seminole stories about the white wars, in military policy, and in federal land settlement policies, white women's power to make homes, materially and symbolically, had extremely important consequences. The presence of white women and children signified and guaranteed the existence, claims, and need to protect American homes in Florida. Gender, in combination with race, sentimentalized the frontier, justified expansionist aggression against indigenous women and their families as defense, facilitated the expansion of American slavery, and established U.S. claims to Florida as organic and unquestionable.

As homemakers, as supplicating victims in need of protection and provisions, and as the partners and mothers of hearty frontier settlers, white women's material and symbolic value made them targets for pro-settler government policy. The wartime aid and land policies that the United States implemented in Florida between 1836 and 1842 took social provisions for deserving, needy widows and turned them into land entitlements for the hard-working, presumably male settler. The Armed Occupation Act of 1842, the culmination of federal and military policy during the Second U.S.-Seminole War, offered land to white settler families willing to relocate to regions of Florida recently stripped of Seminole residents. The AOA was certainly not the first land grant policy used to attract white settlers in North America. France, England, and Spain had previously used land to lure settlers (European and sometimes Native American) to their colonies, and the United States had rewarded veterans with land bounties since the American Revolution. The AOA marked a new departure in U.S. land policy. It was the first of several major land donation acts that U.S. leaders passed as incentives in order to encourage settlement along distant and dangerous borders, rather than as a reward for those who had served the nation in war. Although Senator Benton had attempted something similar in Missouri in the 1820s (where support for it helped to elect Jackson in 1828), his land scheme did not pass there. It finally found success in Florida. Subsequently, he proposed similar policies to colonize the Oregon Territory (an idea that he first introduced in 1838) and to encourage whites to settle along the "Highway to the Pacific" in 1851. In 1862 the Homestead Act opened up much of the North American West to settlers under a policy that was nearly identical to the AOA in Florida. Many of these later homestead bills reflected the designs of the Free-Soilers, and therefore precluded the spread of slavery alongside national boundaries, unlike Florida. Nevertheless, the Free-Soil commitment to containing slavery was hardly an antiracist campaign but one that intended to allow white men of all classes the opportunity to settle on their own land and extend national terrain at the same time, a goal shared by proslavery whites in Florida.[9]

Race drove American expansion in conjunction with gender. White settler claims to Florida relied on their presumed superiority and dominance over nonwhite others—autonomous indigenous and black peoples—who whites believed needed to be removed, destroyed, or enslaved in order for white American homes and families to inhabit and flourish in Florida. Symbolically, white womanhood in Florida assembled its meanings (vulnerable, domestic, innocent) against the white male protector and defender, the Indian attacker or abject squaw, and the black person who had to be enslaved and managed.

Although vital to American colonization, white women were not necessarily empowered by their role in expansionist domesticity, which has perhaps discouraged women's historians from focusing on their role in national expansion. In Florida, women were cast not as independent pioneers but as the vulnerable victims of indigenous violence and as the helpers of hearty, white, male frontiersmen. Yet some savvy individuals benefited from their willingness to colonize a dangerous territory. Hundreds received rations from the U.S. Army during the war. Many women (and men) profited as members of settler families rewarded with transportation, protection, provisions, and cheap or free land in recolonization and frontier settlement schemes. These benefits are hardly cause for celebration, however, given their consequences for Seminoles and blacks.

Expansionist domesticity not only brings women into focus in discussions of national expansion but it also puts the home on the imperial stage, denaturing its status as an apolitical location. The masculine empire needed homemakers to make its claim, to carry out its policies, and to spread its culture. White settler colonialism relied on mothers and homemakers to reproduce the colonizers' culture in a new place. In their quest to create permanent, nonindigenous communities, white settlers built homes on the land in order to render it their property. They produced children who would subsequently claim native status for themselves by virtue of their birthplace. Finally, domestic and heteronormative discourses helped frame colonization as natural or inevitable, joining white settler colonialism to Manifest Destiny.

Political and military leaders thus not only used gender and white women for political leverage but also relied upon them to conquer and settle Florida. As victims in depredation narratives and as the supportive partners of white male settlers, white women were indeed useful in the propagandistic discourse that supported the Second U.S.-Seminole War and the nation's first homestead bill. Further, women's material contributions were vital. Their property, labor, and indeed their fecundity were as important to expansion as war and politics. That Americans used them symbolically to obscure the racial and national violence that made the nation's destiny manifest does not lessen their material contributions. Yet the long-standing assumption that women and gender had little to do with war and politics has often obscured the significance of white women. White wives, mothers, sisters, and daughters shared the risks and gains of Manifest Destiny with white men. They also shared in the moral burden of national expansion: a project that purposely spread slavery and all of its horrors and that required the terrorizing and removal of Native American peoples in order to privilege and benefit whites. White women planted new lives in Florida and made its "gardens begin to blossom," but the "spear of American enterprise" privileged them at the expense of others.

APPENDIX

Table A1. Florida Population by Race and Gender, 1830–1860

	White males	White females	Enslaved blacks	Enslaved black males	Enslaved black females
1830	10,236	8,149	15,501	7,985	7,516
% within race	55.68	44.32		51.51	48.49
% of total population	29.47	23.46	44.63	22.99	21.64
1840	16,456	11,487	25,717	13,038	12,679
% within race	58.89	41.11		50.7	49.3
% of total population	30.21	21.1	47.21	23.93	23.27
1850	25,705	21,498	39,310	19,804	19,506
% within race	54.46	45.54		50.38	49.62
% of total population	29.4	24.58	44.95	22.65	22.31
1860	41,127	36,619	61,745	31,348	30,397
% within race	53	47		50.77	49.23
% of total population	29	26.08	43.97	22.32	21.65

Source: Social Explorer Dataset, U.S. Census 1830, 1840, 1850 and 1860 [database online].

Table A2. Florida Population by Age, 1830–1840

	1830			1840		
	Territory of Florida	% within race	Nation-wide %	Territory of Florida	% within race	Nation-wide %
Population	34,730			54,477		
Whites	18,385			27,943		
Under age 15	8,319	45.25	45.00	11,372	40.70	43.70
Age 15 and over	10,066	54.75	55.00	16,571	59.30	56.30
White males	10,236			16,456		
Under age 15	4,280	41.81	45.28	5,922	35.99	43.80
Age 15 and over	5,956	58.19	54.72	10,534	64.01	56.20

White females	8,149			11,487		
Under age 15	4,039	49.56	44.70	5,450	47.44	43.60
Age 15 and over	4,110	50.44	55.30	6,037	52.56	56.40
Enslaved blacks	15,501			25,717		
Under age 10	5,061	32.65	34.90	8,036	31.25	33.90
Under age 24	9,992	64.46	65.80	16,226	63.09	65.30
Age 10 and over	10,440	67.35	65.10	17,681	68.75	66.10
Age 24 and over	5,509	35.54	34.20	9,491	36.91	34.70
Enslaved black males	7,985			13,038		
Under age 10	2,501	31.32	34.90	4,044	31.02	33.90
Under age 24	4,983	62.40	65.76	8,114	62.23	65.29
Age 10 and over	5,484	68.68	65.10	8,994	68.98	66.10
Age 24 and over	3,002	37.60	34.24	4,924	37.77	34.71
Enslaved black females	7,516			12,679		
Under age 10	2,560	34.10	34.90	3,992	31.49	34.00
Under age 24	5,009	66.64	65.90	8,112	63.98	65.40
Age 10 and over	4,956	65.93	65.10	8,687	68.51	66.04
Age 24 and over	2,507	33.36	34.10	4,567	36.02	34.60

Source: SE Dataset, U.S. Decennial Census 1830, 1840. It is difficult to compare age statistics across race, because the U.S. census collected age data differently among whites and blacks before 1850. Another of the grotesque traces of the slave trade, the age categories reflect marketing strategies that related to gender, age, mortality, labor, and reproduction. Census takers in 1830 and 1840 recorded the number of slaves who were under the age of 10 and between the ages of 10 and 24, for example, rather than using the same categories used for white residents (birth to 5 years, 5 to 9 years, 10 to 14 years, 15 to 19 years, 20 to 30 years, and so on). By periodizing life stages differently for whites and blacks, census enumerators assisted in the reproduction of race as a meaningful category. In 1850, the census began to record the exact age of all people enumerated.

Table A3. Florida Population by Age, 1850–1860

	1850			1860			
	State of Florida	% within race	Nation-wide %	State of Florida	% within race	Notes to 1860 Census	Nation-wide %
Population	87,445			140,424		*includes 1 "Indian"	
Whites	47,203			77,746			
Under age 15	21,148	44.80	40.93	34,621	44.53	*1,103 whites of unknown age	40
Age 15 and over	26,050	55.19	59.02	42,022	54.05		59.9
White males	25,705			41,127		*556 white men of unknown age	
Under age 15	10,904	42.42	40.6	17,785	43.24		39.6
Age 15 and over	14,797	57.56	59.34	22,786	55.40		60.3
White females	21,498			36,619		*547 white women of unknown age	
Under age 15	10,244	47.65	41.28	16,8364	5.98		40.3
Age 15 and over	11,253	52.34	58.7	19,236	52.53		60.3
Enslaved blacks	39,310			61,745		*268 slaves of unknown age	
Under age 15	17,384	44.22	45.43	27,470	44.49		44.8
Age 15 and over	21,886	55.68	54.45	34,007	55.08		54.6
Enslaved black males	19,804			31,348		*127 enslaved men of unknown age	
Under age 15	8,699	43.93	45.41	13,913	44.38		44.7
Age 15 and Over	11,065	55.87	54.47	17,308	55.21		54.6
Enslaved black females	19,506			30,397		*141 enslaved women of unknown age	
Under age 15	8,685	44.52	45.45	13,557	44.6		44.8
Age 15 and over	10,821	55.48	54.43	16,699	54.94		54.5

Source: SE Dataset, U.S. Decennial Census, Florida Census 1850 and 1860. Subtotals may not add up to the total because of missing data (persons of unknown age) or groups omitted from this table (such as free blacks).

NOTES

Introduction

1. English speakers used various spellings for Chucochatti, such as Chichuchaty and Chocochatti. "Roll of Persons Forming New Settlements, Returning to Plantations, and Suffering Inhabitants," 1842, Record Group (hereafter RG) 94, Microcopy No. 567 (Washington: National Archives Microfilm, 1964), Roll 262, W217–405, 295; "Correspondence, Reports, and Lists Relating to Feeding of 'Suffering Inhabitants of Florida,' June 1841–June 1842," Vol. 1, Entry 74, extracts from RG 393, National Archives (University of Florida Library), 28, 50, 57, 66; "Florida," *Niles' National Register*, October 7, 1837, 2; Armed Occupation Act Permit No. 576-Newnansville, General Land Office Records, Title and Land Records Section, Division of State Lands, Department of Environmental Protection, Tallahassee, Florida (hereafter DEP); 1840 U.S. Census, Alachua County, Florida, population schedule, p. 161, Elizabeth Berry; U.S. Bureau of Land Management (hereafter US BLM), *Florida Pre-1908 Homestead and Cash Entry Patents* (Springfield, VA: General Land Office Automated Records Project, 1993) [CD-ROM], see entry for Elizabeth A. Barry; 1850 U.S. Census, Benton County, Florida, population schedule, p. 23, Elizabeth A. Barry.

2. Brent Richards Weisman, *Like Beads on a String: A Culture History of the Seminole Indians in North Peninsular Florida* (Tuscaloosa: University of Alabama Press, 1989), 67–69; Henry Prince, *Amidst a Storm of Bullets: The Diary of Lt. Henry Prince in Florida, 1836–1842*, ed. Frank Laumer (Tampa, FL: University of Tampa Press, 1998), 38, 70; An act to provide for the armed occupation and settlement of the unsettled part of the peninsula of East Florida, August 4, 1842, *U.S. Statutes at Large*, Vol. 5, ed. Richard Peters (Boston: Little, Brown, 1856), 502–504; Thomas Hart Benton, "Armed Occupation of Florida: Debate in the Senate," Appendix to Cong. Globe, 26th Cong., 1st Sess. 71–73 (1840); Richard J. Stanaback, *A History of Hernando County, 1840–1976* (Brooksville, FL: Action '76 Steering Committee, 1976); 1850 U.S. Census, Benton County, Florida, population schedule, p. 23–29; Kenneth W. Porter, rev. and ed. Alcione M. Amos and Thomas P. Senter, *The Black Seminoles: History of a Freedom-Seeking People* (Gainesville: University Press of Florida, 1996), 25–27; Virginia B. Peters, *The Florida Wars* (Hamden, CT: Archon Books, 1979), 30; Daniel F. Littlefield Jr., *Africans and Seminoles: From Removal to Emancipation* (Westport, CT: Greenwood Press, 1977), 3.

3. Daiva Stasiulis and Nira Yuval-Davis, eds., *Unsettling Settler Societies: Articulations of Gender, Race, Ethnicity, and Class* (London: Sage, 1995); Walter Hixson, *American Settler Colonialism: A History* (New York: Palgrave Macmillan, 2013).

4. Patrick Wolfe, *Settler Colonialism and the Transformation of Anthropology* (London: Cassell, 1999), 163; Lorenzo Veracini, *Settler Colonialism: A Theoretical Overview* (New York:

Palgrave Macmillan, 2010); Margaret D. Jacobs, *White Mother to a Dark Race: Settler Colonialism, Maternalism, and the Removal of Indigenous Children in the American West and Australia, 1880–1940* (Lincoln: University of Nebraska Press, 2009), 2–11.

5. Jacobs, *White Mother*, 3.

6. Patrick Wolfe, "Land, Labor, and Difference: Elementary Structures of Race," *American Historical Review* 106 (2001): 868.

7. Stephen Aron, *How the West Was Lost: The Transformation of Kentucky from Daniel Boone to Henry Clay* (Baltimore: Johns Hopkins University Press, 1996), and *American Confluence: The Missouri Frontier from Borderland to Border State* (Bloomington: Indiana University Press, 2006); John R. Van Atta, "'A Lawless Rabble': Henry Clay and the Cultural Politics of Squatters' Rights, 1832–1841," *Journal of the Early Republic* 28 (2008): 337–378; Jacobs, *White Mother*, 4.

8. David Weber, *The Spanish Frontier in North America* (New Haven, CT: Yale University. Press, 1992), 64–75, 95, 100–101, 141–145, 179–199; Paul Hoffman, *Florida's Frontiers* (Bloomington: Indiana University Press, 2002), 183; John E. Worth, *The Timucuan Chiefdoms of Spanish Florida*, Vol. 1, *Assimilation* (Gainesville: University Press of Florida, 1998), 199; Gregory A. Waselkov and Kathryn E. Holland Braund, eds., *William Bartram on the Southeastern Indians* (Lincoln: University of Nebraska Press, 1995), 52–53; John Paul A. Nuño, "Making Africans and Indians: Colonialism, Identity, Racialization, and the Rise of the Nation-State in the Florida Borderlands, 1765–1837" (PhD diss., University of Texas, El Paso, 2010), 59–65; Mikaëla M. Adams, "Who Belongs? Becoming Tribal Members in the South" (PhD diss., University of North Carolina at Chapel Hill, 2012), 221; Richard A. Sattler, "Remnants, Renegades, and Runaways: Seminole Ethnogenesis Reconsidered," in *History, Power and Identity: Ethnogenesis in the Americas, 1492–1992*, Jonathan David Hill, ed. (Iowa City: University of Iowa Press, 1996), 36–69; Patricia R. Wickman, *The Tree That Bends: Discourse, Power, and the Survival of the Maskókî People* (Tuscaloosa: University of Alabama Press, 1999); Susan A. Miller, *Coacoochee's Bones: A Seminole Saga* (Lawrence: University Press of Kansas, 2003), 6–11; Kevin Mulroy, *Freedom on the Border: The Seminole Maroons in Florida, the Indian Territory, Coahuila, and Texas* (Lubbock: Texas Tech University Press, 1993), 6–7; Jane F. Lancaster, *Removal Aftershock: The Seminoles' Struggle to Survive in the West, 1836–1866* (Knoxville: University of Tennessee Press, 1994), 3; Brent Richards Weisman, *Unconquered People: Florida's Seminole and Miccosukee Indians* (Gainesville: University Press of Florida, 1999), 14, 27, 49; Christina Snyder, *Slavery in Indian Country: The Changing Face of Captivity in Early America* (Cambridge, MA: Harvard University Press, 2010).

9. Weber, *Spanish Frontier*, 12–13, 337; Philip D. Rasico, "The Minorcan Population of St. Augustine in the Spanish Census of 1786," *Florida Historical Quarterly* 66 (1987): 160–184; William S. Coker, "Pensacola, 1686–1763," in *The New History of Florida*, ed. Michael Gannon (Gainesville: University Press of Florida, 1996), 122; Robin F. A. Fabel, "British Rule in the Floridas," in *The New History of Florida*, ed. Gannon, 134; Nuño, "Making Africans and Indians," 45–100, 241–243; cf. Wolfe, "Land, Labor, and Difference," 878.

10. Weber, *Spanish Frontier*, 33–38, 64–75, 95, 100–101, 141–145, 179–199; J. Leitch Wright, *Anglo-Spanish Rivalry in North America* (Athens: University of Georgia Press, 1971); Amy Turner Bushnell, *Situado and Sabana: Spain's Support System for the Presidio and Mission Provinces of Florida* (Athens: University of Georgia Press, 1994); Amy Turner Bushnell, "The Menéndez Marquéz Cattle Barony at La Chua and the Determinants of Economic Expansion

in Seventeenth-Century Florida," *Florida Historical Quarterly* 56 (April 1978): 408; Jane Landers, *Black Society in Spanish Florida* (Chicago: University of Illinois Press, 1999), 29–60; Nuño, "Making Africans and Indians," 64.

11. There is much historiographical debate about the status of the people called "Black Seminoles," "*estelusti*," or "Seminole maroons." Some scholars argue that they were enslaved, while others (including Seminoles in 1970s oral history interviews) argue that Seminoles claimed them as slaves only to protect them from enslavement by whites, but otherwise granted them independence. Some scholars consider them a distinct ethnic group, while others argue for viewing them as a maroon culture within Seminole society. See "Transcript, 70 year old Seminole Creek lady (Bird Clan) and her husband (Tiger Clan) who was a Miccosukee from the Tamiami Trail," Oral History Interview with Jean Chaudhuri, n.d., 7–9, Samuel Proctor Oral History Program Collection, P. K. Yonge Library of Florida History, University of Florida (hereafter SPOHP); Jane Landers, "A Nation Divided?: Blood Seminoles and Black Seminoles on the Florida Frontier," in *Coastal Encounters: The Transformation of the Gulf South in the Eighteenth* Century, ed. Richmond F. Brown (Lincoln: University of Nebraska Press, 2007), 103; Larry Eugene Rivers, *Slavery in Florida: Territorial Days to Emancipation* (Gainesville: University Press of Florida, 2000), 189–192, 196–197; Melinda Beth Micco, "Freedmen and Seminoles: Forging a Seminole Nation" (PhD diss., University of California, Berkeley, 1995); Melinda Micco, "'Blood and Money': The Case of Seminole Freedmen and Seminole Indians in Oklahoma," in *Crossing Waters, Crossing Worlds: The African Diaspora in Indian Country*, ed. Tiya Miles and Sharon Holland (Durham, NC: Duke University Press, 2006), 121–144; Snyder, *Slavery in Indian Country*, 213–243; Shirley Boteler Mock, *Dreaming with the Ancestors: Black Seminole Women in Texas and Mexico* (Norman: University of Oklahoma Press, 2010), 29, 30–31, 36; Kevin Mulroy, *The Seminole Freedmen: A History* (Norman: University of Oklahoma Press, 2007) and *Freedom on the Border*; Kevin Kokomoor, "A Reassessment of Seminoles, Africans and Slavery on the Florida Frontier," *Florida Historical Quarterly* 88 (2009): 234–236.

12. Landers, *Black Society*, 29–60, 66, 74–79, 80–83; Nuño, "Making Africans and Indians," 241–243; Weber, *Spanish Frontier*, 12–13; John K. Mahon, *History of the Second Seminole War, 1835–1842*, rev. ed. (Gainesville: University Press of Florida, 1985), 18–28; Joe Knetsch, *Florida's Seminole Wars, 1817–1858* (Charleston, SC: Arcadia Press, 2003), 13–15, 23–41, 61; John Missall and Mary Lou Missall, *The Seminole Wars: America's Longest Indian Conflict* (Gainesville: University Press of Florida, 2004), 2–7, 32–51; Bruce Edward Twyman, *The Black Seminole Legacy and North American Politics, 1693–1845* (Washington, DC: Howard University Press, 1999), 3, 13; William C. Davis, *The Rogue Republic: How Would-Be Patriots Waged the Shortest Revolution in American History* (New York: Houghton Mifflin Harcourt, 2011); David A. Bice, *The Original Lone Star Republic: Scoundrels, Statesmen and Schemers of the 1810 West Florida Rebellion* (Clanton, AL: Heritage Publishing, 2004); James G. Cusick, *The Other War of 1812: The Patriot War and the American Invasion of Spanish East Florida* (Athens: University of Georgia Press, 2007), 301; Robert Remini, *Andrew Jackson and His Indian Wars* (New York: Viking, 2001), 54–79; Michael Paul Rogin, *Fathers and Children: Andrew Jackson and the Subjugation of the American Indian* (New York: Knopf, 1975), 150–159; Daniel Scallet, "'This Inglorious War': The Second Seminole War, the Ad Hoc Origins of American Imperialism, and the Silence of Slavery" (PhD diss., Washington University in St. Louis, 2011), 59–62; "Treaty of Amity, Settlement, and Limits Between the United States of America and His Catholic Majesty," 1819, reprinted in Francis Newton Thorpe, *The Federal and State Constitutions, Colonial*

Charters, and Other Organic Laws of the States, Territories, and Colonies Now or Heretofore Forming the United States of America, Vol. 2 (Washington, DC: Government Printing Office, 1909), 649–655.

13. Claudio Saunt, *A New Order of Things: Property, Power, and the Transformation of the Creek Indians, 1733–1816* (New York: Cambridge University Press, 1999); Theda Perdue and Michael D. Green, *The Cherokee Nation and the Trail of Tears* (New York: Viking, 2007); Cecil Eby,"*That Disgraceful Affair," the Black Hawk War* (New York: Norton, 1973); Scallet, "This Inglorious War," 6, 39–95; Knetsch, *Florida's Seminole Wars*, 13.

14. Aron, *American Confluence*; Mark Carroll, *Homesteads Ungovernable: Families, Sex, Race, and the Law in Frontier Texas, 1823–1860* (Austin: University of Texas Press, 2001); Laura Gómez, *Manifest Destinies: The Making of the Mexican American Race* (New York: New York University Press, 2007); Deena González, *Refusing the Favor: The Spanish-Mexican Women of Santa Fe, 1820–1880* (New York: Oxford University Press, 1999).

15. Veracini, *Settler Colonialism*, 12–14; Jacobs, *White Mother*, 4–5.

16. Jacobs, *White Mother*, 9–10; Stasiulis and Yuval-Davis, *Unsettling Settler Societies*, 2.

17. Ann Laura Stoler, *Carnal Knowledge and Imperial Power: Race and the Intimate in Colonial Rule* (Berkeley: University of California Press, 2010); Jacobs, *White Mother*; Adele Perry, *On the Edge of Empire: Gender, Race, and the Making of British Columbia, 1849–1871* (Toronto: University of Toronto Press, 2001); Lora Wildenthal, *German Women for Empire, 1884–1945* (Durham, NC: Duke University Press, 2001); Wolfe, "Land, Labor, and Difference," 866–867, 885–886. For discussion of the highly gendered policies carried out under assimilationist Indian programs before 1830, see Theda Perdue, *Cherokee Women: Gender and Culture Change, 1700–1835* (Lincoln: University of Nebraska Press, 1998).

18. On U.S. expansion, see Amy S. Greenberg, *Manifest Manhood and the Antebellum American Empire* (New York: Cambridge University Press, 2005); Robert E. May, *Manifest Destiny's Underworld: Filibustering in Antebellum America* (Chapel Hill: University of North Carolina Press, 2002), and "Reconsidering Antebellum U.S. Women's History: Gender, Filibustering, and America's Quest for Empire," *American Quarterly* 57 (2005): 1155–1188; Kristin L. Hoganson, *Fighting for American Manhood: How Gender Politics Provoked the Spanish-American and Philippine-American Wars* (New Haven, CT: Yale University Press, 1998); Anders Stephanson, *Manifest Destiny: American Expansionism and the Empire of Right* (New York: Hill and Wang, 1995); Frederick Merk, *Manifest Destiny and Mission in American History: A Reinterpretation* (New York: Knopf, 1963); Alexander Saxton, *The Rise and Fall of the White Republic: Class Politics and Mass Culture in Nineteenth-Century America* (London: Verso, 1990), 39; Frank Lawrence Owsley Jr. and Gene A. Smith, *Filibusters and Expansionists: Jeffersonian Manifest Destiny, 1800–1821* (Tuscaloosa : University of Alabama Press, 1997), 2–4; Reginald Horsman, "The Dimensions of an 'Empire for Liberty': Expansion and Republicanism, 1775–1825," *Journal of the Early Republic* 9 (1989): 1–20; Eliga H. Gould, *Among the Powers of the Earth: The American Revolution and the Making of a New World Empire* (Cambridge, MA: Harvard University Press, 2012), 1–3. On settler colonialism, Indian removal, and U.S. imperialism/foreign policy, see Hixson, *American Settler Colonialism*; Scallet, "This Inglorious War"; William Savage Jr., *The Cherokee Strip Live Stock Association: Federal Regulation and the Cattleman's Last Frontier* (Norman: University of Oklahoma Press, 1990); Francis Paul Prucha, *The Great Father: The United States Government and the American Indians*, Vol. 2 (Lincoln: University of Nebraska Press, 1984); Frederick Hoxie, *A Final Promise: The Campaign to Assimilate the Indians, 1880–1920* (Lincoln: University of Nebraska Press, 1984); Stuart

Banner, *How the Indians Lost Their Land: Law and Power on the Frontier* (Cambridge, MA: Belknap Press of Harvard University Press, 2005). On the connections between continental expansion and the seizure of the Philippines, see David C. Hendrickson, *Union, Nation, or Empire: The American Debate over International Relations, 1789–1941* (Lawrence: University Press of Kansas, 2009), 268–272; Sean McEnroe, "Painting the Philippines with an American Brush: Visions of Race and National Mission among the Oregon Volunteers in the Philippine Wars of 1898 and 1899," *Oregon Historical Quarterly*, 104 (2003): 24–61; David Burton, "The Influence of the American West on the Imperialist Philosophy of Theodore Roosevelt," *Arizona and the West* 4 (1962): 5–26; Richard Slotkin, "Nostalgia and Progress: Theodore Roosevelt's Myth of the Frontier," *American Quarterly* 33 (1981): 608–637.

19. Hixson, *American Settler Colonialism*, chapter 4; Scallet, "This Inglorious War"; Greenberg, *Manifest Manhood*, 20; Weber, *Spanish Frontier*, 179, 280–281, 337–338; James A. Sandos, "From 'Boltonlands' to 'Weberlands': The Borderlands Enter American History," *American Quarterly* 46 (1994): 595–604; Thomas R. Hietala, *Manifest Design: Anxious Aggrandizement in Late Jacksonian America* (Ithaca, NY: Cornell University Press, 1985), x.

20. Edward E. Baptist, *Creating an Old South: Middle Florida's Plantation Frontier before the Civil War* (Chapel Hill: University of North Carolina Press, 2002); Gould, *Among the Powers of the Earth*, 1; "Treaty of Amity, Settlement, and Limits . . . 1819," in Thorpe, *Federal and State Constitutions*.

21. Catharine E. Beecher (quoting Tocqueville), *Treatise on Domestic Economy* (Boston: T. H. Webb, 1842), 37–38; Amy Kaplan, "Manifest Domesticity," *American Literature* 70 (1998): 581–606; Baptist, *Creating an Old South*, 27–28; Greenberg, *Manifest Manhood*, 258; Stoler, *Carnal Knowledge*; Wildenthal, *German Women for Empire*.

22. Bruce Dorsey, *Reforming Men and Women: Gender in the Antebellum City* (Ithaca, NY: Cornell University Press, 2002); Stephanie McCurry, *Masters of Small Worlds: Yeoman Households, Gender Relations, and the Political Culture of the Antebellum South Carolina Low Country* (New York: Oxford University Press, 1995); Joan E. Cashin, *A Family Venture: Men and Women on the Southern Frontier* (New York: Oxford University Press, 1991); John Mack Faragher, *Women and Men on the Overland Trail* (New Haven, CT: Yale University Press, 1979); Anya Jabour, "'It Will Never Do for Me to Be Married': The Life of Laura Wirt Randall, 1803–1833," *Journal of the Early Republic* 17 (1997): 193–236, and Anya Jabour, "'The Privations and Hardships of a New Country': Southern Women and Southern Hospitality of the Florida Frontier," *Florida Historical Quarterly* 75 (1997): 259–275.

23. On southern women, see Laura F. Edwards, *Scarlett Doesn't Live Here Anymore: Southern Women in the Civil War Era* (Urbana: University of Illinois Press, 2000), 27–28; Victoria Bynum, *Unruly Women: The Politics of Social and Sexual Control in the Old South* (Chapel Hill: University of North Carolina Press, 1992), 52–55; Elizabeth Varon, *We Mean to Be Counted: White Women and Politics in Antebellum Virginia* (Chapel Hill: University of North Carolina Press, 1998); Elizabeth Fox-Genovese, *Within the Plantation Household: Black and White Women of the Old South* (Chapel Hill: University of North Carolina Press, 1988): 224–225, 231–235, 281–289. On domesticity see Nancy F. Cott, *The Bonds of Womanhood: "Woman's Sphere" in New England, 1780–1835* (New Haven, CT: Yale University Press, 1977); Barbara Welter, "The Cult of True Womanhood, 1800–1860," *American Quarterly* 18 (1966): 151–174; Kathleen Anne McHugh, *American Domesticity: From How-To Manual to Hollywood Melodrama* (New York: Oxford University Press, 1999); Christine Stansell, *City of Women: Sex*

and Class in New York, 1789–1860 (Urbana: University of Illinois Press, 1987); Lora Romero, *Home Fronts: Domesticity and Its Critics in the Antebellum United States* (Durham, NC: Duke University Press, 1997); Karen Sánchez-Eppler, "Bodily Bonds: The Intersecting Rhetorics of Feminism and Abolition," and Laura Wexler, "Tender Violence: Literary Eavesdropping, Domestic Fiction, and Educational Reform" both in *The Culture of Sentiment: Race, Gender, and Sentimentality in Nineteenth-Century America*, ed. Shirley Samuels (New York: Oxford University Press, 1992), 92–114 and 9–38; Laura Wexler, *Tender Violence: Domestic Visions in an Age of U.S. Imperialism* (Chapel Hill: University of North Carolina Press, 2000); Jane E. Simonsen, *Making Home Work: Domesticity and Native American Assimilation in the American West, 1860–1919* (Chapel Hill: University of North Carolina Press, 2006); Mark Rifkin, *When Did Indians Become Straight? Kinship, the History of Sexuality, and Native Sovereignty* (New York: Oxford University Press, 2010); Linda Kerber, "Separate Spheres, Female Worlds, Woman's Place: The Rhetoric of Women's History," *Journal of American History* 75 (1988): 9–39; Tracy Revels, *Grander in Her Daughters: Florida's Women During the Civil War* (Columbia: University of South Carolina Press, 2004).

24. Kerber, "Rhetoric of Women's History"; Gerda Lerner, "The Lady and the Mill Girl: Changes in the Status of Women in the Age of Jackson," *Midcontinent American Studies Journal* 10 (1969): 5–15; Aileen S. Kraditor, ed., *Up from the Pedestal: Selected Writings in the History of American Feminism* (Chicago: University of Chicago Press, 1968); Alice Kessler-Harris, *Out to Work: A History of Wage-Earning Women in the United States* (New York: Oxford University Press, 1982).

25. Kaplan, "Manifest Domesticity," 584.

26. Lynnea Magnuson, "In the Service of Columbia: Gendered Politics and Manifest Destiny Expansion" (PhD diss., University of Illinois, Urbana-Champaign, 2001); Amy Kaplan, *The Anarchy of Empire in the Making of U.S. Culture* (Cambridge, MA: Harvard University Press, 2002); Gretchen Murphy, *Hemispheric Imaginings: The Monroe Doctrine and Narratives of U.S. Empire* (Durham, NC: Duke University Press, 2005); Greenberg, *Manifest Manhood*; Wexler, "Tender Violence: Literary Eavesdropping," and *Tender Violence: Domestic Visions*; Hoganson, *Fighting for American Manhood*; Shelley Streeby, *American Sensations: Class, Empire, and the Production of Popular Culture* (Berkeley: University of California Press, 2002).

27. Hoganson, *Fighting for American Manhood*; Greenberg, *Manifest Manhood*; Wexler, *Tender Violence*; Brian Rouleau, "Maritime Destiny as Manifest Destiny: American Commercial Expansion and the Idea of the Indian," *Journal of the Early Republic* 30 (2010): 377–411.

28. Racial projects include any attempt to define racial identity in order to structure social interactions and control resources, see Michael Omi and Howard Winant, *Racial Formation in the United States: From the 1960s to the 1980s* (New York: Routledge, 1986); Matthew Dennis, "Red Jacket's Rhetoric: Postcolonial Persuasions on the Native Frontiers of the Early American Republic," in *American Indian Rhetorics of Survivance: Word Medicine, Word Magic*, ed. Ernest Stromberg (Pittsburgh: University of Pittsburgh Press, 2006), 15–33, 25; Theda Perdue and Michael D. Green, eds., *The Cherokee Removal: A Brief History with Documents* (Boston: Bedford/St. Martin's, 2004), 15.

29. Alan Taylor argues that the United States fought a series of interconnected wars between 1810 and 1818 in a drive to remove any obstacles to western expansion. He includes in these "wars of 1810s" U.S. attempts to annex West Florida in 1810 and 1813, the Patriot War

in Florida during 1812, the Creek War in Georgia in 1813, and U.S. invasions of Florida in 1814 and 1818. Alan Taylor, "Settling and Unsettling Borders: Continental Legacies of the War of 1812," biennial J. J. Talman Lecture at the University of Western Ontario, November 4, 2013. Richard White, *The Middle Ground: Indians, Empires, and Republics in the Great Lakes Region, 1650–1815* (New York: Cambridge University Press, 1991). On race in Florida, see Nuño, "Making Africans and Indians"; Landers, *Black Society*, 229–248; Frank Marotti, *Heaven's Soldiers: Free People of Color and the Spanish Legacy in Antebellum Florida* (Tuscaloosa: University of Alabama Press, 2013); Weber, *Spanish Frontier*, 337; Baptist, *Creating an Old South*, 281–284.

30. 1830 U.S. Census, Florida, population schedules, and 1860 U.S. Census, Florida, population schedules (National Archives, Washington, DC); Rivers, *Slavery in Florida*, 8–10, 69–84.

31. Sattler, "Seminole Ethnogenesis Reconsidered," 36–69; Weisman, *Like Beads*, 107; Weisman, *Unconquered People*, 25–26; Susan Micco Snow and Susan Enns Stans, *Healing Plants: Medicine of the Florida Seminole Indians* (Gainesville: University Press of Florida, 2001), 13; James Leitch Wright, *Creeks and Seminoles: The Destruction and Regeneration of the Muscogulge People* (Lincoln: University of Nebraska Press, 1990), 306–308; Kokomoor, "Reassessment of Seminoles, Africans and Slavery," 234–236; Nuño, "Making Africans and Indians," 6, 107; Scallet, "This Inglorious War," 49–50. For Seminole perspectives on their history in Florida see Wickman, *Tree That Bends*.

32. Ramón A. Gutiérrez, *When Jesus Came, the Corn Mothers Went Away: Marriage, Sexuality, and Power in New Mexico, 1500–1846* (Stanford, CA: Stanford University Press, 1991), 298–336; Juliana Barr, *Peace Came in the Form of a Woman: Indians and Spaniards in the Texas Borderlands* (Chapel Hill: University of North Carolina Press, 2007); James F. Brooks, *Captives and Cousins: Slavery, Kinship, and Community in the Southwest Borderlands* (Chapel Hill: University of North Carolina Press, 2002), 215–228; White, *Middle Ground*; Perdue, *Cherokee Women*, 65–85; Baptist, *Creating an Old South*, 90–96; 111–119.

33. Weisman, *Unconquered People*, 24–28, 42–50; Grant Foreman, *Indian Removal: The Emigration of the Five Civilized Tribes*, 3rd ed. (Norman: University of Oklahoma Press, 1972), 318–324; Miller, *Coacoochee's Bones*, 25–30.

34. New Protestant migrants supported Methodist, Baptist, Presbyterian, Episcopalian, Lutheran, and Universalist congregations. By 1850, when the census first counted them, there were 177 churches in Florida, 5 of which were Roman Catholic. By 1860, 319 churches served Florida's growing population; 17 of them were Roman Catholic. There were 69 schools in Florida in 1840, as well as ten newspapers. By 1850, 103 schools educated the free, white children of Florida. U.S. Census Bureau, Population Schedules, Florida, 1830, 1840, 1850, and 1860, in Social Explorer Dataset (electronic resource), digitally transcribed by Inter-university Consortium for Political and Social Research, verified by Michael Haines, compiled, edited and verified by Social Explorer (Bronxville, NY: Social Explorer, 2003). Estimates of the number of Seminoles that the U.S. military removed vary from 3,824 to 6,000. John Mahon concluded that the United States sent 3,824 Seminoles to Oklahoma; *Second Seminole War*, 321; Brent Weisman and Grant Foreman both report that Americans shipped 4,420 Seminoles west during the Second U.S.-Seminole War, see Weisman, *Unconquered People*, 54–57, and Foreman, *Indian Removal*, 315–386, 323; Patsy West claims that "some 6000 Florida Indians" surrendered or were captured in the nineteenth century, see Patsy West, *The Seminole and Miccosukee Tribes of Southern Florida* (Charleston, SC: Arcadia Publishing, 2002), 9. Today there are just over 4,000 Seminoles and 600 Miccosukees in Florida; Betty Mae Tiger Jumper

and Patsy West, *A Seminole Legend: The Life of Betty Mae Tiger Jumper* (Gainesville: University Press of Florida, 2001), 12; Paul N. Backhouse to Laurel Clark Shire, personal email correspondence, September 2, 2015.

35. In 1814, 19 percent of Spanish East Florida's black population (387 people) were free; see Landers, *Black Society*, 75–83. Very few free people of color remained after 1821, and most who stayed continued to live near St. Augustine and Pensacola, U.S. Census, Florida, 1830, 1840, 1850, and 1860, in Social Explorer Dataset.

36. Albert H. Roberts, "The Dade Massacre," *Florida Historical Quarterly* 5, no. 3 (1927): 128–129; Missall and Missall, *Seminole Wars*, 91–100; Mahon, *Second Seminole War*, 87–134; Knetsch, *Florida's Seminole Wars*, 70–91; Scallet, "This Inglorious War," 94–95.

37. Missall and Missall, *Seminole Wars*, 1–3; Mahon, *Second Seminole War*, 1–25; Knetsch, *Florida's Seminole Wars*, 1–3; Robert V. Hine and John Mack Faragher, *Frontiers: A Short History of the American West* (New Haven, CT: Yale University Press, 2007), 70–71. To put the cost of Seminole removal in perspective, yearly federal expenditures totaled between $24.3 and $37.2 million between 1836 and 1842, so the Second Seminole War cost roughly what the U.S. government spent in total in one year, if not more. See *Historical Statistics of the United States 1789–1945* (Washington, DC: United States Department of Commerce, 1949), 300–301.

38. Missall and Missall, *Seminole Wars*, 104–121; Mahon, *Second Seminole War*, 135–189; Knetsch, *Florida's Seminole Wars*, 83–95; Scallet, "This Inglorious War," 27, 30–32.

39. Missall and Missall, *Seminole Wars*, 104–121; Mahon, *Second Seminole War*, 135–189; Knetsch, *Florida's Seminole Wars*, 83–95; Scallet, "This Inglorious War," 27, 30–32.

40. Other southern frontier states had similar white gender patterns: in 1830 55.3 percent of all whites in Arkansas Territory were male, as were 54.6 percent of Mississippi whites and 53 percent of Alabama whites. Settled states had more equal white gender ratios, such as South Carolina (50.6 percent of whites were male) and Georgia (51.7 percent of whites were male). Compared to Florida, the percentage of white males older than fifteen in other southern states was smaller. In 1830, when 58.2 percent of Florida's white males were over age fifteen, that percentage was significantly lower in nearby Alabama (50 percent) and Georgia (50.9 percent), and after Florida, the Arkansas Territory (another southern frontier territory) had the next highest percentage, 53 percent of white males were over age fifteen. The age of Florida's white female population was more similar to neighboring states: in 1830 50.4 percent of white females in Florida were over age fifteen, as was 50.2 percent in Georgia, 47.3 percent in Alabama, and 46.2 percent in Arkansas (in settled states, there were more adult white women, probably because they lived longer: 54.1 percent of white females in South Carolina and 55.5 percent in Virginia, were over age fifteen). U.S. Census Bureau, Population Schedules, Arkansas, Mississippi, Alabama, South Carolina, Georgia, Virginia, and Florida, 1830, 1840, 1850, and 1860, in Social Explorer Dataset.

41. Mock, *Dreaming with the Ancestors*, 34

42. Missall and Missall, *Seminole Wars*, 122–178, 182–188, 206–208; Mahon, *Second Seminole War*, 190–293; Knetsch, *Florida's Seminole Wars*, 95–132; Scallet, "This Inglorious War," 30–32, 119–152, 302–311, 317–318; Foreman, *Indian Removal*, 346–386; Mulroy, *Freedom on the Border*, 29, 57.

43. An Act to Provide for the Armed Occupation and Settlement . . . , 502–504; James W. Covington, "The Armed Occupation Act of 1842," *Florida Historical Quarterly* 40 (1961): 41–53; Missall and Missall, *Seminole Wars*, 189–202; Mahon, *Second Seminole War*, 294–320; Knetsch, *Florida's Seminole Wars*, 128–141; Scallet, "This Inglorious War," 300–301.

44. Mahon, *Second Seminole War*, 188, 323, 325; Knetsch, *Florida's Seminole Wars*, 129; Edward M. Coffman, *The Old Army: A Portrait of the American Army in Peacetime, 1784–1898* (New York: Oxford University Press, 1986), 51–52.

Chapter 1. Property, Settlement, and Slavery

Epigraphs: William Wirt to Laura Randall, December 8, 1827, Randall-Wirt Collection, Maryland Historical Society, Baltimore (hereafter MHS), 1912, 4. *Victoria LeSassier v. Pedro de Alba*, Records of the Probate Court, Escambia County Clerk of Court Archives, Pensacola, Florida (hereafter ECCA), 1831, 2. Reproduced in Loren Schweninger, ed., *Race, Slavery and Free Blacks, Series 2, Petitions to Southern County Courts, Part A* (Bethesda, MD: LexisNexis, 2003), microform, reel 5.

1. The letter was translated from French for the court and included in *LeSassier* (1831), 2. I edited the original awkward English translation, which was as follows: "Thou sayed that thou never gavest me the slightest motive? a slave of thine would have complained of it; but as for me, thou believest I was too much obliged to suffer them. But, Alba, that time of slavery is over. Consider myself thy equal in every respect."

2. *LeSassier* (1831). The enslaved people in her estate included Marie and her son Phillip; Jerome, Frederick and Antonio; Esther, Charlotte and Leandro; Matilde and her two children Laurentine and Manuel; Augustine and her freed young children Diana, Maria Louisa, Joseph and Cecile; Isabel and her freed children Virginia and Alodia; and Judith aged 80 or 90 years (free).

3. *LeSassier* (1831); Leora Sutton, "Victoria Le Sassier," from *Women in Pensacola, 1765–1965*, unpublished manuscript, ECCA.

4. Carole Shammas, "Anglo-American Household Governance in Comparative Perspective," *William and Mary Quarterly* 52 (1995): 138; Charles Donahue Jr., "What Causes Fundamental Legal Ideas? Marital Property in England and France in the Thirteenth Century," *Michigan Law Review* 78 (1979): 80–81; Marylynn Salmon, *Women and the Law of Property in Early America* (Chapel Hill: University of North Carolina Press, 1986), 81–119; Susan Socolow, *The Women of Colonial Latin America* (New York: Cambridge University Press, 2000), 9–12; Deborah A. Rosen, "Women and Property across Colonial America: A Comparison of Legal Systems in New Mexico and New York," *William and Mary Quarterly* 60 (2003): 355–382.

There was a controversy over the legality of three enormous land grants that Spain made after treaty negotiations began and, in the midst of that dispute, it appears that no one considered that some property owners in Florida were married women who would face an ambiguous legal position as the territory shifted from Spanish to U.S. governance. If upheld, those three land grants would have put almost all of the unoccupied land in Florida into private hands. Philip C. Brooks, *Diplomacy in the Borderlands: The Adams-Onís Treaty of 1819* (Berkeley: University of California Press, 1939), 62, 65, 135, 147–163.

"An Act Providing for the Adoption of the Common Law," *Acts of the Legislative Council of the Territory of Florida, 1822* (Pensacola: Floridian Press, 1823), 53–54, http://ufdc.ufl.edu/UF00073402/00001?search=1822; "An Act to Secure the Rights to Property of Husband and Wife," *Acts of the Legislative Council of the Territory of Florida, 1824* (Tallahassee: Office of the Florida Intelligencer, 1825), 189, https://archive.org/stream/actsoflegis24flor#page/n3/mode/2up; *John Brosnaham v. Heirs of D. and Catherine Duval* (ECCA 1833); *In re: Margarita de la Rua, née Bonifay* (ECCA 1833); *T. Pla v. C. Evans and P. Palmes, Executors of L. Pla* (ECCA 1843).

5. "An Act to Secure Certain Rights to Women," *Laws of the Territory of Florida, 1845* (Tallahassee: Office of *The Star of Florida* by W. and C. J. Bartlett, 1845), 24–25; Norma Basch, *In the Eyes of the Law: Women, Marriage, and Property in Nineteenth-Century New York* (Ithaca, NY: Cornell University Press, 1982). Texas was not part of the United States until 1846. Louisiana adopted civil law in 1808 but did not pass an act specifically about married women's property, George Dargo, *Jefferson's Louisiana: Politics and the Clash of Legal Traditions* (Cambridge, MA: Harvard University Press, 1975), 156–160.

6. Salmon, *Women and the Law of Property*, 81–119; Shammas, "Anglo-American Household Governance," 138; Donahue, "Marital Property," 80–81.

7. Socolow, *Women of Colonial Latin America*, 9–12; Rosen, "Women and Property Across Colonial America," 355–382.

8. Adeline E. Townsend v. Daniel Griswold et al., St. Johns County Court Records, St. Augustine Historical Society, St. Augustine, Florida (hereafter SAHS) 1838.

9. Kirsten Wood, *Masterful Women: Slaveholding Widows from the American Revolution Through the Civil War* (Chapel Hill: University of North Carolina Press, 2004), 16–17. Shammas, "Anglo-American Household Governance," 136–137.

10. LeSassier, 1831; Nancy Johnson v. William Johnson (ECCA 1822); J. G. Gagnet v. L. Gagnet (ECCA 1829).

11. Susan Parker quoted in "Women Big Property Owners here in 18th century," *St. Augustine Record*, February 22, 1993; *LeSassier*, 1831; *Gagnet*, 1829; William Wirt to Laura Randall, December 8, 1827 (Randall-Wirt Collection, MHS), 4; Julia Smith, *Slavery and Plantation Growth in Antebellum Florida, 1821–1860* (Gainesville: University of Florida Press, 1973), 213–222.

12. Territory of Florida v. Eliza Hutchinson (SAHS 1824); Pemberton v. McVoy (ECCA 1828). Property-holding patterns in Florida were typical, see Suzanne Lebsock, *The Free Women of Petersburg: Status and Culture in a Southern Town, 1784–1860* (New York: Norton, 1986); Salmon, *Women and the Law of Property*.

13. Bynum, *Unruly Women*, 59–87; Caroline Dunham v. David Dunham, John Stewart, Jeremiah Randolph, and Reuben Withers, Executors of Mary Dunham, deceased (SAHS 1834).

14. *Nancy Johnson*, 1822.

15. Deed Book A, Hillsborough County Court Archives (hereafter HCCA), Edgecombe Courthouse, Tampa, Florida, 103–104, 171–172, 234.

16. Deed Book A, HCCA, 35. In the spring of 1848, Robert Jackson appeared in Hillsborough County Court for assault and battery, "Sixth Judicial Circuit/Hillsborough County Court Dockets," HCCA. The law protected a wife's property from her husband's creditors and required mutual consent for any property decisions, but a wife could not sue her husband, see "An Act to Secure Certain Rights to Women."

17. I use "cracker" here descriptively, not pejoratively. A "cracker" was generally a white, backcountry settler in the American South. Americans in territorial Florida used it to refer to "cowhunters" (cowboys) and to independent pioneer settlers. Dana Ste. Claire, *Cracker: The Cracker Culture in Florida History* (Gainesville: University Press of Florida, 2006). On women's work in antebellum Florida see Jabour, "Privations and Hardships," 259–275; Revels, *Grander in Her Daughters*, 2–7; Baptist, *Creating an Old South*, 47–49. On southern women's work see Catherine Clinton, *The Plantation Mistress: Woman's World in the Old South* (New York: Pantheon Press, 1982); Fox-Genovese, *Within the Plantation Household*; McCurry, *Masters of Small Worlds*; Marli Weiner, *Mistresses and Slaves: Plantation Women in South Carolina, 1830–80* (Urbana: University of Illinois Press, 1998).

18. Eliza Bagley for minors v. Hart et al. (SAHS 1831); Michael B. Dougan, "The Arkansas Married Woman's Property Law," *Arkansas Historical Quarterly* 46 (1987): 3, 13–15; Wood, *Masterful Women*, 1–14, 35–60; Jane Turner Censer, *North Carolina Planters and Their Children, 1800–1860* (Baton Rouge: Louisiana State University Press, 1990), 123–126.

19. Fox-Genovese, *Within the Plantation Household*, 30; McCurry, *Masters of Small Worlds*, 79–80; Walter Johnson, *Soul by Soul: Life Inside the Antebellum Slave Market* (Cambridge, MA: Harvard University Press, 1999): 92–100; Baptist, *Creating an Old South*, 43–44, 94–96. On mortgaged enslaved property see Andrew and Julia Burgevin v. Ambrose and Mary Cooper (SAHS 1834); Francisco Moreno v. Maria Machado Caro (ECCA 1841); on rented enslaved people see Davis v. Parsons (ECCA 1842) and *LeSassier* (ECCA 1831). On financial uses of slaves, see Rivers, *Slavery in Florida*, 44, 80–82, 254; Johnson, *Soul by Soul*, 78–115; James Oakes, *The Ruling Race: A History of American Slaveholders* (New York: Norton, 1982), 170–179.

20. Using slaves that belonged to their wives, aspiring planters like Thomas Randall and John Bunch carved plantations out of an "Indian wilderness," see Daybook of Thomas Randall, March 5, 1828 (Randall-Wirt Collection, MHS), 1912, pp. 1, 12; William Warren Rogers, "'As to the People': Thomas and Laura Randall's Observations on Life and Labor in Early Middle Florida," *Florida Historical Quarterly* 75 (1997): 441–446; and Elizabeth Bunch vs. Cicely Green Munnsings (SAHS 1835). Cashin, *Family Venture*, 58–72; Rivers, *Slavery in Florida*, 44, 80–82, 254.

21. I surveyed the indices of Escambia County and Circuit court cases at the ECCA for all cases between 1821 and 1845 and read most of the cases in which a woman was involved. I surveyed the electronic database of St. John's County and Circuit Court cases at the SAHS for all cases between 1821 and 1845, and read a random sample of cases (78 of 215) that involved any woman's property.

22. "Petition of Sarah Stone and John Robinson," in Loren Schweninger, ed., *Race, Slavery, and Free Blacks: Series I, Petitions to Southern Legislatures* (Bethesda, MD: University Publications of America, 1998), microform, reel 23; "Petition of Mary Helen Alston," in Schweninger, ed., *Race, Slavery, and Free Blacks: Series II*, reel 6; In re: Margarita de la Rua, née Bonifay (ECCA 1833); Brosnaham (ECCA 1833).

23. Fox-Genovese, *Within the Plantation Household*; McCurry, *Masters of Small Worlds*.

24. Jabour, "It Will Never Do," 193–236; Jabour, "Privations and Hardships," 259–275; Rogers, "As to the People," 441–446; Anya Jabour, *Marriage in the Early Republic: Elizabeth and William Wirt and the Companionate Ideal* (Baltimore: Johns Hopkins University Press, 1998).

25. William Wirt to Laura Randall, December 8, 1827 (Randall-Wirt Collection, MHS).

26. Rogers, "As to the People," 441–446.

27. Daybook of Thomas Randall, May 17, 1828 (Randall-Wirt Collection, MHS).

28. Cowkeeper's band made up the third major community, with settlements in the Alachua district of central East Florida, near present-day Gainesville. James W. Covington, *The Seminoles of Florida* (Gainesville: University Press of Florida, 1993), 9–27, 53–54; Nuño, "Making Africans and Indians," 63–64, 193, 212–213; Saunt, *New Order of Things*, 289; Nathaniel Millett, "Defining Freedom in the Atlantic Borderlands of the Revolutionary Southeast," *Early American Studies: An Interdisciplinary Journal* 5 (2007): 379; Owsley and Smith, *Filibusters and Expansionists*, 117.

29. Larry Rivers, "'Dignity and Importance': Slavery in Jefferson County, Florida—1827 to 1860," *Florida Historical Quarterly* 61 (1983): 405.

30. Rivers, "Dignity and Importance," 404–430.

31. Covington, *Seminoles of Florida*, 66–71.

32. Jabour, "It Will Never Do," 193–236; Jabour, "Privations and Hardships," 259–275; on laudanum see Stephen Kandall, *Substance and Shadow: Women and Addiction in the United States* (Cambridge, MA: Harvard University Press, 1999), 14–80.

33. Kaplan, "Manifest Domesticity," 581–606; Anne McClintock, *Imperial Leather: Race, Gender and Sexuality in the Colonial Contest* (New York: Routledge, 1995), 31–36.

34. Marotti, *Heaven's Soldiers*, 13; "Treaty of Amity, Settlement, and Limits . . . 1819," in Thorpe, *Federal and State Constitutions*, 651.

35. Weber, *Spanish Frontier*, 337; Marotti, *Heaven's Soldiers*, 9.

36. Marotti, *Heaven's Soldiers*, 12–25, 33–79, 91–115, 120–151.

37. Since she never officially married Zephaniah Kingsley under U.S. Florida law (which disallowed interracial marriage), Kingsley's case did not turn on her marital status but on her citizenship rights. I include her here as an example of a free black person successfully using Article 6, not a wife claiming separate property. Daniel L. Schafer, *Anna Madgigine Jai Kingsley: African Princess, Florida Slave, Plantation Slaveowner* (Gainesville: University Press of Florida, 2003), 26, 70–76.

38. Marotti, *Heaven's Soldiers*, 92, 43–60, 71–77, 147.

39. A five-dollar "head tax" was levied only on free black households. James Denham, *A Rogue's Paradise: Crime and Punishment in Antebellum Florida, 1821–1861* (Tuscaloosa: University of Alabama Press, 1997), 98; Russell Garvin, "The Free Negro in Florida Before the Civil War," *Florida Historical Quarterly* 46 (1967): 15–17; Marotti, *Heaven's Soldiers*, 134–138. On taxation as an obligation of citizenship see Linda Kerber, *No Constitutional Right to Be Ladies: Women and the Obligations of Citizenship* (New York: Hill and Wang, 1998), 81–123.

40. Marotti, *Heaven's Soldiers*, 140–141.

41. Mahon, *Second Seminole War*, 39; Buckra Woman v. Philip R. Yonge (SAHS 1824). "Buckra Woman" may have been of mixed indigenous and African descent.

42. Margaret Cook v. William Everitt (SAHS 1826 and 1831). Philatouche (or "Black Factor") was of Creek and African descent. His name derived from his complexion and his role as a factor, or trading agent. In one deposition, the witness refers to the patrilineal inheritance rule as "M'Intosh's Law." Creek mestizo leader William McIntosh supported the "plan of civilization" for the Creeks, which included promoting patrilineal descent, but that plan originated in the late eighteenth century, and there is no record that Creeks passed an 1819 law regarding inheritances. Prior to the nineteenth century, Creeks had been a matrilineal society, but patrilineal bequests also began to appear in the late eighteenth century. Perhaps patrilineal inheritance was called "McIntosh's law" in the 1810s because McIntosh was powerful in that period. Andrew Frank, *Creeks and Southerners: Biculturalism on the Early American Frontier* (Lincoln: University of Nebraska Press, 2005), 101, 108; Robbie Ethridge, *Creek Country: The Creek Indians and Their World* (Chapel Hill: University of North Carolina Press, 2003), 173–174; Saunt, *New Order of Things*, 89, 168–171. On similar continuities and changes among the Cherokee, see Perdue, *Cherokee Women*, and Tiya Miles, *Ties That Bind: The Story of an Afro-Cherokee Family in Slavery and Freedom* (Berkeley: University of California Press, 2005).

43. The Louisiana Purchase Treaty protected the property rights of inhabitants under the U.S. Constitution, not under the laws of Spain or France; "The Louisiana Purchase, Treaty between the United States of America and The French Republic," http://www.archives.gov/exhibits/american_originals/louistxt.html, Article III. Texas was annexed by a joint resolution of Congress on March 1, 1845, not by treaty, see Joint resolution for annexing Texas to the United States in Peters, ed., *Public Statutes*, Vol. 5, 797–798. Lands annexed at the end of the U.S.-Mexico War fell under the Treaty of Guadalupe Hidalgo, which did not include explicit provisions protecting the property and citizenship rights of Mexican residents, see María Montoya, *Translating Property: The Maxwell Land Grant and the Conflict over Land in the American West, 1840–1900* (Berkeley: University of California Press, 2002), 168–170. See also Dolores Labbé, "Women in Nineteenth Century Louisiana" (PhD diss., University of Delaware, 1975); Kathleen Lazarou, *Concealed Under Petticoats: Married Women's Property and the Law of Texas, 1840–1913* (New York: Garland Press, 1986); González, *Refusing the Favor*; Gómez, *Manifest Destinies*; Jean Stuntz, *Hers, His, and Theirs: Community Property Law in Spain and Early Texas* (Lubbock: Texas Tech University Press, 2005); Dougan, "Arkansas Married Woman's Property Law," 3–26.

44. Louisiana's established white population continued to follow civil law rules as was their custom, as confirmed in legal statutes of 1808 and 1828; Dargo, *Jefferson's Louisiana*, 156–160. U.S. policies in Texas favored married couples by giving them more land, and by 1840 Texas wives could claim half of their homesteads. By 1848, Texas brought the "definition of separate property in line with the pre-independence Hispanic regime"; Carroll, *Homesteads Ungovernable*, 105–106, 130. Leonard Richards, *The California Gold Rush and the Coming of the Civil War* (New York: Knopf, 2007), 76–78; John Ross Browne, *Report of the Debates in the Convention of California, 1849* (Washington, DC: J. T. Towers, 1850), 258–259.

45. Basch, *In the Eyes of the Law*. When noted at all, these earlier acts are dismissed as accidents of expansion. Richard Chused, "Married Women's Property Law, 1800–1850," *Georgetown Law Journal* 71 (1983): 1359–1425; Sara L. Zeigler, "Uniformity and Conformity: Regionalism and the Adjudication of the Married Women's Property Acts," *Polity* 28 (1996): 473, n. 2; Carole Shammas, "Re-Assessing the Married Women's Property Acts," *Journal of Women's History* 6 (1994): 9–30. Cf. Patricia Seed, "American Law, Hispanic Traces: Some Contemporary Entanglements of Community Property," *William and Mary Quarterly* 52 (1995): 157–162. On intersectionality, see Kimberlé Crenshaw, "Demarginalizing the Intersection of Race and Sex: A Black Feminist Critique of Antidiscrimination Doctrine, Feminist Theory, and Antiracist Politics," *University of Chicago Legal Forum* (1989): 139–67.

46. Christopher Tomlins, "The Many Legalities of Colonization: A Manifesto of Destiny for Early American Legal History," in Christopher L. Tomlins and Bruce H. Mann, eds., *The Many Legalities of Early America* (Chapel Hill: University of North Carolina Press, 2001), 3.

Chapter 2. Innocent Victims of a "Savage" War

Epigraphs: "From the Emancipator. Florida," *Liberator*, July 10, 1840, 110. "War in Florida," *Niles' Weekly Register*, October 1, 1836, 67.

1. Andrew Welch, "A Narrative of the Life and Sufferings of Mrs. Jane Johns" (1837), reprinted in *A Narrative of the Early Days and Remembrances of Oceola Nikkanochee, Written by His Guardian* (Gainesville: University Presses of Florida, 1977), 15, 7–30; "Latest from Florida: More Indian Butcheries!" *Charleston Mercury*, September 24, 1836; "From Florida, Latest

Intelligence, Another Battle," *Charleston Mercury*, September 26, 1836; "From Our Correspondent," and "Indians-Butchery-Pursuit-Escape," *Daily Georgian* (Savannah), September 27, 1836; "War in Florida," *Niles' Weekly Register*, October 1, 1836; "Florida," *New-Yorker*, October 1, 1836; no title, *Daily Georgian*, October 3, 1836; "The War," *Daily Georgian*, November 11, 1836; "Mrs. Johns," *Daily Georgian*, February 16, 1837.

2. Jabour, "Privations and Hardships," 260.

3. "Roll of . . . Suffering Inhabitants," 434–445. Estimates of the number of Seminoles that the United States removed vary from 3,824 to 6,000, Mahon, *Second Seminole War*, 321; Weisman, *Unconquered People*, 54–57; Foreman, *Indian Removal*, 315–386, 323; West, *Seminole and Miccosukee Tribes*, 9.

4. Larry C. Skogen, *Indian Depredation Claims, 1796–1920* (Norman: University of Oklahoma Press, 1996).

5. "War in Florida," *Niles' Weekly Register*, October 1, 1836, 67.

6. Richard Slotkin, *Regeneration Through Violence: The Mythology of the American Frontier, 1600–1860* (Norman: University of Oklahoma Press, 1973), 18; on indiscriminate indigenous violence, see the American Declaration of Independence, www.ushistory.org/declaration/document/index.htm, and Skogen, *Indian Depredation Claims*, 24; for accusations of indiscriminate Seminole violence, see John Quincy Adams, "American Reply," *Niles' Weekly Register*, January 9, 1819, 370–373; Corinna Brown to Mannevillette Brown, February 3, 1836, quoted in James M. Denham and Keith L. Huneycutt, eds., *Echoes from a Distant Frontier: The Brown Sisters' Correspondence from Antebellum Florida* (Columbia: University of South Carolina Press, 2004), 21; "A True and Authentic Account of the Indian War in Florida, Giving the Particulars Respecting the Murder of the Widow Robbins, and the Providential Escape of her Daughter Aurelia, and her Lover, Mr. Charles Somers, After Suffering Almost Innumerable Hardships" (New York: Saunders and Van Welt, 1836), http://palmm.fcla.edu/fhp/, 5; on captivity narratives, see Michelle Burnham, *Captivity and Sentiment: Cultural Exchange in American Literature, 1682–1861* (Hanover, NH: University Press of New England, 1997); June Namias, *White Captives: Gender and Ethnicity on the American Frontier* (Chapel Hill: University of North Carolina Press, 1993); Kathryn Z. Derounian-Stodola, ed., *Women's Indian Captivity Narratives* (New York: Penguin Putnam, 1998); on the uses of women and domesticity to make war look like peace, see Wexler, *Tender Violence: Domestic Visions*.

7. The *Jacksonville Courier* article was reprinted in "The Seminole War," *Niles' Weekly Register*, February 6, 1836, 393–396.

8. David Haven Blake, "'The Man That Was Used Up': Edgar Allan Poe and the Ends of Captivity," *Nineteenth-Century Literature* 57 (2002): 331; Burnham, *Captivity and Sentiment*, 95–102; Shirley Samuels, ed., *The Culture of Sentiment: Race, Gender, and Sentimentality in Nineteenth-Century America* (New York: Oxford University Press, 1992), 3–8.

9. Indian captivity narratives often featured a "babe at the breast," Derounian-Stodola, *Women's Indian Captivity Narratives*, xxi–xxii; Patricia Cline Cohen, *The Murder of Helen Jewett: The Life and Death of a Prostitute in Nineteenth-Century New York* (New York: Vintage, 1998); Amy Gilman Srebnick, *The Mysterious Death of Mary Rogers: Sex and Culture in Nineteenth-Century New York* (New York: Oxford University Press, 1995); Streeby, *American Sensations*; Jesse Alemán and Shelley Streeby, eds., *Empire and the Literature of Sensation: An Anthology of Nineteenth-Century Popular Fiction* (New Brunswick, NJ: Rutgers University Press, 2007), xvii–xviii.

10. I uncovered only two instances of white captivity among Florida Native Americans: Duncan McKrimmon, see T. Frederick Davis, "Milly Francis and Duncan McKrimmon: An Authentic Florida Pocahontas," *Florida Historical Quarterly* 21 (1943): 254–265; and a woman known only as William Cooley's wife, who died in an Native American depredation in 1836 and reportedly had been a captive among them earlier in her life, "Murder of the Widow Robbins," 10.

11. As quoted in Denham and Huneycutt, *Echoes from a Distant Frontier*, 21–22; on the fear generated by the Haitian Revolution, see Edward B. Rugemer, *The Problem of Emancipation: The Caribbean Roots of the American Civil War* (Baton Rouge: Louisiana State University Press, 2009).

12. Robert Raymond Reid to John Forsyth, December 3, 1835, Florida Miscellaneous Manuscripts Collection, P. K. Yonge Library of Florida History, University of Florida libraries, Special Collections, Gainesville (hereafter PKY), Box 5, Folder 23.

13. Stephanie D. Moussalli, "Florida's Frontier Constitution: The Statehood, Banking and Slavery Controversies," *Florida Historical Quarterly* 74 (1996): 431–435; Landers, *Black Society*; Rivers, *Slavery in Florida*; Twyman, *Black Seminole Legacy*.

14. Skogen does not explain why these claims were even investigated given the ongoing war, but they were ultimately rejected on the grounds of a treaty signed with the Creeks in 1866 that granted them amnesty for all past offenses, which the U.S. Court of Claims interpreted to include the Seminoles as well, Skogen, *Indian Depredation Claims*, 49–50, 80–81, 124, 135.

15. Knetsch, *Florida's Seminole Wars*; Joe Knetsch, *Fear and Anxiety on the Florida Frontier: Articles on the Second Seminole War, 1835–1842* (Dade City, FL: Seminole Wars Foundation, 2008); Robert M. Utley and Wilcomb E. Washburn, *Indian Wars* (Boston: Houghton Mifflin, 2002), 130–135; Missall and Missall, *Seminole Wars*; Mahon, *Second Seminole War*; James W. Covington, *The Billy Bowlegs' War, 1855–1858: The Final Stand of the Seminoles Against the Whites* (Chuluota, FL: Mickler House, 1982); Weisman, *Unconquered People*, 56.

16. Nancy Cone Hagan papers (Florida State University Libraries, Special Collections, Tallahassee), Box 149, Folder 1.

17. Gamble family, John Grattan Gamble, and Robert Gamble, *Family History Notes*, 1898, State Archives of Florida, Tallahassee (hereafter SAF), 57–58. Microfilm.

18. Hagan papers, Folder 1.

19. Newspapers reports of the attack on the Carrs corroborate that it was Native resistance to white encroachment. A U.S. judge convicted five Seminoles of murder for this crime; one died, one escaped, and three were executed in Milledgeville, Georgia, in June 1827. See William Pope Duval, "Florida Indians," *Niles' Weekly Register*, January 13, 1827, 312; no title, *New-London Gazette* (Connecticut), January 10, 1827, 2; "Executions," *Niles' Weekly Register*, July 28, 1827, 353; "Domestic: *Sang froid*," *Western Recorder*, August 14, 1827, 131. In 1826, Eliza McIntosh Clinch wrote to her father John Houston McIntosh in St. Mary's, Georgia (just over the Florida border), requesting a slave trade but apologizing for any inconvenience as she had heard about the "recent depredations of the Indians." See letter of December 27, 1826, Correspondence of General Clinch's family, General Duncan Lamont Clinch Family Papers, PKY, Folder 1.

20. Hagan papers, Folder 1.

21. Reginald Horsman, *Race and Manifest Destiny: The Origins of American Racial Anglo-Saxonism* (Cambridge, MA: Harvard University Press, 1981), 192–202; Michael D. Green, *The*

Politics of Indian Removal: Creek Government and Society in Crisis (Lincoln: University of Nebraska Press, 1985), 47, 155–173; Perdue and Green, *Cherokee Removal*, 7–24.

22. October 27, 1838, Daniel Wiggins Diaries, 1816–1834, 1838–1841, 1862, SAF, Folder 11.

23. January 13, 1839, Ibid., Folder 12.

24. Wiggins mentions rumors and depredations on October 27; November 5, 14, 30; December 2, 9, 30, 1838; and on February 5, 17, 19, 20, April 4 and 5, and July 13 and 14, 1839; Ibid., Folders 11 and 12.

25. January 5, 1839, Ibid., Folder 11.

26. February 20, 1839, Ibid., Folder 12.

27. March 24, 1839, Ibid.

28. The figure of the frontier "Indian Hater," motivated to kill Native Americans to avenge the deaths of family members killed by them, was a popular literary trope in eighteenth- and nineteenth-century American fiction, James Hall, *"The Indian Hater" and Other Stories*, edited by Edward Watts (Kent, OH: Kent State University Press, 2009), vii–xxvii.

29. See Finding Aid, Daniel Wiggins Diaries, 1816–1834, 1838–1841, 1862 (SAF).

30. Gamble, *Family History Notes*, 77–90; "Life and Times of Jane Murray Sheldon, written at her dictation in 1889, An Autobiography," unpublished manuscript, Florida Miscellaneous Manuscripts Collection (hereafter Florida Misc. Mss.), PKY, Box 30, Folder 47; John L. Day, "Reminisces of Mrs. Sheldon," 1911, unpublished manuscript, Florida Misc. Mss., PKY, Box 30, Folder 10; Denham and Huneycutt, eds., *Echoes from a Distant Frontier*, 27, 30–32, 37, 39, and 41; Susan L'Engle, *Notes of My Family and Recollections of My Early Life* (New York: Knickerbocker Press, 1888), 61; "Savannah, February 16. Extract of a Letter from St. Mary's," *Connecticut Gazette*, March 17, 1802, Florida Misc. Mss., PKY, Box 33, Folder 10; J. B. Mason to Mary S. Mason, January 21, July 19, and November 10, 1836, and to Sarah Mason, February 24, 1840, Florida Misc. Mss., PKY, Box 78, Folders 12 and 13.

31. Mary Macomb to Eleanor Worthington, December 15, 1835, newspaper clippings and letters, 1771–1862, SAF, Carton 1, Folder 7. Other letters that mention news reports of Native American depredations include: letter from Mr. Wiggins to Daniel Wiggins, n.d., in Daniel Wiggins Diaries Collection, SAF, Folder 18; Corinna Brown to Mannevillette Brown, May 25, 1836, in Denham and Huneycutt, eds., *Echoes from a Distant Frontier*, 22, 26, 30, 41, 22.

32. Quoted in Jabour, "It Will Never Do," 231.

33. Cashin, *Family Venture*, 53–59; Baptist, *Creating an Old South*, 61–87.

34. Quoted in Baptist, *Creating an Old South*, 140, n. 38.

35. Quoted in Jabour, "Privations and Hardships," 263.

36. Cashin, *Family Venture*, 53–59; Baptist, *Creating an Old South*, 61–87.

37. Cashin, *Family Venture*, 58; Baptist, *Creating an Old South*, 85, 197, 208.

38. Baptist, *Creating an Old South*, 140.

39. Cashin, *Family Venture*, 53–59; Baptist, *Creating an Old South*, 61–72, 139–145; Rivers, *Slavery in Florida*, 95–99; Rogers, "As to the People," 441–446.

40. See Chapter 1 for examples of wealthy white women who brought property into frontier households; Jabour, *Marriage in the Early Republic*, 152–161; Baptist, *Creating an Old South*, 44–48, 69–73.

41. Cashin, *Family Venture*, 67.

42. Quoted in Jabour, "Privations and Hardships," 263, 267.

43. Denham and Huneycutt, eds., *Echoes from a Distant Frontier*, 80–82.

44. Cashin, *Family Venture*, 67–68.
45. Baptist, *Creating an Old South*, 53.
46. Baptist, *Creating an Old South*, 46, 53; Revels, *Grander in Her Daughters*, 9.
47. Scallet, "This Inglorious War," 10–11.
48. For examples, see Chapter 2, nn. 3, 52–57, and "From Florida," *Charleston Mercury*, January 6, 1836; "From Jacksonville, Army Movements, From Tampa," *Charleston Mercury*, October 19, 1836; "From St. Augustine," *Charleston Mercury*, January 8, 1836; "Important Intelligence from Florida copied from *Jacksonville Courier*," *Charleston Mercury*, January 12, 1836; "Indian Hostilities: Latest Intelligence," *Charleston Mercury*, January 12, 1836; "Later from Florida, More Indian Depredations," *Charleston Mercury*, October 4, 1836; "Later from Florida. From the Charleston Courier, 26th inst.," *Daily Georgian*, September 28, 1836; "Latest from Florida," *Charleston Mercury*, September 22, 1836; "Latest from Florida: More Indian Butcheries!," *Charleston Mercury*, September 24, 1836; "Latest Intelligence-Army Movements, &c.," *Charleston Mercury*, September 13, 1836; "More Trouble with the Indians," *Atkinson's Saturday Evening Post*, January 2, 1836; "Seminole War, from the *Tallahassee Floridian*, December 26," *Charleston Mercury*, January 5, 1836; "The Creeks Again, from the Tallahassee Floridian, December 10," *Daily Georgian*, December 17, 1836; "The Seminole War," *Niles' Weekly Register*, February 6, 1836; "Later from Florida—More Indian Hostilities," *Daily Georgian*, September 22, 1836; "Latest from Florida," *Charleston Mercury*, September 22, 1836; various untitled articles in the *Daily Georgian*, October 3, 1836; "From the Charleston Courier," *Daily Georgian*, November 14, 1836; several untitled articles in the *Daily Georgian*, February 17, 1837; "Indian and Negro War," *Liberator*, March 18, 1837; "The War Ended," *Florida Herald*, August 4, 1838; "From the Southern Patriot, Further Particulars of the Late Indian Murders in Georgia," *Times and Commercial Intelligencer*, August 8, 1838; no title, *Times and Commercial Intelligencer*, New York, August 18, 1838, Florida State Archives, M97–24, Carton 1, Folder 9; "Summary of News, From Florida," *Jeffersonian*, December 29, 1838, vol. 1, no. 46, page 368; "Escape from the Indians, from the St. Augustine Herald, Oct. 14," *Army and Navy Chronicle*, November 7, 1839; "From Florida" and "Correspondence of the Journal of Commerce, Key West," *Charleston Mercury*, July 31, 1839; "From St. Augustine," *Charleston Mercury*, June 7, 1839; "Gen. Macomb and the Florida War; Army Intelligence," *St. Augustine News*, June 1, 1839; "From St. Augustine," *Charleston Mercury*, June 7, 1839; "Lieut. W. F. Hanson," *St. Augustine News*, August 10, 1839; "Pleasant News," *St. Augustine News*, June 22, 1839; "The War Renewed!" *St. Augustine News*, August 3, 1839; "From Florida," *Charleston Mercury*, August 25, 1840; "From Florida—Destruction of Indian Key," *Charleston Mercury*, August 20, 1840; "From the Savannah Georgian," *Charleston Mercury*, August 24, 1840; "From the South: Attack on, and Destruction of Indian Key," "An Increasing Interest for East Florida," "A Card," and "Obituary for Dr. Perrine," *St. Augustine News*, August 21, 1840; "Late from Florida: continued outrages of Indians," *National Intelligencer*, November 12, 1840; "The Policy of the Government," *St. Augustine News*, January 1, 1841; "Correspondence of the Savannah Republican, Florida Dec. 20," *Charleston Mercury*, January 6, 1841; "From Florida," *Charleston Mercury*, January 7, 1841; "Glorious News from the South," "More Indian Murders," "General Humbug," "The Policy of the Government," *St. Augustine News*, January 1, 1841; "Important News from Florida," *Charleston Mercury*, January 4, 1841; "Interesting from Florida," *Charleston Mercury*, January 11, 1841; "The Army," *Niles' National Register*, January 16, 1841. On the political affiliations of these publications see Charles Sellers, *The Market

Revolution: Jacksonian America, 1815–1846 (New York: Oxford University Press, 1992); William W. Freehling, *Prelude to the Civil War: The Nullification Controversy in South Carolina, 1816–1836* (New York: Oxford University Press, 1992), 182, 353; Stephen L. Vaughn, *Encyclopedia of American Journalism* (New York: Taylor and Francis, 2008), 202; Marvin N. Olasky, "Early Nineteenth Century Christian Libertarian Newspapers: Rise and Decline of the Boston Recorder, 1816–1849," paper presented at the Sixty-Eighth Annual Meeting of the Association for Education in Journalism and Mass Communication, Memphis, TN, August 3–6, 1985, ERIC.

49. Gould, *Among the Powers of the Earth*, 182.

50. "The Jacksonville Courier," *Charleston Mercury*, October 25, 1836. Examples from the *Jacksonville Courier* are not included here as there are few extant issues, although often items in other papers were reprints from the *Courier*.

51. "From the Macon Messenger, June 30, Indian Depredations and Murders." *Atkinson's Saturday Evening Post*, July 16, 1836, 3.

52. "Another Indian Massacre," *Daily Georgian*, March 14, 1837, 1.

53. "More Victims of Savage Barbarity," *Charleston Mercury*, July 21, 1838, 2.

54. "The Indians and Their Truce," *St. Augustine News*, July 27, 1839, 1.

55. "Indians," *St. Augustine News*, August 21, 1840, 1.

56. "The Florida War, from Mr. Underwood's (of Kentucky) late speech in Congress," *Hartford Daily Courant*, January 30, 1838, 2.

57. Mahon, *Second Seminole War*, 261, 323; John Ellis, *From the Barrel of a Gun: A History of Guerrilla, Revolutionary and Counter-Insurgency Warfare, from the Romans to the Present* (Mechanicsburg, PA: Stackpole Books, 1995), 12.

58. "More Indian Murders," *St. Augustine News*, January 1, 1841; "The Army," *Niles' National Register*, January 16, 1841, 307; untitled article, *Charleston Mercury*, January 11, 1841, 2.

59. "From Our Correspondent, More Indian Depredations," *Daily Georgian*, October 3, 1836, 1; also reported in the *Charleston Mercury*, see "More Indian Depredations," *Charleston Mercury*, October 14, 1836, 2.

60. "The Policy of the Government," *St. Augustine News*, January 1, 1841, 1.

61. "Indian and Negro War," *Liberator*, March 18, 1837. Italics mine.

62. These numbers vary in different sources. Knetsch, *Florida's Seminole Wars*, 131; Missall and Missall, *Seminole Wars*, 55, 221; Mahon, *Second Seminole War*, 232, 283, 320; West, *Seminole and Miccosukee Tribes*, 9; Jacob Rhett Motte, *Journey into the Wilderness: An Army Surgeon's Account of Life in Camp and Field During the Creek and Seminole Wars, 1836–1838*, James F. Sunderman, ed. (Gainesville: University Press of Florida, 1963), 182–183; Bartholomew Lynch journal, 1837–1839, Special Collections Department, Florida State University Libraries, Tallahassee; Felix P. McGaughy, "The Squaw Kissing War: Bartholomew M. Lynch's Journal of the Second Seminole War, 1836–1839" (M.A. thesis, Florida State University, 1965).

63. Patrick J. Jung, *The Black Hawk War of 1832* (Norman: University of Oklahoma Press, 2007), 172–174; Eby, *That Disgraceful Affair*, 17; Kerry A. Trask, *Black Hawk: The Battle for the Heart of America* (New York: Henry Holt, 2006), 197, 262–263, 286–308; on Osceola and other Seminoles as "noble savages," see Patricia R. Wickman, *Osceola's Legacy* (Tuscaloosa: University of Alabama Press, 1991), 134, and Mikaëla Adams, "Savage Foes, Noble Warriors, and Frail Remnants: Florida Seminoles in the White Imagination, 1865–1934," (M.A. thesis, University of North Carolina at Chapel Hill, 2009).

64. William P. Edwards, *Narrative of the Capture and Providential Escape of Misses Frances and Almira Hall, Two respectable young women (sisters) of the ages of 16 and 18—who were taken prisoners by the Savages, at a Frontier settlement, near Indian Creek, in May last, when fifteen of the inhabitants fell victims to the bloody Tomahawk and Scalping Knife; among whom were the parents of the unfortunate females* (New York, 1833); Trask, *Black Hawk*, 209–218.

65. Brian DeLay, *War of a Thousand Deserts: Indian Raids and the U.S.-Mexican War* (New Haven, CT: Yale University Press, 2008).

66. Paul Foos, *A Short, Offhand Killing Affair: Soldiers and Social Conflict During the Mexican-American War* (Chapel Hill: University of North Carolina Press, 2002); Mark E. Neely Jr., *The Civil War and the Limits of Destruction* (Cambridge, MA: Harvard University Press, 2008), 6–40; Justin Smith estimated the war cost the United States about $100 million, of which war expenditures totaled over $66 million, plus $12 million paid to Mexico, see *The War with Mexico*, vol. 2 (New York: Macmillan, 1919), 266–267.

67. Foreman, *Indian Removal*; Prucha, *The Great Father*; United States Congress, Indian Removal Act of May 28, 1830, reprinted in Perdue and Green, eds., *Cherokee Removal*, 123–125.

68. Revels, *Grander in Her Daughters*, 3.

69. Revels, *Grander in Her Daughters*, 3–11; Rivers, *Slavery in Florida*, 16–65, 82–83; Baptist, *Creating an Old South*, 69.

70. Baptist, *Creating an Old South*, 48.

71. Ellen Call Long, *Florida Breezes; or, Florida, New and Old* (Gainesville: University Press of Florida, 1962), 186.

72. Revels, *Grander in Her Daughters*, quote p. 3, 4–8; Baptist, *Creating an Old South*, 50–51.

73. Quoted in Cashin, *Family Venture*, 69; Jabour, "Privations and Hardships," 269; Baptist, *Creating an Old South*, 48; Denham and Huneycutt, *Echoes from a Distant Frontier*, 29–39, 68, 92–127.

74. Rivers, *Slavery in Florida*, 18–21, 34–47; Revels, *Grander in Her Daughters*, 9–10; Armed Occupation Act permits (permit number) for Almira Dixon (811), Bee Crews (419), Henrietta Pool (330), Mary Ann Garrason (86), Mary Hall (177), and Ora Carpenter (274), which cite various "Indian" landmarks, including a prairie, field, trail, village, and the "Indian River," in their descriptions of intended white settlements in Florida, see AOA permits, General Land Office Records, DEP, Tallahassee.

75. Rivers, *Slavery in Florida*, 73.

76. Two are included below, the third is "An Authentic Narrative of the Seminole War; and of the Miraculous Escape of Mrs. Mary Godfrey, and Her Four Female Children" (New York: D. F. Blanchard, 1836), reprinted in Derounian-Stodola, *Women's Indian Captivity Narratives*, 211–234.

77. "Captivity and Sufferings of Mrs. Mason, with an account of the Massacre of her youngest child," reprinted in Josiah Priest, *The Captivity and Sufferings of Gen. Freegift Patchin*, Garland Library of Narratives of North American Indian Captivities, vol. 52 (New York: Garland, 1977), 56.

78. Ibid.

79. "Murder of the Widow Robbins," 3–6.

80. Ibid., 8.

81. Ibid., xiii.

82. Ibid., 5.

83. Andrew Welch, "A Narrative of the Life and Sufferings of Mrs. Jane Johns" (1837), reprinted in *A Narrative of the Early Days and Remembrances of Oceola Nikkanochee*, 229–260 (original pagination, 7–30).

84. Frank Laumer, "Introduction," *A Narrative of the Early Days and Remembrances of Oceola Nikkanochee*, xiii–xlvii.

85. Welch, "Life and Sufferings of Mrs. Jane Johns," 12, 7–8; Cusick, *The Other War of 1812*.

86. Welch, "Life and Sufferings of Mrs. Jane Johns," 16–17.

87. Ibid., 10.

88. "For the Benefit of Mrs. Johns," *Charleston Mercury*, March 29, 1837, 3; "To the Benevolent," *Charleston Mercury*, March 29, 1837, 2.

89. Untitled advertisement for Dr. Welch's lecture, *Charleston Mercury*, April 1, 1837, 3.

90. A Mrs. Johns also was listed in passenger lists arriving in Charleston and Savannah in 1837, see *Charleston Courier*, March 2, 1837, 2; *Daily Georgian*, April 15, 1837, 2; Stephen Nissenbaum, *Sex, Diet, and Debility in Jacksonian America: Sylvester Graham and Health Reform* (Chicago: Dorsey Press, 1980); Mary Hershberger, "Mobilizing Women, Anticipating Abolition: The Struggle Against Indian Removal in the 1830s," *Journal of American History* 86 (1999): 15–40.

91. Jennifer Morgan, *Laboring Women: Reproduction and Gender in New World Slavery* (Philadelphia: University of Pennsylvania Press, 2004).

92. Quoted in Jabour, "It Will Never Do," 233

93. Judith Walzer Leavitt, "Under the Shadow of Maternity: American Women's Responses to Death and Debility Fears in Nineteenth-Century Childbirth," *Feminist Studies* 12 (1986): 129–154; Richard W. Wertz and Dorothy C. Wertz, *Lying-in: A History of Childbirth in America* (New Haven, CT: Yale University Press, 1989), 18–22; Daniel Scott Smith and J. David Hacker, "Cultural Demography: New England Deaths and the Puritan Perception of Risk," *Journal of Interdisciplinary History* 26 (1996): 367–392; Baptist, *Creating an Old South*, 74–77, 140; Cashin, *Family Venture*, 66.

94. Baptist, *Creating an Old South*, 139, 51; Revels, *Grander in Her Daughters*, 4; Susan E. Klepp, *Revolutionary Conceptions: Women, Fertility, and Family Limitation in America, 1760–1820* (Chapel Hill: University of North Carolina Press, 2009), 15, 28, 31, 74.

95. U.S. Census Bureau, Population Schedules, Florida, 1850, in Social Explorer Dataset.

96. Rivers, *Slavery in Florida*, 86–87, 88–97, 105–123, 128; Morgan, *Laboring Women*; Baptist, *Creating an Old South*, 48.

97. Susan Klepp notes, "Staples of anti-Indian propaganda were graphic (and usually imaginary) accounts of killer Indians who would rip out fetuses from the bellies of dying wives and mothers. Savages were out to destroy not just the present generation but the future of the colonies," *Revolutionary Conceptions*, 74.

98. Baptist, *Creating an Old South*, 145–151.

99. Jabour, "Privations and Hardships," 264–274.

100. Quotes from Baptist, *Creating an Old South*, 148 and 147; see also 145–151; Donald G. Mathews, *Religion in the Old South* (Chicago: University of Chicago Press, 1977), 47–48, 102.

101. Rivers, *Slavery in Florida*, 210–228.

Chapter 3. Seminole Resistance

1. Transcript, Mrs. H. M. Weiss Oral History Interview with Jean Chaudhuri, n.d., 5–6.

2. See Introduction, n. 34; Mulroy, *Freedom on the Border*, 35–60; Weisman, *Like Beads on a String*, 85–100; Jane Lancaster, *Removal Aftershock*, 1–62.

3. See Introduction, n. 11. Some American political leaders in the 1830s used the history of Seminole migration and ethnogenesis to delegitimize Seminole claims on Florida. Hugh Young suggested to Andrew Jackson in 1818 that the Seminoles' only "title to territory rests on forcible occupancy and the dispossession of other tribes," and therefore that they had no legitimate claim to their lands. Not only was that incorrect, but by that argument no Euro-American has the right to any territory in North America at all. Andrew Jackson sought any justification for Indian removal and at some points claimed all the Seminoles were really just Creeks who had not long occupied Florida and should reunite with their (now enemy) kin in the West. These arguments were (and are) specious for several reasons. First, Native people understood human claims to territory as group- and clan-based and not absolute (not as private property, or territory waiting to become private property), many had hunted in Florida before they moved there, and included it in their own idea of their homeland. Second, state borders in the Southeast were made by whites and not by indigenous people, for whom the difference between southern Georgia and Alabama (or eastern Louisiana) and northern Florida was totally irrelevant. Third, Florida's Native peoples had fled to Florida to escape white encroachment elsewhere, and as refugees from many prior colonial-Indian conflicts one can hardly fault them for being relatively new to Florida. Fourth, by Euro-American ideas about lend tenure, possession is nine-tenths of the law, and those who occupy a place not yet recorded as the private property of someone else have the legal claim on it. Native people in Florida were, without dispute, residents of the region before anyone called an "American"; and under international law, by the terms of the Adams-Onís Treaty, they could have been granted property and citizenship rights as residents of Spanish colonial Florida (although of course the United States never imagined doing so). Finally, although perhaps as much as one-third of their population arrived after 1814 (two thousand out of six thousand), the other two-thirds descended from people who had arrived in the eighteenth century, in plenty of time for Native people in Florida to have buried their parents and grandparents and developed an attachment to the ground where they had done so. For all these reasons, then, the people who became the Seminoles in the early nineteenth century legitimately believed that Florida was their homeland, and went to war to defend their right to stay there. See Scallet, "This Inglorious War," 61; Wickman, *Tree That Bends*, 1–8, 67–81.

4. Jumper and West, *Seminole Legend*, 12; Snow and Stans, *Healing Plants*, 13–15; Micco, "Blood and Money," 212–244; Landers, "A Nation Divided?" 99–116; Kevin Mulroy, "Behind the Rolls: Pompey Bruner Fixico," in Gabrielle Tayac, ed., *IndiVisible: African-Native American Lives in the Americas* (Washington, DC: Smithsonian National Museum of the American Indian, 2009), 133–137; Paul N. Backhouse to Laurel Clark Shire, personal email correspondence, September 2, 2015.

5. Patricia Galloway, *Practicing Ethnohistory: Mining Archives, Hearing Testimony, Constructing Narrative* (Lincoln: University of Nebraska Press, 2006), 1–32, quote 7.

6. Ibid., 22.

7. "Memorandum, " Andrew Jackson to Duncan Clinch, December 16, 1835, Florida Misc. Mss., PKY, Box 5, Folder 16.

8. Journal of Bartholomew Lynch, March 9, 1839, as quoted in McGaughy, "Squaw Kissing War," 192. I checked all quotations from McGaughy's transcription against the original diary.

9. Ernest Stromberg, *American Indian Rhetorics of Survivance: Word Medicine, Word Magic* (Pittsburgh: University of Pittsburgh Press, 2006), 1–14. The Seminoles were not the only Native Americans to accuse whites of depredations against indigenous people, see Angela Pulley Hudson, "Forked Justice: Elias Boudinot, the U.S. Constitution, and Cherokee Removal" in Stromberg, *American Indian Rhetorics*, 63; Janice Schuetz, *Episodes in the Rhetoric of Government-Indian Relations* (Westport, CT: Praeger, 2002), xi–xxii, 80–85, 92.

10. He would not allow his interview to be recorded, but Chaudhuri later recorded what she remembered of their four and a half hour conversation. Transcript, Jean Chaudhuri Monologue (recollections of a conversation with a Seminole man she had seen carving out wood images), n.d., 1, 7, SPOHP, PKY.

11. Weisman, *Unconquered People*, 45; Foreman, *Indian Removal*, 318–320.

12. Foreman, *Indian Removal*, 320–322.

13. Foreman, *Indian Removal*, 324; Miller, *Coacoochee's Bones*, 13–44; Lancaster, *Removal Aftershock*, 32–85; Mulroy, *Freedom on the Border*, 11, 40–63.

14. Mulroy, *Seminole Freedmen* and *Freedom on the Border*; Mock, *Dreaming with the Ancestors*, 29, 30–31, 36; West, *Seminole and Miccosukee Tribes*, 15; Snyder, *Slavery in Indian Country*, 213–243; Kokomoor, "Re-assessment of Seminoles, Africans and Slavery," 234–236.

15. Transcript, Jean Chaudhuri Monologue, n.d., 3, SPOHP, PKY.

16. Ibid., 4.

17. Wickman, *Tree That Bends*, 18–19, 48–63, 82–93, 156, 210.

18. Transcript, Charlie Gopher Oral History Interview with Jean Chaudhuri, May 1971, 6–7, SPOHP, PKY.

19. Jean Chaudhuri Monologue (account of conversations with Mrs. B, a Miccosukee Lady, and Mary Huff), n.d., 3, SPOHP, PKY.

20. Wickman, *Tree That Bends*, 95; Jumper and West, *Seminole Legend*, 55; Harry A. Kersey Jr. and Helen M. Bannan, "Patchwork and Politics: The Evolving Roles of Florida Seminole Women in the Twentieth Century," in Nancy Shoemaker, ed., *Negotiators of Change: Historical Perspectives on Native American Women* (New York: Routledge, 1995), 194.

21. Patsy West, *The Enduring Seminoles: From Alligator Wrestling to Ecotourism* (Gainesville: University Press of Florida, 2008), 28–29, 51–68; Weisman, *Unconquered People*, 30, and *Like Beads on a String*, 28–29, 32–36. Although they may or may not have participated in hunting and fishing in the early nineteenth century, there are twentieth-century accounts of Seminole girls and women who hunted, fished, and guided canoes alongside boys and men, Snow and Stans, *Healing Plants*, 50; West, *Seminole and Miccosukee Tribes*, 31–39, 47; Kevin Mulroy states that Seminole women held title to many slaves as well as livestock, but other scholars believe that when Seminoles claimed blacks as "slaves" they were mainly protecting them from white claimants, not counting them as personal property, Mulroy, *Freedom on the Border*, 25; Kokomoor, "Reassessment of Seminoles, Africans and Slavery," 219–220.

22. Theda Perdue notes similar patterns among the Cherokees in the nineteenth century, *Cherokee Women*, 86–108, 194.

23. Weisman, *Like Beads on a String*, 80, and *Unconquered People*, 24, 37, 40; Kersey and Bannan, "Patchwork and Politics," 193–212; West, *Seminole and Miccosukee Tribes*, 19; Wickman, *Tree that Bends*, 156. Female tribal leaders, as well as wives of powerful men who wielded

influence, ruled among the indigenous peoples encountered by the Spanish in Florida between the sixteenth and eighteenth centuries. There is archaeological evidence that Seminole ancestors revered female as well as male statuary figures. Weisman, *Unconquered People*, 108–111, and *Like Beads on a String*, 28, 46; Wickman, *Tree That Bends*, 82–102.

24. Shirley Mock's ethnography of Black Seminole women indicates that modern Black Seminole women inherited a syncretic culture borne out of contact with African, Anglo-American, Native American, Spanish, and Mexican cultures. Today, they trace their ancestry along both paternal and maternal lines. Generosity, cooperation, and hospitality, especially in the form of food for visitors, are also cultural values and a matter of pride for them (as they were to nineteenth-century Seminole and white and black southern women). They continue to nourish their families and to welcome adopted children into them. Their naming traditions still resonate with the creole Afro-Seminole language their ancestors spoke. Many tell stories today about the children their foremothers lost to kidnapping and slavery. Mock, *Dreaming with the Ancestors*, 18, 29–31, 33.

25. Transcript, Jean Chaudhuri Monologue (recollections of a conversation with a Seminole man she had seen carving out wood images), n.d., SPOHP, PKY. While this story likely refers to an attack during the Second U.S.-Seminole War, American soldiers attacked and burned Seminole villages during all three Seminole Wars, so it might have occurred anytime between 1817 and 1858.

26. Ibid., 1–2.

27. Ibid., 3.

28. Nancy Shoemaker, *A Strange Likeness: Becoming Red and White in Eighteenth-Century North America* (New York: Oxford University Press, 2004), 59.

29. Transcript, Mrs. H. M. Weiss Oral History Interview with Jean Chaudhuri, n.d., 5–6, SPOHP, PKY.

30. Ibid., 3–6.

31. Andrea Smith, "Not an Indian Tradition: The Sexual Colonization of Native Peoples," *Hypatia* 18 (2003): 77; Derounian-Stodola, *Women's Indian Captivity Narratives*, xvi; James Axtell, *The Invasion Within: The Contest of Cultures in Colonial North America* (New York: Oxford University Press, 1986), 310.

32. Journal of Bartholomew Lynch, March 9, 1839, as quoted in McGaughy, "Squaw Kissing War," 192.

33. Quoted in McGaughy, "Squaw Kissing War," 163.

34. Quoted in ibid., 169.

35. Quoted in ibid., 192.

36. Lieutenant Colonel William Sewell Foster's journals from early 1837 mention "squaw" prisoners and the information they supplied. John Irwin, a Tennessee volunteer who served in Florida from July through December 1836, recalled, "If it had not been for Gen. Call, Governor of Florida, we would have caught Oceola [*sic*] that night.... The next morning there were a number of bottles thrown out from the tents at Headquarters, which had been emptied the night previous by the Generals and their escorts, and I do not doubt but that the drunkenness of our General Officers prevented us from striking a decisive if not final blow to the war that night; for liquor there was as it is now a great hindrance to our important duties." While it is not explicit, the officer's "escorts" may have been Native American women captives. A few days later, Irwin wrote that four Seminole women and eight children were

taken captive in battle, and one woman and child were killed. John R. Irwin, "Memoir of the Florida War," Florida Misc. Mss., PKY, Box 70, Folder 2, 16–19.

37. In his interview with William Stiles, John Mahon mentioned to Stiles that Seminole oral history interviews referenced the rape of Native American women by white troops during the Seminole wars, but rape was never mentioned in the written record. Stiles responded that the oral tradition was probably right that sexual abuse had been widespread. Transcript, Mr. William F. Stiles Oral History Interview with Dr. John Mahon, November 29, 1973, 19, SPOHP, PKY.

38. Jumper is a twentieth-century Seminole woman who served as the leader of her tribe from 1967 to 1971. The oral history narrative probably originates in events that took place during a brief peace during the Second U.S.-Seminole War in the spring of 1837. Jumper and West, *Seminole Legend*, 3.

39. Ibid.

40. Ibid., 5–6.

41. Derounian-Stodola, *Women's Indian Captivity Narratives*, xxii.

42. Jumper and West, *Seminole Legend*, 7.

43. Transcript, Jean Chaudhuri Monologue, n.d., 3–4, SPOHP, PKY.

44. Transcript, Charlie Gopher Oral History Interview with Jean Chaudhuri, May 1971, 6, SPOHP, PKY.

45. E. Susan Barber and Charles F. Ritter note, Section 30 of Senate Bill 511 (March 3, 1863) "broke new ground" by providing sexual justice to wartime rape victims for the first time in U.S. history. See their chapter, "'Physical Abuse . . . and Rough Handling': Race, Gender, and Sexual Justice in the Occupied South," in LeeAnn Whites and Alecia P. Long, eds., *Occupied Women: Gender, Military Occupation, and the American Civil War* (Baton Rouge: Louisiana State University Press, 2009), 49–64, quote 51.

46. Quoted in McGaughy, "Squaw Kissing War," 186.

47. Daniel Littlefield reproduces several lists of the Black Seminoles who emigrated (including many women and children) in the appendix to *Africans and Seminoles*; Mock, *Dreaming with the Ancestors*, 32.

48. Claudia Card, "Rape as a Weapon of War," *Hypatia* 11 (1996): 5–18, 7.

49. Card, "Rape as a Weapon," 9. As Andrea Smith states, "When a Native woman suffers abuse, this abuse is not just an attack on her identity as a woman, but on her identity as Native," see "Not an Indian Tradition," 71. I thank Kent Blansett for encouraging me to think about this at the Native American and Indigenous Studies Association annual meeting in 2012.

50. Card, "Rape as a Weapon," 10.

51. Quoted in McGaughy, "The Squaw Kissing War," 186.

52. Card, "Rape as a Weapon," 7; Edward E. Baptist, "'Cuffy,' 'Fancy Maids,' and 'One-Eyed Men': Rape, Commodification, and the Domestic Slave Trade in the United States," *American Historical Review* 106 (2001): 1619–1650; Adrienne Davis, "'Don't Let Nobody Bother Yo' Principle': The Sexual Economy of American Slavery," in *Sister Circle: Black Women and Work*, edited by Sharon Harley and the Black Women and Work Collective (New Brunswick, NJ: Rutgers University Press, 2002), 103–127; Andrea Smith, *Conquest: Sexual Violence and American Indian Genocide* (Cambridge, MA: South End Press, 2005), 16–17.

53. Smith, "Not an Indian Tradition," 70–85.

54. Theda Perdue, "Columbus Meets Pocahontas in the American South," *Southern Cultures* 3 (1997): 16; Kathleen Brown, "The Anglo-Algonquian Gender Frontier," in *Negotiators of Change: Historical Perspectives on Native American Women*, ed. Nancy Shoemaker (New York: Routledge, 1995), 26–48. Rape continues to be used as a weapon of war, see Card, "Rape as a Weapon," 7–8; Smith, "Not an Indian Tradition," 73–75; *Conquest*, 7–33, esp. 25 and 28.

55. Rayna Green, "The Pocahontas Perplex: The Image of Indian Women in American Culture," *Massachusetts Review* 16 (1975): 698–714; Devon Mihesuah, *American Indians: Stereotypes and Realities* (Atlanta: Clarity Press, 1996), 64–69; Raymond W. Stedman, *Shadows of the Indian: Stereotypes in American Culture* (Norman: University of Oklahoma Press, 1982), 25; Shoemaker, *Strange Likeness*, 123–124; Kersey and Bannan, "Patchwork and Politics," 199.

56. Entry dated April 20, 1837, Diary of Thomas Sidney Jesup, 1836–1837, microfilm, SAF.

57. Quoted in Foreman, *Indian Removal*, 346.

58. Motte, *Journey into the Wilderness*, 207–208.

59. Ibid.

60. Mahon, *Second Seminole War*, 243.

61. "From Tampa Bay," *St. Augustine News*, March 16, 1839, 2.

62. Sherman quoted in Mahon, *Second Seminole War*, 285.

63. Captured Native American women are mentioned giving intelligence during the Second U.S.-Seminole War in Knetsch, *Florida's Seminole Wars*, 31; *Charleston Mercury*, October 26, 1836, November 2, 1836, February 13, 1839, and January 4, 1841; Mahon, *Second Seminole War*, 232. Brigadier General Thomas Jesup threatened captives with hanging if they did not reveal what they knew, Mahon, *Second Seminole War*, 204–209. On Cloud's niece, see the Papers of William Sewell Foster, Florida Misc. Mss., PKY, Box 87, Folder 8.

64. Mahon, *Second Seminole War*, 283.

65. Green, "Pocahontas Perplex," 698–714; Mihesuah, *American Indians*, 64–69; Stedman, *Shadows of the Indian*, 25; Perdue, "Columbus Meets Pocahontas," 4–21; Helen C. Rountree, "Pocahontas: The Hostage Who Became Famous," in *Sifters: Native American Women's Lives*, edited by Theda Perdue (New York: Oxford University Press, 2001), 14–28.

66. The daughter of Hillis Hadjo (Josiah Francis), Creek leader and prophet of the Redstick movement, Milly and her family were among the defeated Redstick Creeks who moved into northwest Florida in 1814. Georgia soldier Duncan McKrimmon got lost in the Florida wilderness in 1818 and some of the migrant Redsticks discovered him. They sentenced him to torture and death as revenge for the deaths of their kin. Milly intervened and his life was spared. In most Anglo-American versions of the story, Milly's involvement appears exceptional and is explained as an emotional and feminine response, she was "moved" by his plight. One historian, finding the typical Indian princess narrative irresistible, wrote that McKrimmon would later "betray the tribe's whereabouts to U.S. forces." While her actions did not directly harm her people, Milly Francis' perceived generosity did nothing to stop the removal of the Creeks and Seminoles during the ethnic cleansing of the American South in the 1830s and 1840s. Whites did not reciprocate sympathy for her family, and when her father was later captured, Andrew Jackson ordered his execution without trial. Milly returned to Creek country after 1818 and was forced west with the Creeks in 1838. She settled in Muskogee and died of tuberculosis in the 1840s. The American Congress passed a bill in 1844 honoring her with a pension and a medal because she had saved McKrimmon, but she did not live to receive them. Covington, *Seminoles of Florida*, 39; Wright, *Creeks and Seminoles*, 201, 312; Davis, "Milly Francis and Duncan McKrimmon," 254–265.

67. Longfellow published the epic poem "Evangeline: A Tale of Acadie" in 1847, a fictional portrayal of a young woman who spends the rest of her life trying to find her lover.

68. Patsy West, "The Seminoles in the 1920s," *Seminole Tribune*, February 11, 2000, 3; Jim Robison, "Osceola's History," *Orlando Sentinel*, May 3, 1998; Jim Robison, "Seminole's Past: Polly Parker," *Orlando Sentinel*, April 21, 1996; Covington, *Seminoles of Florida*, 139–144.

69. Snyder, *Slavery in Indian Country*, 237–238; Nuño, "Making Africans and Indians," 272–275; Mock, *Dreaming with the Ancestors*, 30–33; "Late and Important from Florida," *Daily Georgian*, December 6, 1836; "Interesting from Florida," *Daily Georgian*, December 10, 1836.

70. Mulroy, *Freedom on the Border*, quote on 57, 29; Snyder, *Slavery in Indian Country*, 237–238; Nuño, "Making Africans and Indians," 272–275; Mock, *Dreaming with the Ancestors*, 30–33; "Late and Important from Florida," *Daily Georgian*, December 6, 1836; "Interesting from Florida," *Daily Georgian*, December 10, 1836.

71. "The Nation Robbing an Indian Chief of his Wife," *The American Anti-Slavery Almanac for 1839* (New York: Published for the American Anti-Slavery Society, Vol. 1, No. 4); Wickman, *Osceola's Legacy*, 14–16, 85; Mock, *Dreaming with the Ancestors*, 22; John T. Sprague, *The Origin, Progress, and Conclusion of the Florida War* (New York: Appleton and Company, 1847), 101. One example of an historical account that names Morning Dew as the part-black wife is Y. N. Kly, ed., *The Invisible War: African-American Antislavery Resistance from the Stono Rebellion Through the Seminole Wars* (Atlanta: Clarity Press, 2006), 21–22, 85 n. 77.

72. Barr, *Peace Came*, 15.

73. Mock, *Dreaming with the Ancestors*, 32–33.

74. Motte, *Journey into the Wilderness*, 209–210, Mahon, *Second Seminole War*, 236.

75. Barr, *Peace Came*, 13.

76. Foreman, *Indian Removal*, 375. Coontie was a starch made by harvesting the roots of the zamia or smilax plants, skinning and pounding them, and then rinsing and drying them into a powder. It was the mainstay of the Seminole diet during the war and for those who remained in the swamps of south Florida after 1858, where there was little land for cultivation. Weisman, *Unconquered People*, 111.

77. Foreman, *Indian Removal*, 344, 346; Mahon, *Second Seminole War*, 209, Diary of Thomas S. Jesup, 1836–1837, SAF, 148, 170. Seminole insistence on proper clothing in this example follows the conventions of a common negotiating technique that forced whites to give gifts, the diplomatically appropriate thing to do in Native society, Greg O'Brien, "The Conqueror Meets the Unconquered: Negotiating Cultural Boundaries on the Post-Revolutionary Southern Frontier," *Journal of Southern History* 67 (2001): 51–52.

78. Covington, *Seminoles of Florida*, 96–97, 106–108, 235; Adams, "Who Belongs?" 226, 235–236; Minnie Moore-Willson, *The Seminoles of Florida* (New York: Moffat, Yard and Company, 1914), 75; Kersey and Bannan, "Patchwork and Politics," 193–212, 196–201; Jumper and West, *Seminole Legend*, 55; Transcript, Ernest Lyons Oral History Interview with R. T. King, September 1973, 1–13, SPOHP, PKY. William Stiles related in November 1973 that he had just been in a Seminole camp and seen two white men plying three or four women and one man with alcohol. His "interpretation of the scene was that the white men were plying the Indian women with liquor, with the intention to couple with them sexually when they were sufficiently softened up. He said one of the women was badly swollen and bruised in the face, and his belief was that she had been struck by one of the white men." Transcript, Stiles Oral History Interview with Mahon, 19.

79. Transcript, Jean Chaudhuri Monologue (includes conversation with Mrs. B and Mary Huff), 4.
80. Transcript, Mrs. H. M. Weiss Oral History Interview with Jean Chaudhuri, 5–6.
81. Transcript, Charlie Gopher Oral History Interview with Jean Chaudhuri, 6.
82. Ibid.
83. Card, "Rape as a Weapon," 5–18; West and Adams both note that mixed Black and Seminole children of mothers who were not members of a Seminole clan were given an identity in "Little Black Snake" Clan, see Adams, "Who Belongs?" 240–246; West and Jumper, *Seminole Legend*, 39–44, 125–126; West, *Seminole and Miccosukee Tribes*, 15.
84. Foreman, *Indian Removal*, 365.
85. West, *Seminole and Miccosukee Tribes*, 37; Ann Marie Plane, "Childbirth Practices Among Native American Women of New England and Canada, 1600–1800," in Judith Walzer Leavitt, *Women and Health in America: Historical Readings* (Madison: University of Wisconsin Press, 1999), 38–47.
86. Motte, *Journey into the Wilderness*, 120.
87. Mahon, *Second Seminole War*, 204–207.

Chapter 4. Turning Sufferers into Settlers

Epigraphs: Delegate Joseph M. White (Terr. of Florida), 12 Reg. Deb. 2445 (1836). R. K. Call to William Davenport, May 20, 1839, William Davenport Papers, 1835–1842, Florida Misc. Mss., PKY, Box 1, Folder 1; see also R. K. Call to Col. Davenport, March 11, 1839, and R. K. Call to Col. Davenport, July 17, 1839, in same.

1. Delegate Joseph M. White (Terr. of Florida), 12 Reg. Deb. 2445 (1836).
2. Resolution authorizing the president to furnish rations to certain inhabitants of Florida, February 1, 1836, in Peters, ed., *Public Statutes*, Vol. 5, 131.
3. Amanda Bleach Willis, Adela Flotard, Eliza L. Crews, Susannah Brown, and Rebecca Munden were suffering inhabitants in 1842 and filed Armed Occupation Act (AOA) land claims in 1842–43. Single or widowed women Eliza Ann Riley, Charlotte Davis, Christian Brown, Mary Darby, Eliza Glenn, Elizabeth Standley, Susan Whitehurst, Mary Hall, Elizabeth Ann Barry, Mary Ann Garrison, Charlotte Ayers, Nancy Campbell, Elizabeth Hogan, and Ann Mangham filed AOA claims. "Roll of . . . Suffering Inhabitants," 434–445; US BLM, *Florida Pre-1908 . . . Patents*; AOA permits, General Land Office Records, DEP, Tallahassee.
4. Susan M. Sterett, *Public Pensions: Gender and Civic Service in the States, 1850–1937* (Ithaca, NY: Cornell University Press, 2003); Linda Gordon, *Pitied but not Entitled: Single Mothers and the History of Welfare, 1890–1935* (Cambridge, MA: Harvard University Press, 1999); Theda Skocpol, *Protecting Soldiers and Mothers: The Political Origins of Social Policy in the United States* (Cambridge, MA: Harvard University Press, 1996); Daniel L. Schafer, "U.S. Territory and State," in *The New History of Florida*, rev. ed., Michael Gannon, ed. (Gainesville: University Press of Florida, 2013), 228.
5. Reid recounted that during a very recent attack on the Stafford family, the husband had distracted Seminole attackers while his wife took their children out the back door. She fled ten miles to a neighbor's house with her three small children, in the cold, as gunshots sounded behind them. Reid clearly hoped that her story would compel national leaders to send military aid to the anxious territory. Robert Raymond Reid to John Forsyth, December 3, 1835, Florida Misc. Mss., PKY, Box 5, Folder 23.

6. R. K. Call to William Davenport, May 20, 1839, William Davenport Papers, 1835–1842, Florida Misc. Mss., PKY, Box 1, Folder 1.

7. In 1839, following several depredations in Madison County, forty-one frontier residents sent a petition to army headquarters at Fort Lawson, requesting that commanders station a company of soldiers near their settlements. Undated petition, William Davenport Papers, 1835–1842, Florida Misc. Mss., PKY, Box 1, Folder 1. Schafer, "U.S. Territory and State," 228.

8. White, quote from "Sufferers in Florida," 12 Reg. Deb. 2438–2448 (1836), quote from 2438–2439; "Domestic Intelligence from the St. Augustine Herald," *Army and Navy Chronicle* (Washington, DC), October 26, 1837; votes for similar policies during other Indian Wars did split along party lines, as Michele Landis discusses, "Let Me Next Time Be Tried by Fire: Disaster Relief and the Origins of the American Welfare State, 1789–1874," *Northwestern University Law Review* 92 (1998): 967–1034.

9. Barbara J. Nelson, "The Gender, Race, and Class Origins of Early Welfare Policy and the Welfare State: A Comparison of Workmen's Compensation and Mothers' Aid," in *Women, Politics, and Change*, ed. Louise Tilly and Patricia Gurin (New York: Russell Sage Foundation, 1989), 413–435; Gordon, *Pitied but not Entitled*; Skocpol, *Protecting Soldiers and Mothers*; Sterett, *Public Pensions*.

10. Granger, 12 Reg. Deb. 2441 (1836); "Hostility of the Seminoles of Florida and Military Operations Against Them in 1836," January 27, 1836, *American State Papers: Military Affairs* 6: 19–22.

11. Kirsten E. Wood, "Broken Reeds and Competent Farmers: Slaveholding Widows in the Southeastern United States, 1783–1861," *Journal of Women's History* 13 (2001): 34–57, and *Masterful Women*.

12. 12 Reg. Deb. 2441–2442 (1836).

13. "Renewal of the War in Florida," *Atkinson's Saturday Evening Post*, May 21, 1836, 3; "The Seminole War," *Niles' Weekly*, March 26, 1836, 53; Granger, 12 Reg. Deb. 2441 (1836).

14. Stokely, quoted in Michael E. Welsh, "Legislating a Homestead Bill: Thomas Hart Benton and the Second Seminole War," *Florida Historical Quarterly* 57 (1978): 169. Senator William Campbell Preston (South Carolina—Whig) expressed a similar view. Florida was "low and dangerous to the health of the Anglo-Saxon blood, and inviting only to those who had slaves to perform their labor," distinguishing it from the West, where "farmers, a man and his wife" would subsist on the land. Real, permanent settlement required the presence of white farmers and their wives, not the absentee slave owners he feared would acquire Florida lands. Preston, Appendix to Cong. Globe, 26th Cong., 1st Sess. 75 (1840).

15. Landis, "Let Me Next Time," 973; Michele L. Landis, "Fate, Responsibility, and 'Natural' Disaster Relief: Narrating the American Welfare State," *Law and Society Review* 33 (1999): 257–318; Michele Landis Dauber, "The Sympathetic State," *Law and History Review* 23 (2005): 387–442, and "The War of 1812, September 11th, and the Politics of Compensation," *DePaul Law Review* 53 (2003): 289–354.

16. 12 Reg. Deb. 2439 (1836); Knetsch, *Florida's Seminole Wars*, 47–48, 54, and *Fear and Anxiety on the Florida Frontier*, 34; Mahon, *Second Seminole War*, 47; Foreman, *Indian Removal*, 314–386.

17. Quote from Gorham Parks (Democrat-Maine), 12 Reg. Deb. 2440 (1836); 12 Reg. Deb.1537, 1592–1593, 4032–50 (1836).

18. 12 Reg. Deb. 2442 (1836).

19. Michael B. Katz, *In the Shadow of the Poorhouse: A Social History of Welfare in America* (New York: Basic Books, 1986), 3–57; Greg Shaw, *The Welfare Debate* (Westport, CT: Greenwood Press, 2007), 19–40.

20. 12 Reg. Deb. 2443–2444 (1836).

21. Skogen, *Indian Depredation Claims*, 23–86.

22. 12 Reg. Deb. 2446 (1836).

23. Anna Maria Dummett, "Remembrances of the Old Plantation," *Literary Florida* (1949): 8–15; "Roll of . . . Suffering Inhabitants," 438.

24. Motte, *Journey into the Wilderness*, 94–96; "War in Florida," *Niles' Weekly*, September 3, 1836, 6.

25. *The Army and Navy Chronicle* reprinted the resolution on February 4, 1836, 2 and 76; and reprinted the War Department regulations on February 11, 1836, 95.

26. *Army and Navy Chronicle*, February 4, 1836, 2 and 76; *Army and Navy Chronicle*, February 11, 1836, 95; Poinsett to Jesup, September 13, 1837, "Letters Relating to the Relief Program Sponsored by Congress for Indigent and Suffering Inhabitants in Florida," Florida Misc. Mss., PKY, Box 48, Folder 15; "Correspondence . . . 'Suffering Inhabitants of Florida,'" 121–122.

27. Clarence E. Carter, ed., *Territorial Papers of the United States*, Vol. 25, *The Territory of Florida, 1834–1839* (Washington, DC: Government Printing Office, 1960), 411–412; "Roll of . . . Suffering Inhabitants," 434–445.

28. "Roll of . . . Suffering Inhabitants," 434–445.

29. Ibid.

30. "Roll of . . . Suffering Inhabitants," 434–445; "Regulations," *Army and Navy Chronicle*, February 11, 1836, 95; Poinsett to Jesup, September 13, 1837, "Letters Relating to the Relief Program," Folder 15.

31. "Roll of . . . Suffering Inhabitants," 434–445; 1850 U.S. Census, Florida, St. Johns County, population schedules, 202–206, 212, 215–216; 1860 U.S. Census, Florida, St. Johns County, population schedules, 609, 623, 628, 633, 634, 642, 651; comparative value calculated using a GDP per capita formula, "Measuring Worth," www.measuringworth.com; Louis Johnston and Samuel H. Williamson, "What Was the U.S. GDP Then?" MeasuringWorth, www.measuringworth.org/usgdp/.

32. There are good reasons to suspect that Jane Baya was the widow on the 1842 ration rolls, but due to the lack of detail in the 1840 census it is not possible to be entirely sure. In 1840, Antonio Baya is listed as the head of a household in St. Augustine that contained a white man between age 40 and age 50, a white woman between 30 and 40, seven white children (one boy under 5, two boys and one girl between 5 and 10, a girl between 10 and 15, two girls between 15 and 20), and one male slave between the ages of 10 and 24. That is consistent with the widow and five children under age 14 listed as suffering inhabitants in 1842. In 1850, Antonio Baya is again listed in the census as the head of a household in St. Augustine, a 45-year-old illiterate butcher with $500 worth of real property. This inconsistency with his exact age is fairly typical of the census in the early nineteenth century, and in the 1860 census Antonio Baya is listed as 61 years old, which would be consistent with the 1840 age (in his 40s twenty years earlier). His wife, named Jane in both 1850 and 1860 censuses, gave her age as 43 in 1850 and 52 in 1860, so she could definitely be the same woman from the 1840 census (then in her 30s, if she had begun to bear children at age 17 or 18, she could have had daughters as

old as 16 at age 33; no names were recorded for household members before 1850, unfortunately). The children are harder to track, since so many would age out of the household in a decade, and no names were given in the 1840 census nor on the rolls of suffering inhabitants. In 1840 the Antonio Baya household had seven children, five under age 14, consistent with the widow with five children under 14 on the rolls of suffering inhabitants. By 1850, the older daughters (now between 20 and 30) would have aged out of the household, but one might expect to find a son between 10 and 15, and maybe a daughter between 15 and 20 (unless she was married already), and two sons between 15 and 20 (unless they had married or left the household to begin working/marry). In 1850, however, they had two sons between 10 and 15 (Francis 14 and Eleuterio 12, who would have been 4 and 2 in 1840). Florence, living nearby, was probably another son, age 23; perhaps he was mistakenly recorded as a daughter between 10 and 15 in 1840 because his name in English was a typical girl's name (he was probably Florencio to his parents). Further, it is entirely possible that the Bayas adopted an orphan from kin or neighbors, so this does not completely rule out the possibility that this is the same family. The family in the 1860 census is definitely the same one from 1850, as the names and ages of the children (now available) match. It is possible that the postwar Antonio is not the same man from 1842, although a man with the same name and a wife the same age seems a bit too coincidental. The 1840 census and suffering inhabitants lists are not detailed enough to be completely confident, but Antonio and Jane Baya's ages and the names and ages of their children suggest that the households listed in the 1850 and 1860 census are the same family as the Antonio Baya family from the 1840 census and the roll of suffering inhabitants; 1840 U.S. Census, Florida, St. Johns County, population schedules, 166; "Roll of . . . Suffering Inhabitants," 437; 1850 U.S. Census, Florida, St. Johns County, population schedules, 215; 1860 U.S. Census, Florida, St. Johns County population schedules, 609; Baya's Minorcan ancestors are enumerated in the 1786 Spanish census, see Philip D. Rasico, "The Minorcan Population of St. Augustine in the Spanish Census of 1786," *Florida Historical Quarterly* 66 (1987): 177. A $3,000 estate in 1860 compares to a 2010 standard of living based on $81,200.00, Johnston and Williamson, "Measuring Worth."

33. Rasico, "The Minorcan Population," 160–184; Weber, *Spanish Frontier*, 337.

34. "Roll of . . . Suffering Inhabitants," 434–445; Rasico, "The Minorcan Population," 160–184; Joseph B. Lockey, "The St. Augustine Census of 1786: Translated from the Spanish with an Introduction and Notes," *Florida Historical Quarterly* 18 (1939): 11–31. These surnames (except Southwick and Goff) are identified with families of Minorcan, Greek, and Italian descent in the 1786 Spanish Census of St. Augustine, and they appear in population records with diverse spellings; Genova was a form of Jenovardy, for example. Catalina (also spelled Catharina) Southwick was likely of Minorcan descent, given her first name. Rafaela Pellicer married Jacob Goff in December 1830 in St. Johns County, Jordan R. Dodd, et al., *Early American Marriages: Florida to 1850*, Ancestry.com, *Florida Marriage Collection, 1822–1875* (database online) (Provo, UT: Generations Network, Inc., 2006); 1840 U.S. Census, Florida, St. Johns County, population schedules, 115, 116, 118, 166; 1850 U.S. Census, Florida, St. Johns County, population schedules, 202, 205, 206, 212, 215; 1860 U.S. Census, Florida, St. Johns County population schedules, 609, 623, 629, 634, 642, 651; Johnston and Williamston, "Measuring Worth."

35. "Roll of . . . Suffering Inhabitants," 434–445; 1840 U.S. Census, Florida, St. Johns County, population schedules, 112; 1850 U.S. Census, Florida, St. Johns County, population

schedules, 203–204, 217; 1860 U.S. Census, Florida, St. Johns County population schedules, 628, 633; Johnston and Williamston, "Measuring Worth"; Lucy Wayne, *Sweet Cane: The Architecture of the Sugar Works of East Florida* (Tuscaloosa: University of Alabama Press, 2010), 73–93.

6. Wendy Gamber, *The Boardinghouse in Nineteenth-Century America* (Baltimore: Johns Hopkins University Press, 2007), 39; William Scott Willis, "A Swiss Settler in East Florida: A Letter of Francis Philip Fatio," *Florida Historical Quarterly* 64 (1985): 174–189; Walter C. Hartridge, "The Fatio Family: A Book Review," *Florida Historical Quarterly* 31 (1952): 140–144; "Roll of . . . Suffering Inhabitants," 434–445; 1850 U.S. Census, Florida, St. Johns County, population schedules, 204; 1860 U.S. Census, Florida, St. Johns County population schedules, 633.

37. It is likely that Frances Wood and Rachael Board were related by marriage, Rachael Silcock married Edward Board in 1838 in Duval County; while her brother Henry Silcox married Mary Ann Woods in 1848 in Alachua County, Dodd et al., *Early American Marriages*. It is unclear where Wood was farming, perhaps she rented a farm or one of her children owned the land. Ann Monroe (also spelled Munro) bought land in 1854, Rachel Board bought land in 1855 and 1857, US BLM, *Florida Pre-1908 . . . Patents*; "Roll of . . . Suffering Inhabitants," 434–445; 1840 U.S. Census, Florida, Duval County, population schedules, 136–137; 1850 U.S. Census, Florida, Duval County, population schedules, 113, 188; 1860 U.S. Census, Florida, Clay County, population schedules, 155, 158, 159; Johnston and Williamson, "Measuring Worth."

38. Worth to Wilcox, June 24, 1841, in "Correspondence . . . 'Suffering Inhabitants of Florida,'" 5; Mahon, *Second Seminole War*, 301.

39. Call, quoted in Daniel Wiggins Diaries, August 11, 1839, SAF, Folder 12; Cooper to Patrick, April 27, 1842, and April 30, 1842; Patrick to the Commanding Officer, May 5, 1842, in "Correspondence . . . 'Suffering Inhabitants of Florida,'" 30, 109.

40. See "Correspondence . . . 'Suffering Inhabitants of Florida'"; Cooper to Wilcox, December 20, 1841, 17; Wilcox to Cooper, October 9, 1841, 67; Worth to Wilcox, July 29, 1841, 9; Wilcox to Headquarters of the Army of Florida, July 6, 1841, 43–44.

41. Worth to Wilcox, June 24, 1841, "Correspondence . . . 'Suffering Inhabitants of Florida,'" 5; Mahon, *Second Seminole War*, 301; "Roll . . . Suffering Inhabitants," 295–405.

42. "Roll . . . Suffering Inhabitants," 445; "Correspondence . . . 'Suffering Inhabitants of Florida,'" 121–122.

43. Foreman, *Indian Removal*, 314–386.

44. Michael Shalev, "The Social Contract Revisited: 'Loyalty Benefits' and the Welfare State" (Oxford: Foundation for Law, Justice, and Society, 2010); Laura Jensen, *Patriots, Settlers, and the Origins of American Social Policy* (New York: Cambridge University Press, 2003); Skocpol, *Protecting Soldiers and Mothers*; Brian Gifford, "The Camouflaged Safety Net: The U.S. Armed Forces as Welfare State Institution," *Social Politics: International Studies in Gender, State and Society* 13 (2006): 372–399.

45. Murray Rothbard, "The Great Society: A Libertarian Critique," in *The Great Society Reader: The Failure of American Liberalism*, ed. Marvin E. Gettleman and David Mermelstein (New York: Random House, 1967), 502–511.

46. Sterett, *Public Pensions*, 3–7.

47. Stuntz, *Hers, His, and Theirs*; Greenberg, *Manifest Manhood*; May, "Reconsidering Antebellum U.S. Women's History."

48. See Appendix.

Chapter 5. Gender and Settler Colonialism

Epigraphs: Appendix to Cong. Globe, 26th Cong., 1st Sess. 71–73 (1840). Aldrich to Mannevillette Brown, April 30, 1843, in Denham and Huneycutt, eds., *Echoes from a Distant Frontier*, 175.

1. Cong. Globe, 27th Cong., 2nd Sess. 764–766 (1842); quotes from Samuel Stokely (Ohio-Whig) and William Cost Johnson (Maryland-Whig), 765.

2. A Bill to Provide for the Armed Occupation and Settlement of the Unsettled Part of the Peninsula of East Florida, S.B. 257, 27th Cong., May 16, 1842, amended July 1, 1842. Signed by the President on August 4, 1842; An Act to Provide for the Armed Occupation and Settlement of the Unsettled Part of the Peninsula of East Florida, in Peters, ed., *Public Statutes*, Vol. 5, 502–504.

3. An Act to Provide for the Armed Occupation and Settlement (5 Stat. 502); Covington, "Armed Occupation Act," 45.

4. An AOA permit was just the promise to settle on a land claim. A patent, the document granting the right to full title to the land claim, was awarded if the settler proved after five years that she had made an actual settlement on that claim. Rebecca Munden, Amanda Bleach, Eliza Crews, Susannah Brown, and Adela Flotard are the five suffering inhabitants who filed AOA permits. "Roll . . . Suffering Inhabitants," 434–445; AOA Permits, DEP, Tallahassee (copies of these permits are also in the National Archives, Record Group 49); US BLM, *Florida Pre-1908 . . . Patents*; An Act to secure Homesteads to actual Settlers on the Public Domain, May 20, 1862, in George P. Sanger, ed., *United States Statutes at Large*, Vol. 12 (Boston: Little, Brown, 1863), 392–393.

5. Policy historian Laura Jensen, for example, assumes that only men applied for and received AOA land, *Origins of American Social Policy*, 181.

6. Leading citizens of Florida sent several petitions supporting Governor Call's idea for a law that would establish the militarized colonization of the Florida frontier, including one on February 24, 1840, see Clarence E. Carter, ed., *Territorial Papers of the United States*, Vol. 26, *The Territory of Florida, 1839–1845* (Washington, DC: National Archives, 1962), 81–88.

7. Appendix to Cong. Globe, 26th Cong., 1st Sess. 73 (1840).

8. A Bill More Effectually to Protect the Lives and Property of the People of Florida, and to Bring the Seminole War to an End, H.R. 466, 26th Cong. (July 6, 1840). There was consistent conflict between militia volunteers and army regulars in Florida, as well as disagreements among Floridians and national leaders about which kind of soldier was more effective against the Seminoles. Floridians typically believed volunteers were better for the job, while army officials disagreed. Mahon, *Second Seminole War*, 242, 268–269, 297; Knetsch, *Florida's Seminole Wars*, 153. Americans in the early nineteenth century commonly assumed that army regulars were lazy and slave-like, unlike the brave, independent men who volunteered for militia duty, see Foos, *Short, Offhand, Killing Affair*, 13–44.

9. Appendix to Cong. Globe, 26th Cong., 1st Sess. 71–73 (1840).

10. As quoted in Jensen, *Origins of American Social Policy*, 123; original, 2 Reg. Deb. 727 (May 16, 1826).

11. A Bill to Provide for the Armed Occupation and Settlement of that Part of Florida Which is Now Overrun and Infested by Marauding Bands of Hostile Indians, S.B. 120, 26th Cong. (January 3, 1840, amended January 10, 1840); S.B. 160, 25th Cong. (January 3, 1839, amended February 9, 1839).

12. Appendix to Cong. Globe, 26th Cong., 1st Sess. 73 (1840).

13. S.B. 120, 26th Cong. (January 3, 1840, amended January 10, 1840).

14. A Bill to Provide for the Armed Occupation and Settlement of That Part of Florida which is Now Overrun and Infested by Marauding Bands of Hostile Indians, S.B. 160, 25th Cong. (January 3, 1839, amended February 9, 1839).

15. Appendix to Cong. Globe, 26th Cong., 1st Sess. 73 (1840).

16. Cong. Globe, 27th Cong., 2nd Sess. 764–765 (1842).

17. Appendix to Cong. Globe, 26th Cong., 1st Sess. 75 (1840).

18. U.S. *House Journal*, 26th Cong., 1st sess., March 16, 1840, 613; on alcohol in Indian-US relations see Peter C. Mancall, "Men, Women, and Alcohol in Indian Villages in the Great Lakes Region in the Early Republic," *Journal of the Early Republic* 15 (1995): 425–448.

19. Appendix to Cong. Globe, 26th Cong., 1st Sess. 75 (1840).

20. Ibid., 73. Italics mine.

21. The United States restricted citizenship to whites in this period, the "high noon of the white republic" and so rights to federal entitlements or social provisions, such as free public lands, were seen by most U.S. leaders as properly restricted to whites. Rogers M. Smith, *Civic Ideals: Conflicting Visions of Citizenship in U.S. History* (New Haven, CT: Yale University Press, 1997), 200. Jensen notes that many wanted to restrict preemption rights to whites only, *Origins of American Social Policy*, 175–176. Allan Kulikoff argues that Democrats and Whigs in this period celebrated the farmer, always presumed white and male, as the ultimate citizen, *The Agrarian Origins of American Capitalism* (Charlottesville: University Press of Virginia, 1992), 80.

22. Appendix to Cong. Globe, 26th Cong., 1st Sess. 71–73 (1840); Eric T. L. Love argues that late nineteenth-century expansionists had to follow a similar strategy in order to bring territories such as Hawaii into the United States; expansion had to promise benefits to whites without extending citizenship rights to nonwhites. See Love, *Race over Empire: Racism and U.S. Imperialism, 1865–1900* (Chapel Hill: University of North Carolina Press, 2004).

23. Appendix to Cong. Globe, 26th Cong., 1st Sess. 73–74 (1840).

24. Stokely, as quoted in Welsh, "Legislating a Homestead Bill," 169.

25. Cong. Globe, 27th Cong., 2nd Sess. 764–765 (1842).

26. A Bill to Provide for the Armed Occupation and Settlement of the Unsettled Part of the Peninsula of East Florida, S.B. 257, 27th Cong. (May 16, 1842, amended July 1, 1842).

27. An Ordinance for Ascertaining the Mode of Disposing of Lands in Western Territory, May 20, 1785, *Journals of the Continental Congress, 1774–1789*, ed. Worthington C. Ford et al. (Washington, DC, 1904–37), 28: 378.

28. When a bill is in conference, members of the House and Senate examine the versions that passed in each house of the legislature and make sure that they match exactly. If one version did not contain the amendment and the other did, then they could either add the amendment to the bill that lacked it, or delete it from the one that contained it.

29. Cong. Globe, 27th Cong., 2nd Sess. 765 (July 18, 1842).

30. Ibid., 766.

31. See this chapter, nn. 54 and 61.

32. Lewis Linn (Missouri-Democrat) believed the Senate should finally pass the amended bill, which would be "an inducement for necessitous, enterprising, and bold men to go to Florida, and save the defenceless women and children from the knife of the savage." Cong. Globe, 27th Cong., 2nd Sess. 818 (1842).

33. An Act to Provide for the Armed Occupation and Settlement.

34. Jensen, *Origins of American Social Policy*, 176.

35. One Florida newspaper exclaimed with pleasure that Congress "would be induced to extend" the provisions of the 1830 preemption law to Floridians, *Tallahassee Floridian and Advocate*, July 13, 1830, cited in Jensen, *Origins of American Social Policy*, 174. The 1830 law that granted preemption rights to all previous squatters (which was renewed almost every other year until 1840), and the final 1841 act that granted preemption to future squatters, had drawn on similar ideas: that bona fide settlers deserved to buy their land at the lowest government price (before speculators could buy it at the first public auction) because the settlers had risked their lives and fortunes in removing to frontier areas. Roy M. Robbins, "Preemption: A Frontier Triumph," *Mississippi Valley Historical Review* 18 (1931): 331–349; Jensen, *Origins of American Social Policy*, 143–150, 172–177, 184–187; James W. Oberly, *Sixty Million Acres: American Veterans and the Public Lands Before the Civil War* (Kent, OH: Kent State University Press, 1990), 17–19; An Act to Secure Homesteads to actual Settlers on the Public Domain (12 Stat. 392).

36. U.S. *Senate Journal*, 27th Cong., 2nd sess., May 11, 1842, 335–336; Welsh, "Legislating a Homestead Bill," 170.

37. Aldrich to Mannevillette Brown, September 12, 1842, quoted in Denham and Huneycutt, *Echoes from a Distant Frontier*, 172.

38. A permit holder could live in another place, on a lot that she or he purchased, so long as it was in Florida, if the AOA land was cleared and cultivated as required (settlers could also live in a house that was already built on the land). It was possible for a white settler to file an AOA claim for a plantation where he or she did not dwell and have slaves farm the claim while the white family lived in a town. See Item No. 14, United States, General Land Office (hereafter US, GLO), *Report of the Commissioner of the General Land Office, communicating an abstract of permits granted under the Acts for the Armed Occupation of Florida* (Washington, DC, 1848). The final bill, amended as of July 1, 1842, still included section 2, which granted wives and children the right to file concurrent permits for their own 160 acres of land adjacent to their husbands/fathers. By August 4, 1842, this section was gone from the bill. A survey of all debates in the House and Senate has not revealed exactly when this occurred; it was not in the debates of July 14 or August 4 noted above. An Act to Provide for the Armed Occupation and Settlement; US, GLO, *Report of the Commissioner . . . Armed Occupation of Florida* (Washington, DC, 1848).

39. US, GLO, *Report of the Commissioner . . . Armed Occupation of Florida*, 14.

40. Female AOA settlers and the men they wed with AOA claims near their own included Amanda Bleach Willis and J. J. Willis, Christian M. Brown Crum and Richard Crum; Mary Ann Garrison and Joseph Robles, Elizabeth Hobkirk and John G. Dampyer (aka Dampeer), and Elizabeth B. Standley and Thomas C. Kettles (aka Kittles). 1850 U.S. Census, Florida, population schedules, Benton County, 24; Putnam County, 195; Marion County, 140; US BLM, *Florida Pre-1908 . . . Patents;* Dodd et al., *Early American Marriages*.

41. *St. Augustine News*, October 1, 1842; Covington, "Armed Occupation Act," 48.

42. Jensen, *Origins of American Social Policy*, 181.

43. An Act to Provide for the Armed Occupation and Settlement.

44. As quoted in Joe Knetsch and Paul S. Camp, "A Problematical Law: The Armed Occupation Act of 1842 and Its Impact on Southeast Florida," *Tequesta: Journal of the Historical Association of South Florida* 53 (1993): 68–70.

45. Walter Eretson, for example, found out that his claim was privately held land, but he was allowed to file an alternative claim after the first one was nullified, see Item No. 9 in US, GLO, *Report of the Commissioner . . . Armed Occupation of Florida*, 17; Deputy Surveyor Thomas Weightman ,who wrote Valentine Conway on June 20, 1843, regarding Seminoles erasing survey markings, "Letters and Reports to Surveyor General Vol. 1, 1825–47," Title and Land Records Section, DEP, Tallahassee, 457, quoted in Joe Knetsch, "Notes from a Presentation on the Impact of the AOA on Marion County," May 19, 1990, unpublished manuscript, 4.

46. Knetsch, "Notes from a Presentation," 6–10; illustration from "Descriptive Notes on Selected Lands," DEP, Tallahassee. Munden to Jones, March 18, 1844, "Newnansville Land Office Correspondence, 1843–1851," Vol. 17, DEP, Tallahassee.

47. The General Land Office allowed permit applications for land not yet seen, presuming that any conflicts would be settled with affidavits from neighbors about who actually settled first. After W. Clark's land flooded in the spring of 1843 he requested a permit for a different parcel, but his request was denied. Twenty-eight permits issued for islands were denied. Eliza S. Crews (AOA permit 832) was a widow on the list of suffering inhabitants drawing rations at St. Augustine in June 1842, "Roll . . . Suffering Inhabitants," 437. US, GLO, *Report of the Commissioner . . . Armed Occupation of Florida*, 11, 17, 24–25; AOA permits, DEP, Tallahassee.

48. A Bill to Amend the Act Entitled 'An Act to Provide for the Armed Occupation and Settlement of the Unsettled Part of the Peninsula of Florida,' H.R. 302, 28th Cong. (April 2, 1844); A Bill for the Relief of the Bona Fide Settlers Under the Acts for the Occupation and Settlement of a Part of the Territory of Florida, S.B. 202, 30th Cong. (April 18, 1848).

49. Kathy Miklus, "Armed Occupation Act Settlers, 1842–43," *Florida Armchair Researcher* (1984): 9–21; Welsh, "Legislating a Homestead Bill," 157–172. The land offices in Florida recorded 459 patents (titles) to lands settled under the AOA. US BLM, *Florida Pre-1908 . . . Patents*.

50. The 1840 and 1850 census population figures in Florida from Historical Census Browser, University of Virginia, Geospatial and Statistical Data Center (2004), http://mapserver.lib.virginia.edu/. Mahon provides Florida population figures circa 1835 when the total population of the Florida territory was 32,000: 18,000 whites and 16,000 slaves, *Second Seminole War*, 130.

51. Twenty-three women filed AOA permits but did not ultimately receive patents: Eliza Attaway, Susannah Brown, Mary Byrd, Eliza Crews, Christian Metilde Brown Crum, Martha Dampeer, Charlotte Davis, Jane C. Demarest, Almira Dixon, Adela Flotard, Delia D. Gibbons, Maria Gunther, Rebecca Jenkins, Jane Knight, Evelina T. Pool, Henrietta Pool, Eliza Ann Riley, Eustatia Thompson, Josephine Walter, Esther Weeks, Ann West, Esther A. Winter. Dicy Whiddon did not patent her claim in Wahoo Swamp, but the heirs of John Whidden did receive the patent to land in the same township and range. The following seventeen women filed AOA permits and *did* receive patents for their AOA claims (or their heirs did if they were deceased by 1849): Rebecca Munden, Amanda Bleach Willis, Nancy Campbell, Mary Darby, Ann Mangham, Elizabeth Ann Berry, Patience Baisden, Elizabeth B. Standley Kettles, Elizabeth Sturges, Elizabeth Hobkirk Dampeer, Susan Whitehurst McClellan, Elizabeth Hogan, Mary Hall (permit 177, patent 23), Mary Hall (permit 277, patent 300), Mary Ann Garrison Robles, Charlotte Ayres, and Eliza Glenn; AOA permits, DEP, Tallahassee; US BLM, *Florida Pre-1908 . . . Patents*.

52. Five titles went to female heirs who were only partial heirs (shared title with siblings or others), seven went to widows of settlers who died before the five-year term of settlement was over, and another eight titles were issued jointly to "widow and heirs" of the deceased AOA permitee. Female heirs included Celia Carruthers; Emily Smith, Harriet Blanchard, Elizabeth Hendricks, and Mary J. Garey; Eliza Burton and Fanny Williams; Eliza Frances Clark; Mary Mackay and Janet Hutchinson; Mary Monroe; widow of Samuel Eigle; Dominga Hernandez; Martha Barker; Ellen Clark; Frances Barnes; Mary Lynch; widow and heirs of William D. Andrews; widow and heirs of Thomas Colding; widow and heirs of Thomas Brooks; widow and heirs of Richard Ridaught; widow and heirs of Michael Severy; widow and heirs of John Harrell; widow and heirs of John F. Miller; widow and heirs of Isaac Conyers. AOA permits, DEP, Tallahassee; US BLM, *Florida Pre-1908 . . . Patents*. On Barker and Baker, see Papers Concerning Permits of Claims for Land under the Armed Occupation Act, RG 49, National Archives, Box 513A and 508.

53. All land entries are recorded in US BLM, *Florida Pre-1908 . . . Patents*, but preemptions are not differentiated from other sales. The correspondence of the land offices contains many preemption claims, however, see entries for Mary Thomas Rollins, Mary Edwards, Margaret McCaskill, Elizabeth Barrows, and Sarah Sanders in Ledger of Monies Received, 1825–33, Tallahassee Land Office; letters regarding preemption laws in Commissioners Letters to Registers of Land Offices, Land Office Correspondence, Newnansville, 1843–1851, Vol. 17; preemption claims of John Bellamy, Thomas Goff, Abram Pringle, William R. Pattison in Letters, Tallahassee Land Office, 1821–1844, Vol. 1; letters regarding preemption claims of Susan Edwards, Ann Ponder, Caroline Wynns, William M. Loftin, and William McNeely in Letters, Tallahassee Land Office, 1845–1847, Vol. 2; preemption claims of Joseph Flower and Penelope Samuels in Letters, Tallahassee Land Office, 1847–1851, Vol. 4, DEP, Tallahassee; see also Letters, Tallahassee Land Office, 1851–1854, Vol. 3, DEP, Tallahassee. At least 120 veterans of Florida wars received land bounties for their service, Oberly, *Sixty Million Acres*, 17–19. Peter S. Genovese, Jr., "The Graduation Act (1854)," in Junius Rodriguez, ed., *The Louisiana Purchase: a Historical and Geographical Encyclopedia* (Santa Barbara, CA: ABC-CLIO, 2002), 128–129. Homestead entries in Florida are recorded in US BLM, *Florida Pre-1908 . . . Patents*; Alicia E. Rodriguez, "The Homestead Act (1862)," in Junius Rodriguez, ed., *The Louisiana Purchase: a Historical and Geographical Encyclopedia* (Santa Barbara, CA: ABC-CLIO, 2002), 140–142.

54. Census Browser, http://mapserver.lib.virginia.edu/. See Appendix.

55. See Appendix.

56. Frank Marotti, "Negotiating Freedom in St. Johns County, Florida, 1812–1862" (PhD diss., University of Hawaii, 2003), 204–205; Marotti, *Heaven's Soldiers*, 91–93; Mulroy, *Freedom on the Border*; Mock, *Dreaming with the Ancestors*.

57. In 1840, this land (south of 9/10 township line) was in Alachua, Dade, Hillsborough, Monroe, and Orange/Mosquito Counties. By 1850, the same area had been further carved into the following counties: Alachua, Dade, Benton/Hernando, Hillsborough, Levy, Marion, Monroe, Orange/Mosquito, Putnam, and St. Lucie Counties. I have included all of Alachua County in this number even though not all of it was available for armed occupation, but including it overestimates the 1840 (pre-AOA) population of the AOA-eligible area. Census Browser, http://mapserver.lib.virginia.edu/. Some scholars estimate that only about two thousand people came to Florida as a direct result of the AOA, while two-thirds of the six thousand

AOA settlers (this number includes an estimate of the number of family members who accompanied those who filed claims) were already Florida residents in 1842, Knetsch, *Florida's Seminole Wars*, 139–140; Schafer, "U.S. Territory and State," 231.

58. See this chapter, n. 53.

59. Christian Brown Crum's in-laws David D. and Andrew A. Crum settled near her husband Richard R. Crum's claim in Benton County, as did her male kin Daniel, Richard, and John Wiggins, township 22 south, range 19 east (Crum's mother's maiden name was Wiggins, Crum's descendant Elaine Crum Sullivan to Laurel Clark Shire, personal email correspondence, May 6, 2015); Mary Ann Garrison Robles settled near Isaac, Seaborn, Joseph N., William M., Richard L., and Michael Garrison (also spelled Garrason) in Benton County, townships 22 and 23 south, range 19 and 20 east. Mary Hall settled near William Hall in Alachua County (now Putnam County) in township 10 south, range 23 east. Another Mary Hall settled next to James Hall in Marion County, township 14 south, range 20 east. Ann Mangham settled near her son-in-law and his relatives, James and William Piles in Marion County, townships 13 and 14 south, ranges 21 and 22 east. Susan Whitehurst McClellan settled near her brother Asa and other relatives, including Levi S., Daniel S., and John Whitehurst in Benton County, townships 21, 22 or 23 south, range 19 east. Rebecca Munden (Mundin) and her son Allen settled AOA claims in Marion County together, in section 29 of township 14 south, range 20 east; Amanda Bleach (also spelled Blitch) Willis settled less than twelve miles from James Blitch in Marion County, her land was in township 12 south, range 19 east, his was in township 13 south, range 20 east. Elizabeth Sturges settled next to her son and eventual heir Nelson Sturges in township 15 south, range 20 east in Marion County. Frances Barnes inherited a Marion County AOA claim from her husband, William T. Barnes, which they had settled near John and Thomas Barnes in township 16 south, range 21 and 22 east; US BLM, *Florida Pre-1908 . . . Patents*.

60. See this chapter, n. 42.

61. The following female applicants for AOA permits indicated that they had arrived in Florida prior to 1835: Mary Hall (Patent 23), Charlotte Ayres, Elizabeth Hobkirk Dampeer, Mary Hall (Patent 300), Susannah Brown, Amanda Melvina Bleach Willis, Rebecca Munden, Elizabeth Hogan, Delia D. Gibbons, Mary Darby, Christian Metilde Brown Crum, Rebecca Jenkins, Elizabeth B. Standley Kettles, Adela Flotard, Nancy Campbell, Susan Whitehurst McClellan, Almira Dixon, Elizabeth Ann Barry, Patience Baisden, Ann Mangham, Eliza Ann Riley, Mary Ann Garrison Robles, and Charlotte Davis. AOA permits, DEP, Tallahassee.

62. The twelve women who filed AOA permits in what are now Hernando, Citrus, Pasco and Sumter Counties were Patience Baisden, Christian Metilde Brown, Mary Darby, Charlotte Davis, Susan McClellan, Nancy Campbell, Mary Ann Garrason (Robles), Maria Gunther, Dicy Whiddon, Esther Weeks, Elizabeth Barry and Eliza Ann Riley, AOA permits, DEP, Tallahassee.

63. The six successful female settlers were Patience Baisden (heirs received Patent 302-Newnansville [hereafter -N]), Susan McClellan (Patent 283-N), Mary Darby (Patent 9-N), Nancy Campbell (Patent 10-N), Elizabeth Barry (Patent 272-N), and Mary Ann Garrason (Patent 249-N). US BLM, *Florida Pre-1908 . . . Patents*.

64. Benton County was renamed Hernando County in 1860, but I continue to refer to it as Benton County throughout this chapter to avoid confusion.

65. The five women who claimed land in township 22 south, range 19 east were Mary Darby, Christian Brown Crum, Susan Whitehurst McClellan, Patience Baisden, and Charlotte

Davis. There were three other settlements in Benton County at Buddy's Lake, Annutelliga, and Melendez; AOA permits, DEP, Tallahassee; US BLM, *Florida Pre-1908 . . . Patents*; Notes on new settlements in "Roll . . . Suffering Inhabitants," 445.

66. Prince, *Amidst a Storm of Bullets*, 38, 70; Porter, *The Black Seminoles*, 26–27; Peters, *Florida Wars*, 30; Littlefield, *Africans and Seminoles*, 3.

67. Curry had recruited most of the people living at "the head of the Annuttelliza Hammock" as well, who numbered fourteen single white men, one white family (man, woman and three children) and two enslaved black people. In "Rolls of Capt. John Curry's party of Settlers to the head of the Chocochattee Savanna, 46 miles North of Tampa" and "Roll of Oscar B. Hart's Party of Settlers at the Head of the Annuttelliza Hammock 10 Miles North of Fort Cross"; information on Tiger Tail's band recorded by Lt. Patrick, 1842, Roll 261, W47–216, all in "Roll . . . Suffering Inhabitants," 12–18.

68. Notes on the Chocochatti settlement in "Roll . . . Suffering Inhabitants," 445.

69. S. Cooper to Headquarters of the Army of Florida, June 5, 1842, in "Correspondence . . . 'Suffering Inhabitants of Florida,'" 30–31.

70. Jane McClenden bought forty acres in 1860 in township 22 south, range 19 east, US BLM, *Florida Pre-1908 . . . Patents*.

71. I calculated their ages by subtracting seven from their ages in the 1850 census. 1850 U.S. Census, Florida, Benton County, population schedules, 23–29.

72. Mary Ann Garrason and Charlotte Davis went out with Curry's initial group, as did Rachel Board, who eventually settled in Clay County (see Chapter 4), Capt. John Curry's Party, "Roll . . . Suffering Inhabitants," 295. In 1840 Elizabeth Berry (also spelled Barry) had been in her thirties, living in Newnansville with a son between ten and fifteen years old and a daughter between five and ten years old (1840 U.S. Census, Florida, Alachua County, population schedules, 166). Barry and two children were included on the Roll of Wm. Cason's Party of Settlers at Fort White, on the Santa Fee River, E. F., "Roll . . . Suffering Inhabitants," 3. The settlement at Fort White was eventually abandoned, "Correspondence . . . 'Suffering Inhabitants of Florida,'" 28, 50, 57, 66.

73. On widows, see Wood, *Masterful Women*, 4–7. The Robles started their family very soon after Mary Ann Garrison had filed her AOA claim in 1843, since their eldest child was seven in the 1850 census. Joseph Robles also settled an AOA claim in the area, and in April 1850 he received patent 339 to 160 acres in township 23 South, range 20 East. US BLM, *Florida Pre-1908 . . . Patents*. In 1850, Joseph (age twenty-seven) and Mary Ann (age twenty-six) Robles lived next to Michael Garrison in the "Chocochatta" Settlement of Benton County. Joseph Robles was a carpenter with $200 in real estate, born in Malaga, Spain. They had three sons: Michael (age seven), John G. (age five), and Frank (age three). 1850 U.S. Census, Florida, Benton County, population schedules, 24. Mark Carroll's research on land policy in frontier Texas cites many examples of couples who married in order to claim more land. The Garrison-Robles family is perhaps the best example of a similar pattern in Florida. However, such alliances were less common in Florida because the land policy did not offer more land to married men but allowed independent female settlers to claim their own 160 acres if they were the "head of a family." Carroll, *Homesteads Ungovernable*, 105–106.

74. Isaac, Joseph, and Richard Garrason and their families were listed on the Roll of Capt. John Curry's party of Settlers to the head of the Chocochattee Savanna, forty-six miles north of Tampa, "Roll . . . Suffering Inhabitants," 13. Richard, William, Joseph, Michael, Isaac,

and Seaborn Garrison received patents for land in Benton County in 1849, see US BLM, *Florida Pre-1908 . . . Patents*. In 1840, Isaac and Michael Garrison were living with their families in Alachua County, 1840 U.S. Census, Florida, Alachua County, population schedules, 166, 161. Isaac carried the permits and affidavits to the land office in Newnansville for many of the settlers in Benton County, Covington, "Armed Occupation Act," 47. Michael Garrison is listed as a land surveyor in the 1850 U.S. census (Benton County, population schedules, 23–29).

75. In addition to the free land they received through the AOA, the Whitehursts purchased Florida land in the 1830s or early 1840s. McClellan (AOA permit 553, patent 283) joined at least four other Whitehursts who applied for and later received title AOA lands in Benton County: Asa, Daniel, John, and Levi Whitehurst. Susan Whitehurst married William McClellan in 1830 in Jefferson County, Florida, Dodd, et al., *Early American Marriages*. The land Susan bought in 1845 was in township 22 south, range 18 east. Her brother, Asa, purchased forty acres at the same time, just north of hers in township 21 south, range 18 east. Elizabeth Barry received AOA permit 576 and patent 272. Her daughter Hannah's husband, Elijah Tucker, had relatives who claimed AOA lands in the same township, John and Pleasant T. Tucker. In 1850, Barry lived with her son, daughter, son-in-law, and several young grandchildren at Chocochatti, 1850 US Census, Florida, Benton County, population schedules, 23. Her children eventually inherited her land claim. AOA permits, DEP, Tallahassee; US BLM, *Florida Pre-1908 . . . Patents*. In 1870 Hannah Tucker and her family of seven children remained in Benton County, 1870 US Census, Florida, Hernando County, population schedules, 77–78.

76. Mary Darby filed AOA permit 104 and received AOA patent 9 in 1848 for 160 acres in Benton County. Born in Georgia, she had come to Florida in 1825 at age seventeen. By 1843, Darby was a thirty-five-year-old widow with two sons and a daughter settled on a successful AOA claim close to the Baisden and McClellan farms west of Chocochatti. In 1880 the Darbys continued to farm in Benton County. Mary, age seventy-two, lived with her forty-nine-year-old son, his wife and children, one of his widowed sisters, and her children. US BLM, *Florida Pre-1908 . . . Patents*. 1850 US Census, Florida, Benton County, population schedules, 28; 1870 US Census, Florida, Hernando County, population schedules, 78; 1880 US Census, Florida, Hernando County, population schedules, Precinct 7, District 60, 371.

77. There was no US census taken in Benton/Hernando County in 1860. 1850 US Census, Florida, Hillsborough County, population schedules, 267–268, Benton County, population schedules, 28, 29. 1860 US Census, Florida, Hillsborough County, population schedules, 665, 674, 677, 691, 694, Tampa Post Office, 673, 691; slave schedules, 175. 1870 U.S. Census, Florida, Monroe County, population schedules, 344, Hernando County, population schedules, 104, Hillsborough County, population schedules, 148, 150 and Tampa Post Office, 134, Benton County, population schedules, Bay Port Post Office, 108. 1880 US Census, Florida, Hernando County, population schedules, Precincts 4 and 7, 376, Monroe County, population schedules, Key West, District 116, 265, Hillsborough County, population schedules, Precinct 3, 394. AOA permits, DEP, Tallahassee. US BLM, *Florida Pre-1908 . . . Patents*.

78. Seminoles killed Charlotte Piles Crum while she was riding in an open carriage between what is now Brooksville and Dade City. John Cole Ley, *Fifty-Two years in Florida* (1899) (State University System of Florida, electronic version, 2000); Stanaback, *History of Hernando County*, 15–16, and n. 16, 27. In 2003, a historic marker was placed at the site of her grave in Brooksville, Florida.

79. Christian Brown's AOA permit (107) was issued at Newnansville in January 1843 for land in Benton County, township 22 south, range 19 east. Richard Crum received patent 45 for 160 acres in Benton County in 1848. Kinsmen David and Andrew Crum patented AOA land in Benton County in 1849. Charlotte Davis attempted to settle in Benton County but did not stay to patent her claim. She had come to Florida from South Carolina with her husband, William Davis, in early 1834. Indians killed Corporal Davis at Fort Clinch in 1838. After his death, Charlotte (in her mid-forties) lived in Madison County (north central Florida) with eight children. In 1841, Charlotte Davis was recorded on a military pension list in Madison County, Florida. In early 1842, perhaps desperate to find support for her family, Davis went with Curry's first group of settlers to Chocochatti. In January 1843 she filed an AOA claim (124) for 160 acres there, but by 1850 she had returned to Madison County. Her sons, three of whom were in their teens or twenties in 1840 and could have farmed in Benton County, apparently preferred to pursue opportunities in Madison County rather than carving out a new farm in Benton County. Davis intended to settle a parcel of land "about half a mile on the west side of Scott's Road and two and half miles from the Chicuchatta Settlement in an arm of the Anutteliza hammock." 1840 US Census, Florida, Madison County, population schedules, 32; Ancestry.com, *Revolutionary War Pensioner Census, 1841* [database online] (Provo, UT: Ancestry.com Operations, 2004), 194; Sprague, *Origin, Progress and Conclusion of the Florida War*, 530; "Roll of Capt. John Curry's party," "Roll . . . Suffering Inhabitants," 13; AOA permits, DEP, Tallahassee; 1850 US Census, Florida, Benton County, population schedules, 24, Madison County, population schedules, 114; US BLM, *Florida Pre-1908 . . . Patents*; Miklus, "Armed Occupation Act Settlers," 9–21; "Women Settlers—Armed Occupation Act of 1842," notebook pages 102–104, Harvey L. Wells Collection, Heritage Village Archives and Library, Largo, Florida.

80. Knetsch notes the pattern of family migration into Florida in *Florida's Seminole Wars*, 140. Edward Baptist's research on the migrants who came to Middle Florida in the antebellum years illustrates a similar pattern there. Further, he notes that planter women were more likely to support a move to Florida if they believed it would not disrupt their kinship networks. *Creating an Old South*, 24–27, 37–60.

81. Mary Kendrick owned five slaves, Mary Sutton owned one, Emily Garrason owned two, and Nancy Harrell owned twenty-six slaves. Ancestry.com, *1850 U.S. Federal Census—Slave Schedules* [database online]. Provo, UT: Generations Network, 2004.

82. Donation Land Claim Act of September 27, 1850 (9 Stat. 496); Richard H. Chused, "The Oregon Donation Act of 1850 and Nineteenth Century Federal Married Women's Property Law," *Law and History Review* 2 (1984): 44–78. Anyone who had ever raised arms against the United States (for the Confederacy) was barred from claiming land under the Homestead Act, which enabled settlers to claim a homestead on any of the unclaimed federal lands in the thirty states created out of the public domain. The Homestead Act of May 20, 1862 (12 Stat. 392); Rodriguez, "The Homestead Act," 140–142.

Conclusion

1. "Florida," *Atkinson's Saturday Evening Post*, May 18, 1833, Florida Misc. Mss., PKY, Box 33, Folder 1. Greenberg, *Manifest Manhood*, 20–21.

2. Aron, *American Confluence*, 78–83, 95–103, 159–160, 192–194, quote 209.

3. Martha Menchaca, *Recovering History, Constructing Race: The Indian, Black, and White Roots of Mexican Americans* (Austin: University of Texas Press, 2001), 172, 201; Alwyn Barr,

Black Texans: A History of African Americans in Texas, 1528—1995, 2nd ed. (Norman: University of Oklahoma Press, 1996), 17. Walter Prescott Webb notes that whites outnumbered Mexicans and Native Americans, *The Texas Rangers: A Century of Frontier Defense* (Austin: University of Texas Press, 1935). David La Vere estimates that there were 4,500 indigenous people in East Texas in 1834, *The Texas Indians* (College Station: Texas A&M University Press, 2003), 167.

4. Gómez, *Manifest Destinies*, 5; González, *Refusing the Favor*, 6–15; Karl Jacoby, *Shadows at Dawn: An Apache Massacre and the Violence of History* (New York: Penguin, 2009), 124–130; Weber, *Spanish Frontier*, 337.

5. Scallet, "This Inglorious War," 14–15; Savage, *Cherokee Strip Live Stock Association*; Prucha, *Great Father*, Vol. 2; Hoxie, *Final Promise*; Banner, *How the Indians Lost Their Land*; Hendrickson, *Union, Nation, or Empire*, 268–272; McEnroe, "Painting the Philippines with an American Brush," 24–61; Burton, "Influence of the American West," 5–26; Slotkin, "Nostalgia and Progress," 608–637.

6. Baptist, *Creating an Old South*, 261–275; in 1858, Senator Joshua Giddings published *The Exiles of Florida*, which decried the treatment of runaway slaves in Florida and the use of federal funds to fight an Indian war that was, in his estimation, just a slave-catching expedition; *The Exiles of Florida, or, the Crimes Committed by Our Government against the Maroons, Who Fled from South Carolina and Other Slave States Seeking Protection Under Spanish Laws* (Gainesville: University of Florida Press, 1964, facsimile reproduction of the 1858 edition).

7. Horsman, *Race and Manifest Destiny*, 218–242.

8. Kennedy, quoted in House debate on Oregon land donation act, January 10, 1846, Cong. Globe, 29th Cong., 1st sess. 180 (1846); Robert V. Hine and John Mack Faragher, *The American West: A New Interpretive History* (New Haven, CT: Yale University Press, 2000), 199–200; Benjamin Franklin, "Observations Concerning the Increase of Mankind, Peopling of Countries, etc." (1755); Gerald Stourzh calls Franklin's essay "the first conscious and comprehensive formulation of 'Manifest Destiny,'" *Benjamin Franklin and American Foreign Policy* (Chicago: University of Chicago Press, 1954), 44, 59.

9. Aron, *American Confluence*, 192–196; Welsh, "Legislating a Homestead Bill," 172; Foos, *Short, Offhand, Killing Affair*, 155–163.

BIBLIOGRAPHY

Archival Sources and Public Records

Acts of the Legislative Council of the Territory of Florida, 1822. Pensacola: Floridian Press, 1823.

Acts of the Legislative Council of the Territory of Florida, 1824. Tallahassee: Office of the *Florida Intelligencer,* 1825.

American State Papers: Military Affairs

Appendix to the Congressional Globe

Armed Occupation Act Permits. General Land Office Records, Title and Land Records Section, Division of State Lands, Department of Environmental Protection. Tallahassee, Florida.

A Census of Pensioners for Revolutionary or Military Services. Washington, DC: Blair and Rives, 1841. Ancestry.com. *Revolutionary War Pensioner Census, 1841* [database online]. Provo, UT: Ancestry.com Operations Inc., 2004.

Clinch, General Duncan Lamont. Family Papers. P. K. Yonge Library of Florida History. University of Florida libraries, Special Collections, Gainesville.

Correspondence of the Land Offices at Newnansville and St. Augustine. Multiple volumes. Title and Land Records Section, Division of State Lands, Florida Department of Environmental Protection, Tallahassee.

Correspondence, Reports, and Lists Relating to Feeding of 'Suffering Inhabitants of Florida,' June 1841–June 1842. Extracted from *Records of U.S. Army Continental Commands, 1821–1920.* National Archives and Records Administration, Record Group 393, Vol. 1, Entry 74. University of Florida Library, Gainesville.

Davenport, William. Papers, 1835–1842. Florida Miscellaneous Manuscripts Collection, Box 1, Folder 1. P.K. Yonge Library of Florida History. University of Florida libraries, Special Collections, Gainesville.

Dodd, Jordan R., et al. *Early American Marriages: Florida to 1850.* Ancestry.com, *Florida Marriage Collection, 1822–1875* [database online]. Provo, UT: Generations Network, Inc., 2006.

Escambia County Clerk of Court Archives. Pensacola, Florida.

Florida Miscellaneous Manuscripts Collection. P.K. Yonge Library of Florida History. University of Florida libraries, Special Collections, Gainesville.

Gamble family, John Grattan Gamble, and Robert Gamble. *Family History Notes,* 1898. State Archives of Florida, Tallahassee. Microfilm.

Hagan, Nancy Cone. Papers. Florida State University Libraries, Special Collections, Tallahassee.

Hillsborough County Court Archives. Edgecombe Courthouse, Tampa, Florida.

Historical Census Browser, University of Virginia, Fischer Library, Geospatial and Statistical Data Center (2004), http://mapserver.lib.virginia.edu/.

Historical Statistics of the United States 1789–1945. Washington: United States Department of Commerce, 1949.

Jesup, Thomas Sidney. Diary, 1836–1837. State Archives of Florida, Tallahassee. Microfilm.

Journals of the Continental Congress

Laws of the Territory of Florida, 1845. Tallahassee: Office of *The Star of Florida* by W. and C. J. Bartlett, 1845.

"Louisiana Purchase, Treaty between the United States of America and The French Republic." National Archives and Records Administration. http://www.archives.gov/exhibits/american_originals/louistxt.html.

Lynch, Bartholomew. Journal, 1837–1839. Florida State University Libraries, Special Collections, Tallahassee.

Papers Concerning Permits of Claims for Land under the Armed Occupation Act. Records of the Bureau of Land Management. National Archives and Records Administration, Record Group 49, Washington, DC.

Proctor, Samuel, Oral History Program Collection. P.K. Yonge Library of Florida History, University of Florida Libraries, Special Collections, Gainesville.

Randall-Wirt Collection. Maryland Historical Society, Baltimore, Maryland.

"Roll of Persons Forming New Settlements, Returning to Plantations, and Suffering Inhabitants." 1842. In *Letters Received by the Adjutant General's Office, 1822–1860*, roll 262. *Records of the Adjutant General's Office, 1780s-1917*, National Archives and Records Administration, Record Group 94. Microfilm.

Social Explorer Dataset (electronic resource). U.S. Census 1830, 1840, 1850, and 1860. Digitally transcribed by Inter-university Consortium for Political and Social Research. Verified by Michael Haines. Compiled, edited, and verified by Social Explorer. Bronxville, NY: Social Explorer, 2003.

St. Johns County Court Records. Saint Augustine Historical Society, St. Augustine, Florida.

Sutton, Leora. *Women in Pensacola, 1765–1965*, unpublished manuscript, Escambia County Clerk of Court Archives, Pensacola, Florida.

United States, Bureau of the Census. *Fifth Census of the United States, 1830.* National Archives and Records Administration, Washington, D.C.

———. *Sixth Census of the United States, 1840.* National Archives and Records Administration, Washington, D.C.

———. *Seventh Census of the United States, 1850.* National Archives and Records Administration, Washington, D.C.

———. 1850 U.S. Census, Slave Schedules.

———. *Eighth Census of the United States, 1860.* National Archives and Records Administration, Washington, D.C.

———. *Ninth Census of the United States, 1870.* National Archives and Records Administration, Washington, D.C.

U.S. Bureau of Land Management. *Florida Pre-1908 Homestead and Cash Entry Patents.* Springfield, VA: General Land Office Automated Records Project, 1993. CD-ROM.

U.S., General Land Office. *Report of the Commissioner of the General Land Office, communicating an abstract of permits granted under the Acts for the Armed Occupation of Florida* (Washington, 1848). Library of Congress.

U.S. *House Journal*
U.S. *Senate Journal*
Wells, Harvey L. Collection. Heritage Village Archives and Library, Largo, Florida.
Wiggins, Daniel. Diaries, 1816–1834, 1838–1841, 1862. State Archives of Florida, Tallahassee.

Books and Other Sources

Adams, Mikaëla M. "Savage Foes, Noble Warriors, and Frail Remnants: Florida Seminoles in the White Imagination, 1865–1934." Master's thesis, University of North Carolina at Chapel Hill, 2009.

———. "Who Belongs? Becoming Tribal Members in the South." PhD diss., University of North Carolina at Chapel Hill, 2012.

Alemán, Jesse, and Shelley Streeby, eds. *Empire and the Literature of Sensation: An Anthology of Nineteenth-Century Popular Fiction*. New Brunswick, NJ: Rutgers University Press, 2007.

Aron, Stephen. *American Confluence: The Missouri Frontier from Borderland to Border State*. Bloomington: Indiana University Press, 2006.

———. *How the West Was Lost: The Transformation of Kentucky from Daniel Boone to Henry Clay*. Baltimore: Johns Hopkins University Press, 1996.

Axtell, James. *The Invasion Within: The Contest of Cultures in Colonial North America*. New York: Oxford University Press, 1986.

Banner, Stuart. *How the Indians Lost Their Land: Law and Power on the Frontier*. Cambridge, MA: Belknap Press of Harvard University Press, 2005.

Baptist, Edward E. *Creating an Old South: Middle Florida's Plantation Frontier Before the Civil War*. Chapel Hill: University of North Carolina Press, 2002.

———. "'Cuffy,' 'Fancy Maids,' and 'One-Eyed Men': Rape, Commodification, and the Domestic Slave Trade in the United States." *American Historical Review* 106 (2001): 1619–1650.

Barber, E. Susan, and Charles F. Ritter. "'Physical Abuse . . . and Rough Handling': Race, Gender, and Sexual Justice in the Occupied South." In *Occupied Women: Gender, Military Occupation, and the American Civil War*, edited by LeeAnn Whites and Alecia P. Long, 49–64. Baton Rouge: Louisiana State University Press, 2009.

Barr, Alwyn. *Black Texans: A History of African Americans in Texas, 1528–1995*. 2nd ed. Norman: University of Oklahoma Press, 1996.

Barr, Juliana. *Peace Came in the Form of a Woman: Indians and Spaniards in the Texas Borderlands*. Chapel Hill: University of North Carolina Press, 2007.

Basch, Norma. *In the Eyes of the Law: Women, Marriage, and Property in Nineteenth-Century New York*. Ithaca, NY: Cornell University Press, 1982.

Beecher, Catharine E. *Treatise on Domestic Economy*. Boston, MA: T. H. Webb, 1842.

Bice, David A. *The Original Lone Star Republic: Scoundrels, Statesmen and Schemers of the 1810 West Florida Rebellion*. Clanton, AL: Heritage Publishing, 2004.

Blake, David Haven. "'The Man That Was Used Up': Edgar Allen Poe and the Ends of Captivity." *Nineteenth-Century Literature* 57 (2002): 323–349.

Brooks, James F. *Captives and Cousins: Slavery, Kinship, and Community in the Southwest Borderlands*. Chapel Hill: University of North Carolina Press, 2002.

Brooks, Philip C. *Diplomacy in the Borderlands: The Adams-Onís Treaty of 1819*. Berkeley: University of California Press, 1939.

Brown, Kathleen. "The Anglo-Algonquian Gender Frontier." In *Negotiators of Change: Historical Perspectives on Native American Women*, edited by Nancy Shoemaker, 26–48. New York: Routledge, 1995.

Browne, John Ross. *Report of the Debates in the Convention of California, 1849*. Washington, DC: J. T. Towers, 1850.

Burnham, Michelle. *Captivity and Sentiment: Cultural Exchange in American Literature, 1682–1861*. Hanover, NH: University Press of New England, 1997.

Burton, David. "The Influence of the American West on the Imperialist Philosophy of Theodore Roosevelt." *Arizona and the West* 4 (1962): 5–26.

Bushnell, Amy Turner. "The Menéndez Marquéz Cattle Barony at La Chua and the Determinants of Economic Expansion in Seventeenth-Century Florida." *Florida Historical Quarterly* 56 (1978): 407–431.

———. *Situado and Sabana: Spain's Support System for the Presidio and Mission Provinces of Florida*. Athens: University of Georgia Press, 1994.

Bynum, Victoria. *Unruly Women: The Politics of Social and Sexual Control in the Old South*. Chapel Hill: University of North Carolina Press, 1992.

Card, Claudia. "Rape as a Weapon of War." *Hypatia* 11 (1996): 5–18.

Carroll, Mark. *Homesteads Ungovernable: Families, Sex, Race, and the Law in Frontier Texas, 1823–1860*. Austin: University of Texas Press, 2001.

Carter, Clarence E., ed. *Territorial Papers of the United States*. Vol. 26, *Territory of Florida, 1839–1845*. Washington, DC: National Archives, 1962.

Cashin, Joan E. *A Family Venture: Men and Women on the Southern Frontier*. New York: Oxford University Press, 1991.

Censer, Jane Turner. *North Carolina Planters and Their Children, 1800–1860*. Baton Rouge: Louisiana State University Press, 1990.

Chused, Richard. "Married Women's Property Law, 1800–1850." *Georgetown Law Journal* 71 (1983): 1359–1425.

———. "The Oregon Donation Act of 1850 and Nineteenth Century Federal Married Women's Property Law." *Law and History Review* 2 (1984): 44–78.

Clinton, Catherine. *The Plantation Mistress: Woman's World in the Old South*. New York: Pantheon Press, 1982.

Coffman, Edward M. *The Old Army: A Portrait of the American Army in Peacetime, 1784–1898*. New York: Oxford University Press, 1986.

Cohen, Patricia Cline. *The Murder of Helen Jewett: The Life and Death of a Prostitute in Nineteenth-Century New York*. New York: Vintage Press, 1998.

Coker, William S. "Pensacola, 1686–1763." In *The New History of Florida*, edited by Michael Gannon, 117–133. Gainesville: University Press of Florida, 1996.

Cott, Nancy F. *The Bonds of Womanhood: "Woman's Sphere" in New England, 1780–1835*. New Haven, CT: Yale University Press, 1977.

Covington, James W. "The Armed Occupation Act of 1842." *Florida Historical Quarterly* 40 (1961): 41–53.

———. *The Billy Bowlegs War, 1855–1858: The Final Stand of the Seminoles Against the Whites*. Chuluota, FL: Mickler House Publishers, 1982.

———. *The Seminoles of Florida*. Gainesville: University Press of Florida, 1993.

Crenshaw, Kimberle. "Demarginalizing the Intersection of Race and Sex: A Black Feminist Critique of Antidiscrimination Doctrine, Feminist Theory, and Antiracist Politics." *University of Chicago Legal Forum* (1989): 139–167.

Cusick, James G. *The Other War of 1812: The Patriot War and the American Invasion of Spanish East Florida*. Athens: University of Georgia Press, 2007.

Dargo, George. *Jefferson's Louisiana: Politics and the Clash of Legal Traditions*. Cambridge, MA: Harvard University Press, 1975.

Dauber, Michele Landis. "The Sympathetic State." *Law and History Review* 23 (2005): 387–442.

———. "The War of 1812, September 11th, and the Politics of Compensation." *DePaul Law Review* 53 (2003): 289–354.

Davis, Adrienne. "'Don't Let Nobody Bother Yo' Principle': The Sexual Economy of American Slavery." In *Sister Circle: Black Women and Work*, edited by Sharon Harley and the Black Women and Work Collective, 103–127. New Brunswick, NJ: Rutgers University Press, 2002.

Davis, T. Frederick. "Milly Francis and Duncan McKrimmon: An Authentic Florida Pocahontas." *Florida Historical Quarterly* 21 (1943): 254–265.

Davis, William C. *The Rogue Republic: How Would-Be Patriots Waged the Shortest Revolution in American History*. New York: Houghton Mifflin Harcourt, 2011.

DeLay, Brian. *War of a Thousand Deserts: Indian Raids and the U.S.-Mexican War*. New Haven, CT: Yale University Press, 2008.

Denham, James M. *A Rogue's Paradise: Crime and Punishment in Antebellum Florida, 1821–1861*. Tuscaloosa: University of Alabama Press, 1997.

Denham, James M., and Keith L. Huneycutt, eds. *Echoes from a Distant Frontier: The Brown Sisters' Correspondence from Antebellum Florida*. Columbia: University of South Carolina Press, 2004.

Dennis, Matthew. "Red Jacket's Rhetoric: Postcolonial Persuasions on the Native Frontiers of the Early American Republic." In *American Indian Rhetorics of Survivance: Word Medicine, Word Magic*, edited by Ernest Stromberg, 15–33. Pittsburgh: University of Pittsburgh Press, 2006.

Derounian-Stodola, Kathryn Z. *Women's Indian Captivity Narratives*. New York: Penguin Putnam, 1998.

Donahue, Charles, Jr. "What Causes Fundamental Legal Ideas? Marital Property in England and France in the Thirteenth Century." *Michigan Law Review* 78 (1979): 59–88.

Dorsey, Bruce. *Reforming Men and Women: Gender in the Antebellum City*. Ithaca, NY: Cornell University Press, 2002.

Dougan, Michael B. "The Arkansas Married Woman's Property Law." *Arkansas Historical Quarterly* 46 (1987): 3–26.

Dummett, Anna Maria. "Remembrances of the Old Plantation." *Literary Florida* (1949): 8–15.

Eby, Cecil. *"That Disgraceful Affair," the Black Hawk War*. New York: Norton, 1973.

Edwards, Laura F. *Scarlett Doesn't Live Here Anymore: Southern Women in the Civil War Era*. Urbana: University of Illinois Press, 2000.

Edwards, William P. "Narrative of the Capture and Providential Escape of Misses Frances and Almira Hall, Two respectable young women (sisters) of the ages of 16 and 18—who were taken prisoners by the Savages, at a Frontier settlement, near Indian Creek, in May last, when fifteen of the inhabitants fell victims to the bloody Tomahawk and Scalping Knife; among whom were the parents of the unfortunate females." New York, 1833.

Ellis, John. *From the Barrel of a Gun: A History of Guerrilla, Revolutionary and Counter-Insurgency Warfare, from the Romans to the Present*. Mechanicsburg, PA: Stackpole Books, 1995.

Ethridge, Robbie. *Creek Country: The Creek Indians and Their World*. Chapel Hill: University of North Carolina Press, 2003.
Fabel, Robin F. A., "British Rule in the Floridas." In *The New History of Florida*, edited by Michael Gannon, 134–149. Gainesville: University Press of Florida, 1996.
Faragher, John Mack. *Women and Men on the Overland Trail*. New Haven, CT: Yale University Press, 1979.
Foos, Paul. *A Short, Offhand Killing Affair: Soldiers and Social Conflict During the Mexican-American War*. Chapel Hill: University of North Carolina Press, 2002.
Foreman, Grant. *Indian Removal: The Emigration of the Five Civilized Tribes of Indians*. 3rd ed. Norman: University of Oklahoma Press, 1972.
Fox-Genovese, Elizabeth. *Within the Plantation Household: Black and White Women of the Old South*. Chapel Hill: University of North Carolina Press, 1998.
Frank, Andrew F. *Creeks and Southerners: Biculturalism on the Early American Frontier*. Lincoln: University of Nebraska Press, 2005.
Franklin, Benjamin. "Observations Concerning the Increase of Mankind, Peopling of Countries, etc." (1755). In *The Papers of Benjamin Franklin*, Vol. 4, edited by Leonard Labaree, 227–234. New Haven, CT: Yale University Press, 1961.
Freehling, William W. *Prelude to the Civil War: The Nullification Controversy in South Carolina, 1816–1836*. New York: Oxford University Press, 1992.
Galloway, Patricia. *Practicing Ethnohistory: Mining Archives, Hearing Testimony, Constructing Narrative*. Lincoln: University of Nebraska Press, 2006.
Gamber, Wendy. *The Boardinghouse in Nineteenth-Century America*. Baltimore: Johns Hopkins University Press, 2007.
Garvin, Russell. "The Free Negro in Florida Before the Civil War." *Florida Historical Quarterly* 46 (1967): 1–17.
Genovese, Peter S., Jr. "The Graduation Act (1854)." In *The Louisiana Purchase: A Historical and Geographical Encyclopedia*, edited by Junius Rodriguez, 128–129. Santa Barbara, CA: ABC-CLIO, 2002.
Giddings, Joshua. *The Exiles of Florida, or, the Crimes Committed by Our Government against the Maroons, Who Fled from South Carolina and Other Slave States Seeking Protection Under Spanish Laws*. Gainesville: University of Florida Press, 1964. Facsimile reproduction of the 1858 edition.
Gifford, Brian. "The Camouflaged Safety Net: The U.S. Armed Forces as Welfare State Institution." *Social Politics: International Studies in Gender, State and Society* 13 (2006): 372–399.
Gómez, Laura E. *Manifest Destinies: The Making of the Mexican American Race*. New York: New York University Press, 2007.
González, Deena. *Refusing the Favor: The Spanish-Mexican Women of Santa Fe, 1820–1880*. New York: Oxford University Press, 1999.
Gordon, Linda. *Pitied but Not Entitled: Single Mothers and the History of Welfare, 1890–1935*. Cambridge, MA: Harvard University Press, 1999.
Gould, Eliga H. *Among the Powers of the Earth: The American Revolution and the Making of a New World Empire*. Cambridge, MA: Harvard University Press, 2012.
Green, Michael D. *The Politics of Indian Removal: Creek Government and Society in Crisis*. Lincoln: University of Nebraska Press, 1985.
Green, Rayna. "The Pocahontas Perplex: The Image of Indian Women in American Culture." *Massachusetts Review* 16 (1975): 698–714.

Greenberg, Amy S. *Manifest Manhood and the Antebellum American Empire*. New York: Cambridge University Press, 2005.

Gutiérrez, Ramón A. *When Jesus Came, the Corn Mothers Went Away: Marriage, Sexuality, and Power in New Mexico, 1500–1846*. Stanford, CA: Stanford University Press, 1991.

Hall, James. *"The Indian Hater" and Other Stories*, edited by Edward Watts. Kent, OH: Kent State University Press, 2009.

Hartridge, Walter C. "The Fatio Family: A Book Review." *Florida Historical Quarterly* 31 (1952): 140–144.

Hendrickson, David C. *Union, Nation, or Empire: The American Debate over International Relations, 1789–1941*. Lawrence: University Press of Kansas, 2009.

Hershberger, Mary. "Mobilizing Women, Anticipating Abolition: The Struggle Against Indian Removal in the 1830s." *Journal of American History* 86 (1999): 15–40.

Hietala, Thomas R. *Manifest Design: Anxious Aggrandizement in Late Jacksonian America*. Ithaca, NY: Cornell University Press, 1985.

Hine, Robert V., and John Mack Faragher. *The American West: A New Interpretive History*. New Haven, CT: Yale University Press, 2000.

———. *Frontiers: A Short History of the American West*. New Haven, CT: Yale University Press, 2007.

Hixson, Walter. *American Settler Colonialism: A History*. New York: Palgrave Macmillan, 2013.

Hoffman, Paul E. *Florida's Frontiers*. Bloomington: Indiana University Press, 2002.

Hoganson, Kristin L. *Fighting for American Manhood: How Gender Politics Provoked the Spanish-American and Philippine-American Wars*. New Haven, CT: Yale University Press, 1998.

Horsman, Reginald. "The Dimensions of an 'Empire for Liberty': Expansion and Republicanism, 1775–1825." *Journal of the Early Republic* 9 (1989): 1–20.

———. *Race and Manifest Destiny: The Origins of American Racial Anglo-Saxonism*. Cambridge, MA: Harvard University Press, 1981.

Hoxie, Frederick E. *A Final Promise: The Campaign to Assimilate the Indians, 1880–1920*. Lincoln: University of Nebraska Press, 1984.

———. "Retrieving the Red Continent: Settler Colonialism and the History of American Indians in the U.S." *Ethnic and Racial Studies* 31 (2008): 1153–1167.

Hudson, Angela Pulley. "Forked Justice: Elias Boudinot, the U.S. Constitution, and Cherokee Removal." In *American Indian Rhetorics of Survivance: Word Medicine, Word Magic*, edited by Ernest Stromberg, 50–65. Pittsburgh: University of Pittsburgh Press, 2006.

Jabour, Anya. " 'It Will Never Do for Me to Be Married': The Life of Laura Wirt Randall, 1803–1833." *Journal of the Early Republic* 17 (1997): 193–236.

———. *Marriage in the Early Republic: Elizabeth and William Wirt and the Companionate Ideal*. Baltimore: Johns Hopkins University Press, 1998.

———. " 'The Privations and Hardships of a New Country': Southern Women and Southern Hospitality on the Florida Frontier." *Florida Historical Quarterly* 75 (1997): 259–275.

Jacobs, Margaret D. *White Mother to a Dark Race: Settler Colonialism, Maternalism, and the Removal of Indigenous Children in the American West and Australia, 1880–1940*. Lincoln: University of Nebraska Press, 2009.

Jacoby, Karl. *Shadows at Dawn: An Apache Massacre and the Violence of History*. New York: Penguin, 2009.

Jensen, Laura. *Patriots, Settlers, and the Origins of American Social Policy*. New York: Cambridge University Press, 2003.

Johnson, Walter. *Soul by Soul: Life Inside the Antebellum Slave Market*. Cambridge, MA: Harvard University Press, 1999.

Johnston, Louis, and Samuel H. Williamson. "What Was the U.S. GDP Then?" Measuring-Worth. http://www.measuringworth.org/usgdp/.

Jumper, Betty Mae Tiger, and Patsy West. *A Seminole Legend: The Life of Betty Mae Tiger Jumper*. Gainesville: University Press of Florida, 2001.

Jung, Patrick J. *The Black Hawk War of 1832*. Norman: University of Oklahoma Press, 2007.

Kandall, Stephen R. *Substance and Shadow: Women and Addiction in the United States*. Cambridge, MA: Harvard University Press, 1999.

Kaplan, Amy. *The Anarchy of Empire in the Making of U.S. Culture*. Cambridge, MA: Harvard University Press, 2002.

———. "Manifest Domesticity." *American Literature* 70 (1998): 581–606.

Katz, Michael B. *In the Shadow of the Poorhouse: A Social History of Welfare in America*. New York: Basic Books, 1986.

Kerber, Linda K. *No Constitutional Right to Be Ladies: Women and the Obligations of Citizenship*. New York: Hill and Wang, 1998.

———. "Separate Spheres, Female Worlds, Woman's Place: The Rhetoric of Women's History." *Journal of American History* 75 (1988): 9–39.

Kersey, Harry A., and Helen M. Bannan. "Patchwork and Politics: The Evolving Roles of Florida Seminole Women in the Twentieth Century." In *Negotiators of Change: Historical Perspectives on Native American Women*, edited by Nancy Shoemaker, 193–212. New York: Routledge, 1995.

Kessler-Harris, Alice. *Out to Work: A History of Wage-Earning Women in the United States*. New York: Oxford University Press, 1982.

Klepp, Susan E. *Revolutionary Conceptions: Women, Fertility, and Family Limitation in America, 1760–1820*. Chapel Hill: University of North Carolina Press, 2009.

Kly, Y. N., ed. *The Invisible War: African American Anti-slavery Resistance from the Stono Rebellion through the Seminole Wars*. Atlanta, GA: Clarity Press, 2006.

Knetsch, Joe. *Fear and Anxiety on the Florida Frontier: Articles on the Second Seminole War, 1835–1842*. Dade City, FL: Seminole Wars Foundation Press, 2008.

———. *Florida's Seminole Wars, 1817–1858*. Charleston, SC: Arcadia Press, 2003.

———. "Notes from a Presentation on the Impact of the AOA on Marion County." Unpublished manuscript, May 19, 1990.

Knetsch, Joe, and Paul S. Camp. "A Problematical Law: The Armed Occupation Act of 1842 and Its Impact on Southeast Florida." *Tequesta* 53 (1993): 68–70.

Kokomoor, Kevin. "A Re-assessment of Seminoles, Africans and Slavery on the Florida Frontier." *Florida Historical Quarterly* 88 (2009): 209–236.

Kraditor, Aileen S., ed. *Up from the Pedestal: Selected Writings in the History of American Feminism*. Chicago: University of Chicago Press, 1968.

Kulikoff, Allan. *The Agrarian Origins of American Capitalism*. Charlottesville: University Press of Virginia, 1992.

Labbé, Dolores. "Women in Nineteenth Century Louisiana." PhD diss., University of Delaware, 1975.

Lancaster, Jane F. *Removal Aftershock: The Seminoles' Struggle to Survive in the West, 1836–1866.* Knoxville: University of Tennessee Press, 1994.
Landers, Jane. *Black Society in Spanish Florida.* Chicago: University of Illinois Press, 1999.
———. "A Nation Divided?: Blood Seminoles and Black Seminoles on the Florida Frontier." In *Coastal Encounters: The Transformation of the Gulf South in the Eighteenth Century,* edited by Richmond F. Brown, 99–116. Lincoln: University of Nebraska Press, 2007.
Landis, Michele L. "Fate, Responsibility, and 'Natural' Disaster Relief: Narrating the American Welfare State." *Law and Society Review* 33 (1999): 257–318.
———. "Let Me Next Time Be Tried By Fire: Disaster Relief and the Origins of the American Welfare State 1789–1874." *Northwestern University Law Review* 92 (1998): 967–1034.
La Vere, David. *The Texas Indians.* College Station: Texas A&M University Press, 2003.
Lazarou, Kathleen Elizabeth. *Concealed Under Petticoats: Married Women's Property and the Law of Texas, 1840–1913.* New York: Garland Press, 1986.
Leavitt, Judith Walzer. "Under the Shadow of Maternity: American Women's Responses to Death and Debility Fears in Nineteenth-Century Childbirth." *Feminist Studies* 12 (1986): 129–154.
Lebsock, Suzanne. *The Free Women of Petersburg: Status and Culture in a Southern Town, 1784–1860.* New York: Norton, 1986.
L'Engle, Susan. *Notes of My Family and Recollections of My Early Life.* New York: Knickerbocker Press, 1888.
Lerner, Gerda. "The Lady and the Mill Girl: Changes in the Status of Women in the Age of Jackson." *Midcontinent American Studies Journal* 10 (1969): 5–15.
Ley, John Cole. *Fifty-Two Years in Florida.* 1899. Gainesville: State University System of Florida, electronic version, 2000.
Littlefield, Daniel F., Jr. *Africans and Seminoles: From Removal to Emancipation.* Westport, CT: Greenwood Press, 1977.
Lockey, Joseph B. "The St. Augustine Census of 1786: Translated from the Spanish with an Introduction and Notes." *Florida Historical Quarterly* 18 (1939): 11–31.
Long, Ellen Call. *Florida Breezes; or, Florida, New and Old.* Gainesville: University Press of Florida, 1962. Facsimile of the 1883 edition.
Love, Eric T. L. *Race over Empire: Racism and U.S. Imperialism, 1865–1900.* Chapel Hill: University of North Carolina Press, 2004.
Magnuson, Lynnea. "In the Service of Columbia: Gendered Politics and Manifest Destiny Expansion." PhD diss., University of Illinois-Urbana-Champaign, 2001.
Mahon, John K. *History of the Second Seminole War, 1835–1842.* Revised edition. Gainesville: University Press of Florida, 1985.
Mancall, Peter C. "Men, Women, and Alcohol in Indian Villages in the Great Lakes Region in the Early Republic." *Journal of the Early Republic* 15 (1995): 425–448.
Marotti, Frank. *Heaven's Soldiers: Free People of Color and the Spanish Legacy in Antebellum Florida.* Tuscaloosa: University of Alabama Press, 2013.
———. "Negotiating Freedom in St. Johns County, Florida, 1812–1862." PhD diss., University of Hawaii, 2003.
Mathews, Donald G. *Religion in the Old South.* Chicago: University of Chicago Press, 1977.
May, Robert E. *Manifest Destiny's Underworld: Filibustering in Antebellum America.* Chapel Hill: University of North Carolina Press, 2002.

———. "Reconsidering Antebellum U.S. Women's History: Gender, Filibustering, and America's Quest for Empire." *American Quarterly* 57 (2005): 1155–1188.

McClintock, Anne. *Imperial Leather: Race, Gender and Sexuality in the Colonial Context.* New York: Routledge, 1995.

McCurry, Stephanie. *Masters of Small Worlds: Yeoman Households, Gender Relations, and the Political Culture of the Antebellum South Carolina Low Country.* New York: Oxford University Press, 1995.

McEnroe, Sean. "Painting the Philippines with an American Brush: Visions of Race and National Mission Among the Oregon Volunteers in the Philippine Wars of 1898 and 1899." *Oregon Historical Quarterly* 104 (2003): 24–61.

McGaughy, Felix P. "The Squaw Kissing War: Bartholomew M. Lynch's Journal of the Second Seminole War, 1836–1839." Master's thesis, Florida State University, 1965.

McHugh, Kathleen Anne. *American Domesticity: From How-To Manual to Hollywood Melodrama.* New York: Oxford University Press, 1999.

Menchaca, Martha. *Recovering History, Constructing Race: The Indian, Black, and White Roots of Mexican Americans.* Austin: University of Texas Press, 2001.

Merk, Frederick. *Manifest Destiny and Mission in American History: A Reinterpretation.* New York: Knopf, 1963.

Micco, Melinda Beth. "'Blood and Money': The Case of Seminole Freedmen and Seminole Indians in Oklahoma." In *Crossing Waters, Crossing Worlds: The African Diaspora in Indian Country*, edited by Tiya Miles and Sharon Holland, 121–144. Durham, NC: Duke University Press, 2006.

———. "Freedmen and Seminoles: Forging a Seminole Nation." PhD diss., University of California, Berkeley, 1995.

Mihesuah, Devon. *American Indians: Stereotypes and Realities.* Atlanta, GA: Clarity Press, 1996.

Miklus, Kathy. "Armed Occupation Act Settlers, 1842–43." *Florida Armchair Researcher* (1984): 9–21.

Miles, Tiya. *Ties That Bind: The Story of an Afro-Cherokee Family in Slavery and Freedom.* Berkeley: University of California Press, 2005.

Miller, Susan A. *Coacoochee's Bones: A Seminole Saga.* Lawrence: University Press of Kansas, 2003.

Millett, Nathaniel. "Defining Freedom in the Atlantic Borderlands of the Revolutionary Southeast." *Early American Studies: An Interdisciplinary Journal* 5 (2007): 367–394.

Missall, John, and Mary Lou Missall. *The Seminole Wars: America's Longest Indian Conflict.* Gainesville: University Press of Florida, 2004.

Mock, Shirley Boteler. *Dreaming with the Ancestors: Black Seminole Women in Texas and Mexico.* Norman: University of Oklahoma Press, 2010.

Montoya, María E. *Translating Property: The Maxwell Land Grant and the Conflict over Land in the American West, 1840–1900.* Berkeley: University of California Press, 2002.

Moore-Willson, Minnie. *The Seminoles of Florida.* New York: Moffat, Yard and Company, 1914.

Morgan, Jennifer L. *Laboring Women: Reproduction and Gender in New World Slavery.* Philadelphia: University of Pennsylvania Press, 2004.

Motte, Jacob Rhett. *Journey into Wilderness: An Army Surgeon's Account of Life in Camp and Field During the Creek and Seminole Wars, 1836–1838.* Edited by James F. Sunderman. Gainesville: University Press of Florida, 1963.

Moussalli, Stephanie D. "Florida's Frontier Constitution: The Statehood, Banking and Slavery Controversies." *Florida Historical Quarterly* 74 (1996): 423–439.

Mulroy, Kevin. "Behind the Rolls: Pompey Bruner Fixico." In *IndiVisible: African-Native American Lives in the Americas*, edited by Gabrielle Tayac, 133–137. Washington: Smithsonian National Museum of the American Indian, 2009.

———. *Freedom on the Border: The Seminole Maroons in Florida, the Indian Territory, Coahuila, and Texas*. Lubbock: Texas Tech University Press, 1993.

———. *The Seminole Freedmen: A History*. Norman: University of Oklahoma Press, 2007.

Murphy, Gretchen. *Hemispheric Imaginings: The Monroe Doctrine and Narratives of U.S. Empire*. Durham, NC: Duke University Press, 2005.

Namias, June. *White Captives: Gender and Ethnicity on the American Frontier*. Chapel Hill: University of North Carolina Press, 1993.

Neely, Mark E., Jr. *The Civil War and the Limits of Destruction*. Cambridge, MA: Harvard University Press, 2008.

Nelson, Barbara J. "The Gender, Race, and Class Origins of Early Welfare Policy and the Welfare State: A Comparison of Workmen's Compensation and Mothers' Aid." In *Women, Politics, and Change*, edited by Louise Tilly and Patricia Gurin, 413–435. New York: Russell Sage Foundation, 1989.

Nissenbaum, Stephen. *Sex, Diet, and Debility in Jacksonian America: Sylvester Graham and Health Reform*. Chicago: Dorsey Press, 1980.

Nuño, John Paul A. "Making Africans and Indians: Colonialism, Identity, Racialization, and the Rise of the Nation-State in the Florida Borderlands, 1765–1837." PhD diss., University of Texas, El Paso, 2010.

Oakes, James. *The Ruling Race: A History of American Slaveholders*. New York: Norton, 1982.

Oberly, James W. *Sixty Million Acres: American Veterans and the Public Lands Before the Civil War*. Kent, OH: Kent State University Press, 1990.

O'Brien, Greg. "The Conqueror Meets the Unconquered: Negotiating Cultural Boundaries on the Post-Revolutionary Southern Frontier." *Journal of Southern History* 67 (2001): 39–72.

Olasky, Marvin N. "Early Nineteenth Century Christian Libertarian Newspapers: Rise and Decline of the Boston Recorder, 1816–1849." Paper presented at the Sixty-Eighth Annual Meeting of the Association for Education in Journalism and Mass Communication, Memphis, TN, August 3–6, 1985. ERIC.

Omi, Michael, and Howard Winant. *Racial Formation in the United States: From the 1960s to the 1980s*. New York: Routledge, 1986.

Owsley, Frank Lawrence, Jr., and Gene A. Smith. *Filibusters and Expansionists: Jeffersonian Manifest Destiny, 1800–1821*. Tuscaloosa: University of Alabama Press, 1997.

Perdue, Theda. *Cherokee Women: Gender and Culture Change, 1700–1835*. Lincoln: University of Nebraska Press, 1998.

———. "Columbus Meets Pocahontas in the American South." *Southern Cultures* 3 (1997): 4–21.

Perdue, Theda, and Michael D. Green. *The Cherokee Nation and the Trail of Tears*. New York: Viking, 2007.

———, eds. *The Cherokee Removal: A Brief History with Documents*. Boston: St. Martin's Press, 2004.

Perry, Adele. *On the Edge of Empire: Gender, Race, and the Making of British Columbia, 1849–1871.* Toronto: University of Toronto Press, 2001.
Peters, Richard, ed. *Public Statutes at Large of the United States of America*, Vol. 5. Boston: Little and Brown, 1846.
Peters, Virginia B. *The Florida Wars.* Hamden, CT: Archon Books, 1979.
Plane, Ann Marie. "Childbirth Practices Among Native American Women of New England and Canada, 1600–1800." In *Women and Health in America: Historical Readings*, edited by Judith Walzer Leavitt, 38–47. Madison: University of Wisconsin Press, 1999.
Porter, Kenneth W. *The Black Seminoles: History of a Freedom-Seeking People.* Edited by Alcione M. Amos, and Thomas P. Senter. Gainesville: University Press of Florida, 1996.
Priest, Josiah. *The Captivity and Sufferings of Gen. Freegift Patchin.* Garland Library of Narratives of North American Indian Captivities, Vol. 52. New York: Garland Publishing, 1977.
Prince, Henry. *Amidst a Storm of Bullets: The Diary of Lt. Henry Prince in Florida, 1836–1842.* Edited by Frank Laumer. Tampa, FL: University of Tampa Press, 1998.
Prucha, Francis Paul. *The Great Father: The United States Government and the American Indians*, Vol. 2. Lincoln: University of Nebraska Press, 1984.
Rasico, Philip D. "The Minorcan Population of St. Augustine in the Spanish Census of 1786." *Florida Historical Quarterly* 66 (1987): 160–184.
Remini, Robert. *Andrew Jackson and His Indian Wars.* New York: Viking, 2001.
Revels, Tracy J. *Grander in Her Daughters: Florida's Women During the Civil War.* Columbia: University of South Carolina Press, 2004.
Richards, Leonard L. *The California Gold Rush and the Coming of the Civil War.* New York: Knopf, 2007.
Rifkin, Mark. *When Did Indians Become Straight? Kinship, the History of Sexuality, and Native Sovereignty.* New York: Oxford University Press, 2010.
Rivers, Larry Eugene. "'Dignity and Importance': Slavery in Jefferson County, Florida—1827 to 1860." *Florida Historical Quarterly* 61 (1983): 404–430.
———. *Slavery in Florida: Territorial Days to Emancipation.* Gainesville: University Press of Florida, 2000.
Robbins, Roy M. "Preemption: A Frontier Triumph." *Mississippi Valley Historical Review* 18 (1931): 331–349.
Roberts, Albert H. "The Dade Massacre." *Florida Historical Quarterly* 5 (1927): 128–129.
Rodriguez, Alicia E. "The Homestead Act (1862)." In *The Louisiana Purchase: a Historical and Geographical Encyclopedia*, edited by Junius Rodriguez, 140–142. Santa Barbara, CA: ABC-CLIO, 2002.
Rogers, William Warren. "'As to the People': Thomas and Laura Randall's Observations on Life and Labor in Early Middle Florida." *Florida Historical Quarterly* 75 (1997): 441–446.
Rogin, Michael Paul. *Fathers and Children: Andrew Jackson and the Subjugation of the American Indian.* New York: Knopf, 1975.
Romero, Lora. *Home Fronts: Domesticity and Its Critics in the Antebellum United States.* Durham, NC: Duke University Press, 1997.
Rosen, Deborah A. "Women and Property Across Colonial America: A Comparison of Legal Systems in New Mexico and New York." *William and Mary Quarterly* 60 (2003): 355–382.
Rothbard, Murray. "The Great Society: A Libertarian Critique." In *The Great Society Reader: The Failure of American Liberalism*, edited by Marvin E. Gettleman and David Mermelstein, 502–511. New York: Random House, 1967.

Rouleau, Brian. "Maritime Destiny as Manifest Destiny: American Commercial Expansion and the Idea of the Indian." *Journal of the Early Republic* 30 (2010): 377–411.
Rountree, Helen C. "Pocahontas: The Hostage Who Became Famous." In *Sifters: Native American Women's Lives*, edited by Theda Perdue, 14–28. New York: Oxford University Press, 2001.
Rugemer, Edward B. *The Problem of Emancipation: The Caribbean Roots of the American Civil War*. Baton Rouge: Louisiana State University Press, 2009.
Salmon, Marylynn. *Women and the Law of Property in Early America*. Chapel Hill: University of North Carolina Press, 1986.
Samuels, Shirley, ed. *The Culture of Sentiment Race, Gender, and Sentimentality in Nineteenth-Century America*. New York: Oxford University Press, 1992.
Sánchez-Eppler, Karen. "Bodily Bonds: The Intersecting Rhetorics of Feminism and Abolition." In *The Culture of Sentiment: Race, Gender, and Sentimentality in Nineteenth-Century America*, edited by Shirley Samuels, 92–114. New York: Oxford University Press, 1992.
Sandos, James A. "From 'Boltonlands' to 'Weberlands': The Borderlands Enter American History." *American Quarterly* 46 (1994): 595–604.
Sanger, George P., ed. *United States Statutes at Large*, Vol. 12. Boston: Little, Brown, 1863.
Sattler, Richard A. "Remnants, Renegades, and Runaways: Seminole Ethnogenesis Reconsidered." In *History, Power and Identity: Ethnogenesis in the Americas, 1492–1992*, edited by Jonathan David Hill, 36–69. Iowa City: University of Iowa Press, 1996.
Saunt, Claudio. *A New Order of Things: Property, Power, and the Transformation of the Creek Indians, 1733–1816*. New York: Cambridge University Press, 1999.
Savage, William W., Jr. *The Cherokee Strip Live Stock Association: Federal Regulation and the Cattleman's Last Frontier*. Norman: University of Oklahoma Press, 1990.
Saxton, Alexander. *The Rise and Fall of the White Republic: Class Politics and Mass Culture in Nineteenth-Century America*. London: Verso, 1990.
Scallet, Daniel. "'This Inglorious War': The Second Seminole War, the Ad Hoc Origins of American Imperialism, and the Silence of Slavery." Ph.D. diss., Washington University in St. Louis, 2011.
Schafer, Daniel L. *Anna Madgigine Jai Kingsley: African Princess, Florida Slave, Plantation Slaveowner*. Gainesville: University Press of Florida, 2003.
———. "U.S. Territory and State." In *The New History of Florida*, revised edition, edited by Michael Gannon, 220–243. Gainesville: University Press of Florida, 2013.
Schuetz, Janice. *Episodes in the Rhetoric of Government-Indian Relations*. Westport, CT: Praeger, 2002.
Schweninger, Loren, ed. *Race, Slavery, and Free Blacks: Series 1, Petitions to Southern Legislatures*. Bethesda, MD: University Publications of America, 1998. Microfilm.
———. *Race, Slavery and Free Blacks, Series 2: Petitions to Southern County Courts, 1775–1867; Part A Georgia (1796–1867), Florida (1821–1867), Alabama (1821–1867), Mississippi (1822–1867)*. Bethesda, MD: LexisNexis, 2003. Microfilm.
Seed, Patricia. "American Law, Hispanic Traces: Some Contemporary Entanglements of Community Property." *William and Mary Quarterly* 52 (1995): 157–162.
Sellers, Charles. *The Market Revolution: Jacksonian America, 1815–1846*. New York: Oxford University Press, 1992.

Shalev, Michael. "The Social Contract Revisited: 'Loyalty Benefits' and the Welfare State." Oxford: Foundation for Law, Justice, and Society, 2010. http://www.fljs.org/sites/www.fljs.org/files/publications/Shalev.pdf.

Shammas, Carole. "Anglo-American Household Governance in Comparative Perspective." *William and Mary Quarterly* 52 (1995): 104–144.

———. "Re-Assessing the Married Women's Property Acts." *Journal of Women's History* 6 (1994): 9–30.

Shaw, Greg M. *The Welfare Debate*. Westport, CT: Greenwood Press, 2007.

Shoemaker, Nancy. *A Strange Likeness: Becoming Red and White in Eighteenth-Century North America*. New York: Oxford University Press, 2004.

Simonsen, Jane E. *Making Home Work: Domesticity and Native American Assimilation in the American West, 1860–1919*. Chapel Hill: University of North Carolina Press, 2006.

Skocpol, Theda. *Protecting Soldiers and Mothers: The Political Origins of Social Policy in the United States*. Cambridge, MA: Harvard University Press, 1996.

Skogen, Larry C. *Indian Depredation Claims, 1796–1920*. Norman: University of Oklahoma Press, 1996.

Slotkin, Richard. "Nostalgia and Progress: Theodore Roosevelt's Myth of the Frontier." *American Quarterly* 33 (1981): 608–637.

———. *Regeneration Through Violence: The Mythology of the American Frontier, 1600–1860*. Norman: University of Oklahoma Press, 1973.

Smith, Andrea. *Conquest: Sexual Violence and American Indian Genocide*. Cambridge, MA: South End Press, 2005.

———. "Not an Indian Tradition: The Sexual Colonization of Native Peoples." *Hypatia* 18 (2003): 70–85.

Smith, Daniel Scott, and J. David Hacker. "Cultural Demography: New England Deaths and the Puritan Perception of Risk." *Journal of Interdisciplinary History* 26 (1996): 367–392.

Smith, Julia. *Slavery and Plantation Growth in Antebellum Florida, 1821–1860*. Gainesville: University of Florida Press, 1973.

Smith, Justin H. *The War with Mexico*, Vol. 2. New York: Macmillan, 1919.

Smith, Rogers M. *Civic Ideals: Conflicting Visions of Citizenship in U.S. History*. New Haven, CT: Yale University Press, 1997.

Snow, Susan Micco, and Susan Enns Stans. *Healing Plants: Medicine of the Florida Seminole Indians*. Gainesville: University Press of Florida, 2001.

Snyder, Christina. *Slavery in Indian Country: The Changing Face of Captivity in Early America*. Cambridge, MA: Harvard University Press, 2010.

Socolow, Susan Migden. *The Women of Colonial Latin America*. New York: Cambridge University Press, 2000.

Sprague, John T. *The Origin, Progress, and Conclusion of the Florida War*. New York: Appleton and Company, 1847.

Srebnick, Amy Gilman. *The Mysterious Death of Mary Rogers: Sex and Culture in Nineteenth-Century New York*. New York: Oxford University Press, 1995.

Stanaback, Richard J. *A History of Hernando County, 1840–1976*. Brooksville, FL: Action '76 Steering Committee, 1976.

Stansell, Christine. *City of Women: Sex and Class in New York, 1789–1860*. Urbana: University of Illinois Press, 1987.

Stasiulis, Daiva, and Nira Yuval-Davis, eds. *Unsettling Settler Societies: Articulations of Gender, Race, Ethnicity, and Class*. London: Sage Publications, 1995.

Ste. Claire, Dana. *Cracker: The Cracker Culture in Florida History*. Gainesville: University Press of Florida, 2006.

Stedman, Raymond W. *Shadows of the Indian: Stereotypes in American Culture*. Norman: University of Oklahoma Press, 1982.

Stephanson, Anders. *Manifest Destiny: American Expansionism and the Empire of Right*. New York: Hill and Wang, 1995.

Sterett, Susan M. *Public Pensions: Gender and Civic Service in the States, 1850–1937*. Ithaca, NY: Cornell University Press, 2003.

Stoler, Ann Laura. *Carnal Knowledge and Imperial Power: Race and the Intimate in Colonial Rule*. Berkeley: University of California Press, 2010.

Stourzh, Gerald. *Benjamin Franklin and American Foreign Policy*. Chicago: University of Chicago Press, 1954.

Streeby, Shelley. *American Sensations: Class, Empire, and the Production of Popular Culture*. Berkeley: University of California Press, 2002.

Stromberg, Ernest, ed. *American Indian Rhetorics of Survivance: Word Medicine, Word Magic*. Pittsburgh: University of Pittsburgh Press, 2006.

Stuntz, Jean. *Hers, His, and Theirs: Community Property Law in Spain and Early Texas*. Lubbock: Texas Tech University Press, 2005.

Thorpe, Francis Newton. *The Federal and State Constitutions, Colonial Charters, and Other Organic Laws of the States, Territories, and Colonies Now or Heretofore Forming the United States of America*, Vol. 2. Washington, DC: Government Printing Office, 1909.

Tomlins, Christopher. "The Many Legalities of Colonization: A Manifesto of Destiny for Early American Legal History." In *The Many Legalities of Early America*, edited by Christopher L. Tomlins and Bruce H. Mann, 1–24. Chapel Hill: University of North Carolina Press, 2001.

Trask, Kerry A. *Black Hawk: The Battle for the Heart of America*. New York: Henry Holt, 2006.

"A True and Authentic Accounts of the Indian War in Florida, Giving the Particulars Respecting the Murder of the Widow Robbins, and the Providential Escape of her Daughter Aurelia, and her Lover, Mr. Charles Somers, After Suffering Almost Innumerable Hardships." New York: Saunders and Van Welt, 1836. Florida Heritage Collection, http://palmm.fcla.edu/fhp/.

Twyman, Bruce Edward. *The Black Seminole Legacy and North American Politics, 1693–1845*. Washington, DC: Howard University Press, 1999.

Utley, Robert Marshall, and Wilcomb E. Washburn. *Indian Wars*. 1st Mariner Books ed. Boston: Houghton Mifflin, 2002.

Van Atta, John R. "'A Lawless Rabble': Henry Clay and the Cultural Politics of Squatters' Rights, 1832–1841." *Journal of the Early Republic* 28 (2008): 337–378.

Varon, Elizabeth R. *We Mean To Be Counted: White Women and Politics in Antebellum Virginia*. Chapel Hill: University of North Carolina Press, 1998.

Vaughn, Stephen L., ed. *Encyclopedia of American Journalism*. New York: Taylor and Francis, 2008.

Veracini, Lorenzo. *Settler Colonialism: A Theoretical Overview*. New York: Palgrave Macmillan, 2010.

Waselkov, Gregory A., and Kathryn E. Holland Braund, eds. *William Bartram on the Southeastern Indians*. Lincoln: University of Nebraska Press, 1995.

Wayne, Lucy B. *Sweet Cane: The Architecture of the Sugar Works of East Florida*. Tuscaloosa: University of Alabama Press, 2010.

Webb, Walter Prescott. *The Texas Rangers: A Century of Frontier Defense*. Austin: University of Texas Press, 1935.

Weber, David J. *The Spanish Frontier in North America*. New Haven, CT: Yale University Press, 1992.

Weiner, Marli F. *Mistresses and Slaves: Plantation Women in South Carolina, 1830–1880*. Urbana: University of Illinois Press, 1998.

Weisman, Brent Richards. *Like Beads on a String: A Culture History of the Seminole Indians in North Peninsular Florida*. Tuscaloosa: University of Alabama Press, 1989.

———. *Unconquered People: Florida's Seminole and Miccosukee Indians*. Gainesville: University Press of Florida, 1999.

Welch, Andrew. *A Narrative of the Early Days and Remembrances of Oceola Nikkanochee, Prince of Econchatti*. Facsimile reproductions of the 1841 ed. and of the pamphlets of 1837 and 1847. Bicentennial Floridiana Facsimile Series. Gainesville: University Presses of Florida, 1977.

Welsh, Michael E. "Legislating a Homestead Bill: Thomas Hart Benton and the Second Seminole War." *Florida Historical Quarterly* 57 (1978): 157–172.

Welter, Barbara. "The Cult of True Womanhood, 1800–1860." *American Quarterly* 18 (1966): 151–174.

Wertz, Richard W., and Dorothy C. Wertz. *Lying-in: A History of Childbirth in America*. New Haven, CT: Yale University Press, 1989.

West, Patsy. *The Enduring Seminoles: from Alligator Wrestling to Ecotourism*. Gainesville: University Press of Florida, 2008.

———. *The Seminole and Miccosukee Tribes of Southern Florida*. Images of America series. Charleston, SC: Arcadia Publishing, 2002.

Wexler, Laura. "Tender Violence: Literary Eavesdropping, Domestic Fiction, and Educational Reform." In *The Culture of Sentiment: Race, Gender, and Sentimentality in Nineteenth-Century America*, edited by Shirley Samuels, 9–38. New York: Oxford University Press, 1992.

———. *Tender Violence: Domestic Visions in an Age of U.S. Imperialism*. Chapel Hill: University of North Carolina Press, 2000.

White, Richard. *The Middle Ground: Indians, Empires, and Republics in the Great Lakes Region, 1650–1815*. New York: Cambridge University Press, 1991.

Wickman, Patricia R. *Osceola's Legacy*. Tuscaloosa: University of Alabama Press, 1991.

———. *The Tree That Bends: Discourse, Power, and the Survival of the Maskoki People*. Tuscaloosa: University of Alabama Press, 1999.

Wildenthal, Lora. *German Women for Empire, 1884–1945*. Durham, NC: Duke University Press, 2001.

Willis, William Scott. "A Swiss Settler in East Florida: A Letter of Francis Philip Fatio." *Florida Historical Quarterly* 64 (1985): 174–189.

Wood, Kirsten E. "Broken Reeds and Competent Farmers: Slaveholding Widows in the Southeastern United States, 1783–1861." *Journal of Women's History* 13 (2001): 34–57.

———. *Masterful Women: Slaveholding Widows from the American Revolution through the Civil War*. Chapel Hill: University of North Carolina Press, 2004.

Wolfe, Patrick. "Land, Labor, and Difference: Elementary Structures of Race." *American Historical Review* 106 (2001): 866–905.

———. *Settler Colonialism and the Transformation of Anthropology*. London: Cassell, 1999.

Worth, John E. *The Timucuan Chiefdoms of Spanish Florida*. Vol. 1, *Assimilation*. Gainesville: University Press of Florida, 1998.

Wright, J. Leitch, Jr. *Anglo-Spanish Rivalry in North America*. Athens: University of Georgia Press, 1971.

———. *Creeks and Seminoles: The Destruction and Regeneration of the Muscogulge People*. Lincoln: University of Nebraska Press, 1990.

Zeigler, Sara L. "Uniformity and Conformity: Regionalism and the Adjudication of the Married Women's Property Acts." *Polity* 28 (1996): 467–495.

INDEX

abolitionism. *See* antislavery
Adams, John, 13–14
Adams, John Quincy, 14, 32
Adams–Onís Treaty, 32, 47, 176
American Revolution, 7, 11, 75, 193, 200
antislavery, 73–74, 76–77, 129, 168, 197
Apalachicola River, 23, 44, 109, 141
Armed Occupation Act, 2, 163–65, 167–69, 171, 173–79, 181–93, 200
Armistead, Walker Keith, 130

Benton County, 2, 177, 186, 188–92. *See also* Chucochatti
Benton, Thomas Hart, 2, 162, 165–71, 175, 177, 186–92, 195, 200
Berry, Elizabeth, 1–2, 155
Buckra Woman, 49

California, 52, 70
Call, Richard Keith, 141, 155, 165
Christianity, 8, 13–14, 19, 66, 68–69, 74, 94, 133, 170, 196
Chucochatti, 1, 2, 186–89, 200. *See also* Benton County
Clinch, Duncan, 102, 107

disease, 6, 7, 25, 59, 71, 95, 98, 103, 148, 192

enslaved blacks, 1, 7–8, 20; Florida population of, 22–24, 40; as property in the creation of households, 42–43, 45, 47, 52, 71, 76, 82, 84, 92; and reproductive labor, 96–97; and women's kinship as resistance, 100–101, 151, 157, 176, 181–82, 191; as used by white migrants to facilitate expansionist domesticity, 195–96, 198. *See also* fugitive slaves; Native Americans
ethnic cleansing, 21, 25, 102, 104, 106, 127, 133, 198

expansionist domesticity, definition of, 14–16, 18, 33–34; as part of the construction of "civilization" and race, 46–47, 53, 56, 103, 106, 132; and aid policy, 138–40, 160–61, 164; as the establishment of the "home front," 172–74, 192, 194, 197–98, 201
expansionist welfare policies, 2, 26, 56, 103, 125, 137–40, 144–46, 149, 158–61, 164, 200

Factor, Billy, 129
Factor, Black. *See* Philatouche
Factor, Rose, 129
Florida: East Florida, 24, 35, 55, 75–76, 83–84, 91, 143, 153, 167, 184; Middle Florida: 9, 23–24, 37, 43–45, 67, 73, 82, 99, 141, 182; North Florida, 1, 79, 83, 109, 173, 178, 183; South Florida, 24, 105–6, 127, 131, 182; West Florida, 6–7, 27, 32, 82, 177
Fort Andrews, 160
Fort Brooke, 24, 116, 119, 121, 145. *See also* Tampa Bay, Florida
Fort Gibson, 110
Fort King, 24
Fort Mellon, 124. *See also* Treaty of Payne's Landing
Fort Micanopy, 179
Fort Mose, 7
Fort Pike, 133
Fort Robert Gamble, 150
Fort White, 1, 156, 188
France, 200
free blacks, 5, 7, 9, 17, 20; Florida population of, 22–24, 33; the inconsistent rights of, 47–49, 51, 54, 63, 151, 176, 183, 196–198. *See also* Fort Mose; Native Americans
fugitive slaves, 7, 56, 77, 86, 91, 109, 120, 167. *See also* enslaved blacks

Index

Gagnet, Josephine, 37
Garvin, Felicia, 49
gender, 2; masculinity, 3, 11–12, 17–19, 142, 14; and white women as colonizers, 16–19, 26–27, 33–34; and property rights, 46; and Manifest Destiny, 57, 72–73, 81, 164; and depredation narratives, 61–63, 68, 81, 83–85, 97, 103–5, 113, 121, 124, 130; and aid policy, 138–43, 146–48, 151–52; and recolonization of Florida, 156–61, 165–68
General Land Office, 176, 178
Georgia, 9–10, 44, 50, 65, 74, 76, 80, 92, 100, 127, 129, 145
Great Britain, 6, 75

Hillsborough River, 38
Homestead Act, 182, 192–93, 200

Indian Creek Massacre, 79
Indian depredation narratives, 2, 9, 25–26, 56–58, 62, 64–69, 76–79; published narratives, 84–85, 92, 94–96, 98, 100; and indigenous perspective, 102–4, 107–8, 114–18, 132, 137, 165, 199, 201. *See also* indigenous resistance; Native Americans
Indian Removal, 11, 13, 18, 22, 27, 46, 53; and depredation narratives, 56–58, 65, 67, 69, 77, 80; framed as domestic defense, 84–86, 94, 105, 109, 118, 132; and aid policy, 160–163, 166–67, 186, 195
Indian Territory, 23, 27, 60, 80, 103, 109, 110, 183
indigenous resistance, 1, 5, 21, 27, 58; and depredation narratives, 64, 76–78, 100, 115–17; and Seminole women, 102–4, 106, 108, 110–11, 119, 125, 127–129, 133, 166

Jackson, Andrew, 18–20, 24–25, 102, 107, 109, 148
Jacksonian politics, 5, 74, 173, 177, 195, 197; Free Soilism, 5, 200
Jacksonville, Florida, 137, 150–151
Jefferson County, 44–45, 67, 150
Jesup, Thomas, 27, 124, 126, 129
Johns, Jane, 55–56, 59, 61, 91–94, 110

Kingsley, Anna, 48–49

Lake Okeechobee, 25
Land Donation Act (Oregon), 192, 200
LeSassier, Victoria, 31–32, 35–37
Lynch, Bartholomew, 118–19, 121–22

Macomb, Alexander, 131
Macomb, Mary, 70
Madeloyee (Polly Parker), 127–28
Manifest Destiny, 2, 3, 10, 13, 18, 28, 34, 53, 57, 63, 67, 79, 146, 159, 161, 187, 195, 197–198, 201–202. *See also* expansionist domesticity
Military Land Bounty Act, 182
Mississippi, 22, 25, 40, 42, 80, 109, 133
Mississippi River, 22, 80, 109, 195
Missouri, 2–3, 10, 13, 165, 195, 200
Montgomery, Cora, 13, 129
Motte, Jacob Rhett, 124–25, 129–30, 134, 148
Munden, Rebecca, 179–80, 185

Native Americans, 1, 4; and kinship, 5–6, 8–11, 16–17, 21, 105, 110, 113, 130; and racial construction, 19–21, 25, 33–34, 44–47, 66–67, 110, 123, 170–71; as slaveholders, 50–52, 54; and depredation narratives, 56, 58–64, 66, 69–70, 73, 75, 79, 83, 86–88, 90–92; and Seminole stories, 104–5, 107–8, 110, 116–17, 120, 123, 126–27, 139–40, 142, 145, 147, 159–60, 167, 174, 176, 192, 194–97, 199; Apalachicolas, 44–45, 56; black Seminoles, 1, 8, 21–22, 25, 27, 47, 56, 89, 100, 106, 108–10, 112, 114, 116, 124, 129, 133, 147, 165, 169–70, 175, 183, 187, 191, 196; Creeks, 6, 8, 22, 44, 50, 56, 80, 109, 110, 129; Miccosukees, 44–5, 66, 106. *See also* ethnic cleansing; Indian Removal; indigenous resistance
New Mexico, 10, 196–97
New Orleans, La., 84, 126, 133. *See* Fort Pike

Ocala, Florida. *See* Fort King
Osceola, 78, 108, 113, 129, 134

Parker, Polly. *See* Madeloyee
Pensacola, Florida, 6, 8, 31–32, 37, 39, 42
Philatouche (Black Factor), 50, 129
Preston, William Campbell, 169–170, 173, 183

rape. *See* sexual violence
Randall, Laura Wirt, 31, 37, 43–44, 46, 67, 71, 83
Randall, Thomas, 43–44, 46, 67, 70, 72
recolonization, 27, 34, 138, 155–56, 161, 163, 168, 187, 192, 201
reproductive labor, 2, 4, 12, 51, 57, 95–96, 101, 104, 112, 174, 198–99. *See also* enslaved blacks; women
Robbins, Aurelia. *See* Widow Robbins

Index   269

settler colonialism, 1, 3, 4–5, 9–16, 18–19, 21, 26, 32, 34, 36, 43, 53–54, 103, 140, 142, 159, 161, 172, 174, 190, 195, 197, 201; Spanish colonization, 2, 6–8, 10, 13–4, 20–1, 31–3, 35–7, 44, 47–8, 50, 52, 63, 70, 92, 129, 183, 195–7; white colonization, 3, 10, 22, 186, 192
sexual violence, 79, 107, 118; against black women, 97; against Seminole women, 104, 108, 111, 113, 117–23, 131–32, 134, 199
Sherman, William Tecumseh, 135
slaveholders, 8–10, 22, 77, 175–76, 195
Spain, 3, 6–10, 13–14, 20, 32–33, 49, 195, 200
Spanish Florida, 7, 32, 47, 92. *See also* settler colonialism; Spain
St. Augustine, Florida, 134, 137, 141, 148, 150–54, 176, 178, 183, 197
"suffering inhabitants," 58–59, 138, 140, 142–46, 148–49; and enslaved and free blacks, 151–52, 154–55, 157–58, 161, 163–64, 168, 174, 186, 192. *See also* expansionist welfare policies; widows

Tampa Bay, Florida, 1, 24, 137, 139, 108, 116, 118, 124, 130, 133, 145, 184, 186, 189–90. *See also* Fort Brooke
territorial expansion, 2–3, 5; and violence, 9–11, 13–15, 18–19, 21, 24, 46, 52–54, 63–64, 79; and law, 32, 40–41, 52–54, 145, 147, 161, 168, 199. *See also* Indian Removal; Manifest Destiny
Texas, 10, 13–14, 27, 45, 52, 129, 183, 194–98
Treaty of Payne's Landing, 109–10, 194

Underwood, Joseph R., 75
U.S. Civil War, 154, 196–97
U.S. Congress, 14, 26–27, 64–65, 75; and expansionist welfare policies, 137–43, 145–48, 153; and land policies, 163–65, 167, 169, 173–75, 177–79, 187, 192, 198
U.S. House of Representatives, 145, 162, 171–73
U.S.–Mexico War, 10, 13, 28, 77, 79, 197
U.S.–Seminole Wars: First U.S.–Seminole War, 9, 10, 21, 28, 33, 59, 102–3, 106, 109, 121, 197; Second U.S.–Seminole War, 2, 3, 6, 8, 10, 21, 25–28, 33, 41, 45, 56–59, 64–65, 70, 73, 77, 84, 102–3, 105–8, 110, 118–19, 121, 127, 131, 138–39, 150, 156, 159, 162, 167, 175, 183, 186, 190, 192, 197, 200, 201; Third U.S.–Seminole War, 33, 59, 103, 106, 127, 197
U.S. Senate, 166, 173
U.S. War Department, 149, 151–52, 155–57, 159

veterans, 140, 156, 159, 174, 182, 193, 200

War of 1812, 10, 43, 144–45, 193
Whig Party, 74, 142, 144, 163, 169, 172,
white anxiety, 26, 45, 62–64, 68–70, 72, 75–76, 88, 114, 127, 148–49, 158, 170, 190. *See also* Indian depredation narratives; indigenous resistance; sexual violence
whiteness, 16, 32, 41, 93, 170
white supremacy, 20, 34, 123, 198
White Wars, 79, 102, 104–7, 111, 113–14, 116, 120, 124, 127, 131. *See also* U.S.–Seminole Wars
widows, 2, 3, 70; as "suffering inhabitants," 138–39, 141–44, 150–54, 156–57, 160, 200; and recolonization of Florida, 164, 173–74, 177, 186, 188, 190
Widow Robbins, 89–91, 93
Wiggins, Daniel, 67, 70
Wilcox, David, 154
Wirt, William, 31, 37, 43–44
Withlacoochee River, 25
women: black, 12, 26, 39, 71, 81–82, 104, 122, 181, 199; Seminole, 70, 102, 104, 106, 111–113, 118–27, 129, 131–34, 198; white, 1–5, 9–12, 14–19, 25–28, 32–43, 46–47, 51–54, 56–58, 60–61, 63, 65, 67, 69–74, 77–78, 80–86, 89–90, 92, 94–96, 98–99, 101–4, 106, 117–18, 122–25, 132, 137–39, 142, 144, 146, 148–49, 154, 156–61, 163–67, 171, 174, 176–77, 181–82, 186–87, 191–92, 197–202; and property rights, 22, 32–36, 39, 41, 46–48, 51–54, 163. *See also* Indian depredation narratives; gender; indigenous resistance; reproductive labor; widows
Worth, William Jenkins, 131, 175

ACKNOWLEDGMENTS

I owe many debts to those who helped me research and write this book and to those who supported me along the way. I am grateful to the many librarians and archivists in Florida and in Washington, D.C., who helped me locate materials. First and foremost I am grateful to Dr. Joe Knetsch, military historian and Florida Department of Environmental Protection land expert, who handed me a microfilm reel in Tallahassee that furnished the records that would eventually become the core of Chapter 4. Joe and his wife, Linda, proved to be keen research contacts and fabulous hosts, and I am forever in their debt. Archivists at the P. K. Yonge Library at the University of Florida, the St. Augustine Historical Society, the State Archives and Library in Tallahassee (especially Boyd Murphree), the Hillsborough County Court Archives, and at the Archives of the Escambia County Clerk of Court's office were very helpful, and I thank them.

I would also like to thank the Williams clan. The generous hospitality of Scott and Maureen Williams—along with their three sons, Daniel, Matthew, and Sean (now grown into handsome young men!)—made research in Florida possible as well as fun. I miss you all, along with Janelle and the late Jeff Williams and their children and grandchildren. D'Ann Williams sustained me in ways too numerous to name, for which she (and Gussie, Cleo, Herc, and Bouncer) deserves many thanks.

The American Studies Department at the George Washington University was an amazing place to start this project and my career. I knew it then, but the years since I left GWU have only sharpened my appreciation for the uniquely warm, smart, and good-natured community nurtured there by a collection of generous and politically engaged scholar-teachers. Terry Murphy was a terrific supervisor and mentor, and James O. Horton, the late Phyllis Palmer, and Chad Heap formed a supportive committee. In addition, the late Jim Miller, Adele Alexander, and Melani McAlister provided me with formative seminar experiences that I will always treasure.

My deepest debt is owed to Laura Cook Kenna, Julie Passanante Elman, Stephanie Ricker Schulte, and Kyle Riismandel, who read and edited every page of my dissertation, and many of the pages of this book, bless them. Their sharp minds, work ethic, and warm friendship made me, and this book, much better. I suppose I could have done it without them, but it would not have been nearly so much fun. Thank you, trustees of my brain, for everything. Other fellow travelers and interlocutors in American Studies at GWU also deserve thanks, especially Paul Gardullo, Kevin Strait, and Yusuke Torii.

A previous version of Chapter 1 appeared in the *Journal of Women's History* in 2010, and some of that research appears here with permission from the Johns Hopkins University Press. The *Journal of the Early Republic* first published an earlier version of parts of Chapter 4 in 2013, and it is reprinted here with permission from the University of Pennsylvania Press and the Society for Historians of the Early American Republic.

At the University of Hartford, the Women's Education and Leadership Fund and a Greenberg Grant in the College of Arts and Sciences provided some needed funds and teaching relief in 2010 and 2011, for which I was very grateful. I extend my thanks to Jennifer Sanborn, Warren Goldstein, and Fred Sweitzer for their support. My colleague and friend Beth Richards read several chapters and also kept me sane in the midst of "program prioritization." My students at the University of Hartford taught me many things, and I became a better historian in the process. I thank them and wish them all the very best.

In the summer of 2011, I was fortunate to attend a National Endowment for the Humanities Summer Institute on the Ethnohistory of Indians in the American South at the University of North Carolina, where Theda Perdue, the late Mike Green, Malinda Maynor Lowery, and Clara Sue Kidwell led a rowdy bunch of academics through four amazing weeks of study and travel to Catawba, Cherokee, and Lumbee country. It was a transformative experience, and it made Chapter 3 possible. Theda's and Mike's unstinting support for me (and many other young scholars) was a generous and lovely gift. They exemplify all the reasons why I wanted to be a scholar and a teacher in the first place, a reminder that came just at the right time in my career.

At the University of Western Ontario, I wish to thank librarian Liz Mantz, as well as Keith Fleming, Nancy Rhoden, Margaret Kellow, Craig Simpson, and many other wonderful colleagues and students who have welcomed me to Western and to Canada. Western is a magnificent place to teach, write, and serve. I am grateful and fortunate to be here.

At Penn Press, I owe many debts to Bob Lockhart and Kathleen Brown, whose critiques have been consistently generous and constructive. I am also thankful for the challenging and productive appraisals of my work proffered by Amy Greenberg and an anonymous reviewer. I am sincerely and deeply grateful.

My family has been a wonderful distraction from writing and an inspiration to keep at it over the years. Support from the Arbers and the Clarks was always generous, for which I am very grateful. Carolyn Shire buoys and pushes me, and I appreciate her support and her good sense of humor. I am especially grateful for our son, Henry, who keeps my feet on the ground and my head in the clouds.